HISTORIC PHOTOS OF
BIRMINGHAM

One of the iconic images of Birmingham: Terminal Station with the Magic City sign out front to greet travelers as they leave the station and head downtown.

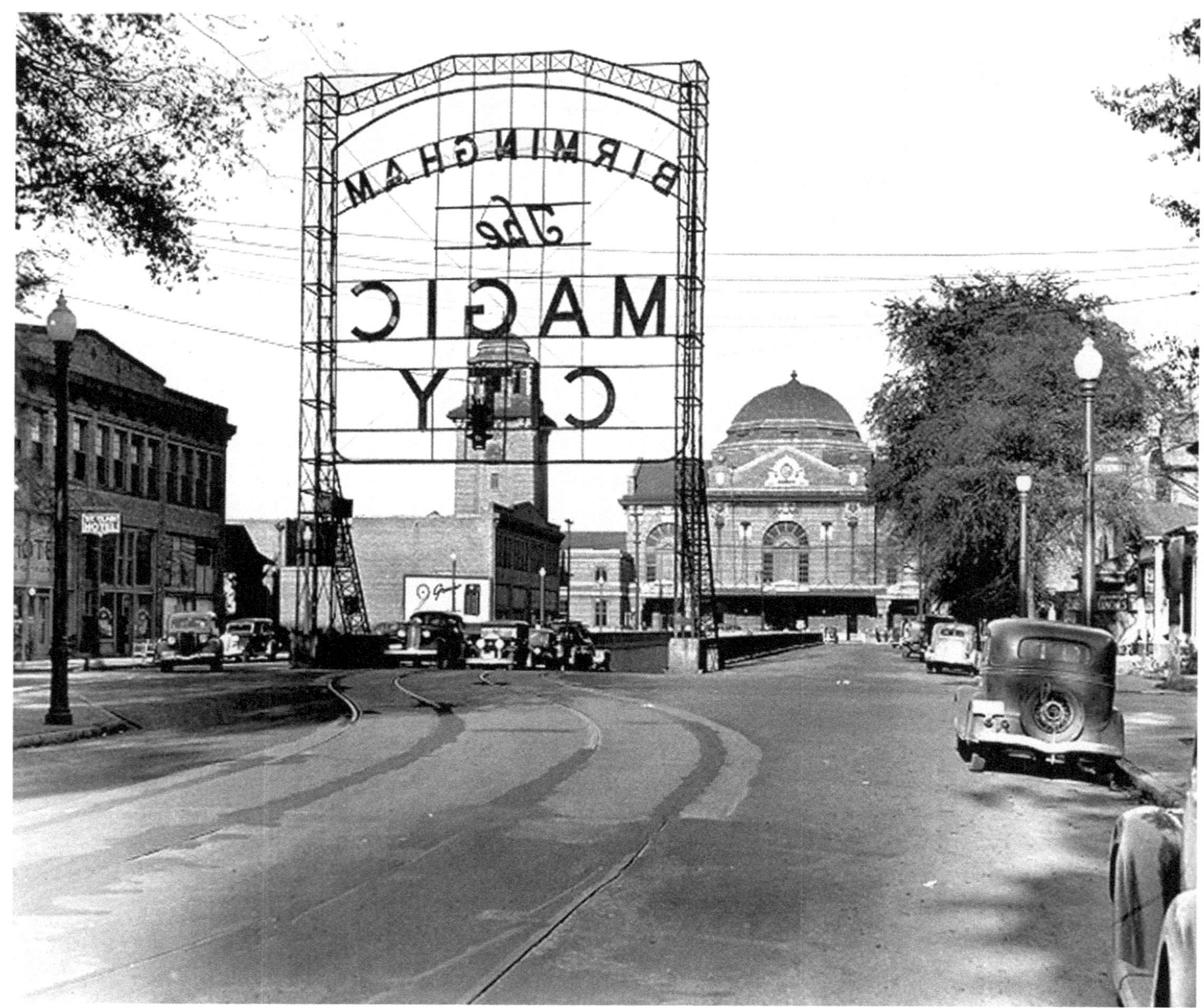

HISTORIC PHOTOS OF
BIRMINGHAM

TEXT AND CAPTIONS BY
JAMES L. BAGGETT

TURNER
PUBLISHING COMPANY

Turner Publishing Company
Historic Photos of Birmingham

Library of Congress Control Number: 2006902319

ISBN-10: 1-59652-254-2
ISBN-13: 978-1-59652-254-1

Printed in the United States of America

ISBN 978-1-68336-911-0 (hc)

Contents

Acknowledgments vii

Preface viii

A City of the New South (1871–1899) 1

A City at the Turn of the Century (1900–1917) 31

A Growing Metropolis and a Great Depression (1918–1939) 87

Difficult Days and Changing Times (1940–1990) 137

Notes on the Photographs 190

Workers place the first steel column for the Tutwiler Hotel, 1913.

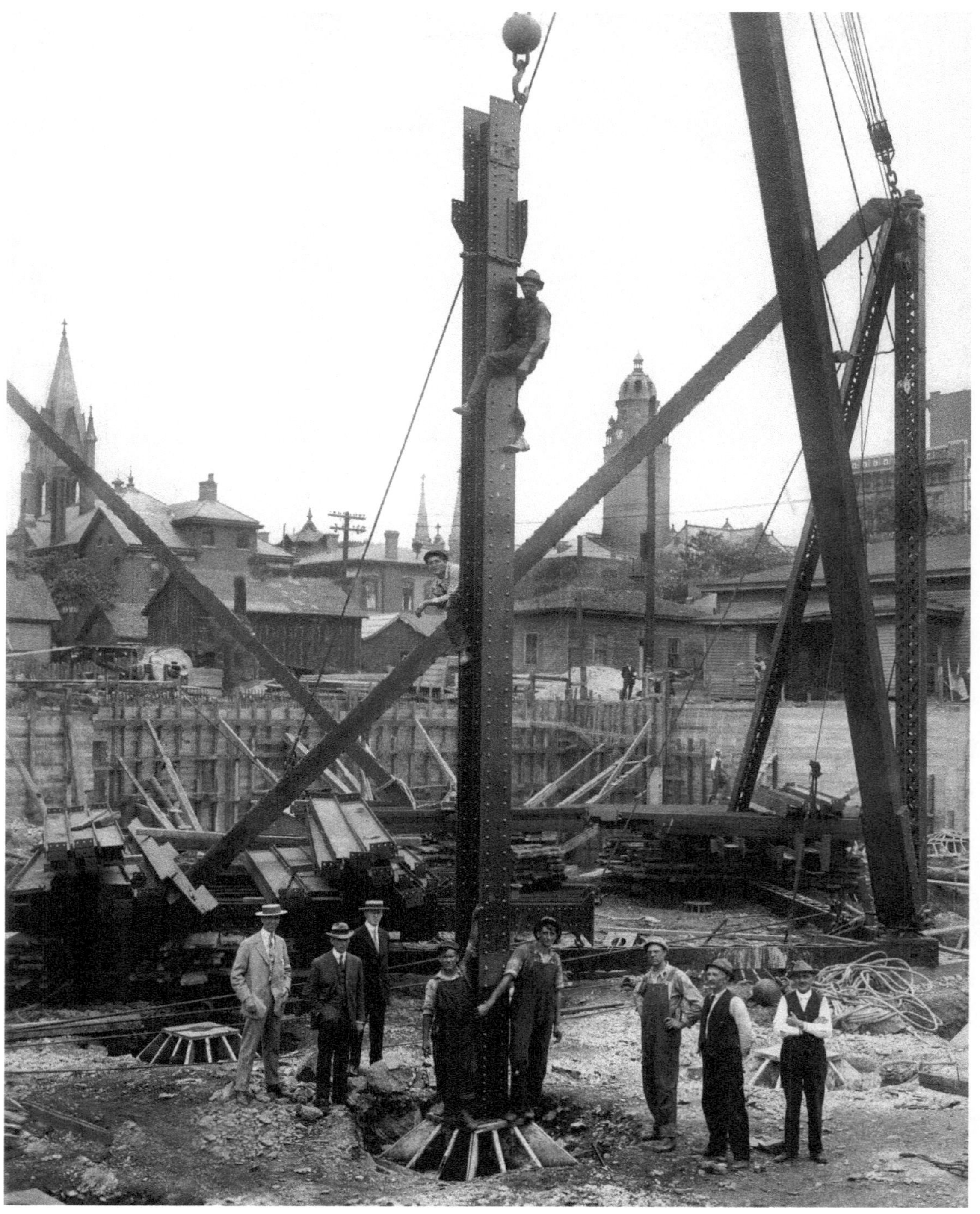

ACKNOWLEDGMENTS

This volume, *Historic Photos of Birmingham*, is the result of the cooperation and efforts of many individuals, organizations, institutions, and corporations. It is with great thanks that we acknowledge the valuable contribution of the following for their generous support.

Alabama Power Company
Birmingham Public Library Archives
Brice Building Company
St. Vincent's Hospital
Vulcan Materials Company
Wachovia Bank

We would also like to thank the following individuals for their valuable contributions and assistance in making this work possible:

Bill Tharpe, Alabama Power Company
Kelsey Bates, Birmingham Public Library Archives
Gigi Gowdy, Birmingham Public Library Archives
Yolanda Valentin, Birmingham Public Library Archives
Don Veasey, Birmingham Public Library Archives
Sherry Denson, Brice Building Company
John English, Vulcan Materials Company
Scott Goggins, St. Vincent's Hospital
John Lotz, Wachovia Bank
Carolyn Wallace, Wachovia Bank

Preface

Birmingham has thousands of historic photographs that reside in archives, both locally and nationally. This book began with the observation that, while those photographs are of great interest to many, not all are easily accessible. During a time when Birmingham is looking ahead and evaluating its future course, many people are asking, How do we treat the past? These decisions affect every aspect of the city—architecture, public spaces, commerce, tourism, recreation, and infrastructure—and these, in turn, affect the way that people live their lives. This book seeks to provide easy access to a valuable, objective look into Birmingham's history.

The power of photographic images is that they are less subjective in their treatment of history. While the photographer can make decisions regarding what subject matter to capture and some limited variation in its presentation, photographs do not provide the breadth of interpretation that text does. For this reason, they provide an original, untainted perspective that allows the viewer to interpret and observe.

This project represents countless hours of research and review. The researchers and author have reviewed thousands of photographs in numerous archives. We greatly appreciate the generous assistance of the archivists listed in the acknowledgments of this work, without whom this project could not have been completed.

The goal in publishing this work is to provide broader access to a set of extraordinary photographs that seek to inspire, provide perspective, and evoke insight that might assist people who are responsible for determining Birmingham's future. In addition, the book seeks to preserve the past with adequate respect and reverence.

The photographs selected have been reproduced using multiple colors of ink to provide depth to the images. With the exception of touching up imperfections caused by the damage of time, no other changes have been made. The focus and clarity of many images is limited to the technology and the ability of the photographer at the time they were taken.

The work is divided into eras. Beginning with some of the earliest known photographs of Birmingham, the first section records photographs from the 1870s through the end of the nineteenth century. The second section spans the beginning of the twentieth century to World War I. Section three moves from World War I to World War II. And finally, Section four covers the World War II era to the 1980s.

In each of these sections we have made an effort to capture various aspects of life through our selection of photographs. People, commerce, transportation, infrastructure, religious institutions, educational institutions, and scenes of natural beauty have been included to provide a broad perspective.

It is the publisher's hope that in utilizing this work, longtime residents will learn something new and that new residents will gain a perspective on where Birmingham has been, so that each can contribute to its future.

—Todd Bottorff, Publisher

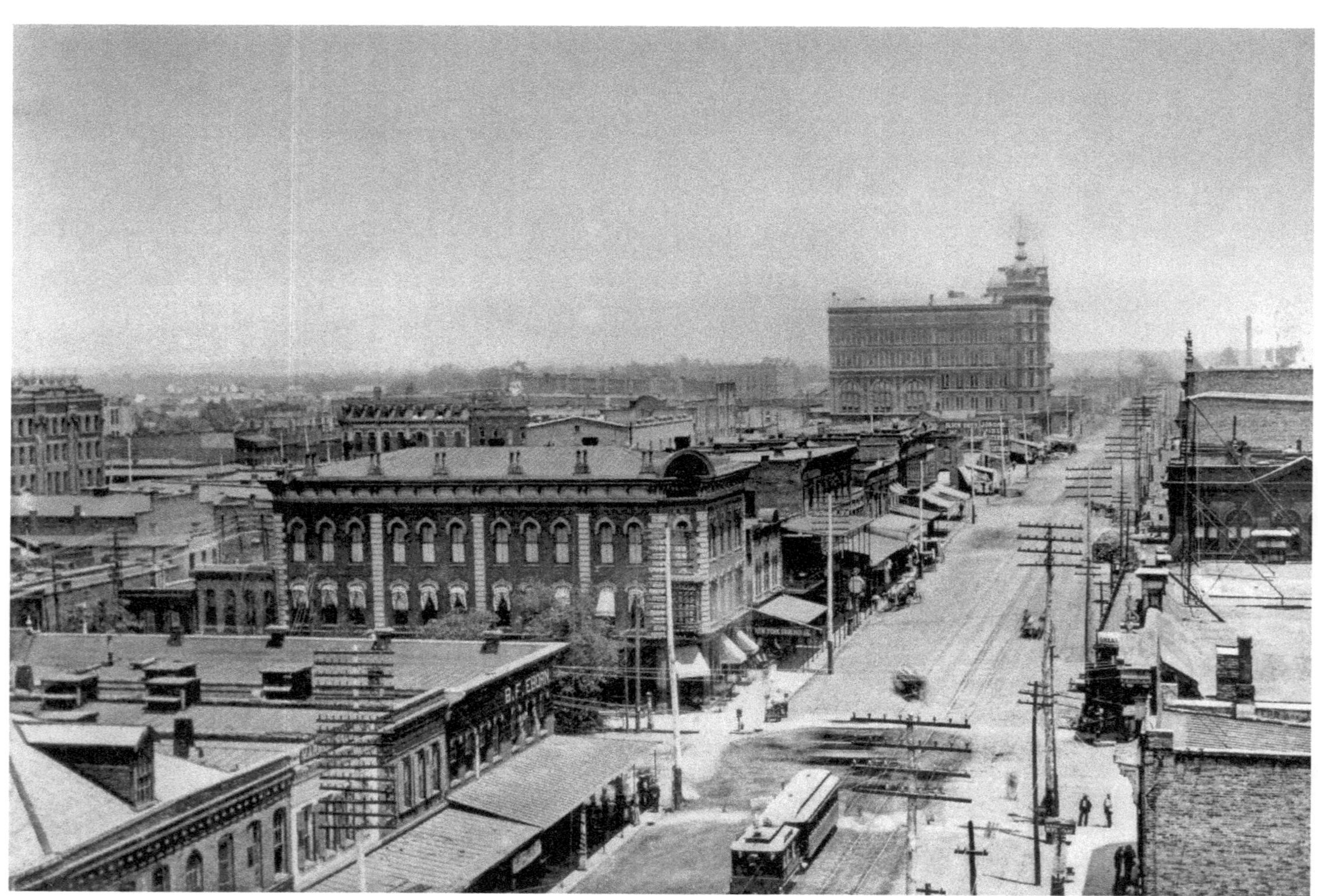

First Avenue North in the 1890s. The tallest building in the distance is the Caldwell Hotel, built in 1886. Promoted as Birmingham's first "fireproof" hotel, the Caldwell burned down in 1894.

A City of the New South

(1871–1899)

On an early spring day in 1872, a team of engineers took their surveying equipment out into a Jones Valley cornfield and began laying off the streets and blocks of Birmingham. Hired by the Elyton Land Company, the firm that founded Birmingham, the surveyors could work with an almost blank slate on the valley floor. With carefully recorded field notes and stakes driven into the ground, they created a city.

The Birmingham area held great industrial promise. All the ingredients needed to produce iron and steel were available in abundance and close proximity, but Birmingham's iron and steel industry developed in fits and starts. Sloss Furnaces began operation in 1882 and Henderson Steel produced Alabama's first steel in 1888, but for almost three decades, Birmingham failed to develop into the "El Dorado of iron-masters" that the city's founders had envisioned. Industrial development took a great leap in 1899 when the Tennessee Coal, Iron and Railroad Company began casting steel at its new Ensley works.

Just two years after Birmingham's founding, James R. Powell, president of the Elyton Land Company, told his stockholders that "this magic little city of ours has no peer in the rapidity of its growth, combined with the character of its population and buildings."

Birmingham did experience remarkable growth in its early decades. The population in 1880, the year of the city's first census, was slightly more than 3,000 people. By the end of the nineteenth century, the city had grown to more than 38,000 people, with more living in surrounding suburbs.

Birmingham did not enter the twentieth century with all of its rough edges smoothed away. But by 1899, Birmingham had developed from a ragged town peopled by land speculators into a community with a modest number of theaters, accomplished musicians, social clubs, and lake resorts.

Taken in 1873, this is the earliest known photograph of Birmingham. The two chimneys in the bottom left corner are probably on the roof of the county jail. The street behind the two houses in the foreground is Fifth Avenue North, about where the Redmont Hotel now stands.

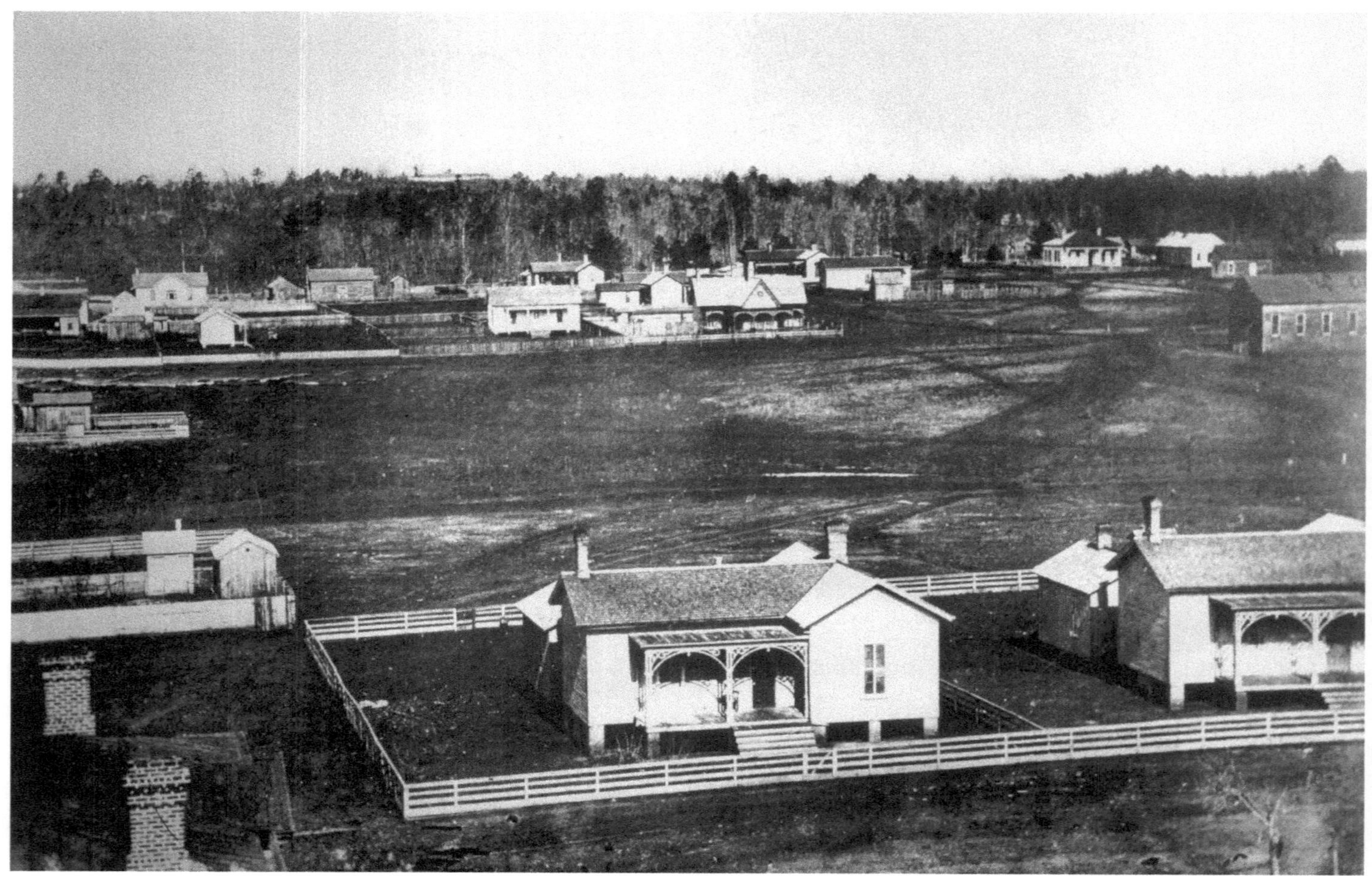

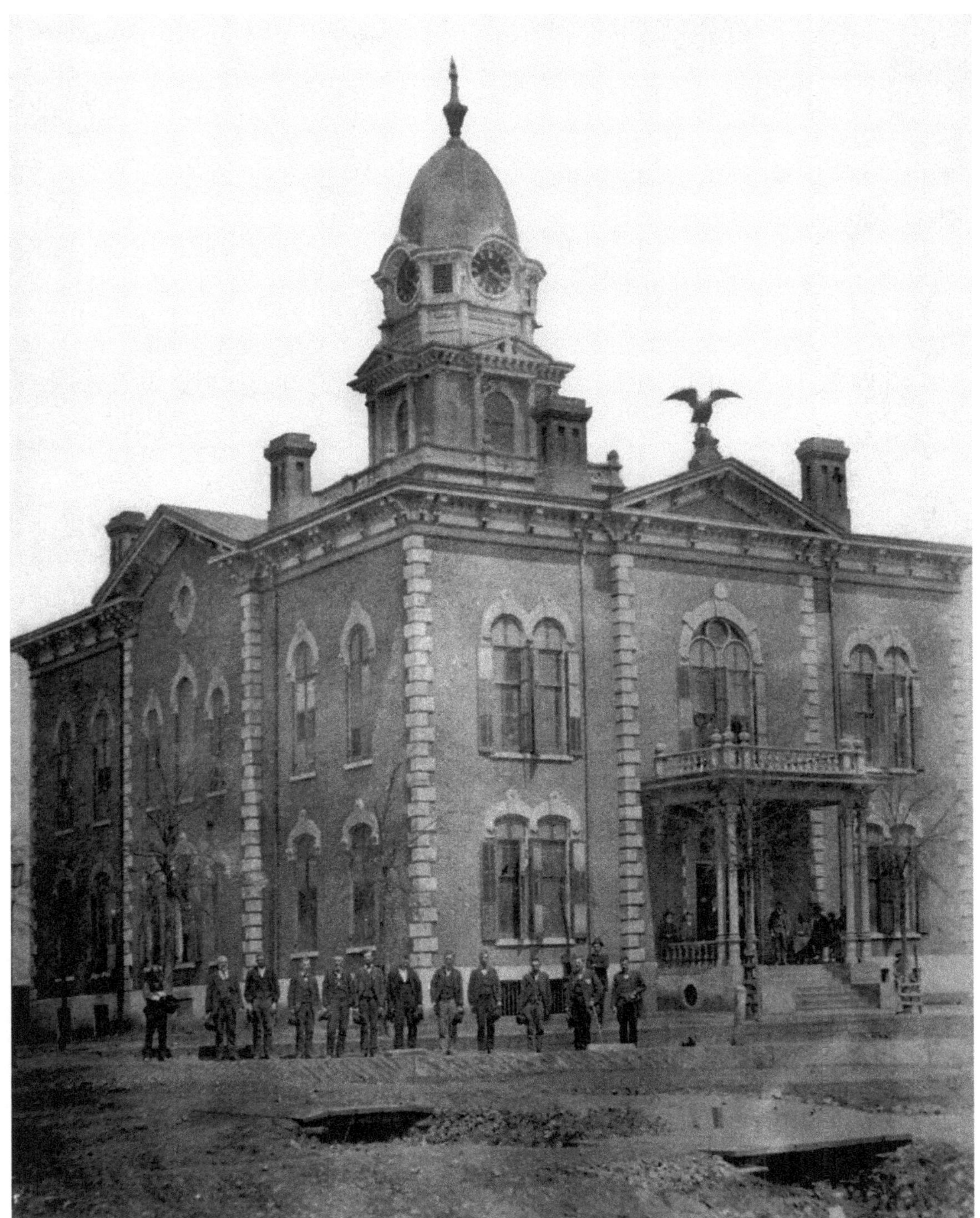

The first Jefferson County courthouse to be located in Birmingham, as it appeared in 1874. In a recent election that included many questionable campaign activities, voters had approved moving the courthouse from the nearby village of Elyton to the new city of Birmingham.

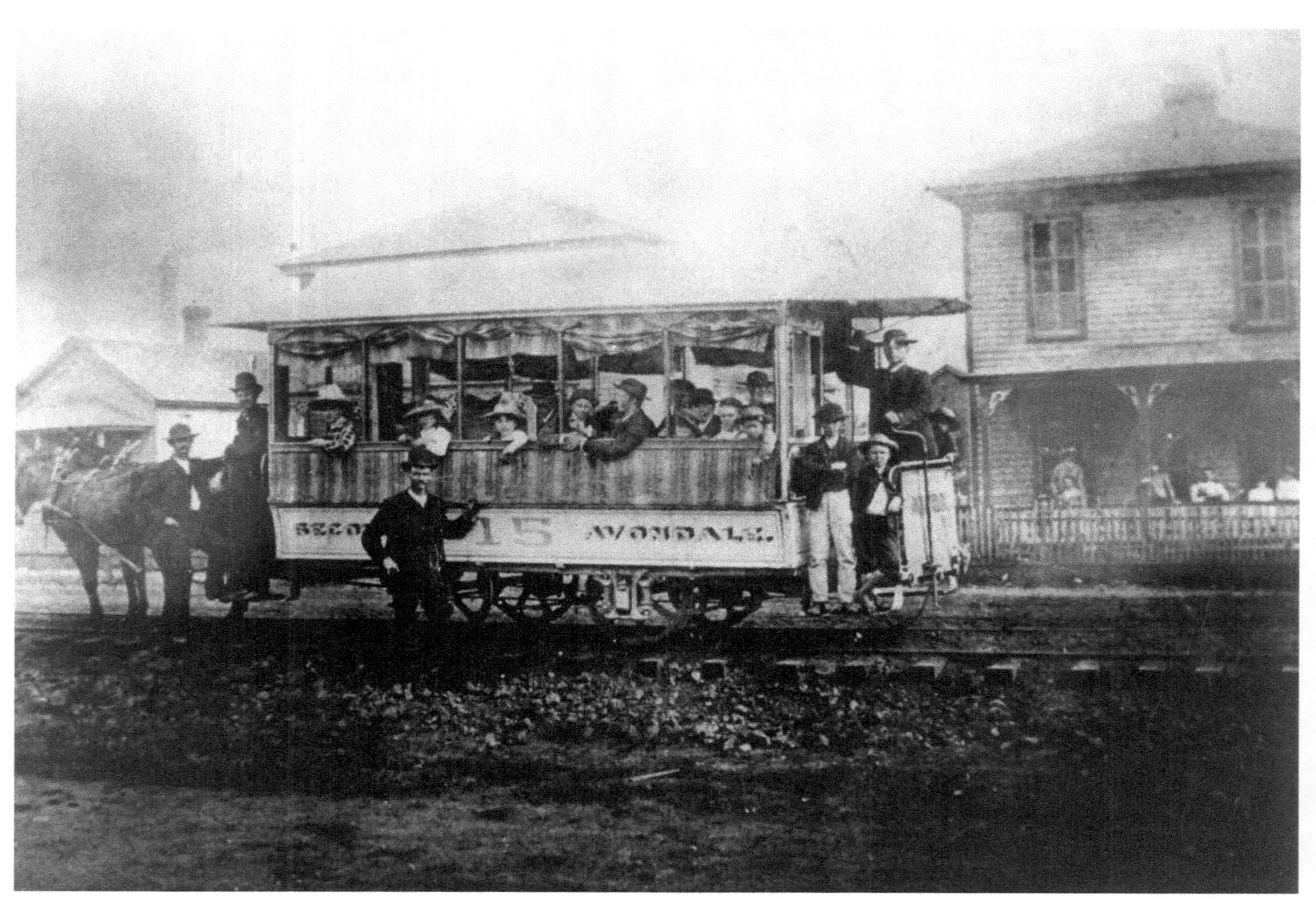

A mule-drawn streetcar on First Avenue North, 1887.

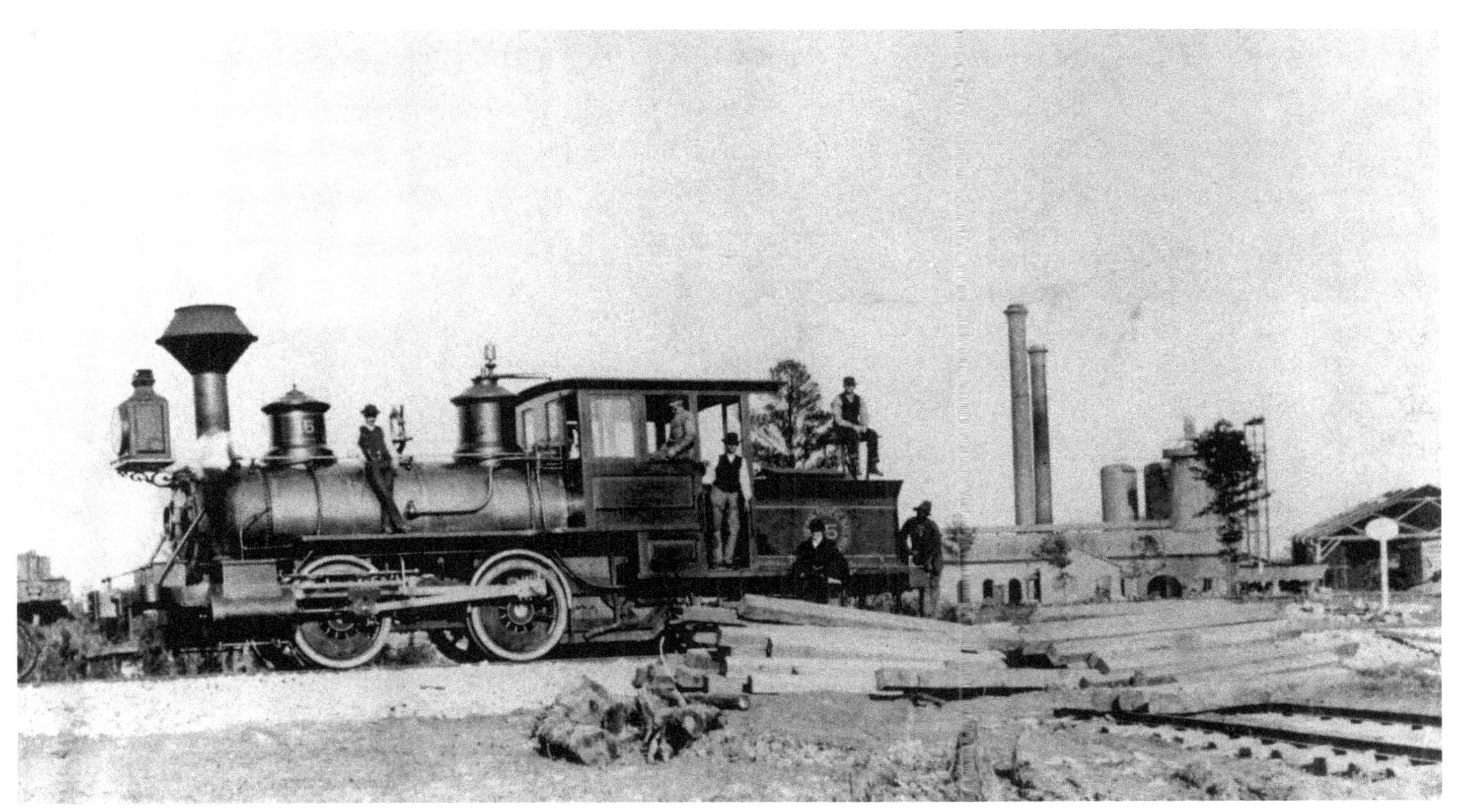

A Georgia-Pacific Railroad engine outside the old Sloss Furnaces, 1881.

A passenger train idles near Birmingham in the 1880s.

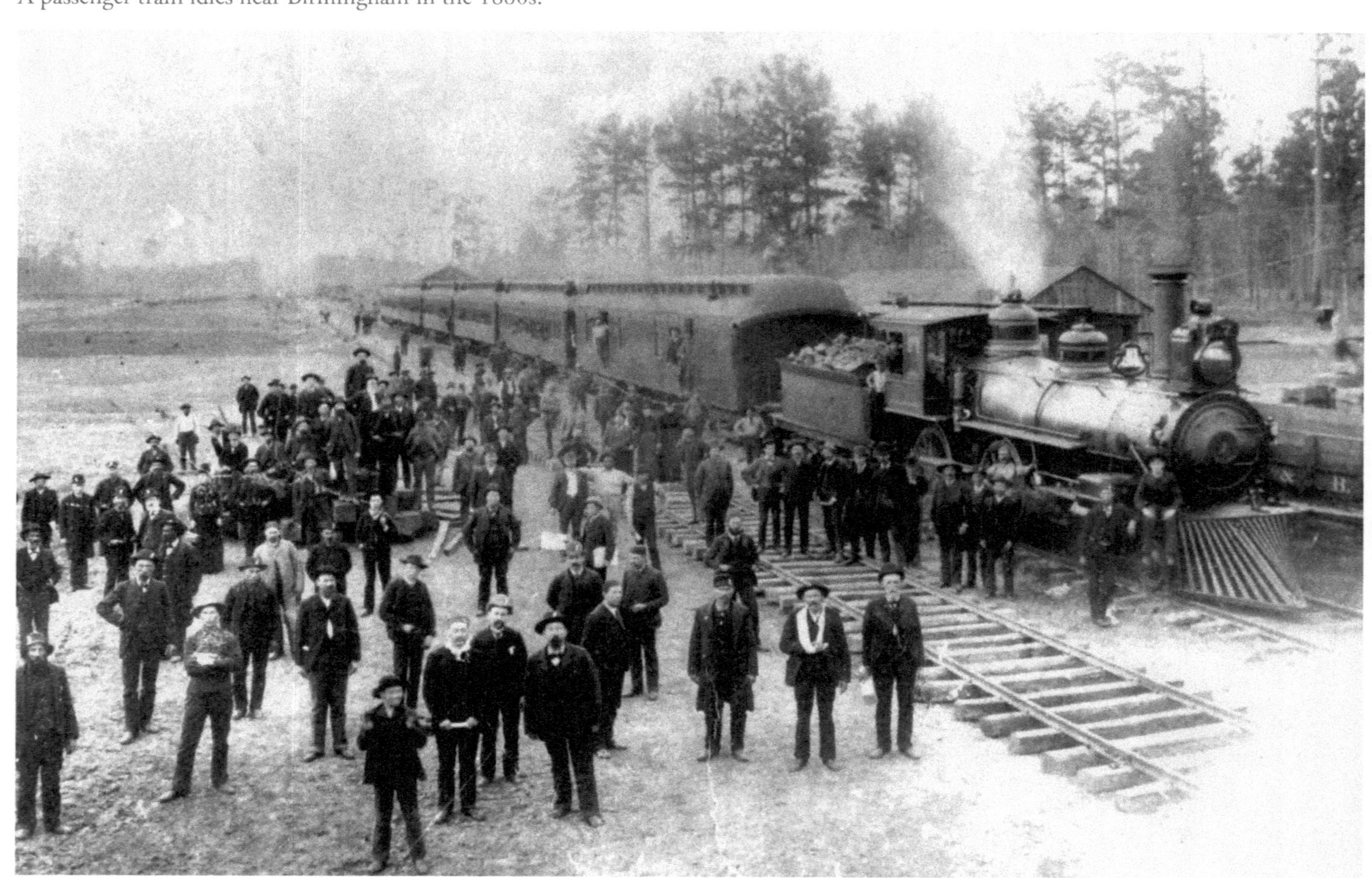

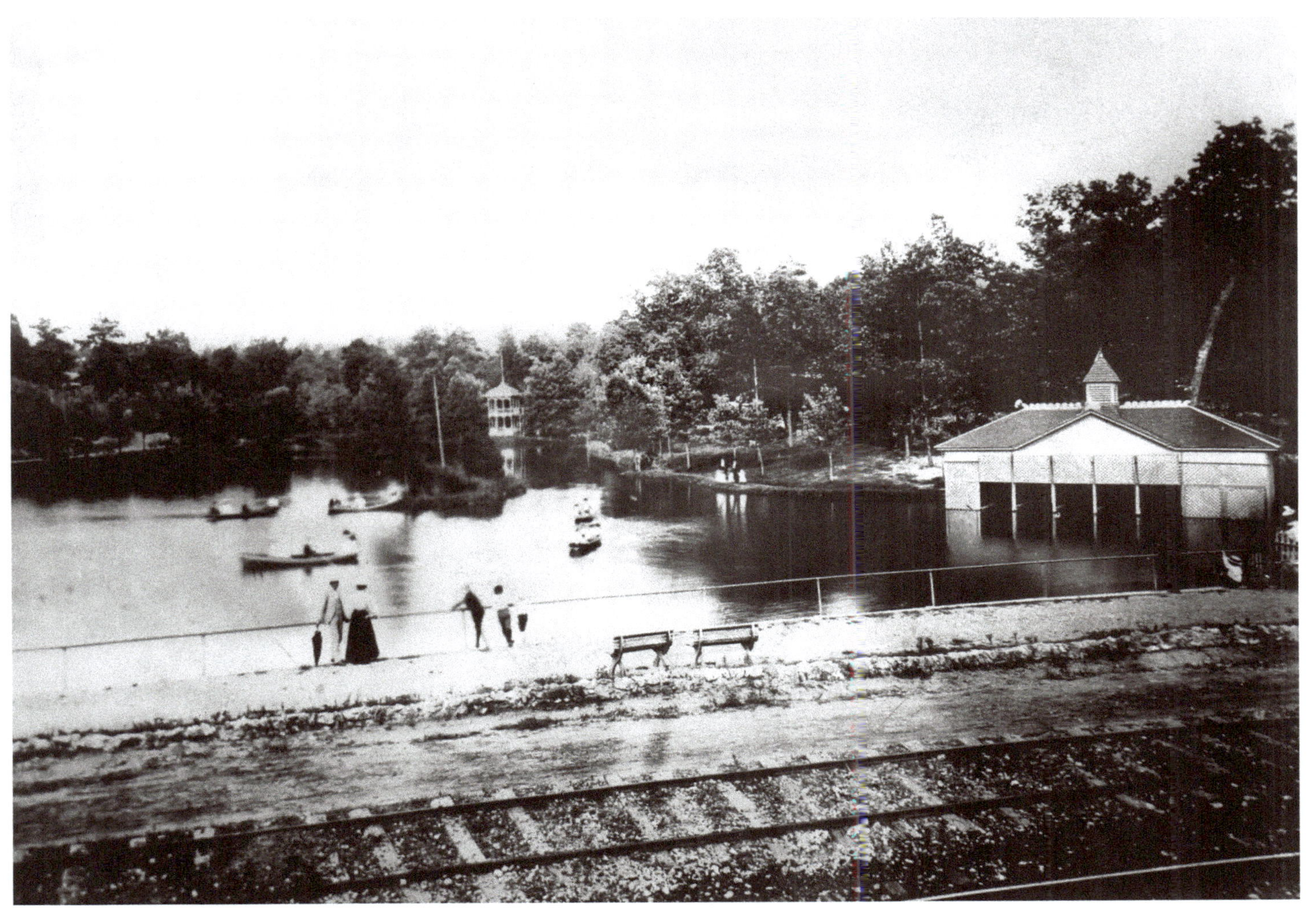

Lakeview resort, seen here from Highland Avenue in 1893. Located on the site that is now the Highland Park Golf Course, Lakeview boasted a hotel, dance pavilion, and boat rides. Streetcars brought residents from Birmingham for the day or weekend.

Roden's Book Store on Second Avenue North near Nineteenth Street, 1884. At far-left is John B. Roden, proprietor.

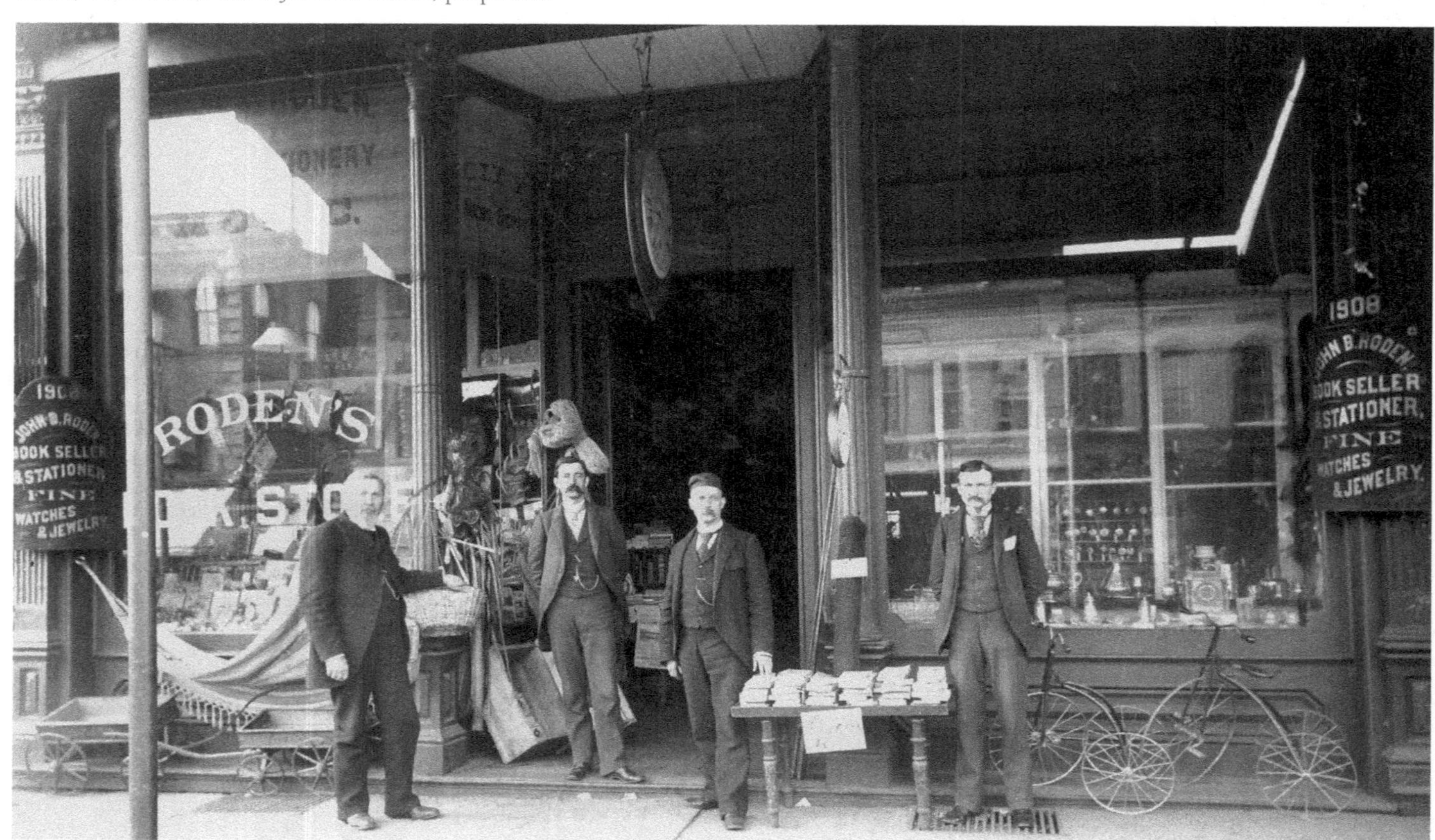

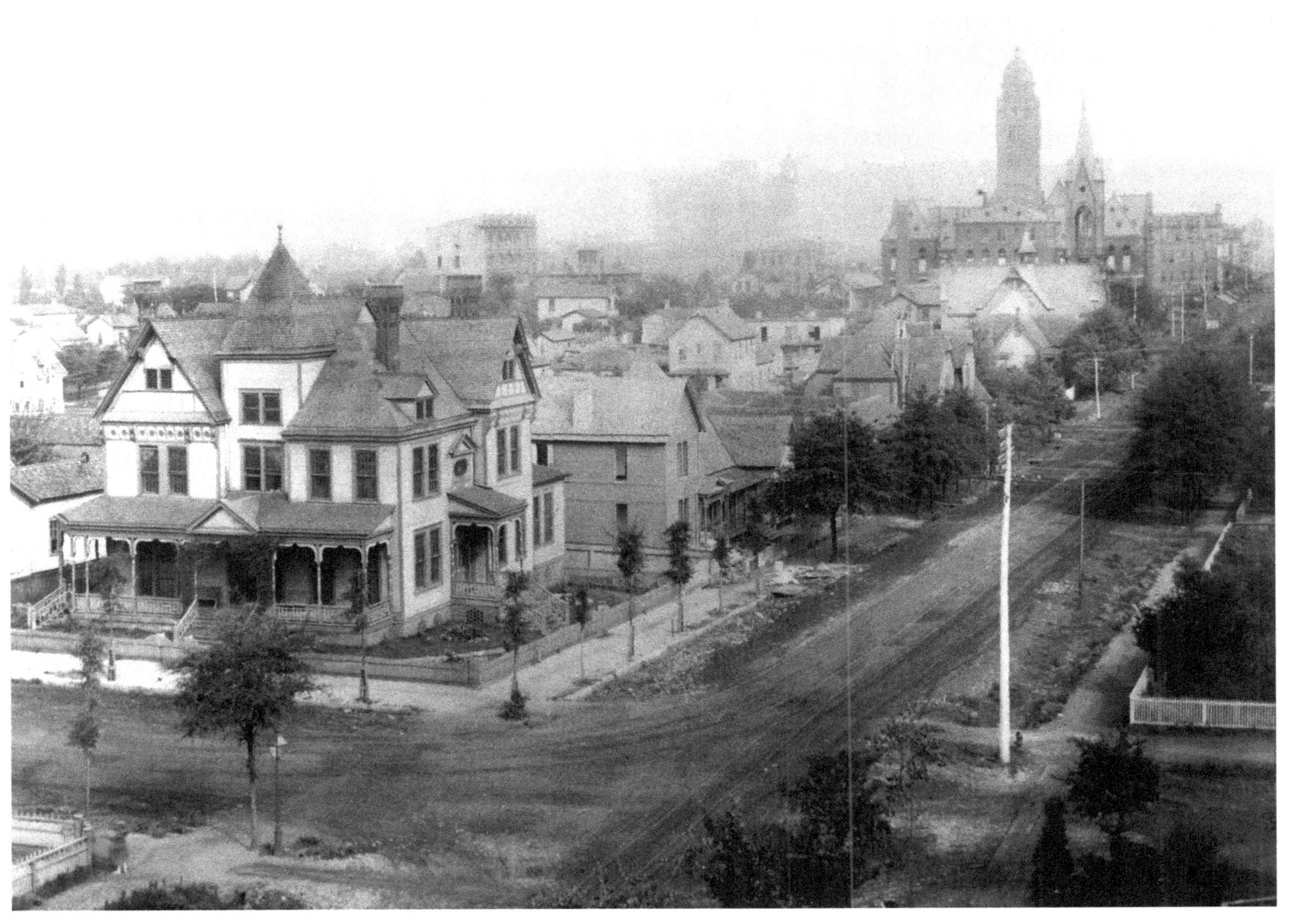

The home of Robert Jemison, Sr., on the corner of Sixth Avenue North and Twenty-first Street, around 1888. Jemison later moved to Glen Iris Park, an area he developed for his family and friends.

This 1890 skyline view of Birmingham shows the Jefferson County Courthouse (building with tower) on the corner of Twenty-first Street and Third Avenue North.

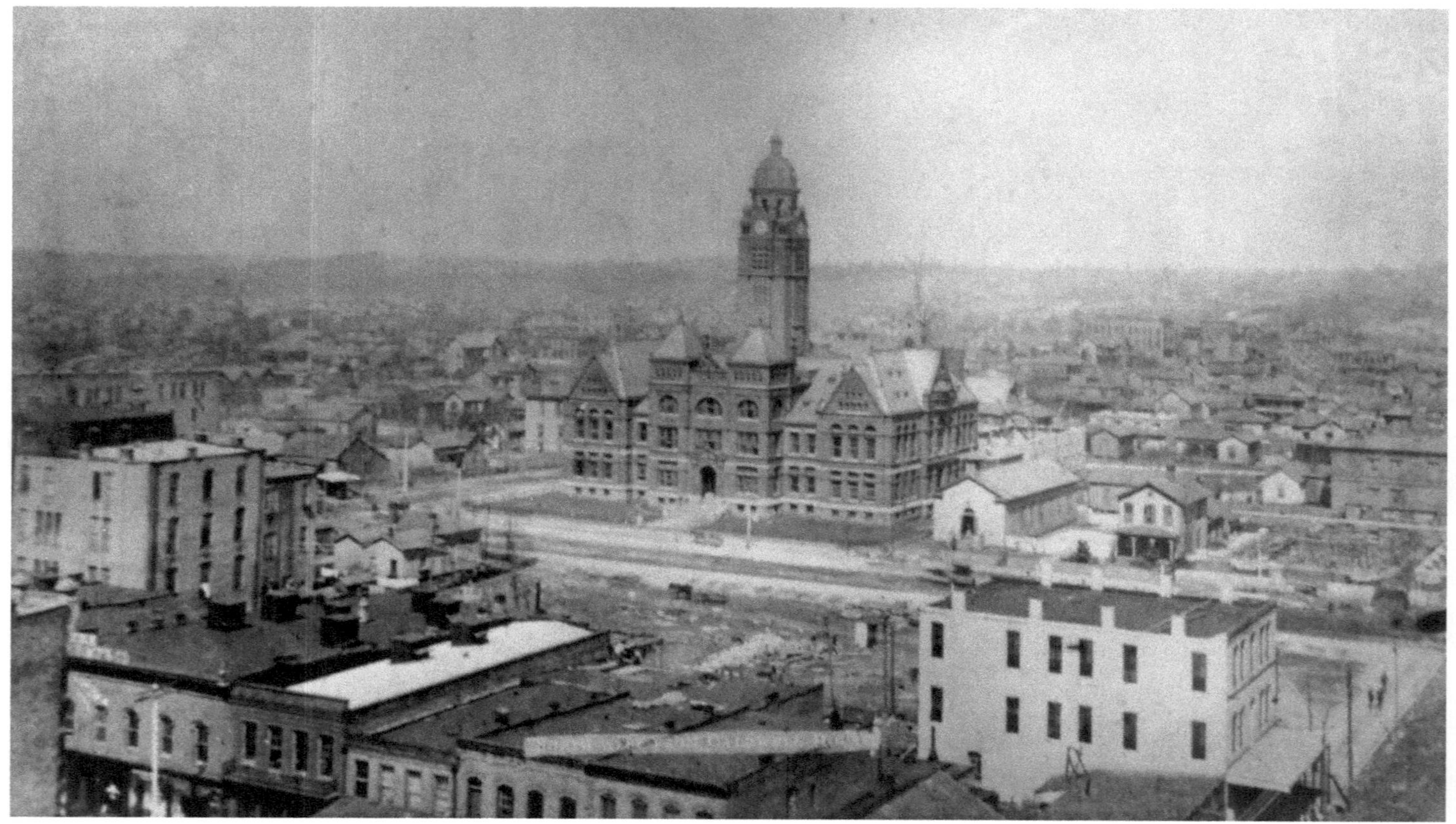

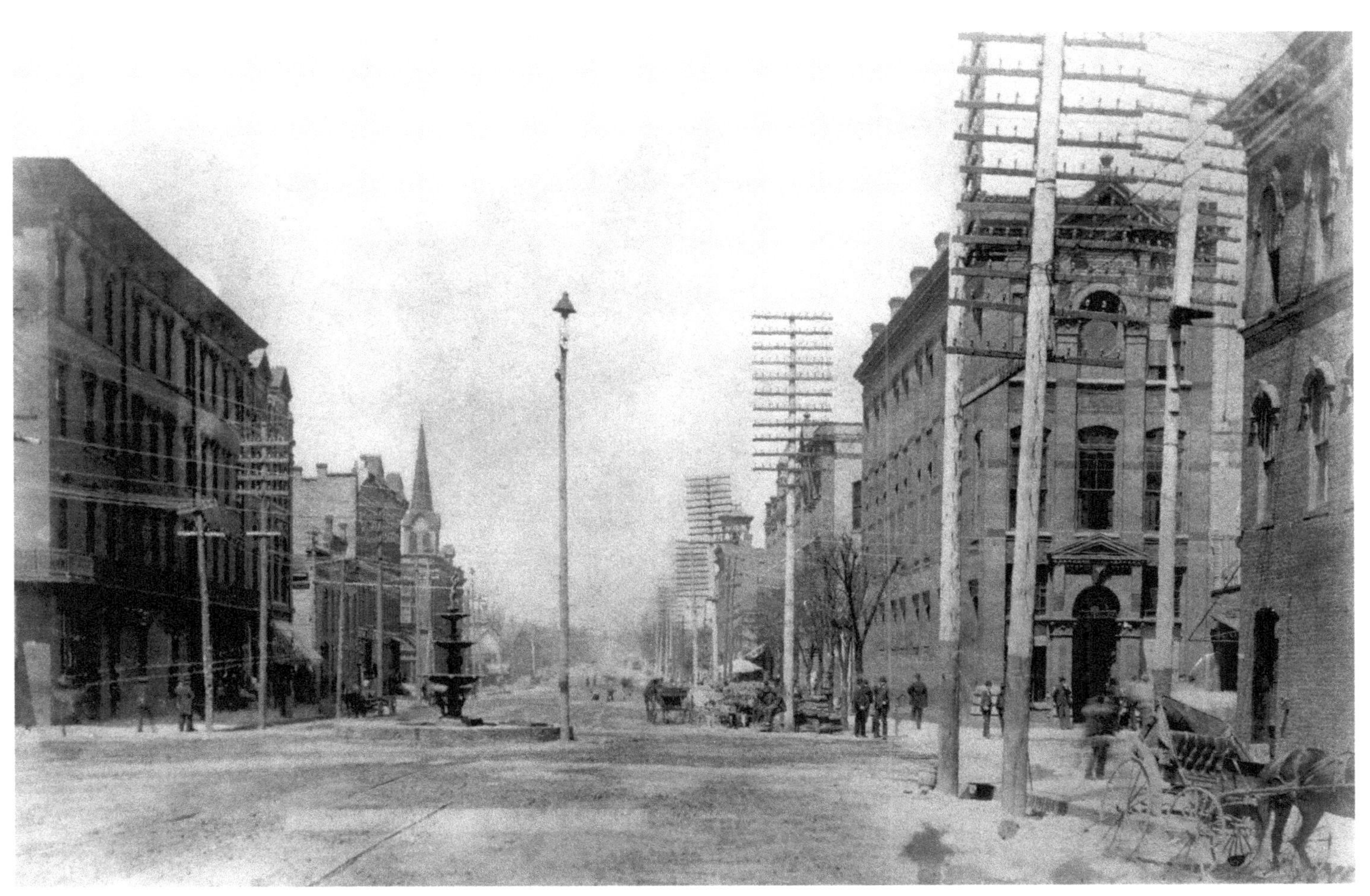

Nineteenth Street North at Second Avenue, around 1890. The fountain in the middle of the intersection was later removed and placed in storage, then lost.

The corner of Third Avenue North and Twenty-second Street, around 1890. The construction on the corner is the laying of the foundation for St. Paul's Catholic Church. The small wood-frame church on the far left is the old St. Paul's.

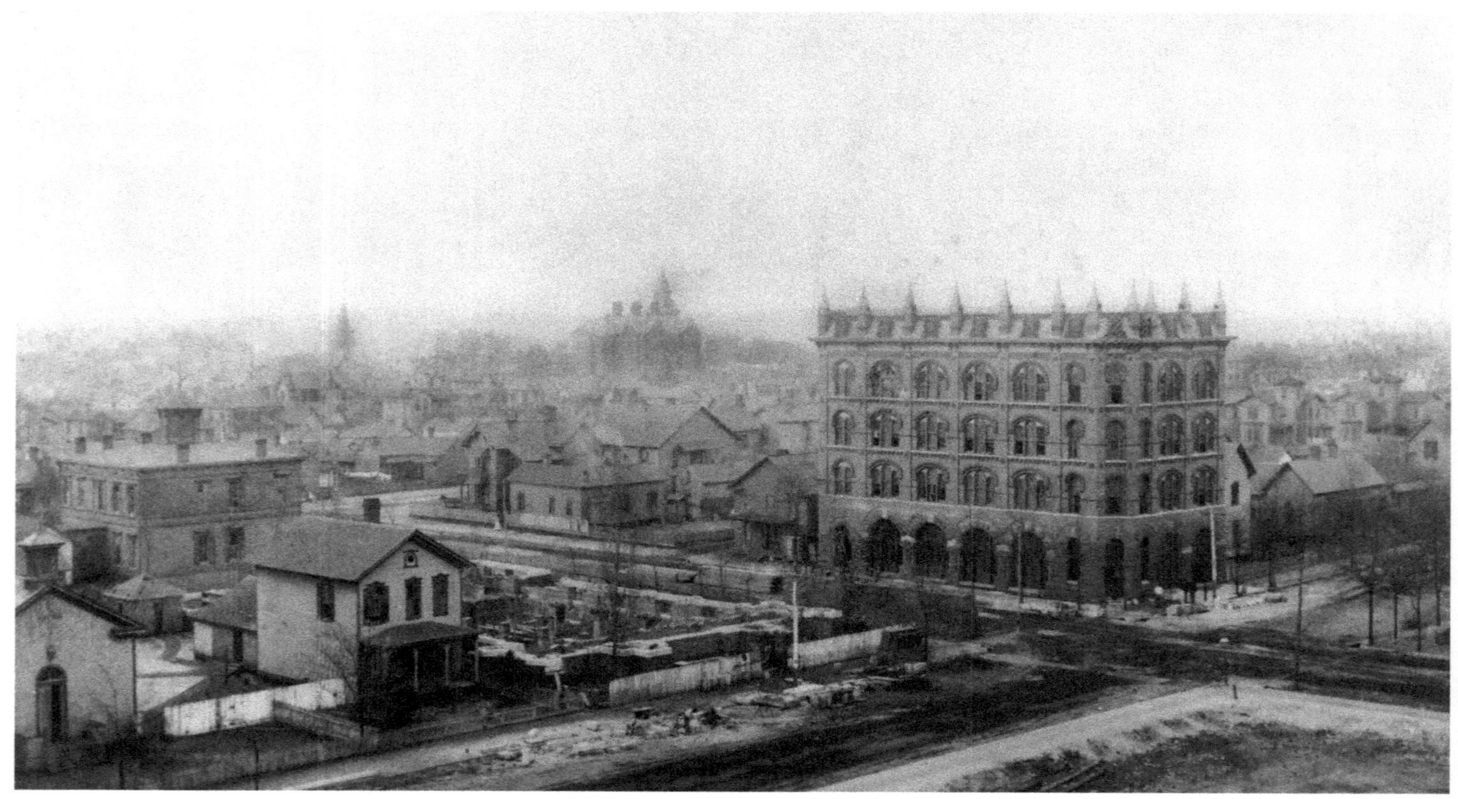

Streetcar lines allowed people to live farther from work and shopping and encouraged the development of Birmingham's first suburbs. Here an early Birmingham streetcar pauses on the tracks to Gate City, around 1890.

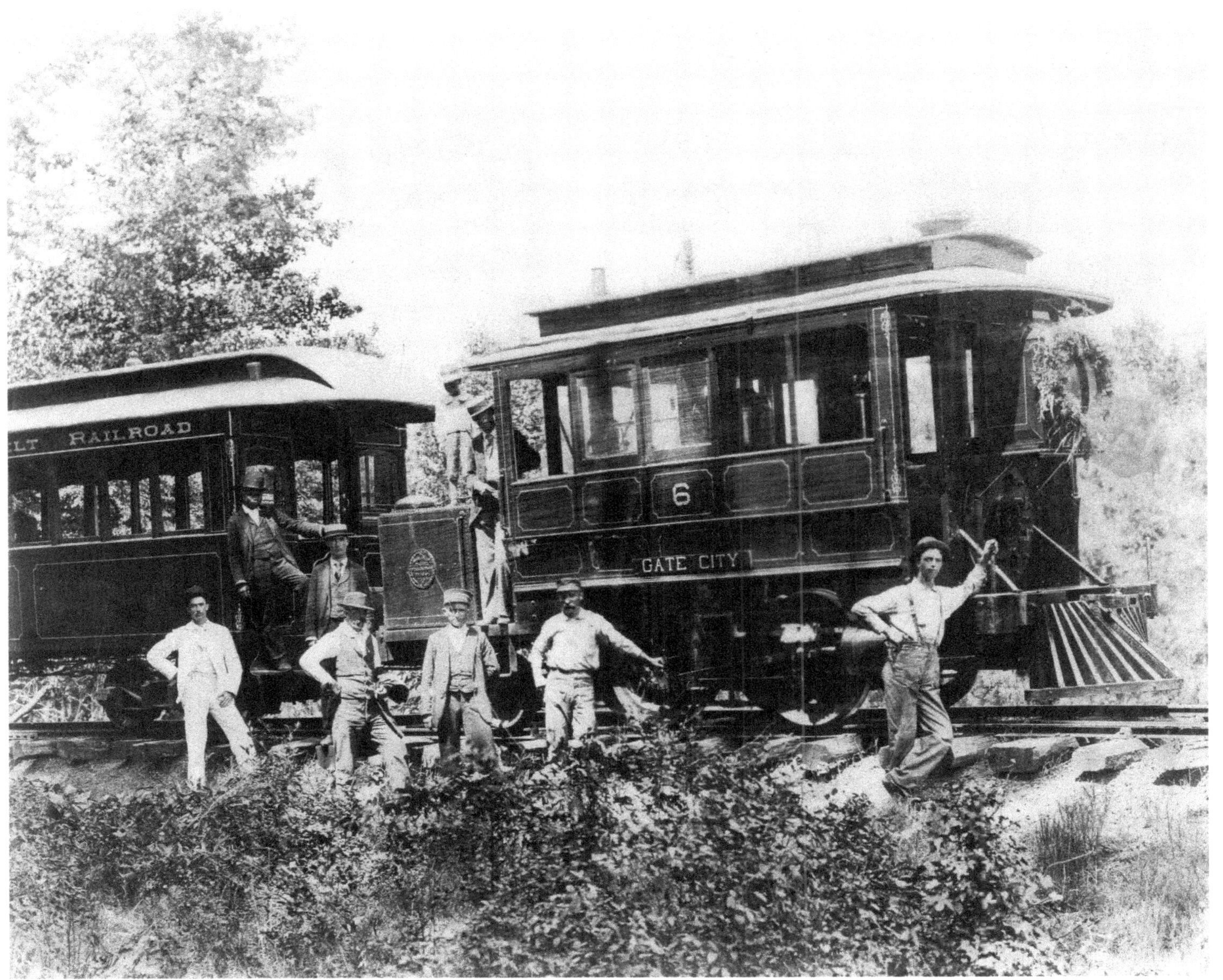

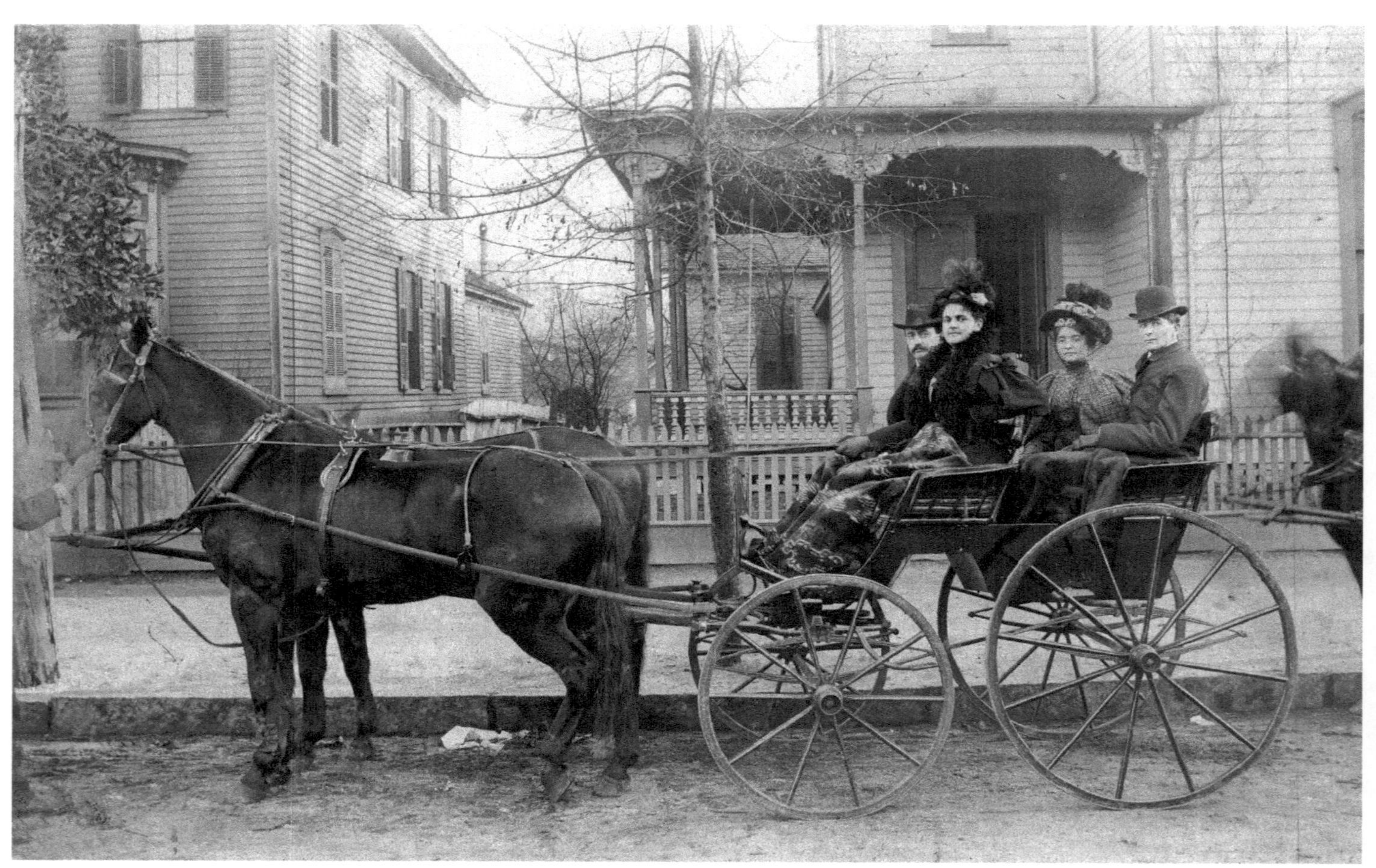

Going for a ride on Fifth Avenue in the late 1890s.

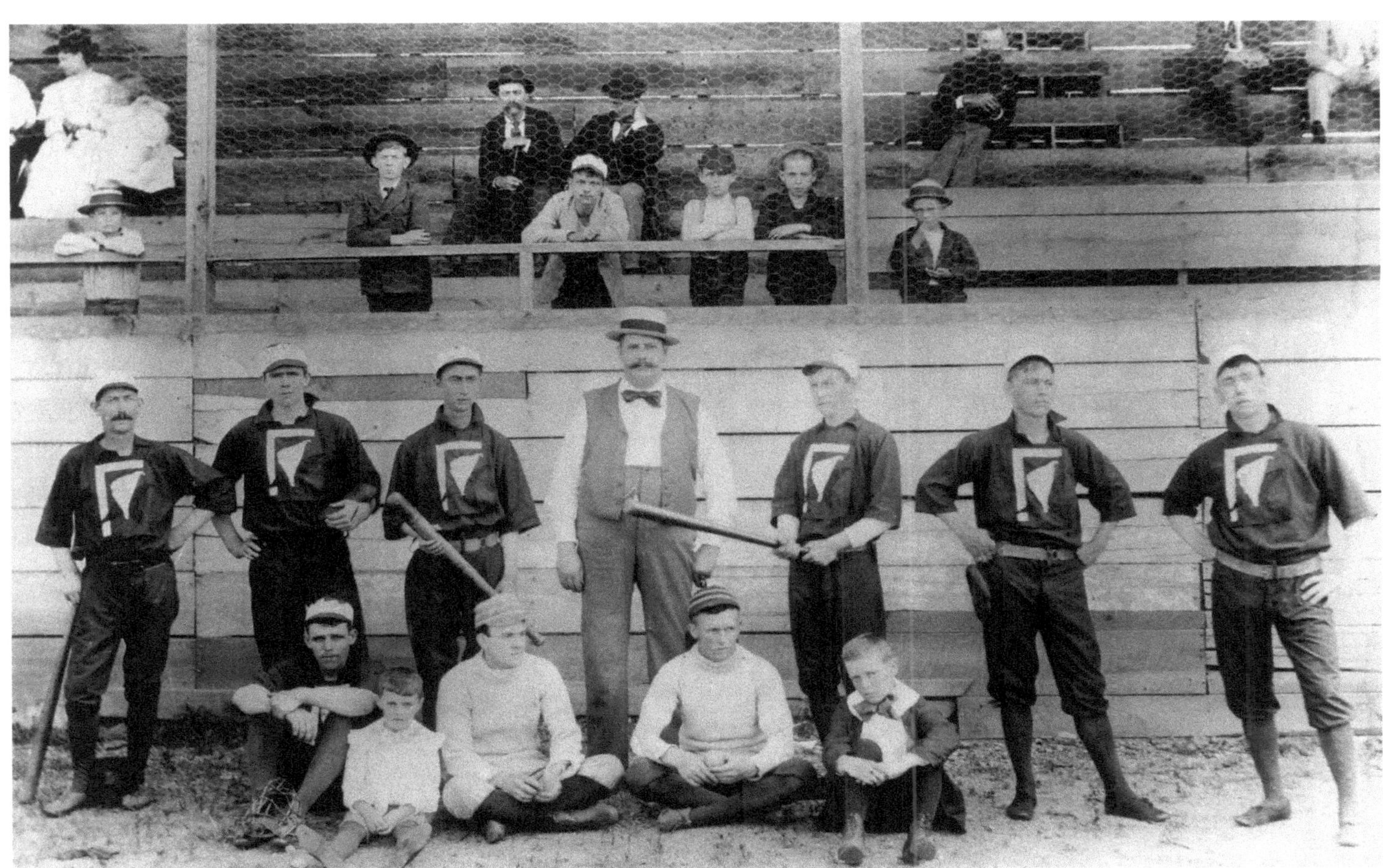

Posing for a team photo at Lakeview ballpark in the 1890s, these players for the Blach's department store team wear a lily and carpenter's square on their jerseys, signifying the store's motto, "fair and square."

Shriners on parade, at First Avenue North near Twentieth Street, around the 1890s.

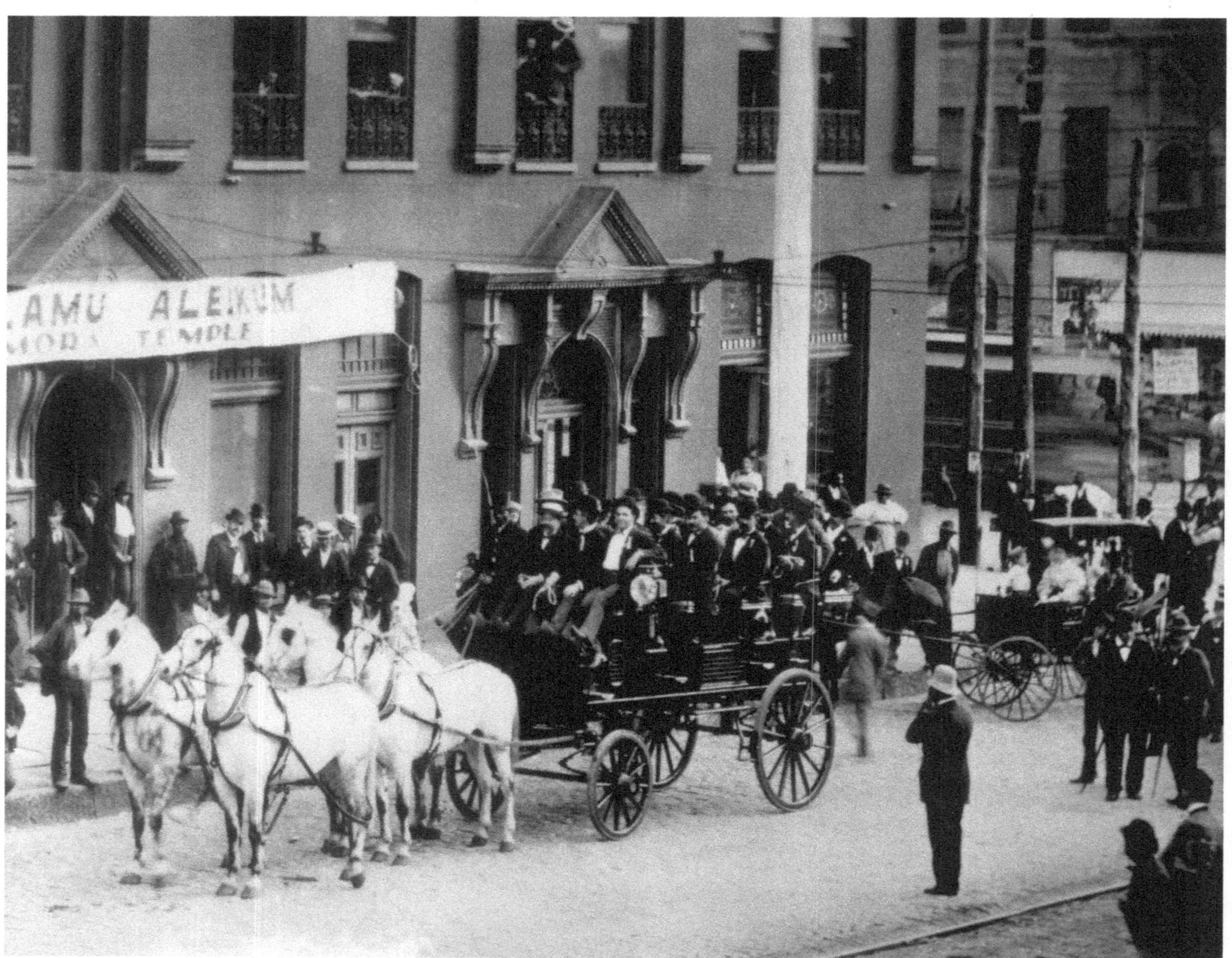

In the early 1890s, Birmingham's streetcar lines began converting from horse-drawn or mule-drawn to electric. Here, the two types of cars are shown on Twentieth Street.

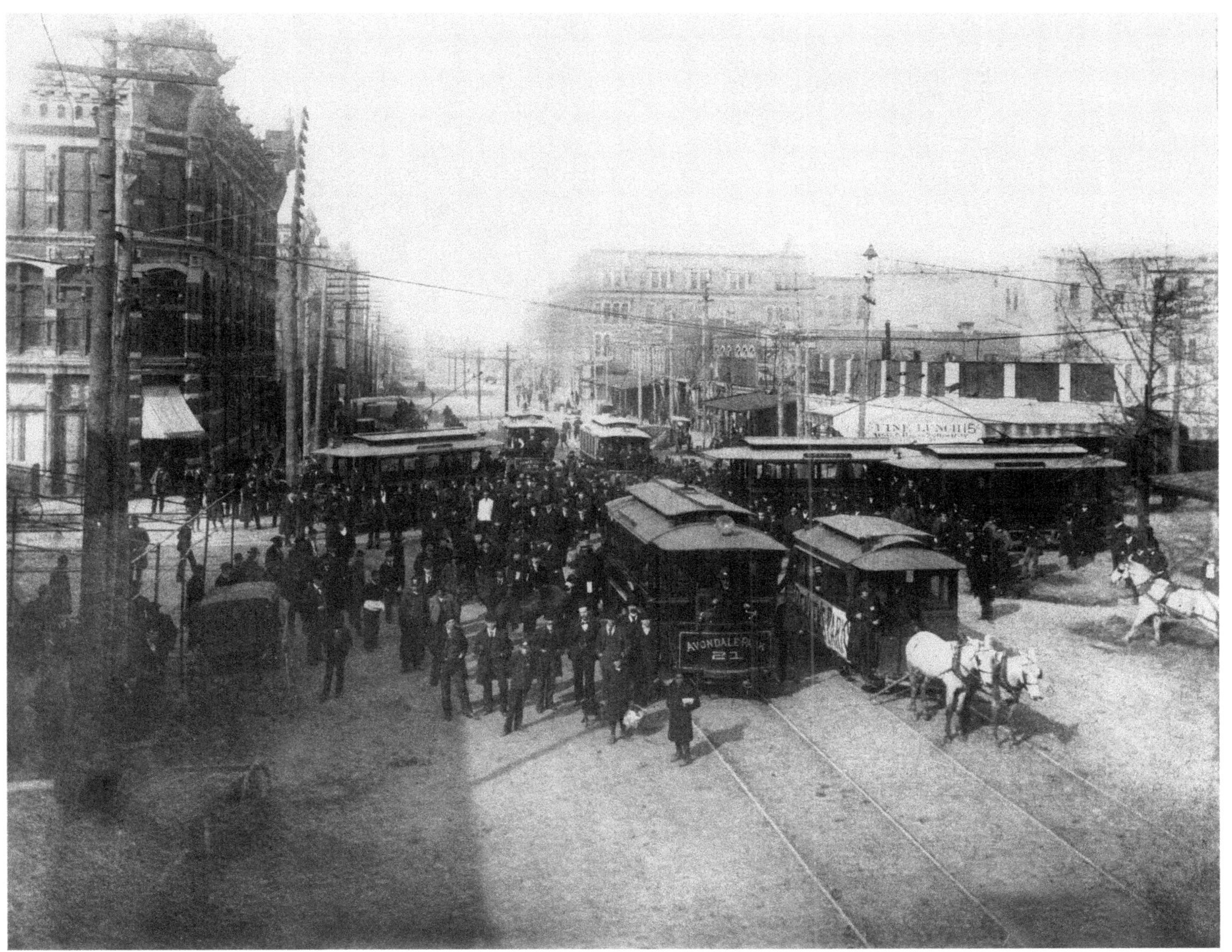

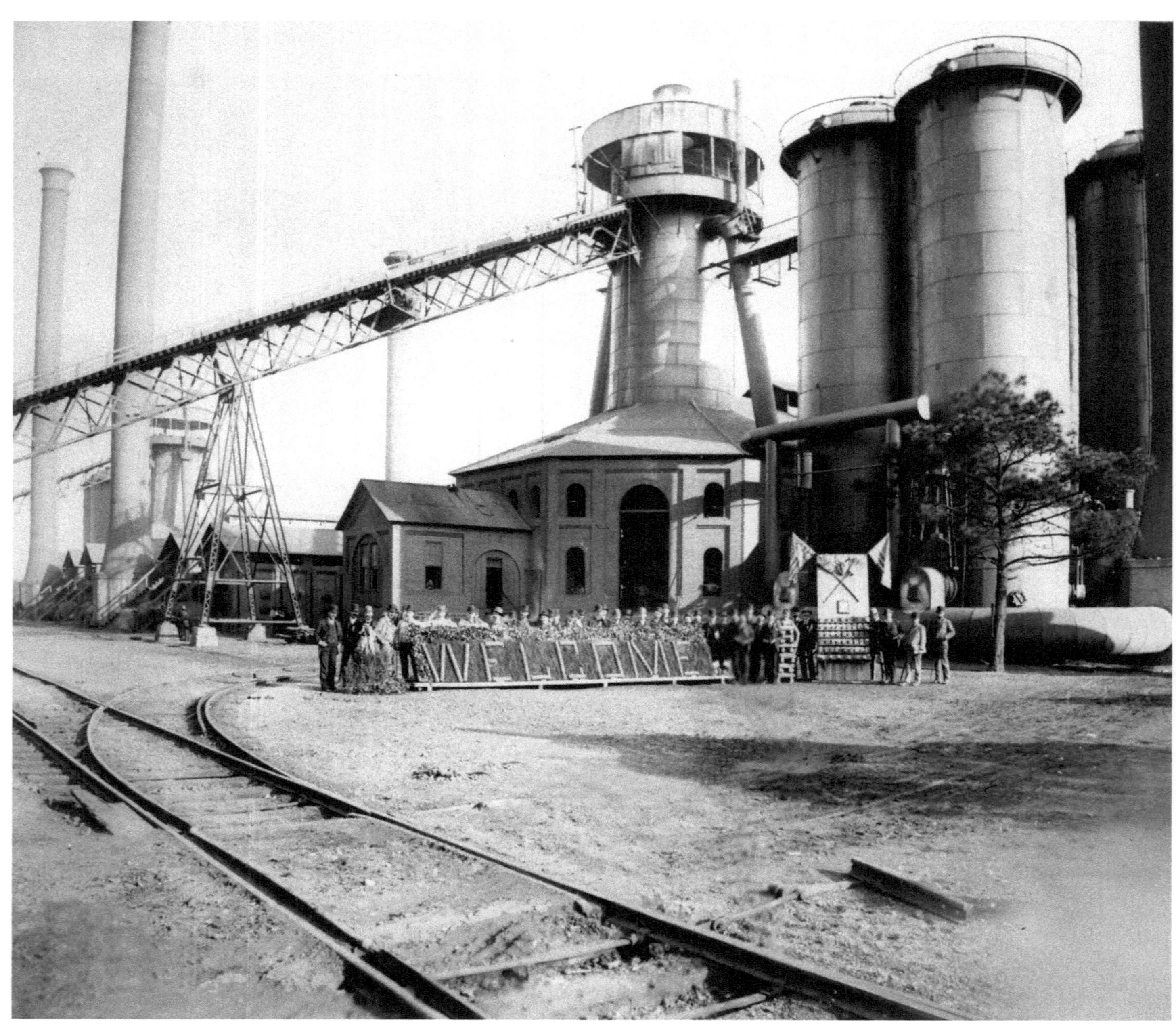

The Pioneer Mining and Manufacturing Company began operations of its blast furnace in Thomas in 1888. Republic Iron and Steel later assumed ownership and operated at the site until 1971.

The Jefferson Volunteers of the Alabama militia, shown here outside the Jefferson County Courthouse, on December 8, 1888. On this date, the Volunteers were called out to help disperse a mob that attacked the courthouse trying to lynch Robert Hawes, a railroad engineer accused of murdering his wife and two daughters.

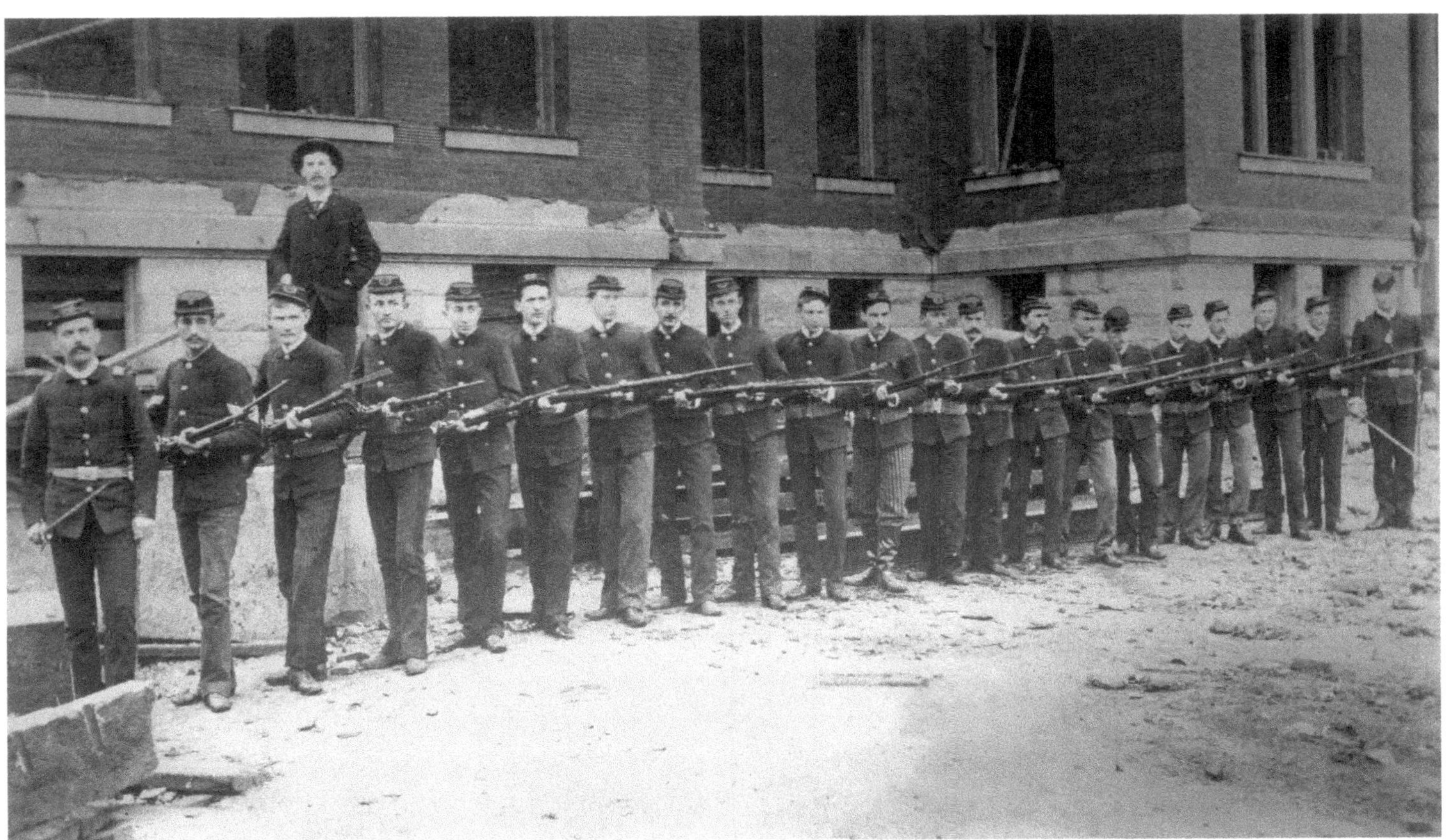

A special train takes picnickers to East Lake Park in June 1893. According to the original caption, B. H. Kelly was the train's engineer, Sherman Arrington the fireman, and Bob Baker and Charles Martin the conductors.

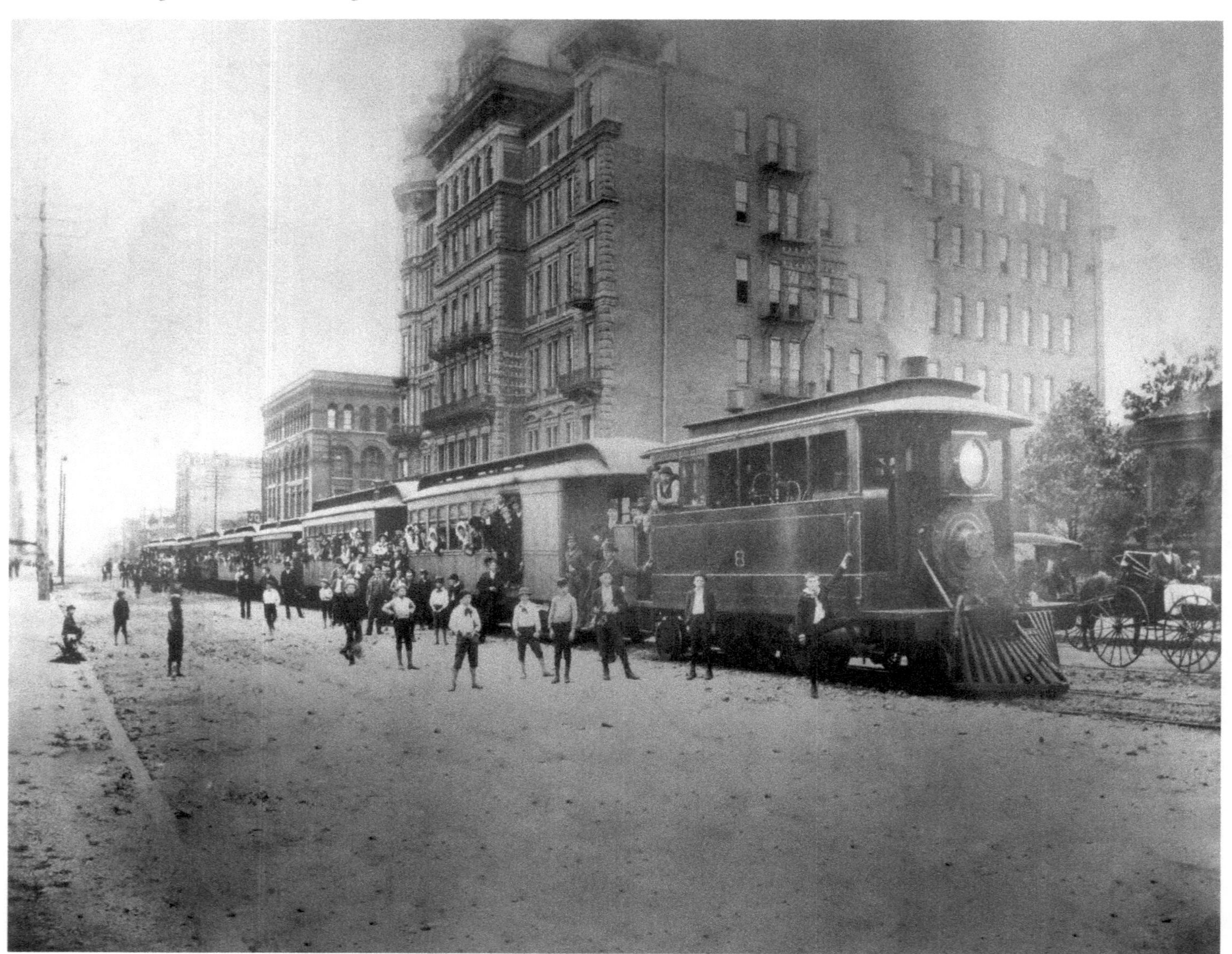

First Avenue North, facing east from Eighteenth Street, around the 1890s.

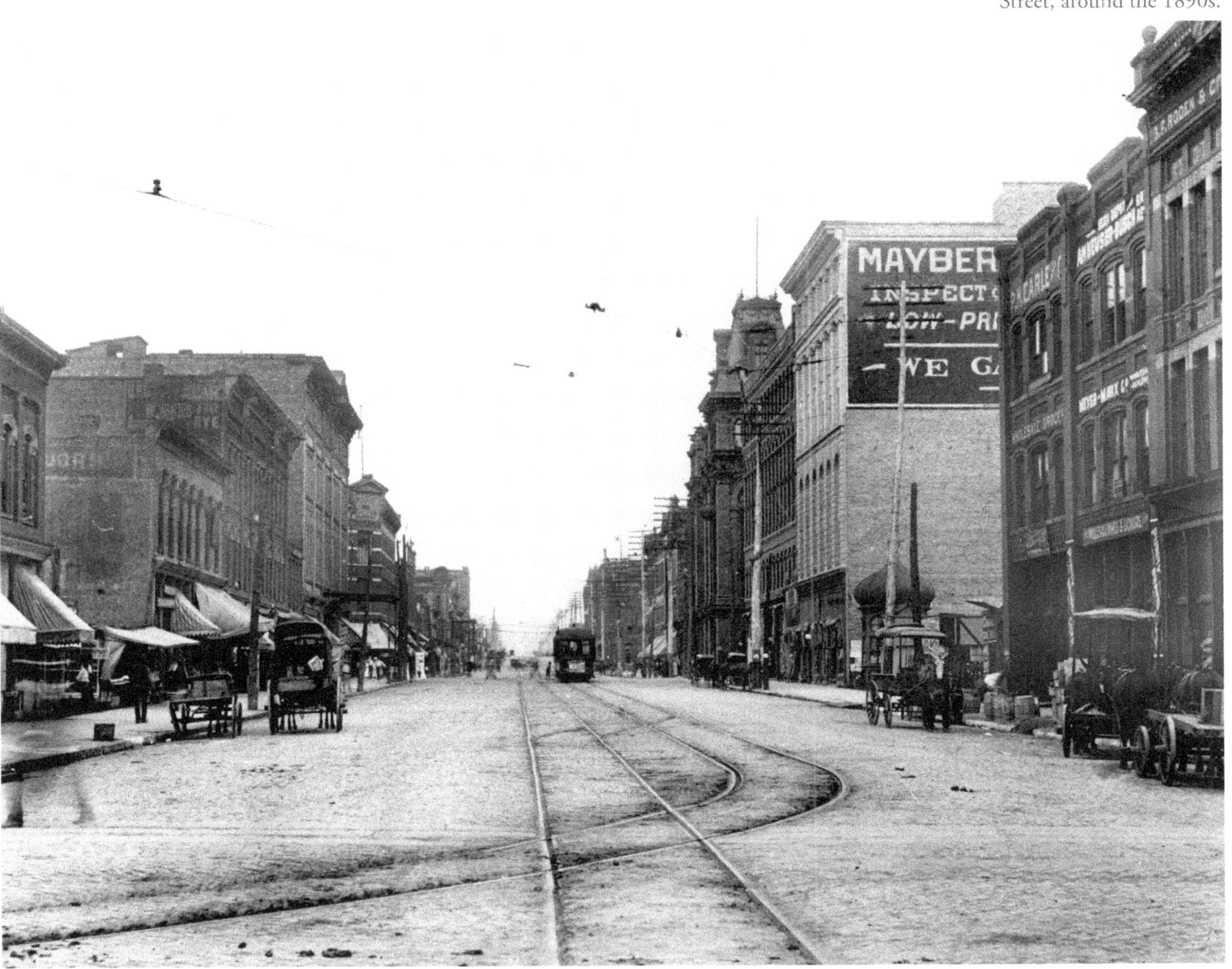

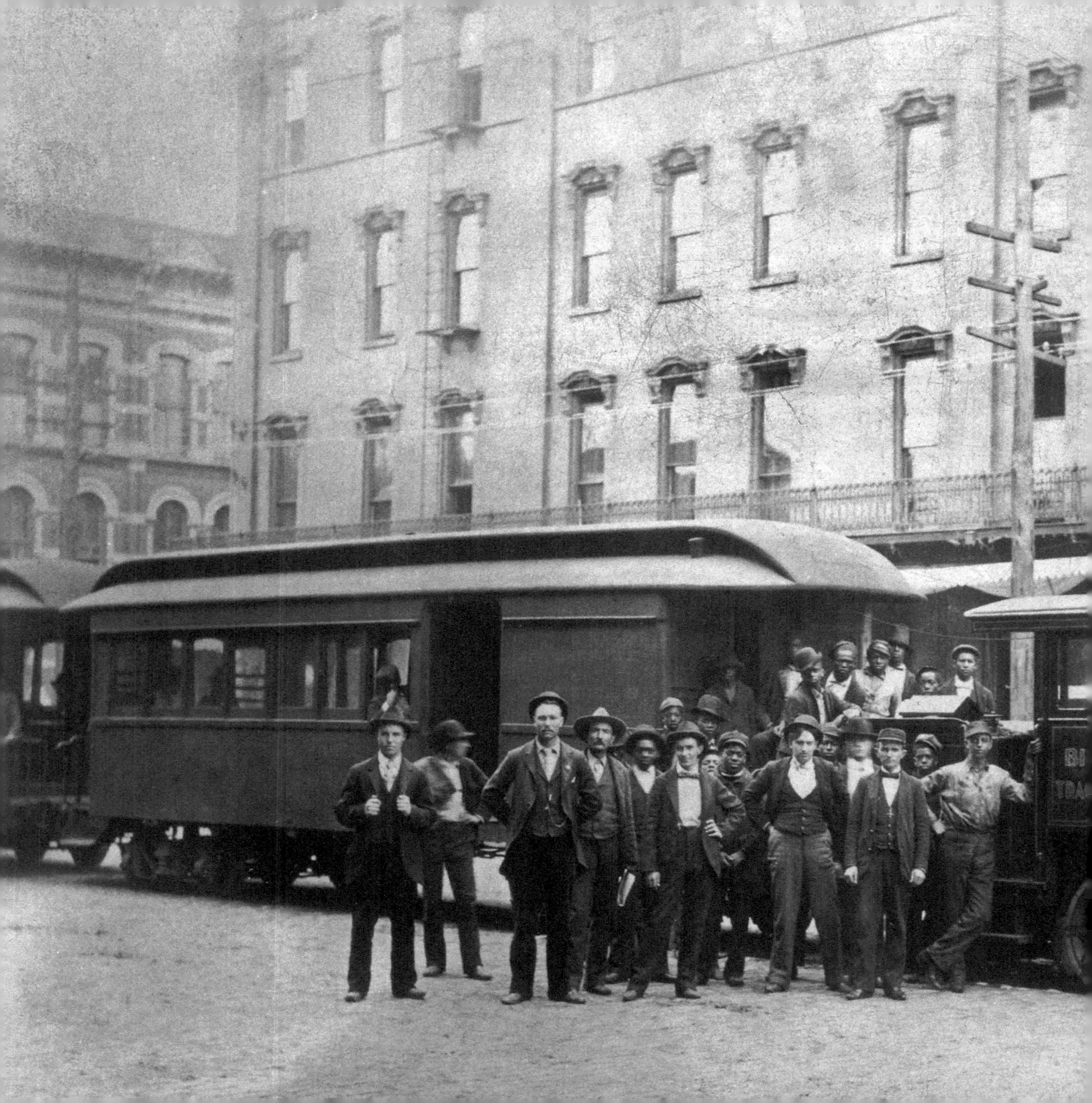

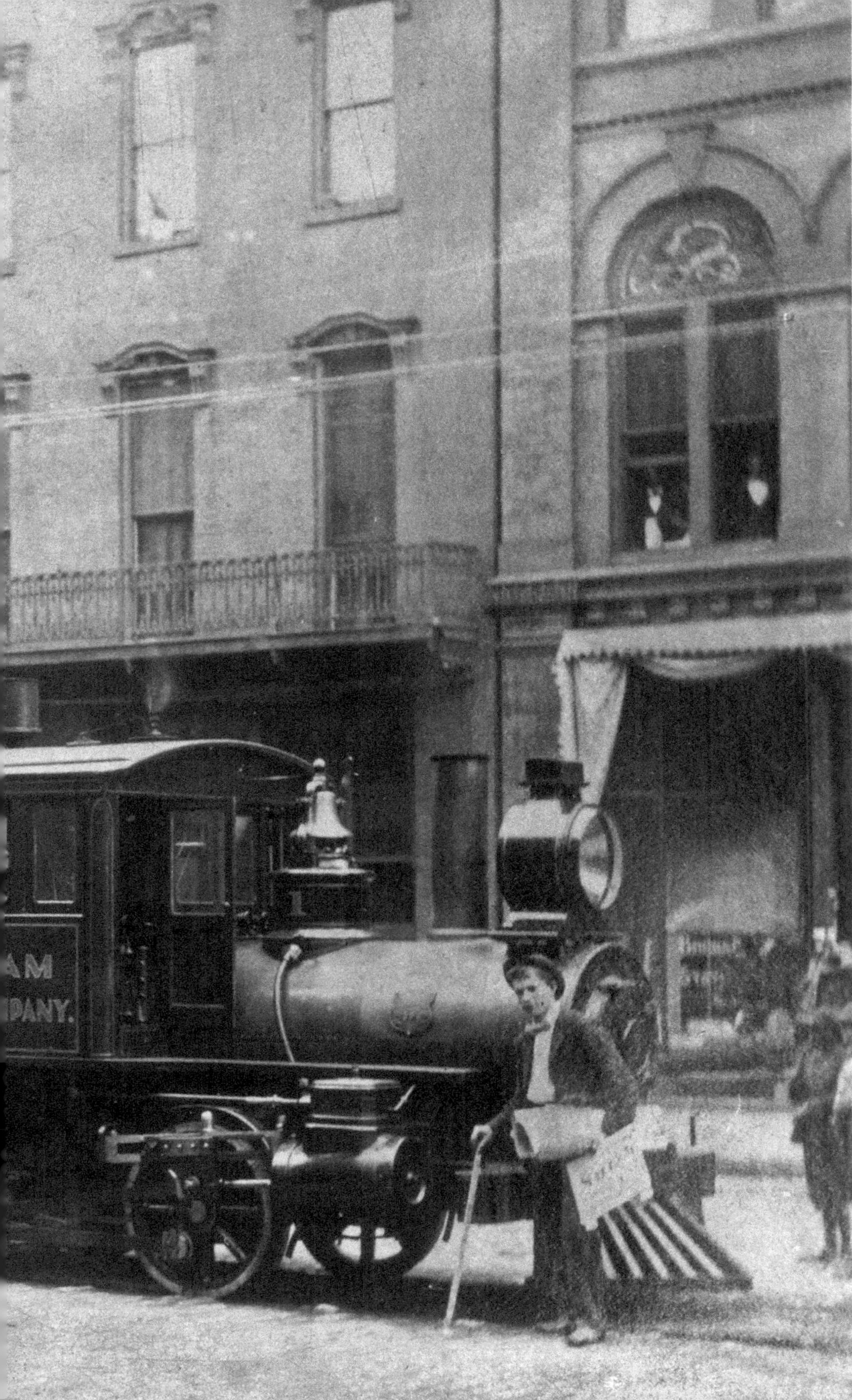

Streetcars of the Birmingham Traction Company carried passengers between downtown and North Birmingham in the 1890s.

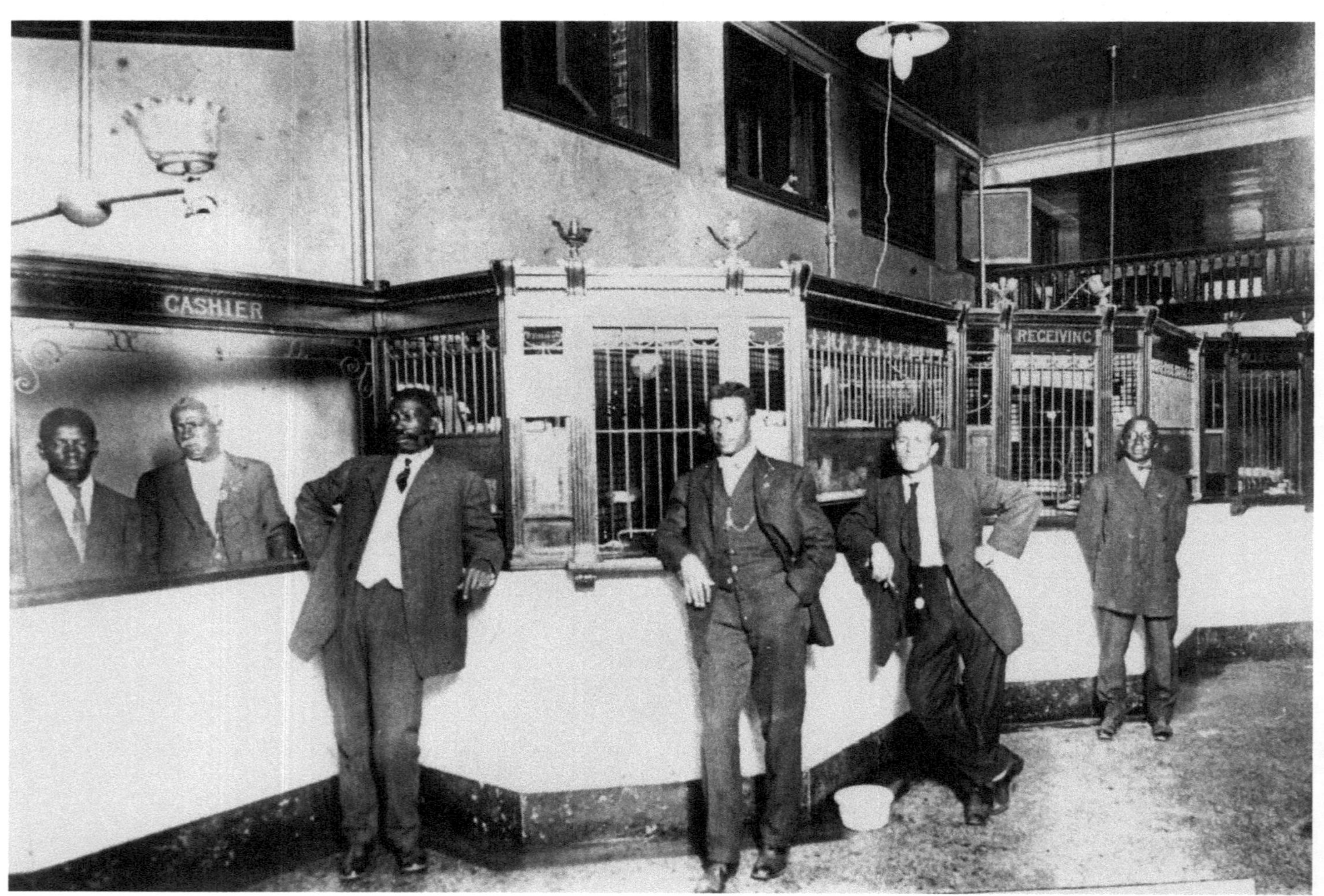

Founded in 1895 when most white-owned banks would not make loans to African Americans, the Alabama Penny Savings Bank was Birmingham's first black-owned financial institution.

Members of the Birmingham Fire Department company number two pose for the camera at their station on Southside, around 1896.

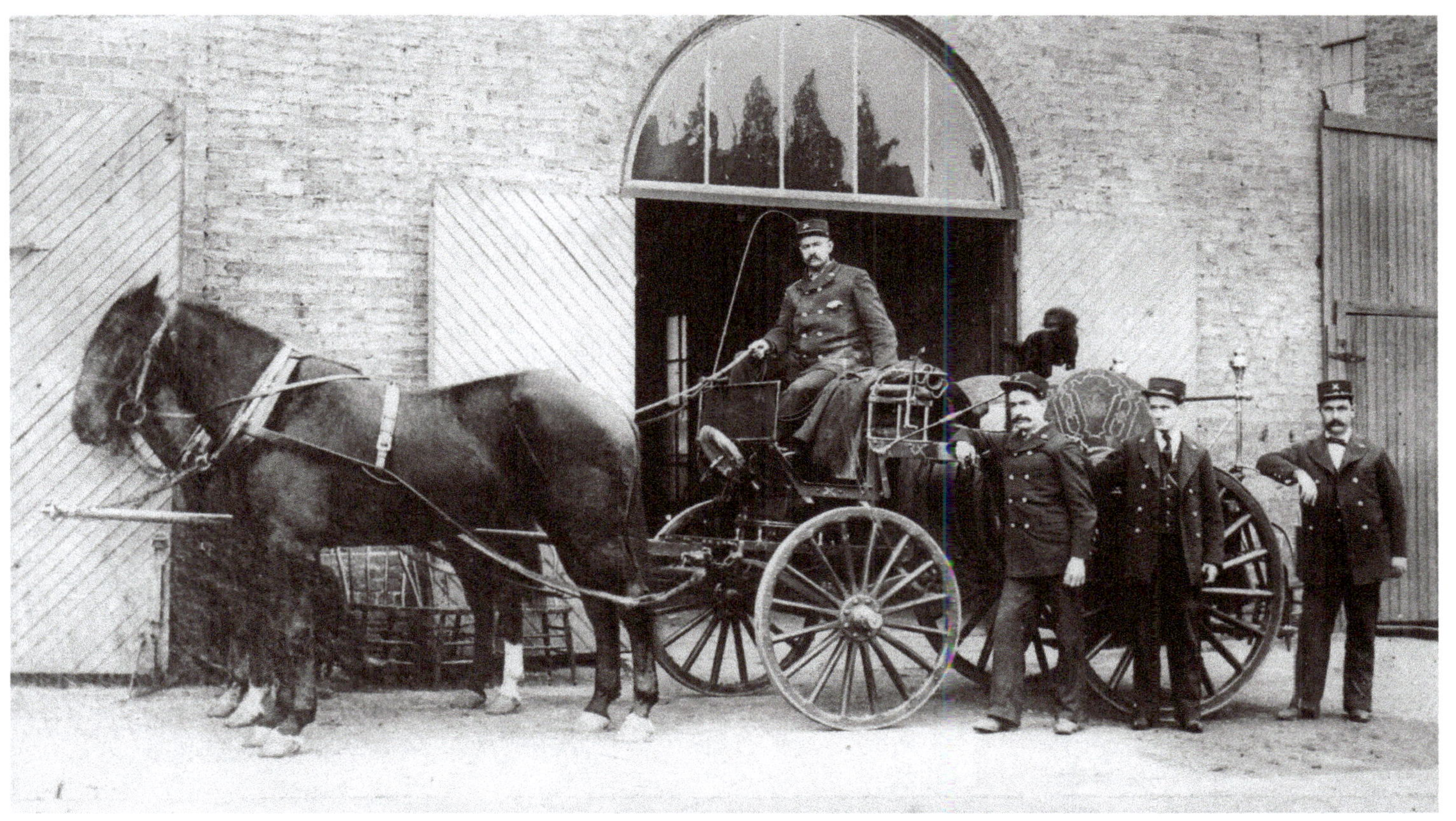

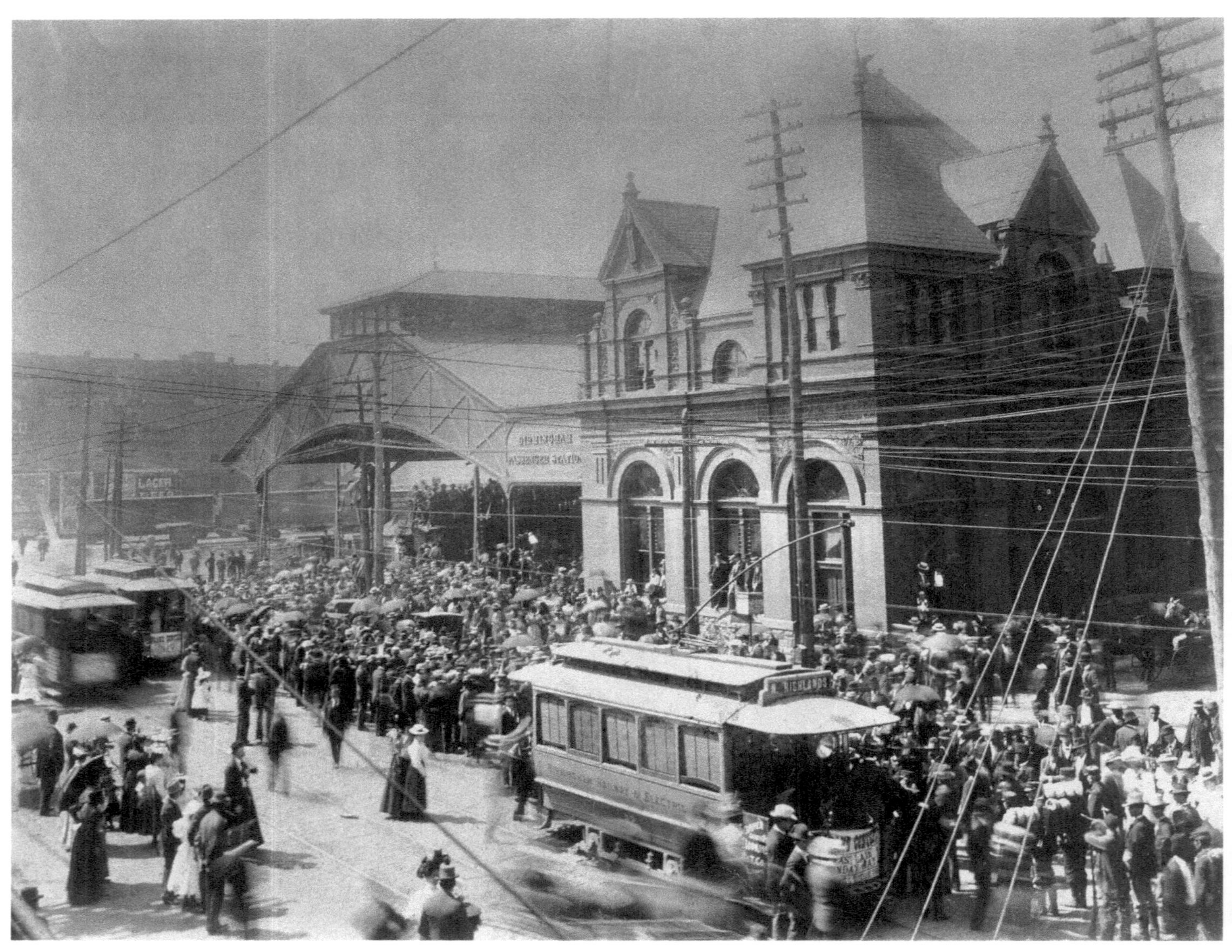

A crowd has gathered at Union Station on Twentieth Street to see local volunteers leave for the Spanish-American War, May 1, 1898.

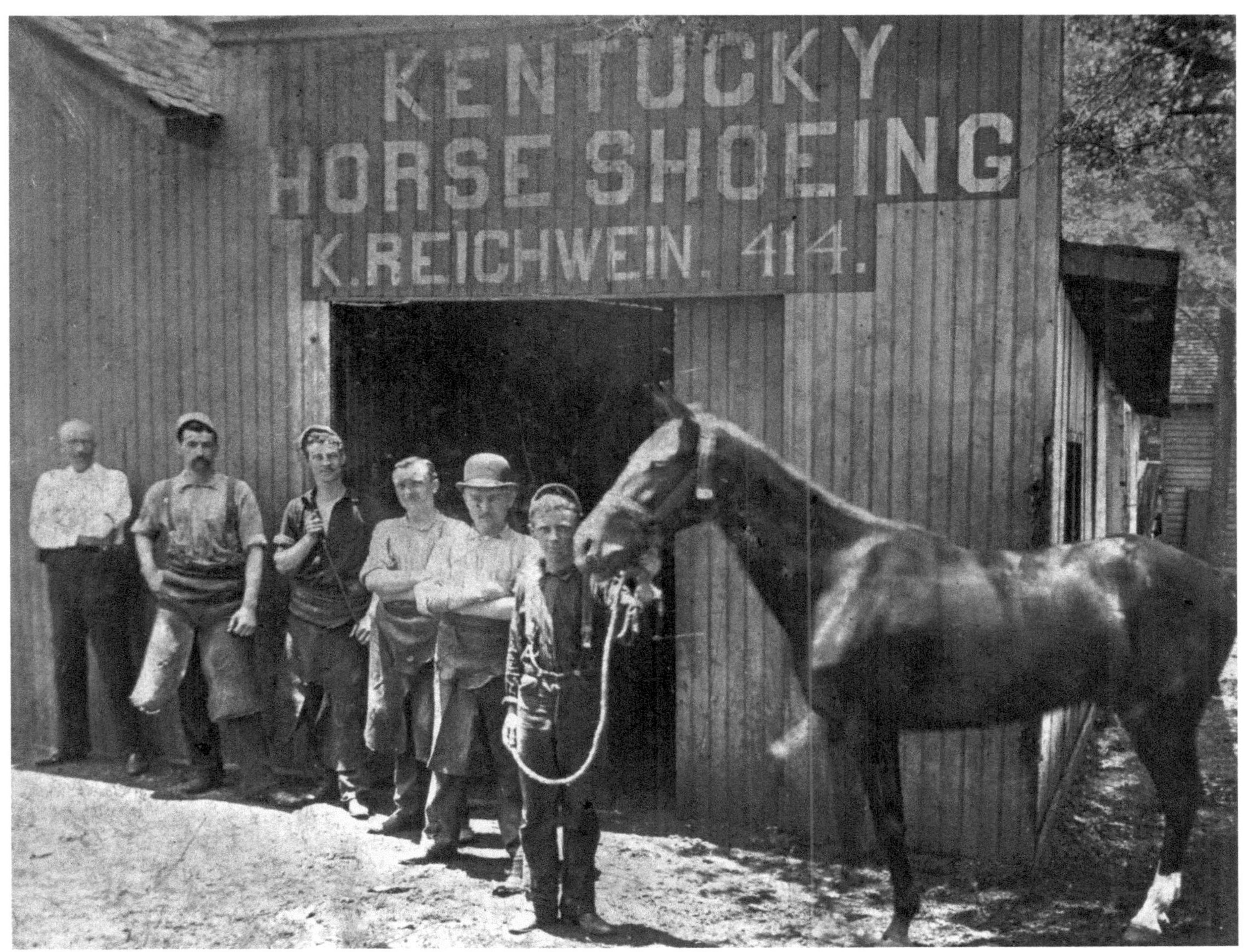

Kentucky Horse Shoeing on Twentieth Street was one of a dozen blacksmiths operating in Birmingham in the 1890s.

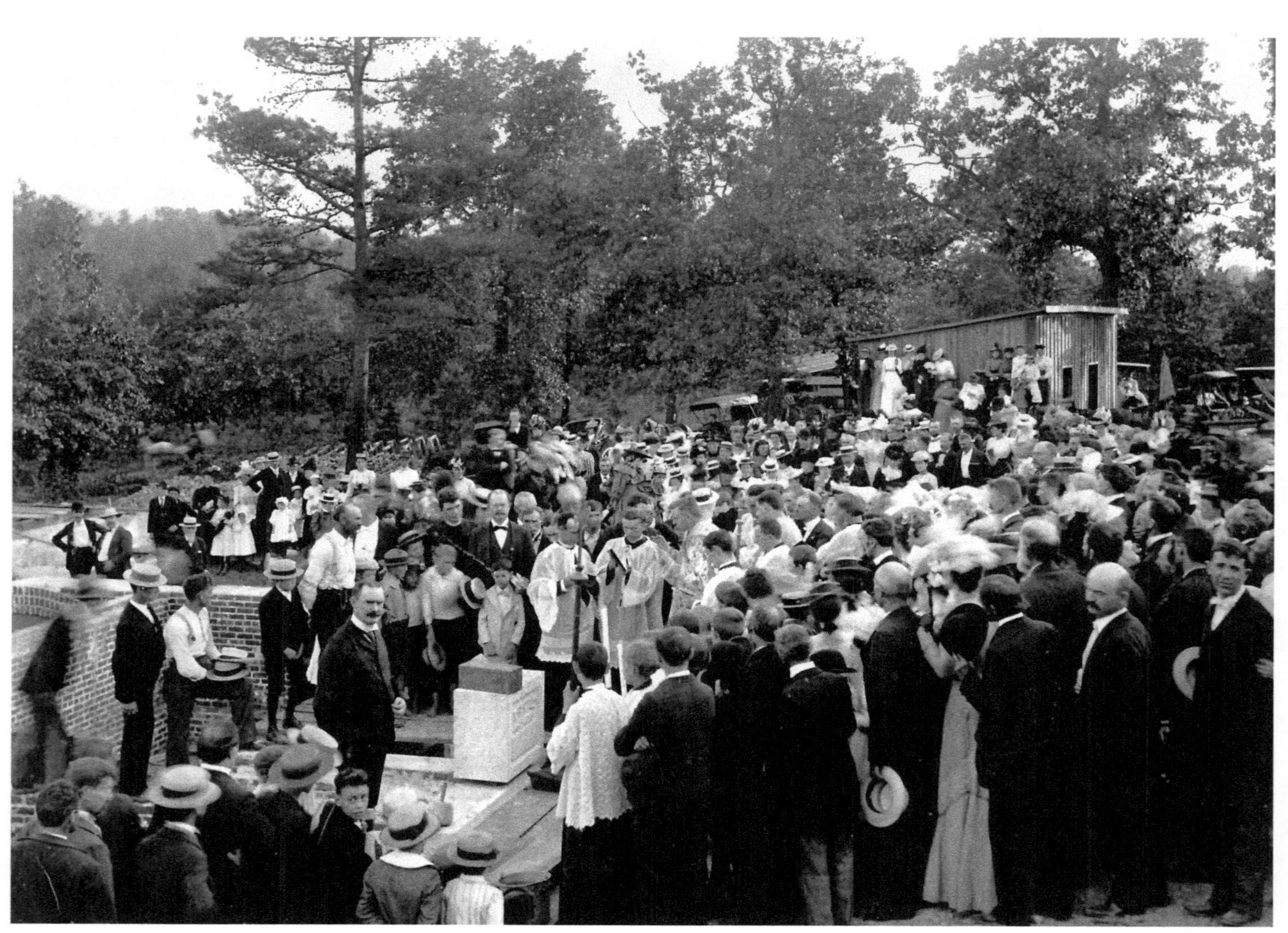

Laying of the cornerstone of St. Vincent's Hospital, May 30, 1899.

The old Watts Building, corner of Twentieth Street and Third Avenue North. Sometimes misidentified as the funeral procession for Louise Wooster, Birmingham's most famous madam, this photograph was made more than a decade before Wooster's death.

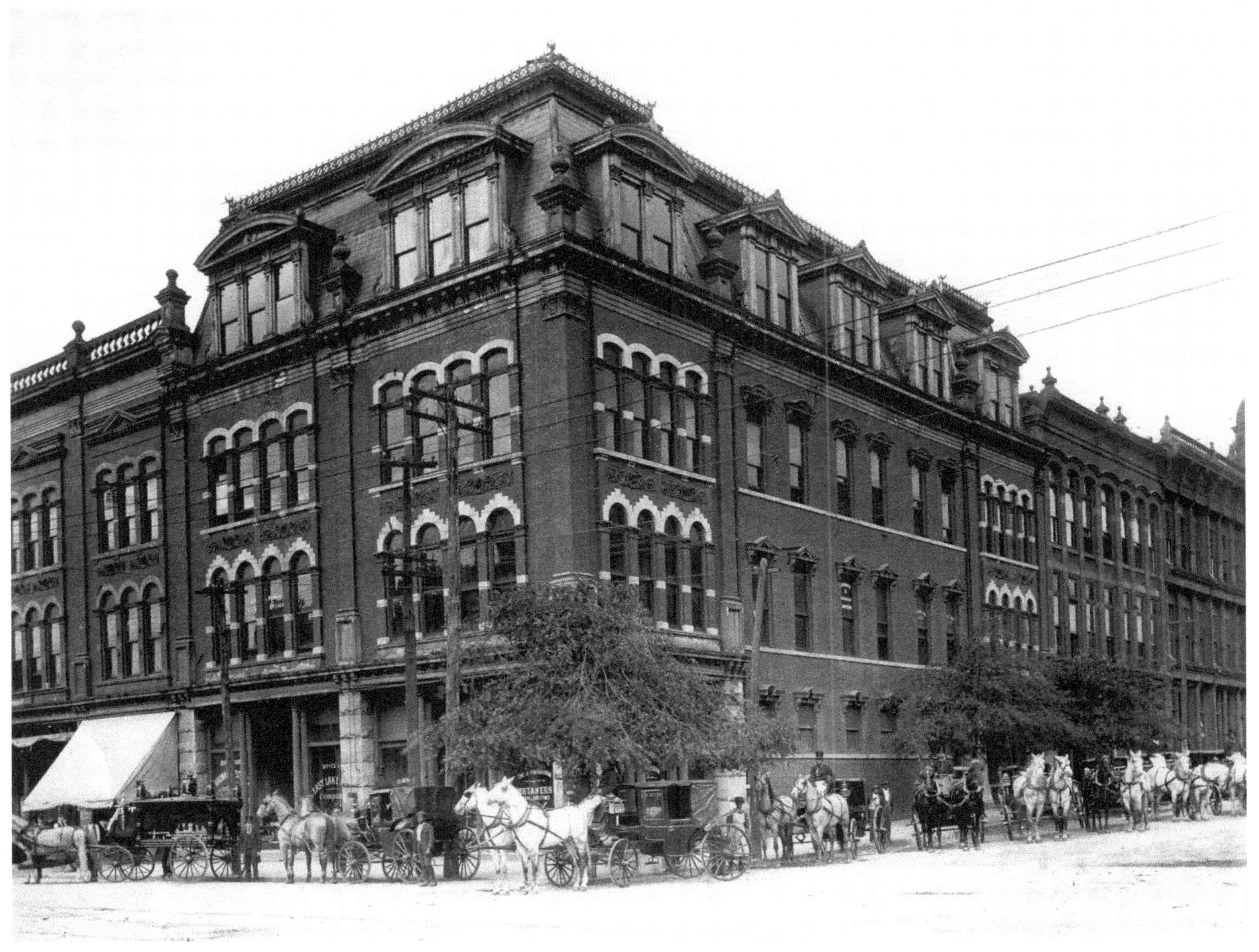

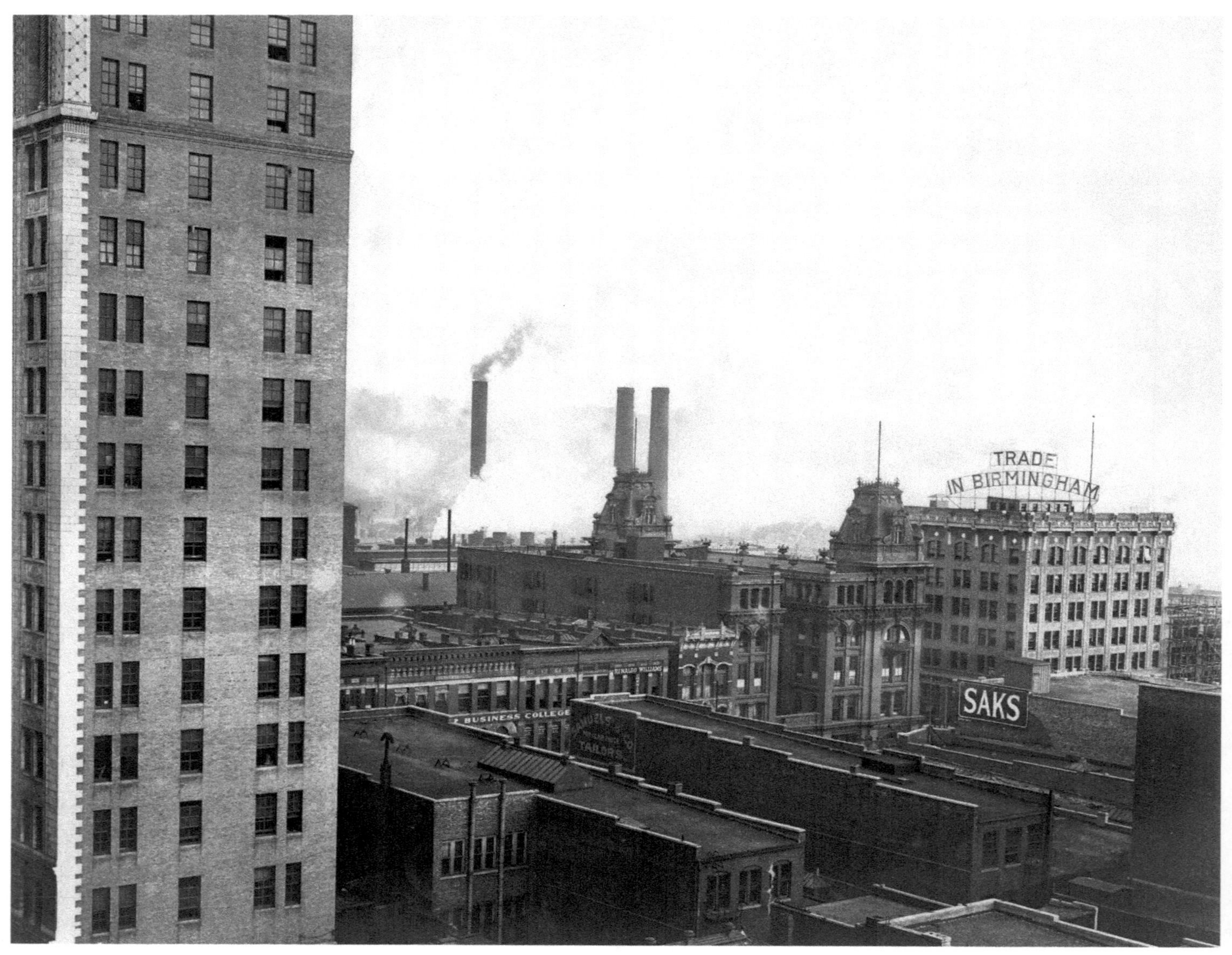

A rooftop view of downtown, around 1910. The Empire Building is in the left foreground. In the distance, with the "Trade in Birmingham" sign on the roof, is the old Chamber of Commerce Building on the corner of First Avenue North and Nineteenth Street. This is now Jemison Flats.

A City at the Turn of the Century

(1900–1917)

For Birmingham, like many American cities, the decade and a half after 1900 was the era of the skyscraper. Rising land values in urban areas led to demands for buildings that were taller than nineteenth-century bricks and mortar could support. With the development of steel-framed construction techniques, and the perfection of safe electric elevators, buildings could rise dozens of floors above their Victorian predecessors.

Birmingham's first steel-frame office building was the Woodward Building, completed in 1902, but it did not dominate the skyline for long. Other skyscrapers followed, including the Frank Nelson Building and the Title Guaranty Building (both in 1903), the Brown-Marx Building (1906), Empire Building (1909), John Hand Building (1912), the Alabama Penny Savings Bank Building and the City Federal Building (both in 1913), and the Tutwiler Hotel (1914). The towering new buildings changed the look and feel of the city, and residents dubbed First Avenue North "the Grand Canyon."

A nationwide financial panic in 1907 nearly led to the bankruptcy of the Tennessee Coal, Iron and Railroad Company (TCI), Birmingham's largest manufacturer. In a deal brokered by New York bankers, United States Steel Corporation bought the majority of TCI's stock at a bargain basement price. Local boosters believed the sale would bring long needed capital to Birmingham's struggling industry, and it did. But the sale also ensured that Birmingham's steel industry would become, and remain, something of a stepchild to U.S. Steel's more established works in the north.

In addition to Birmingham's upward growth with new skyscrapers, the city expanded outward. In 1908, voters in Birmingham and several outlying communities approved the creation of a Greater Birmingham, annexing into the city the suburbs of Avondale, West End, East Lake, Woodlawn, Pratt City, Elyton, North Birmingham, and others. Swelling the city's population to well over 100,000, the annexation made Birmingham the largest city in Alabama and one of the largest in the South.

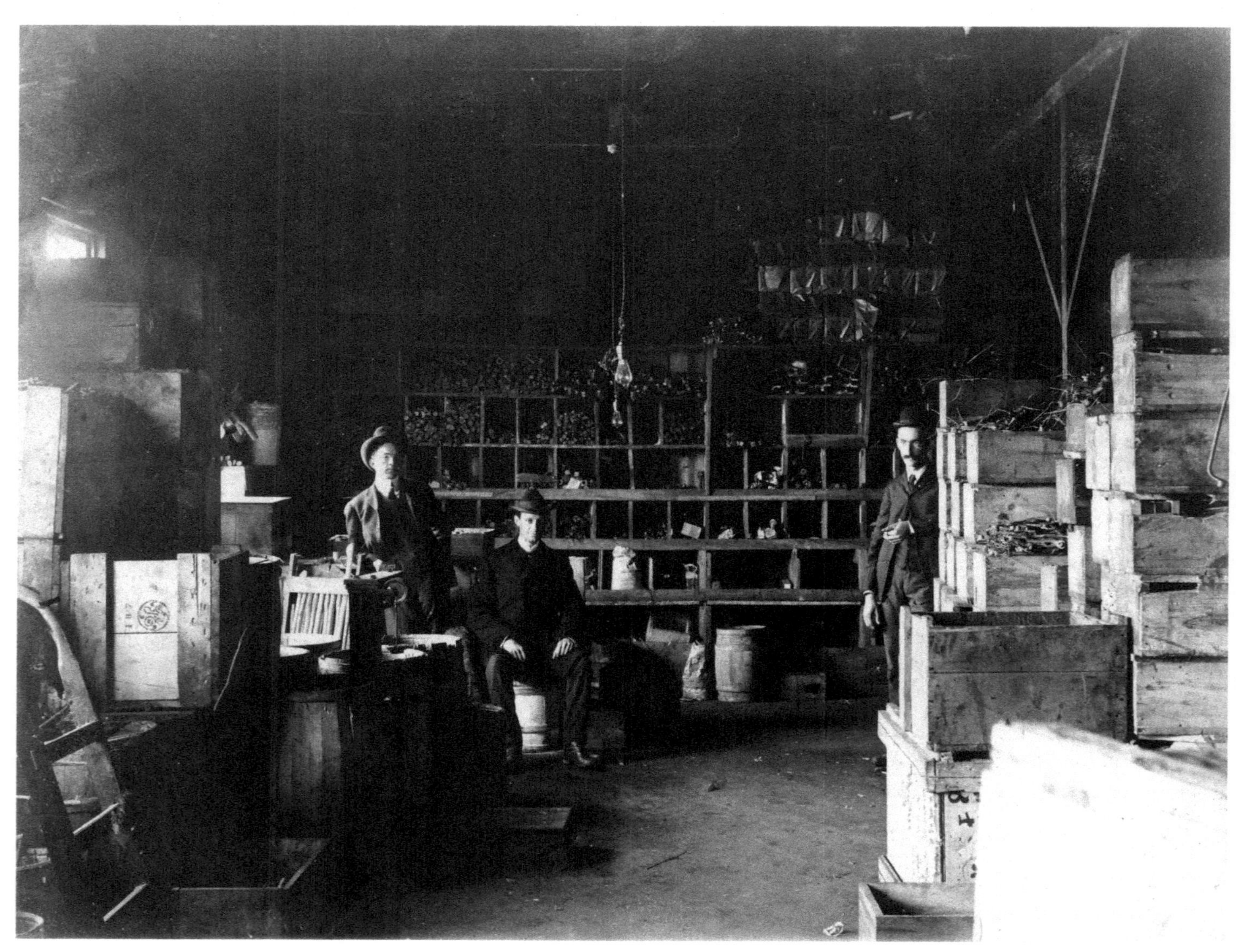

Shop for the Birmingham Railway, Light and Power Company, around 1900.

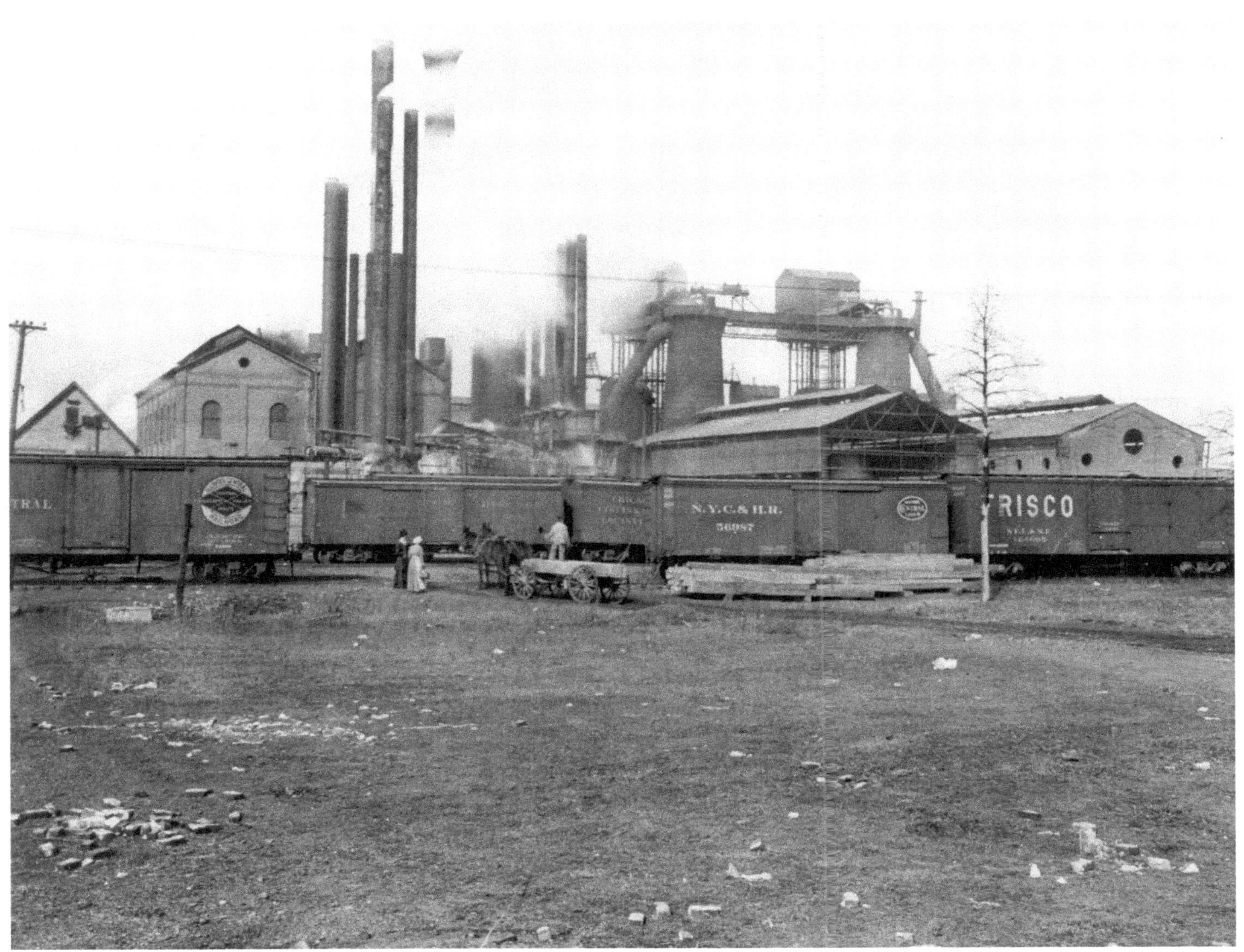

Outside the furnaces of the Bessemer Coal, Iron and Land Company, around 1900.

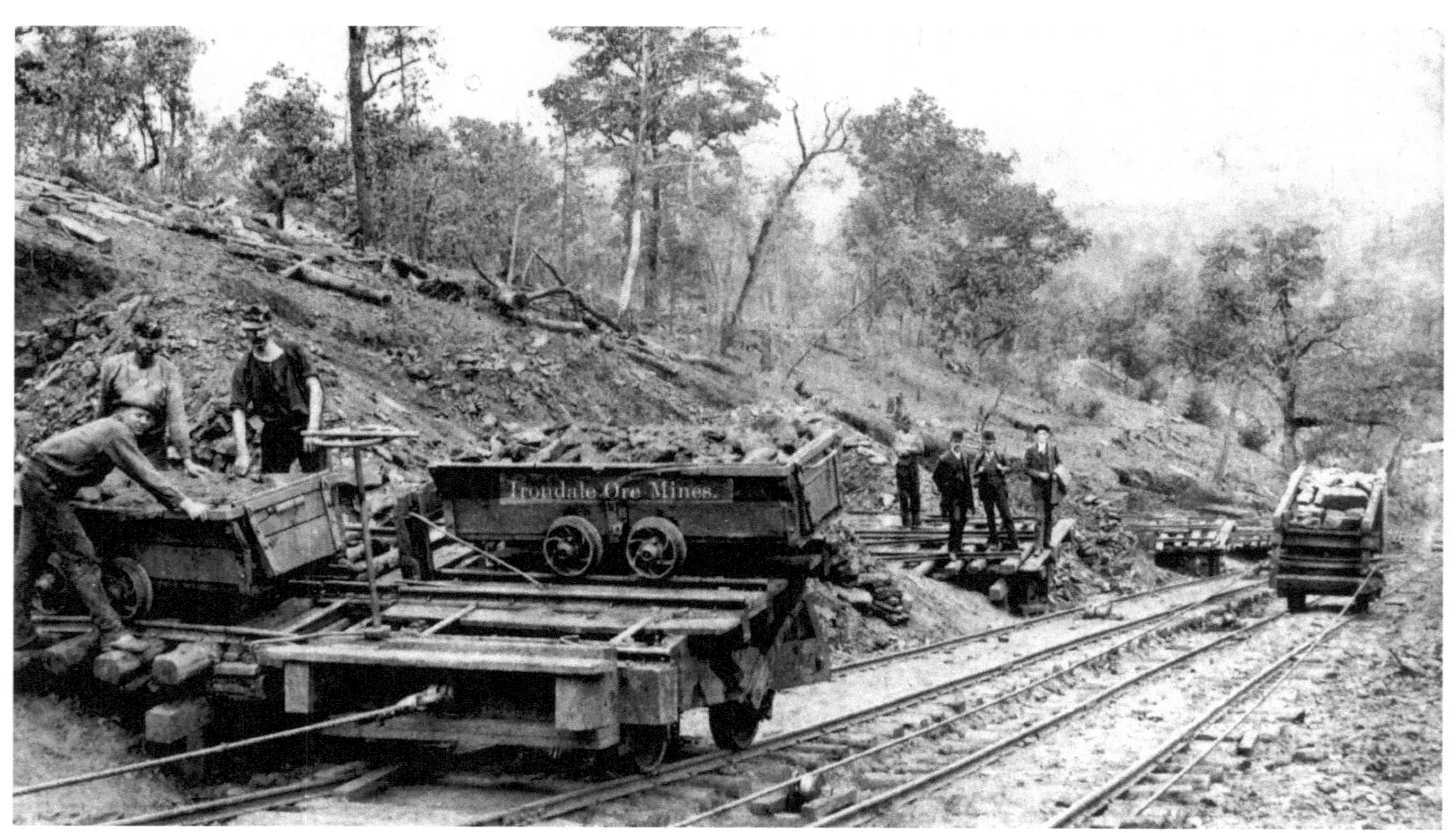

Outside the ore mines at Irondale, around 1900.

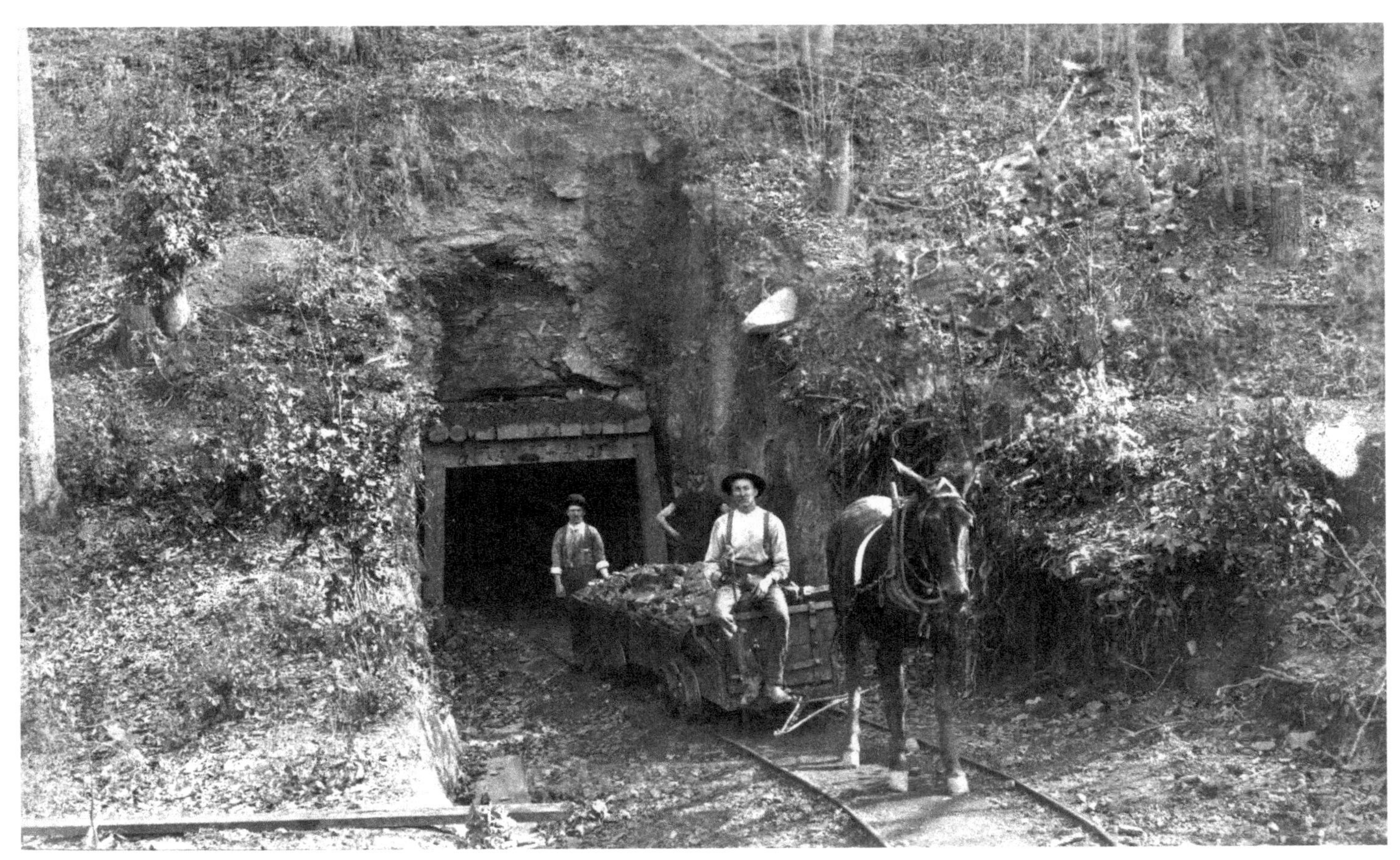

Entrance to an unidentified turn-of-the-century coal mine.

Starting line for a bicycle race at the Alabama State Fairgrounds.

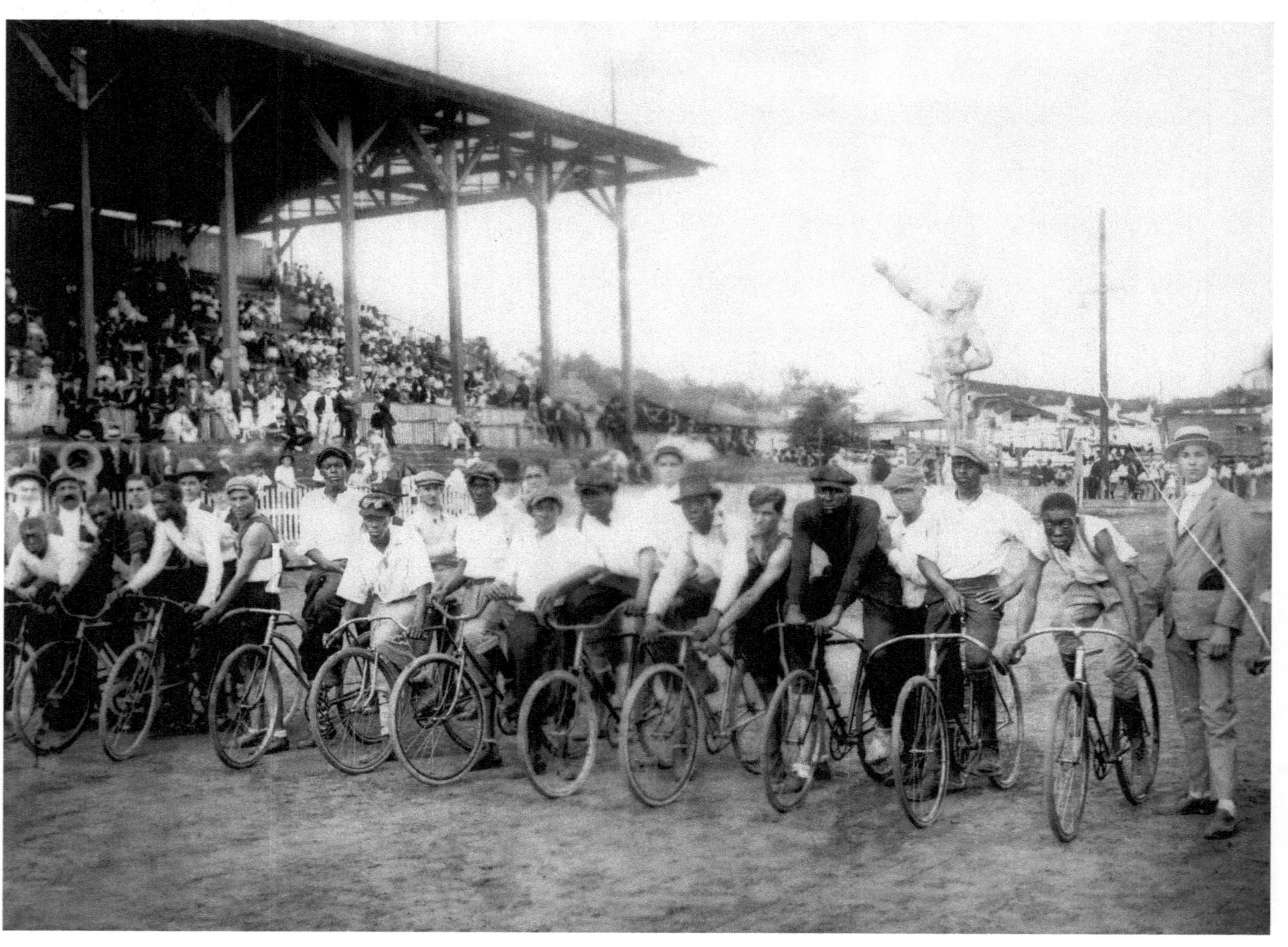

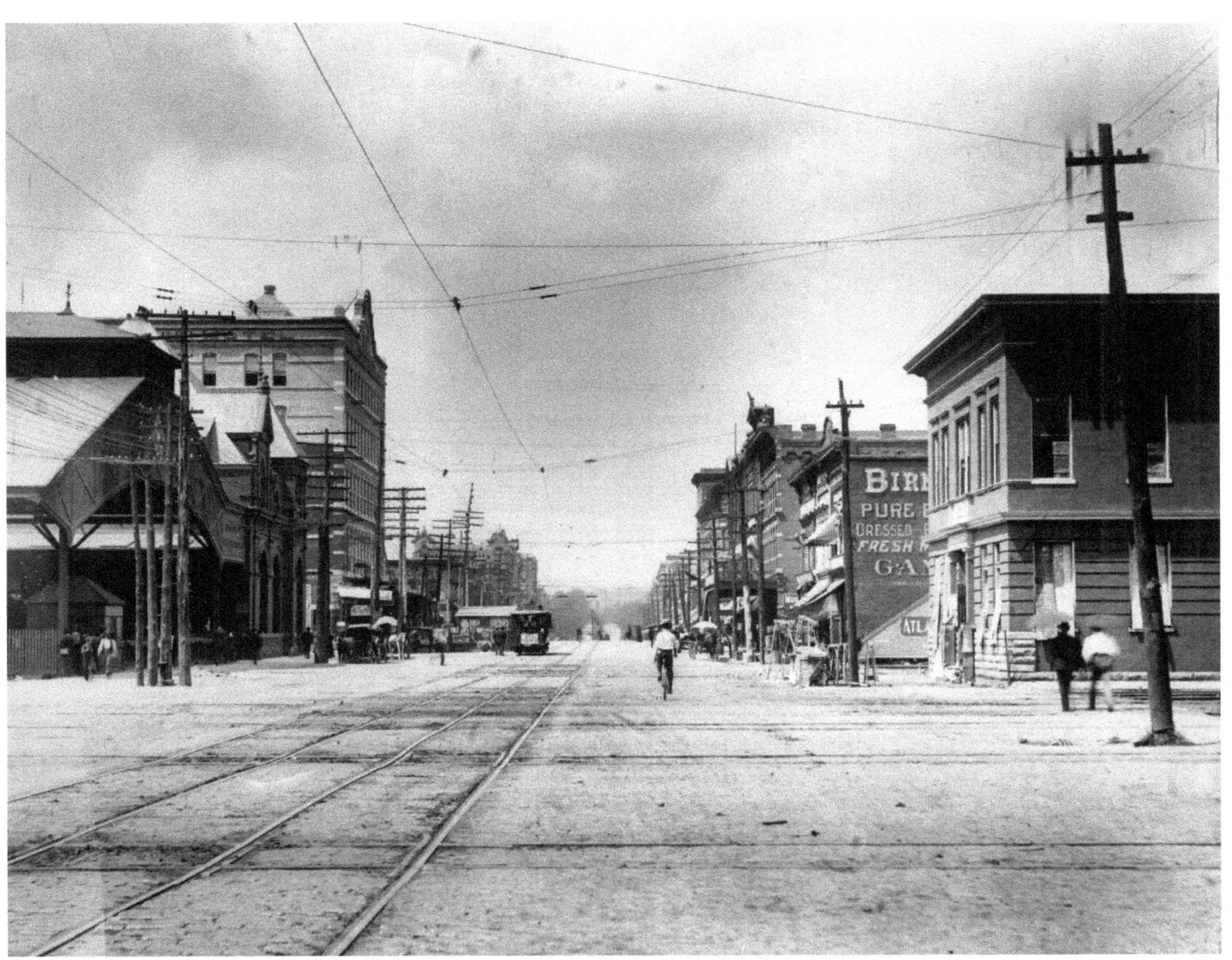

Facing north on Twentieth Street from Morris Avenue, around 1903. On the left is the train station with train shed and just beyond it the recently constructed Metropolitan Hotel.

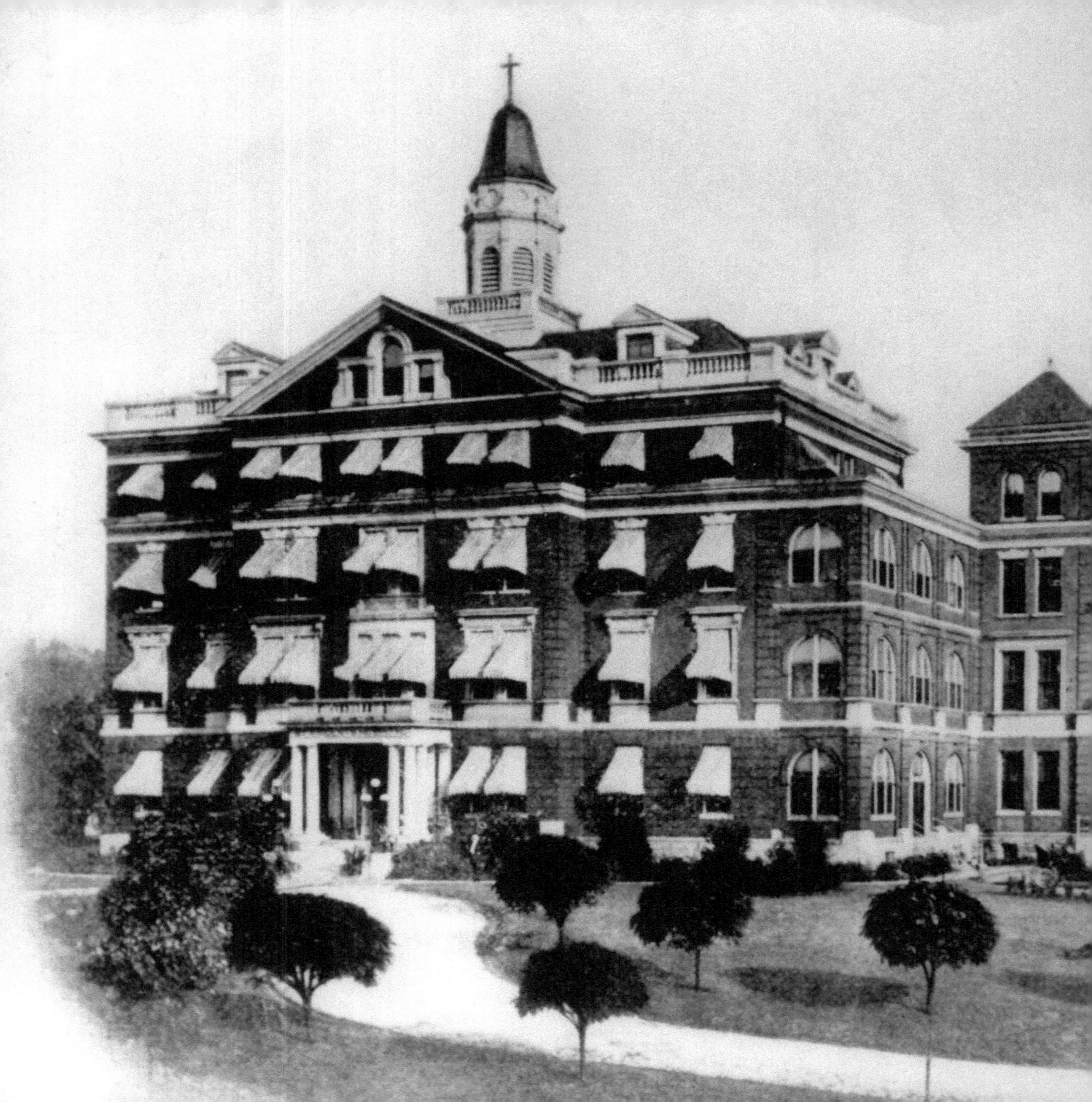

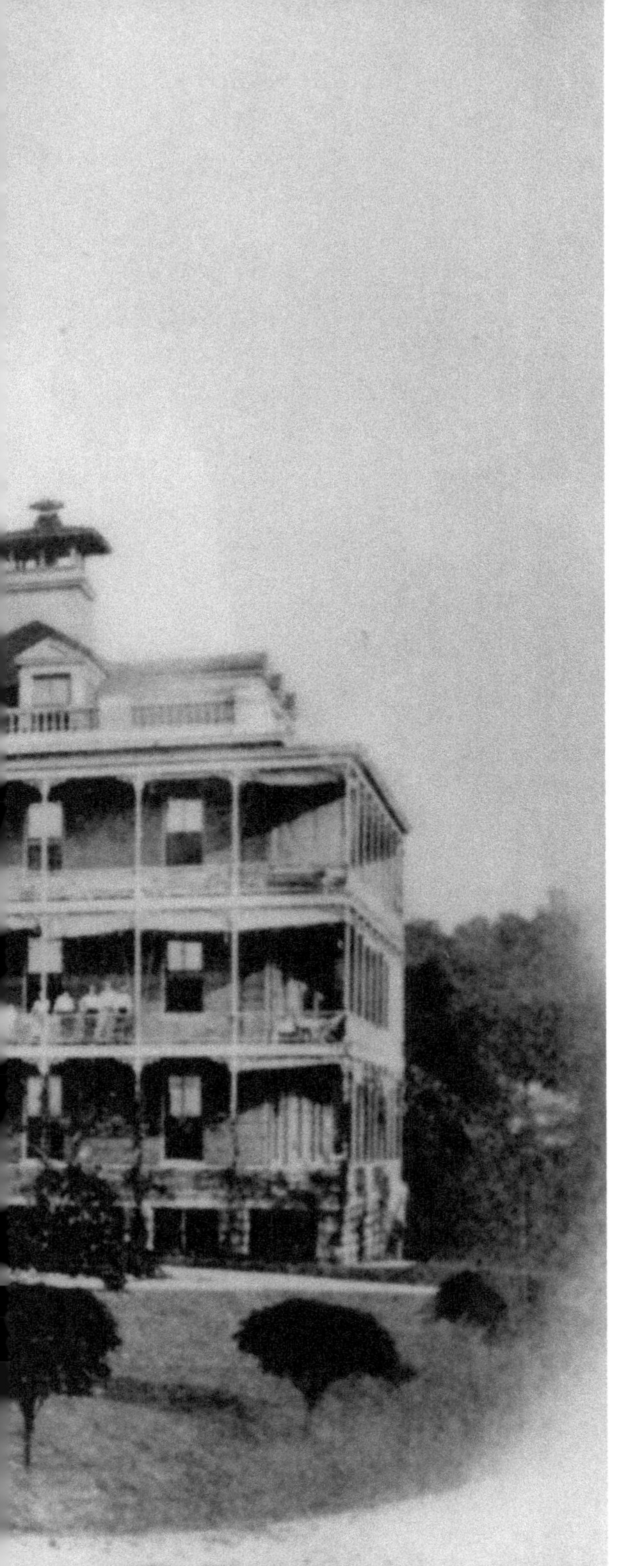

St. Vincent's Hospital, 1900.

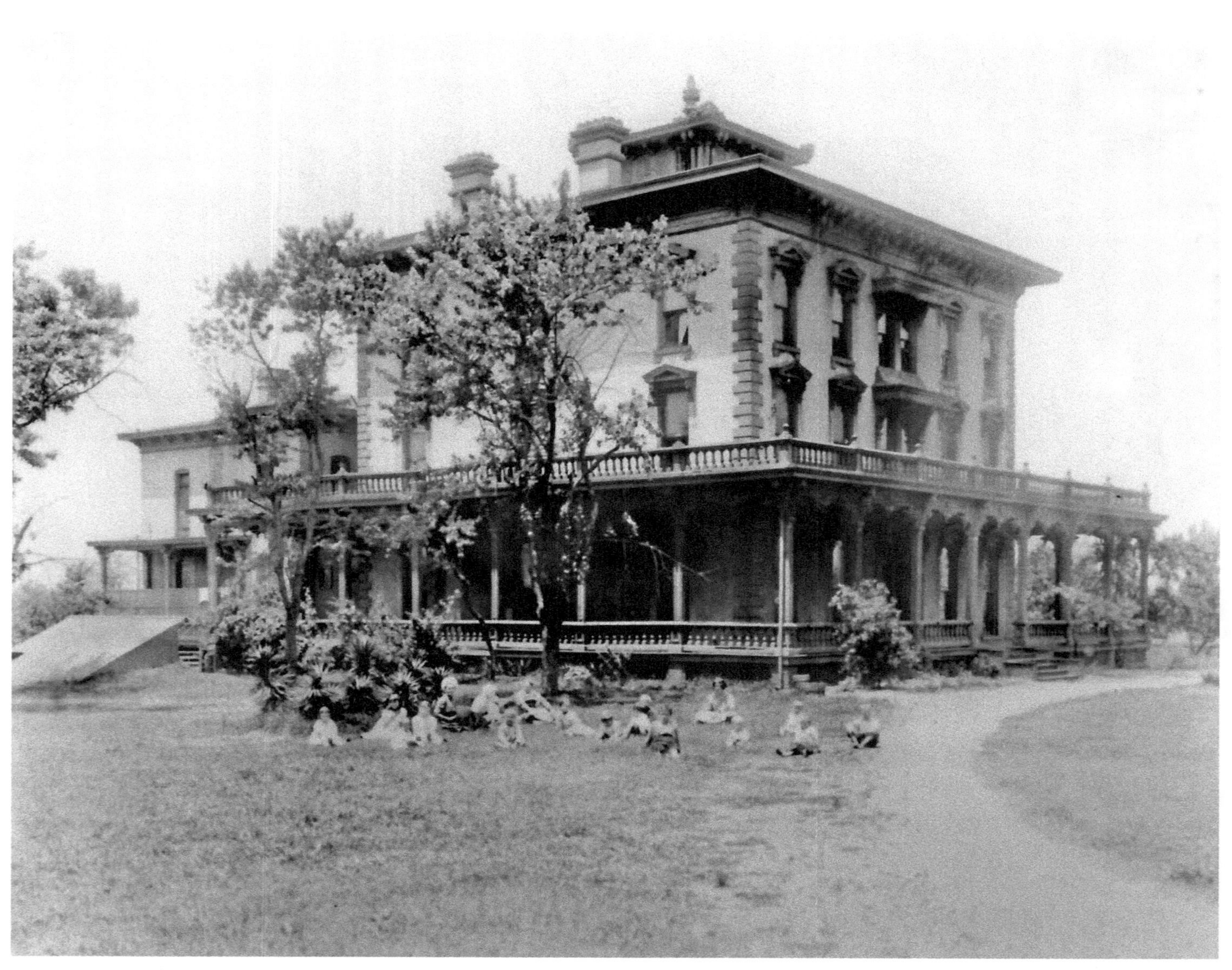

St. Vincent's opened in this three-story mansion that Henry F. DeBardeleben had built in the 1800s.

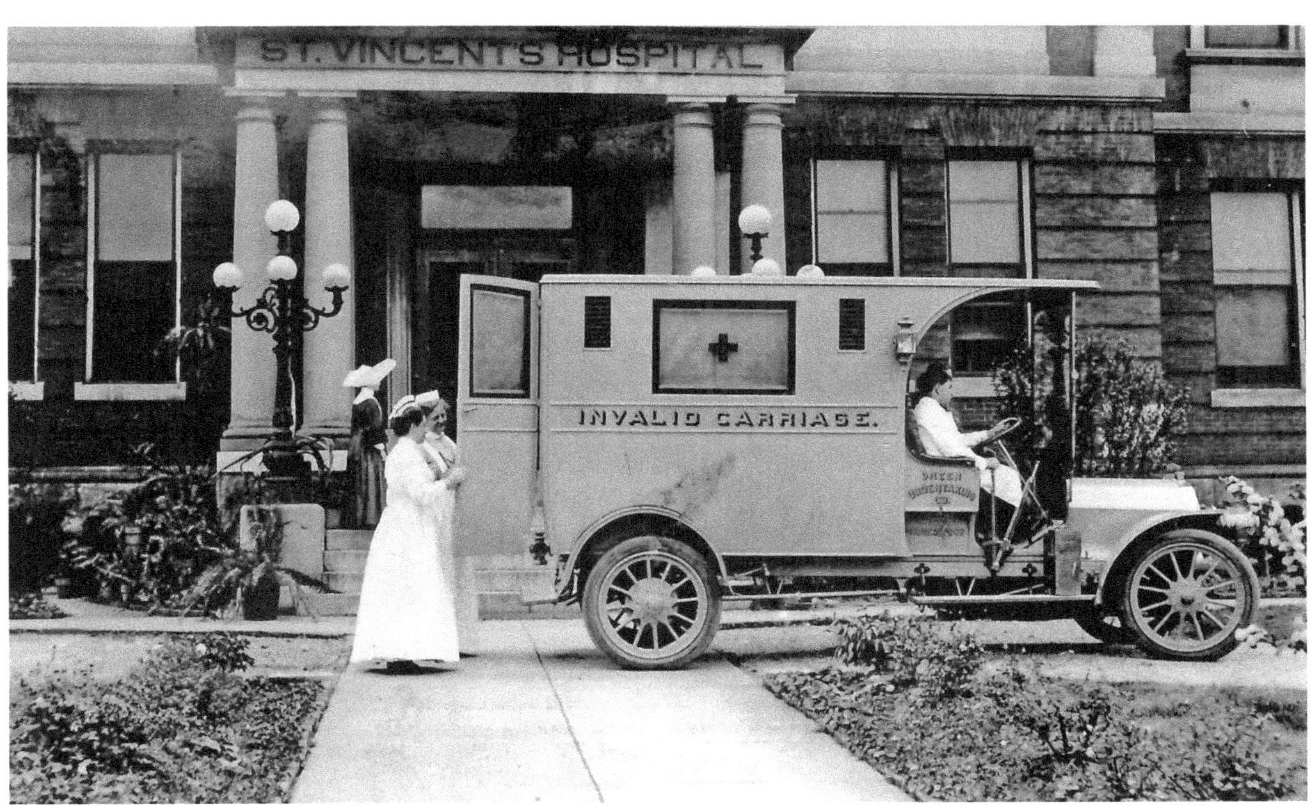

Nurses with ambulance at St. Vincent's, 1909.

The old Loveman, Joseph and Loeb Department Store on Third Avenue North and facing Nineteenth Street. A few years after this photo was taken, the Alabama Theatre was built just past Loveman's on Third.

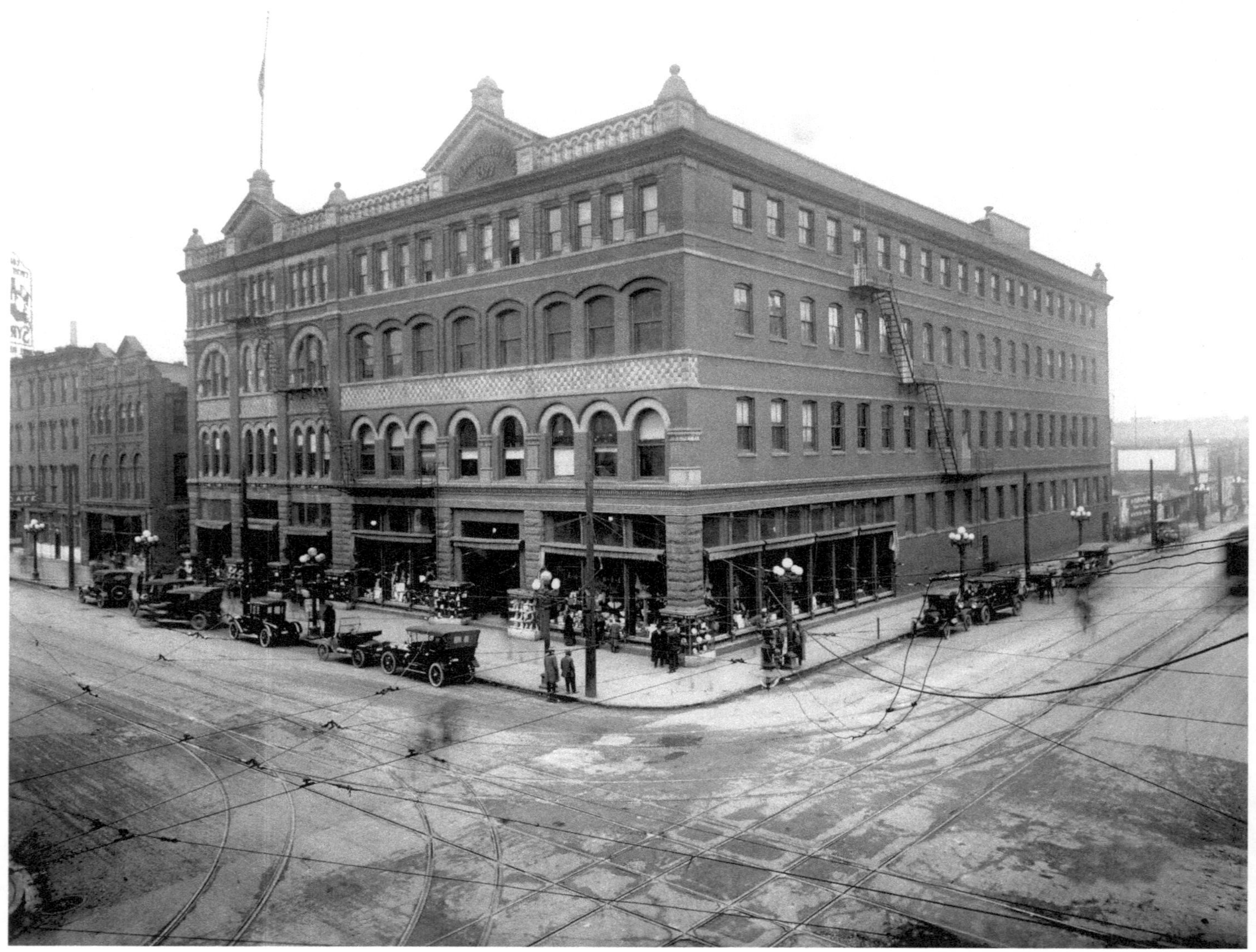

In the early twentieth century, motion pictures and Vaudeville shows were often promoted with elaborate displays like this one at the Lyric Theater.

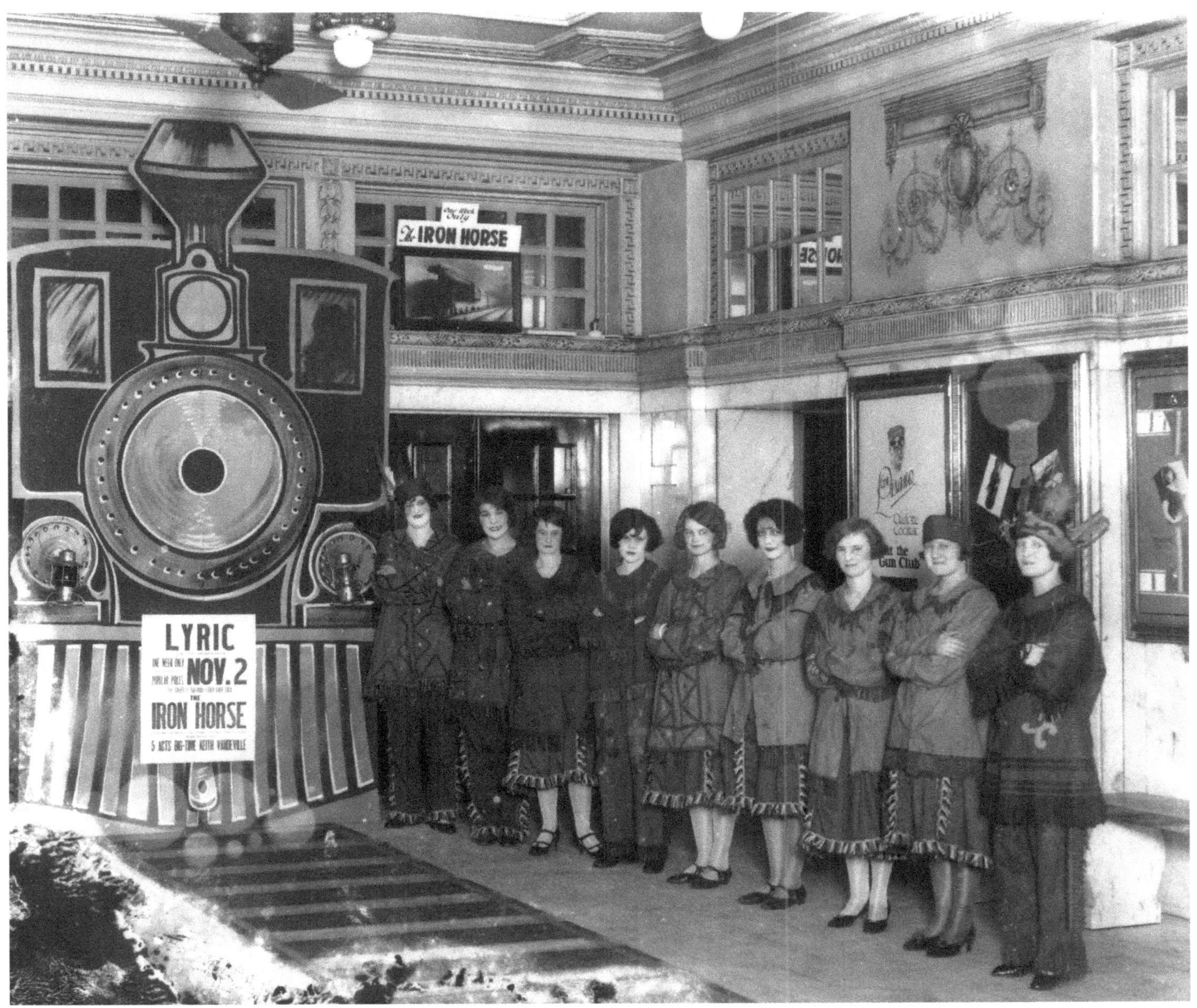

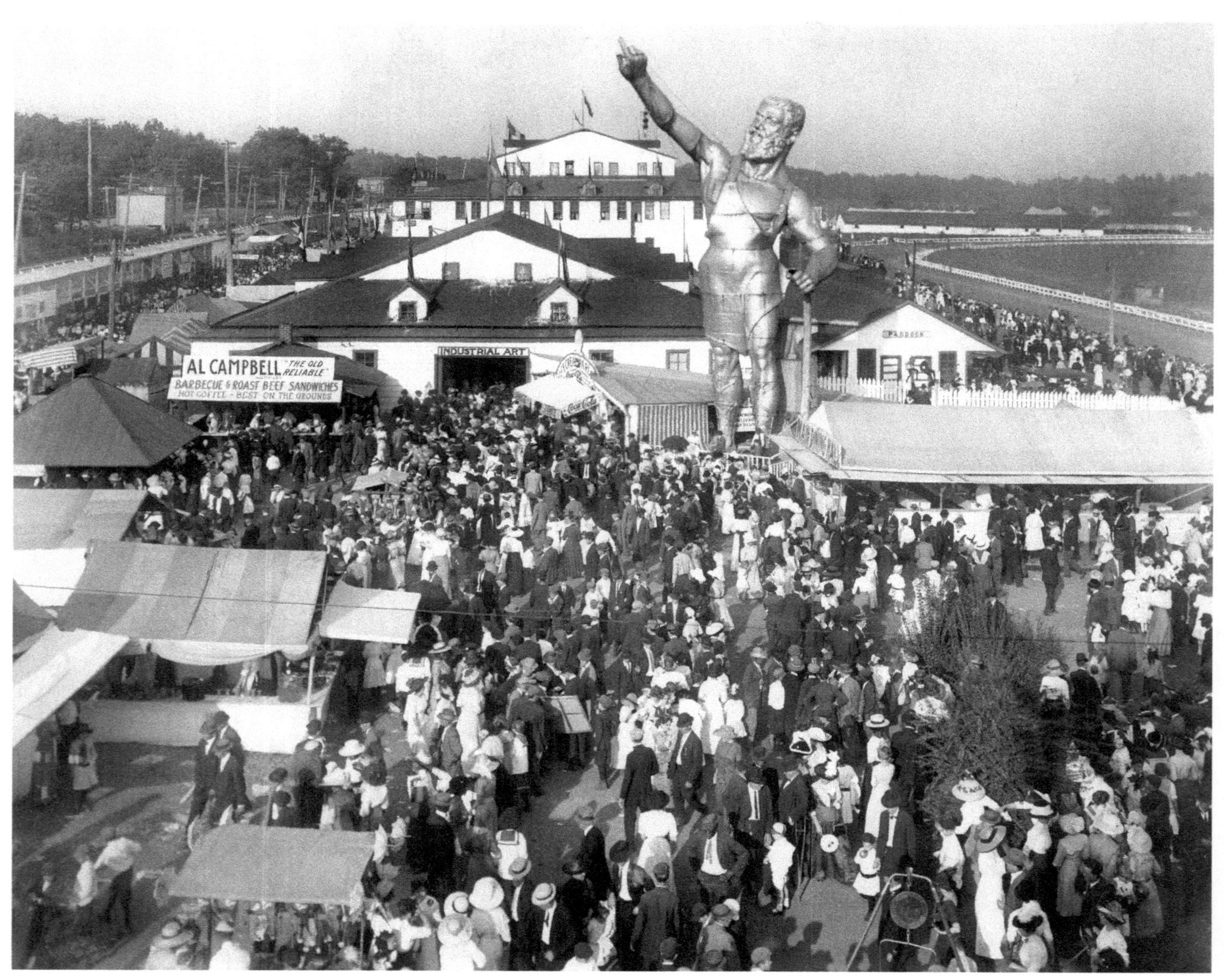

Between his triumph at the St. Louis World's Fair and his final home atop Red Mountain, Vulcan suffered a variety of indignities. Here he is shown at the state fair around 1910, assembled incorrectly so that his right arm is backward.

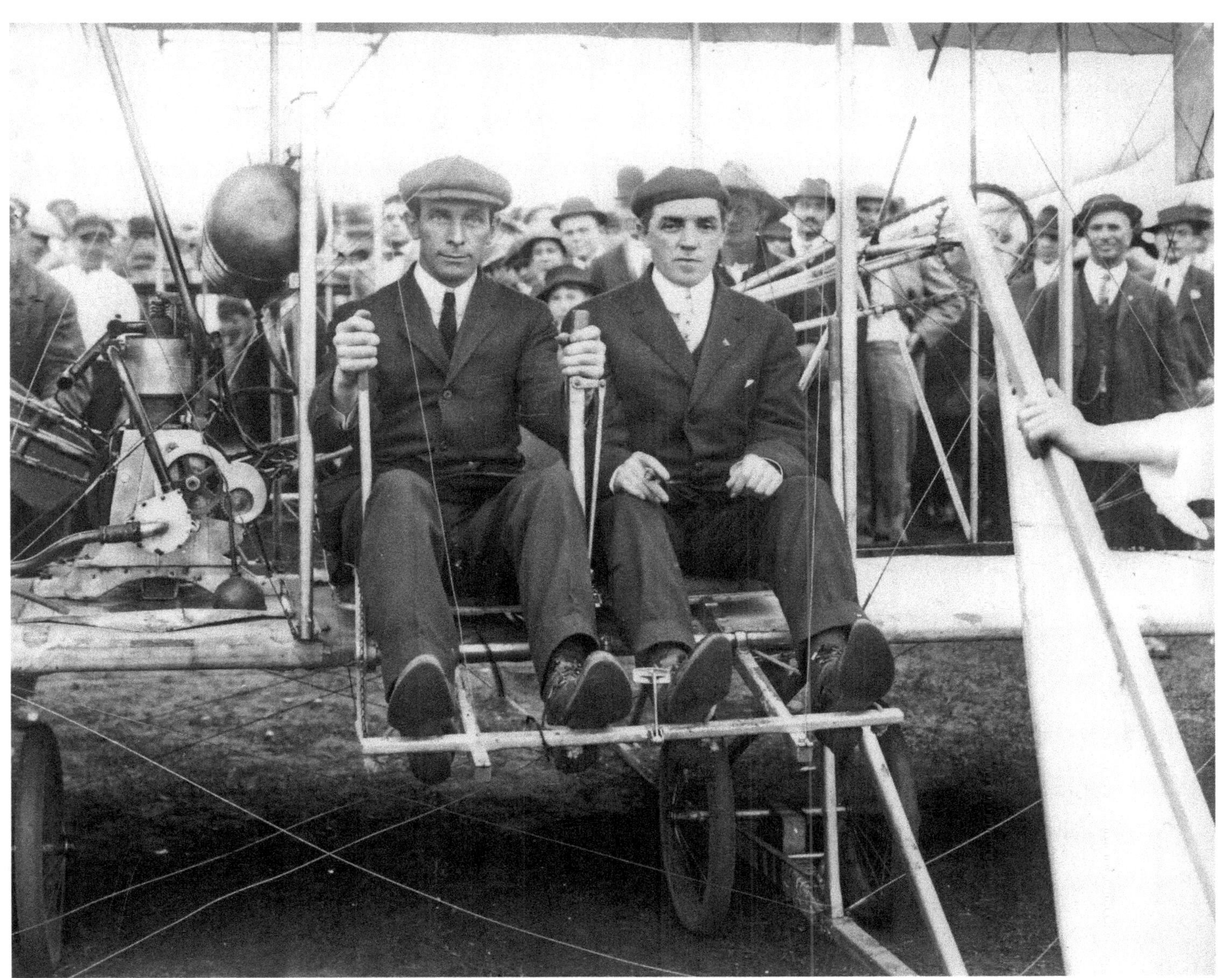

An early airplane, photographed at the Alabama State Fairgrounds, around 1910.

Once the site of a resort hotel, East Lake's amusement park made it a popular destination for day trippers in the 1910s.

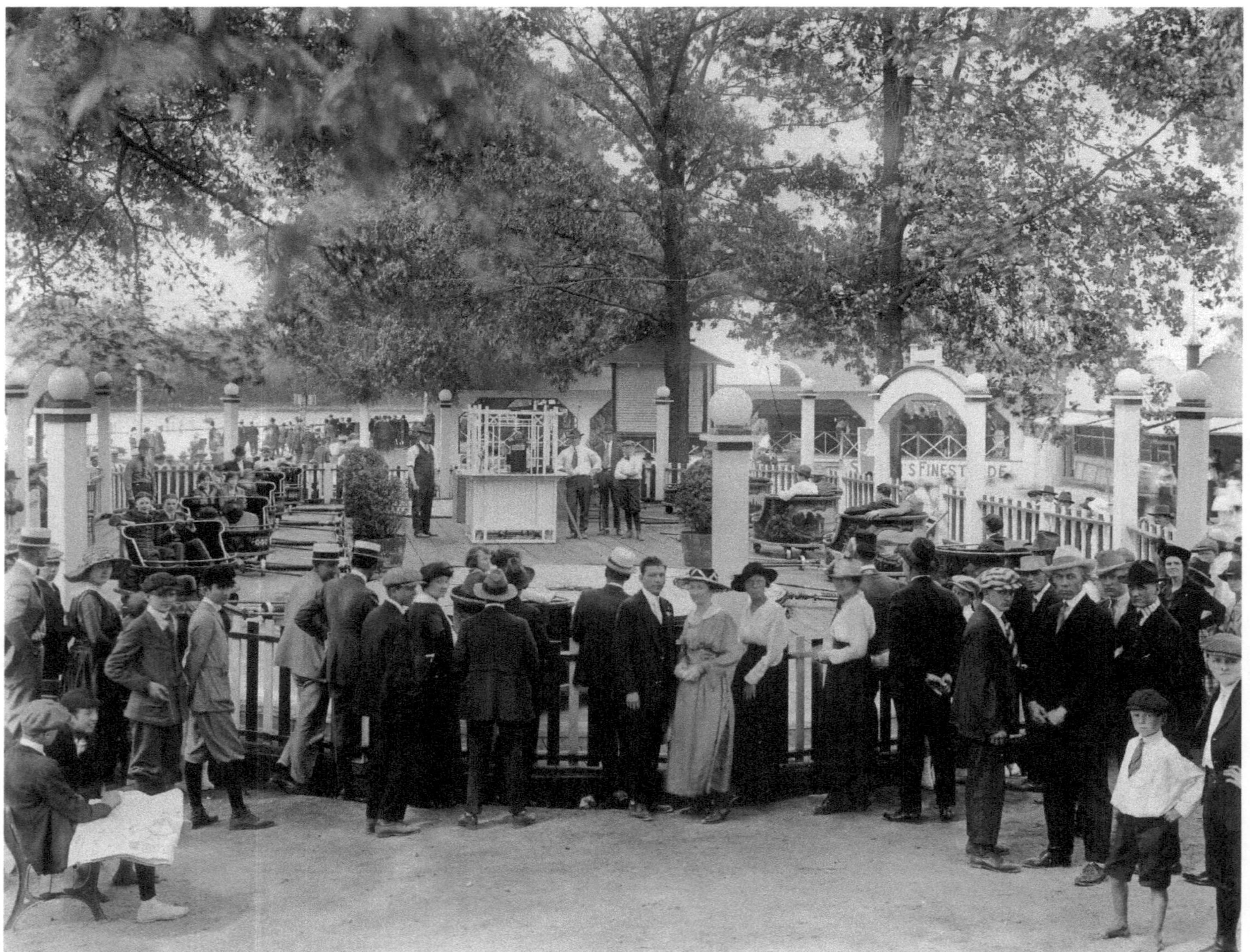

An early twentieth-century view of Five Points South when the area was still largely residential. The cut intersecting the circle median is for the streetcar track.

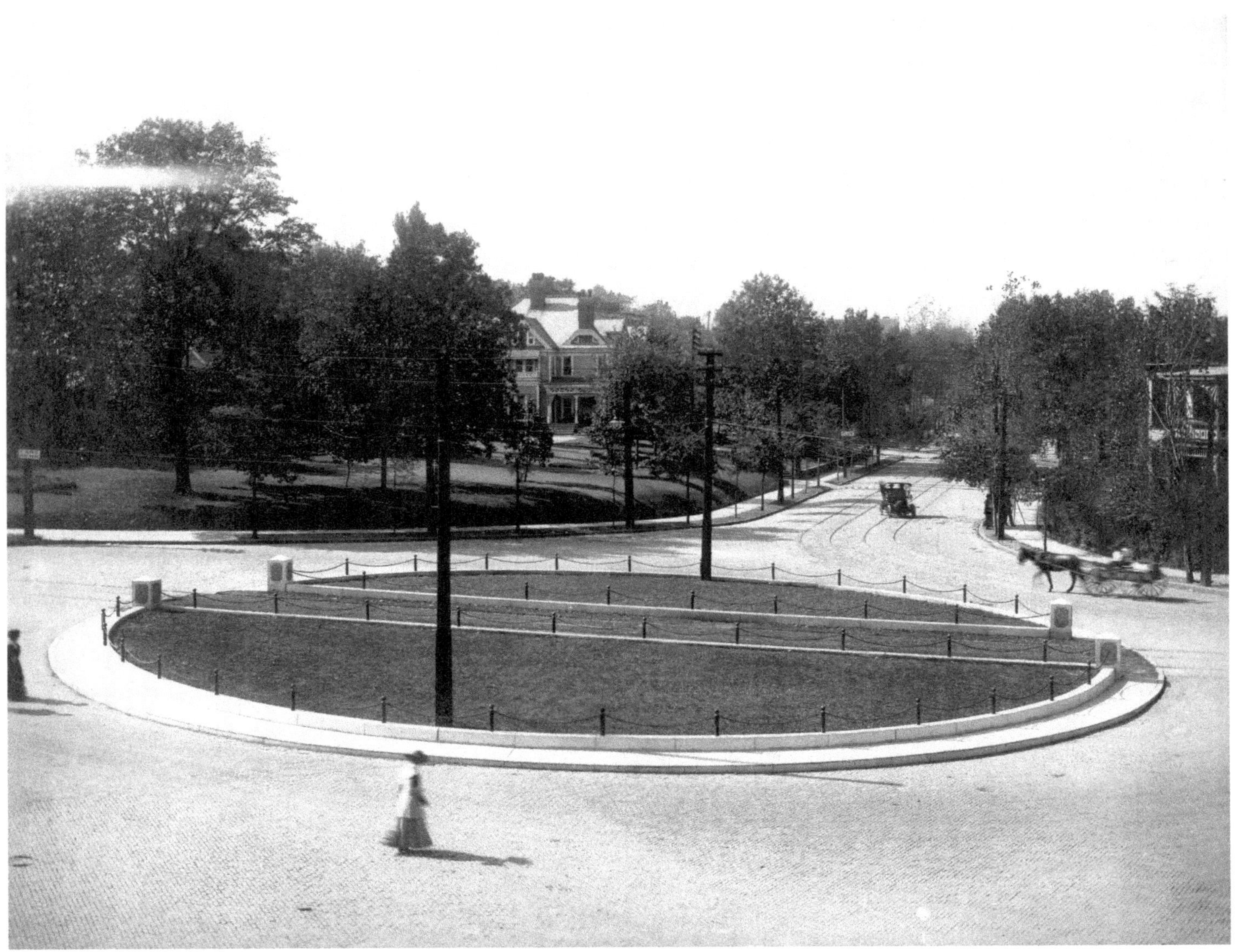

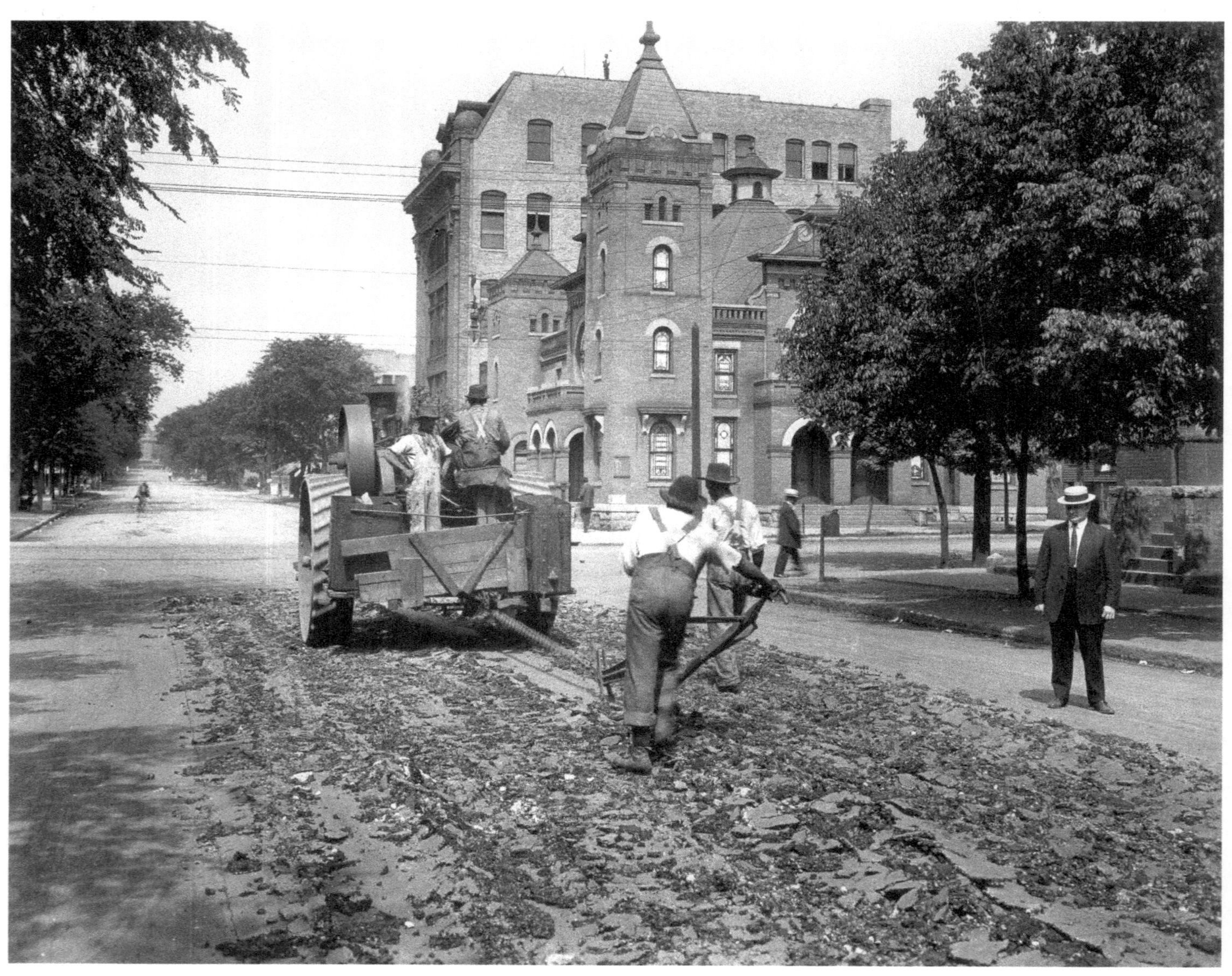

A road crew lays tracks for the Tidewater streetcar line along Fifth Avenue North in the spring of 1912. The church on the corner, First Christian, was later demolished, and the Redmont Hotel now occupies the site. The Birmingham Age-Herald building, visible just beyond, still stands.

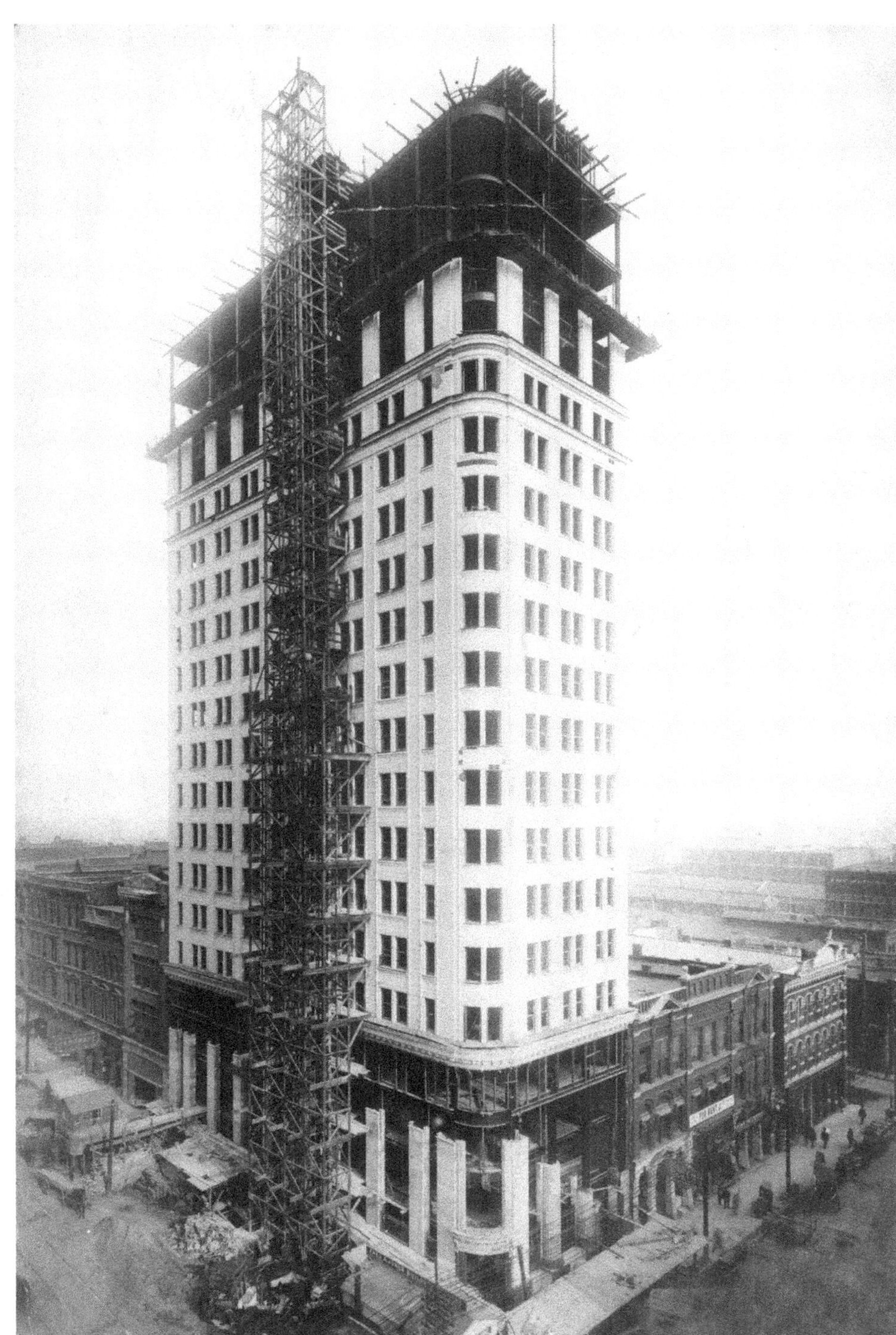

American Trust & Savings Bank, 1912. This 20-story building was completed in record time (less than one year) by Houston A. Brice, project manager for Houston, Texas contractor Fred A. Jones. It is now known as the John Hand Building.

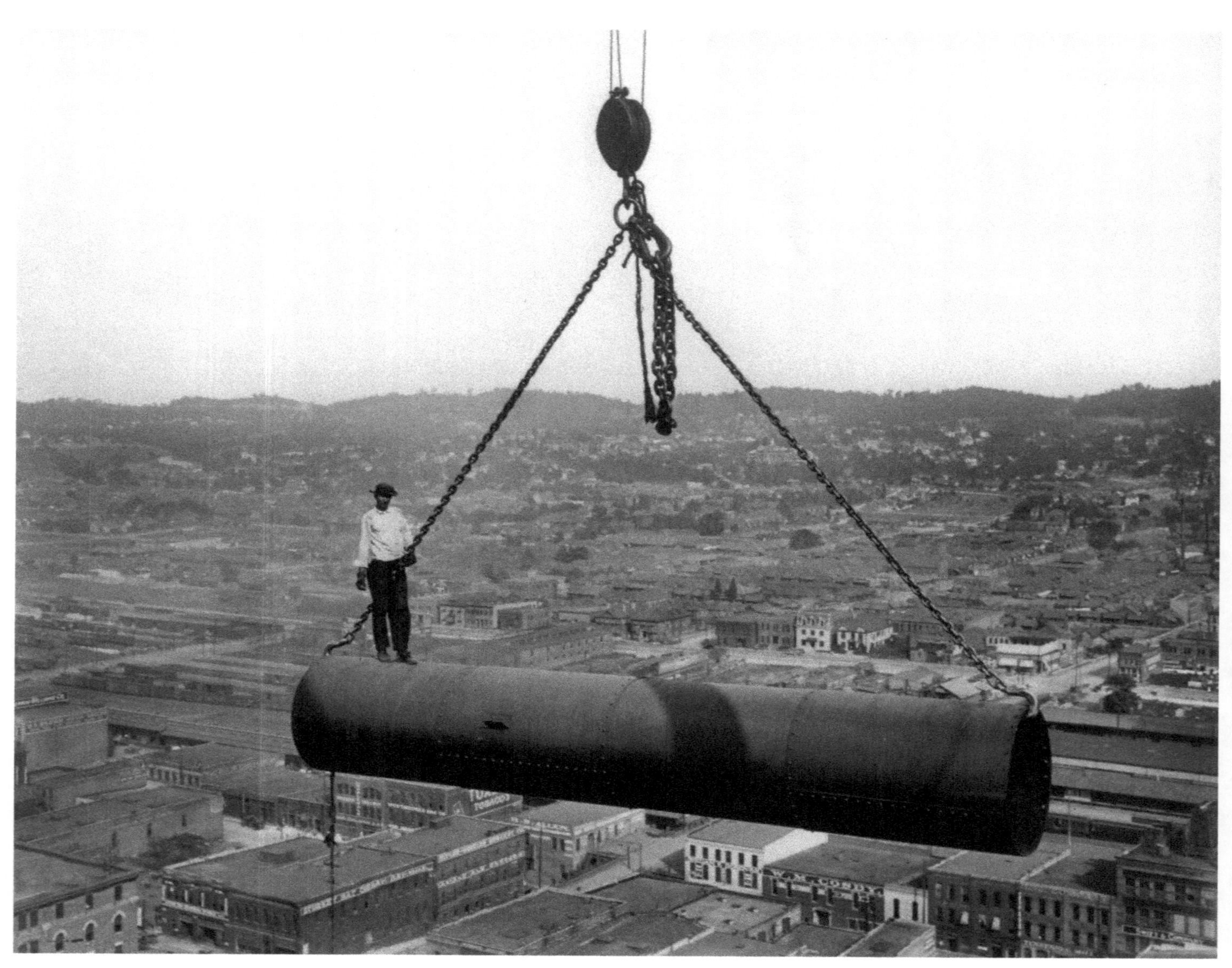

A daring worker stands suspended high above the construction site of the Jefferson County Savings Bank Building, around 1913.

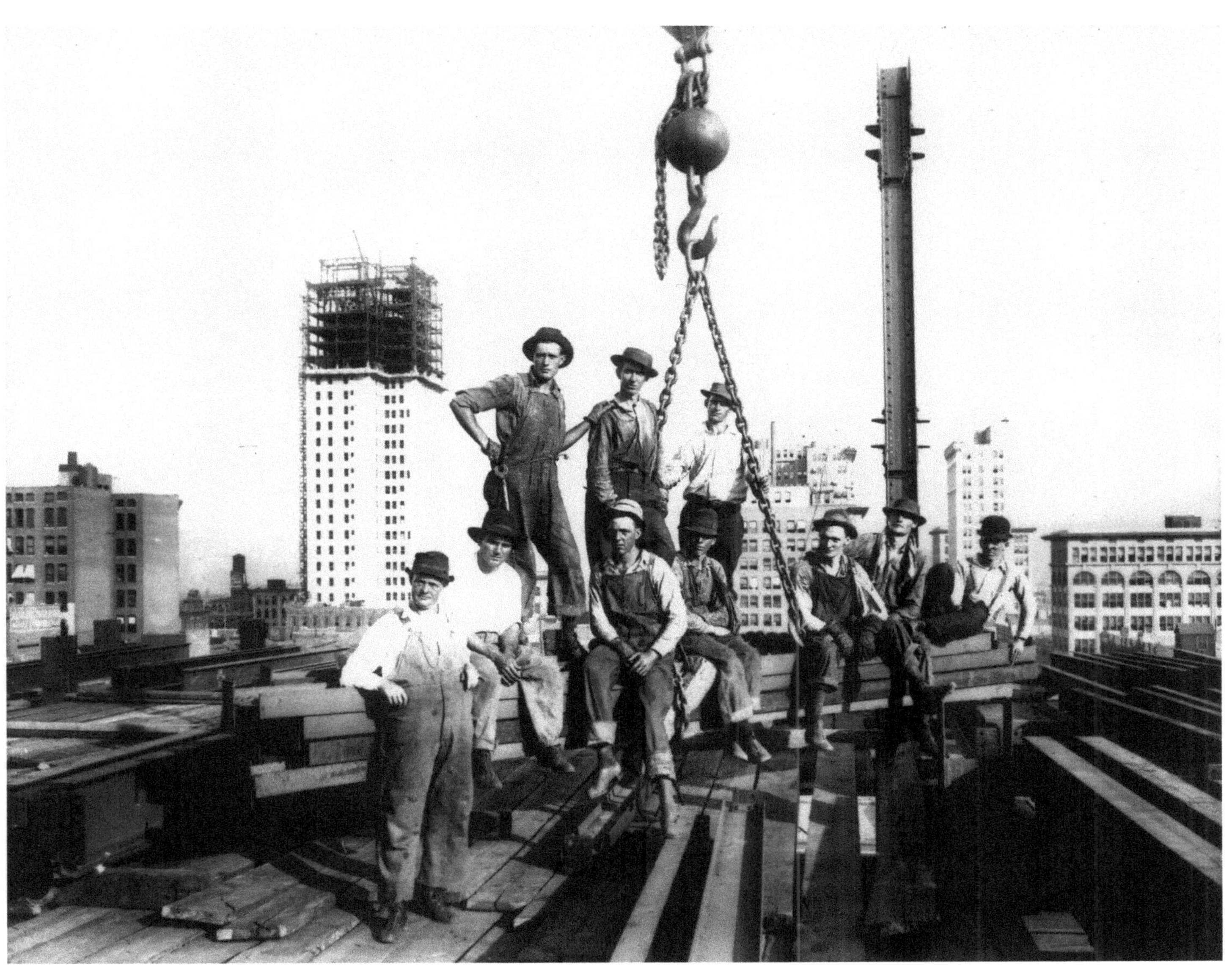

Construction workers on the frame of the unfinished Tutwiler Hotel, 1913. Under construction behind them is the Jefferson County Savings Bank Building, now the City Federal Building.

The Tutwiler, for decades Birmingham's finest hotel, was located on the corner of Fifth Avenue North and Twentieth Street (now the location of Regions Bank). Built in 1914, the hotel was demolished in 1974, one of the first buildings in the United States to be imploded.

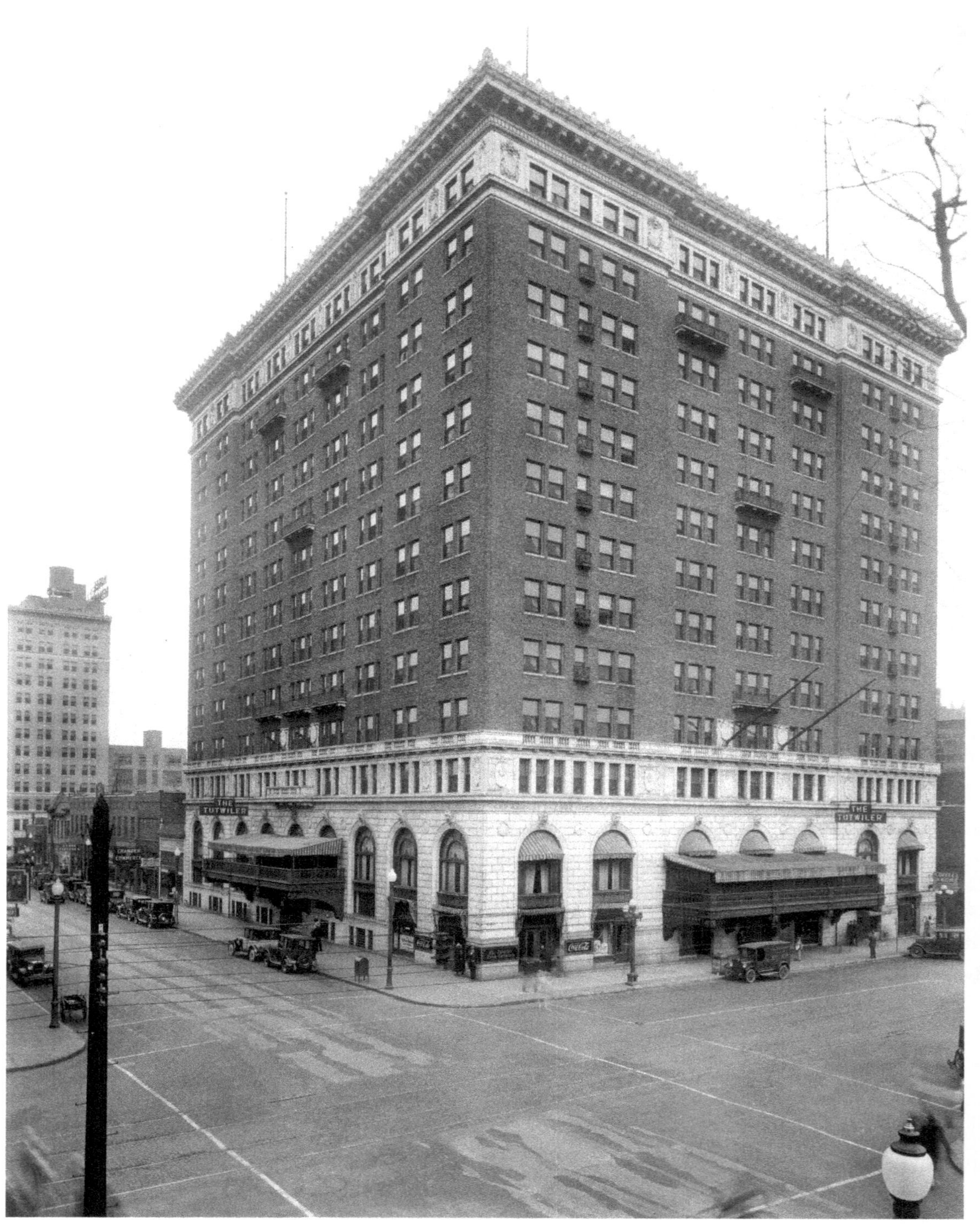

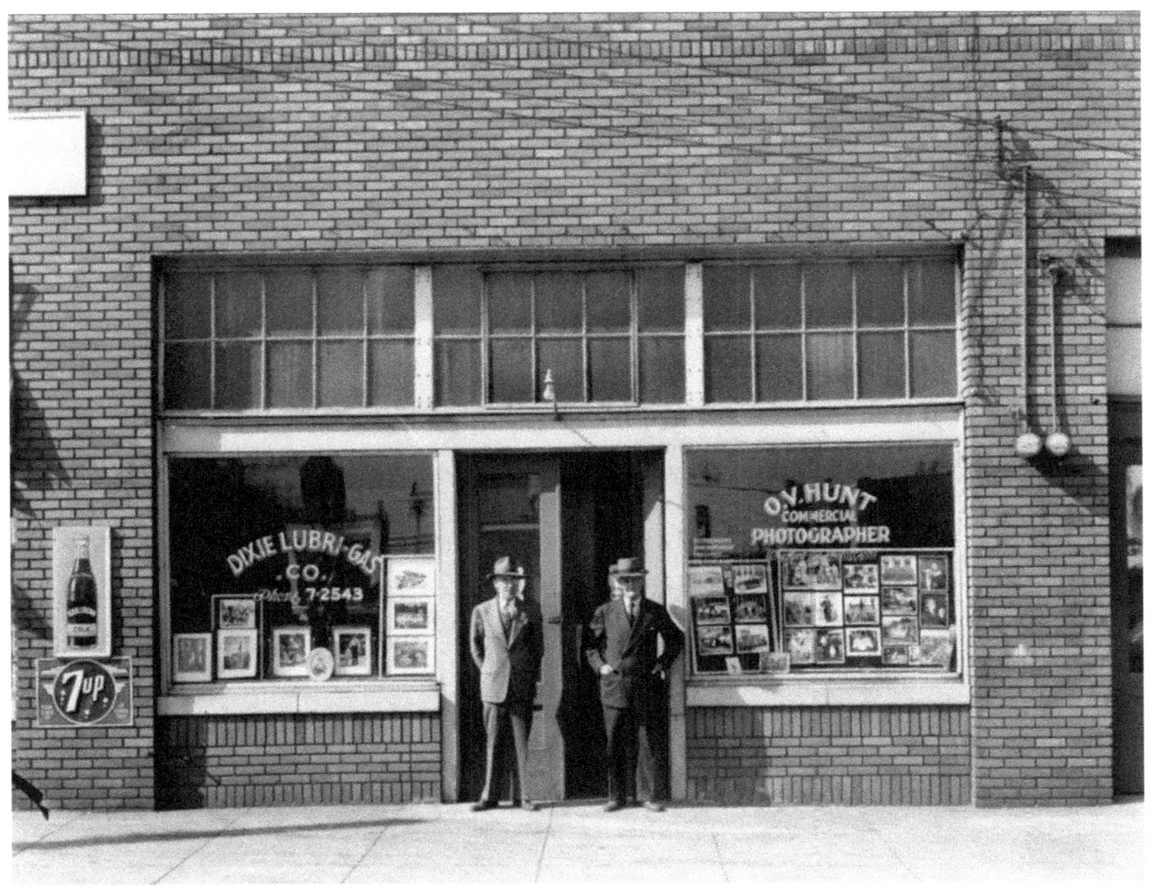

Studio of O. V. Hunt, Birmingham's best-known early commercial photographer. Hunt took many of the photographs featured in this book.

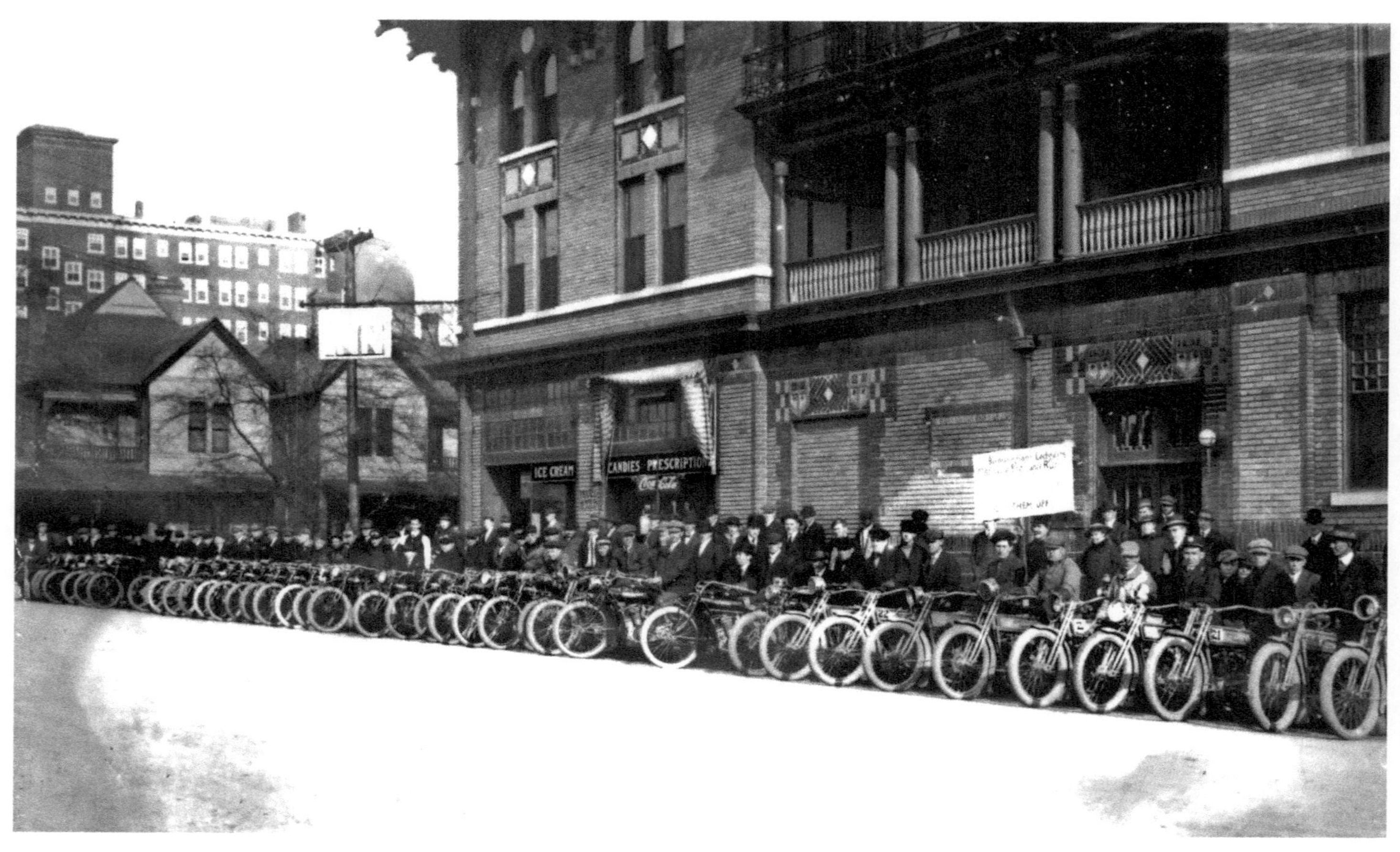

Motorcyclists along Seventh Avenue North, around 1915. The Ridgley Apartments building, now the Tutwiler Hotel, is visible at upper-left.

Delivery wagons line up outside Moore & Handley Hardware Company, at the corner of First Avenue North and Twentieth Street, around 1915.

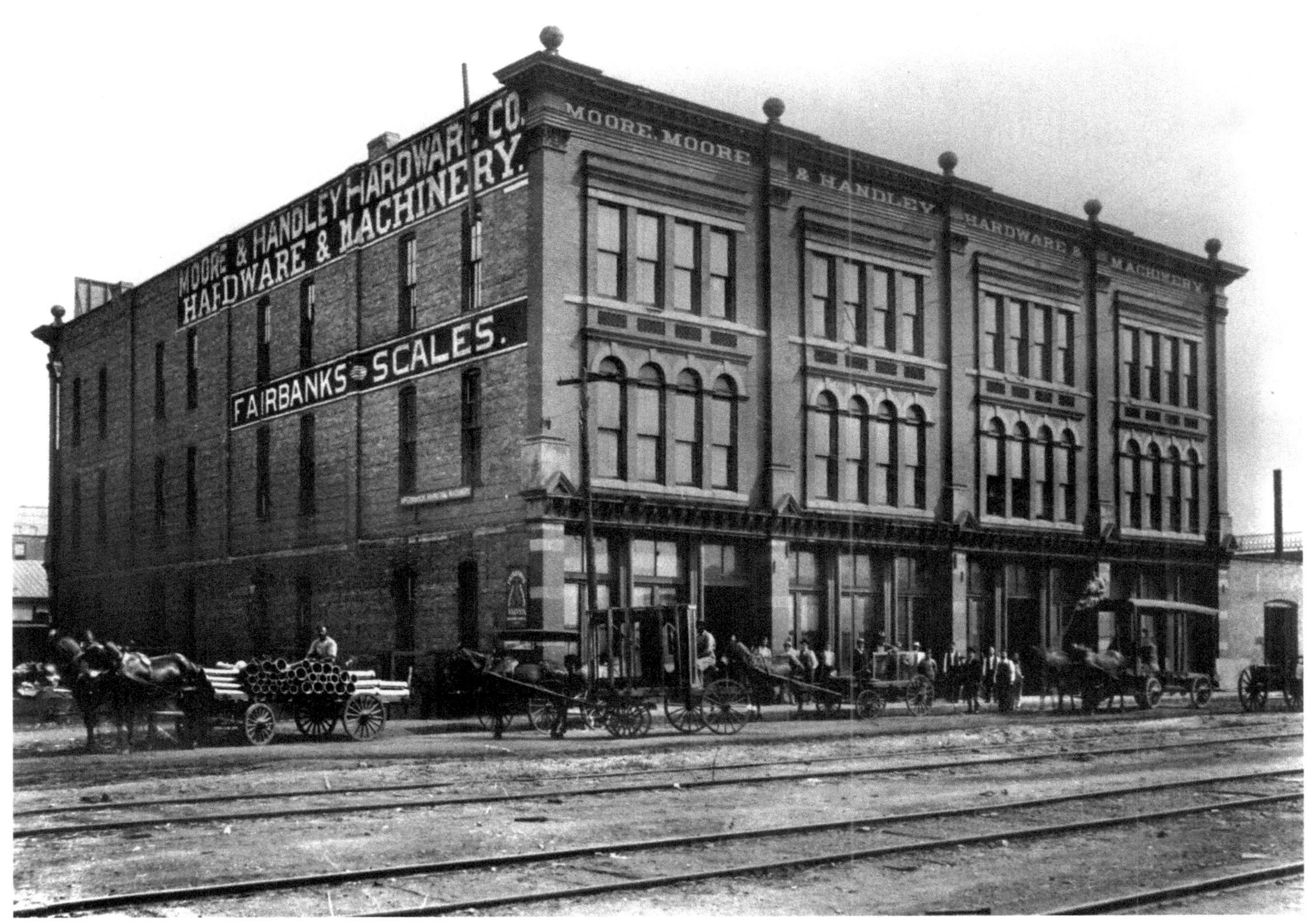

Advertising Indian Motorcycles on Twentieth Street North, 1915.

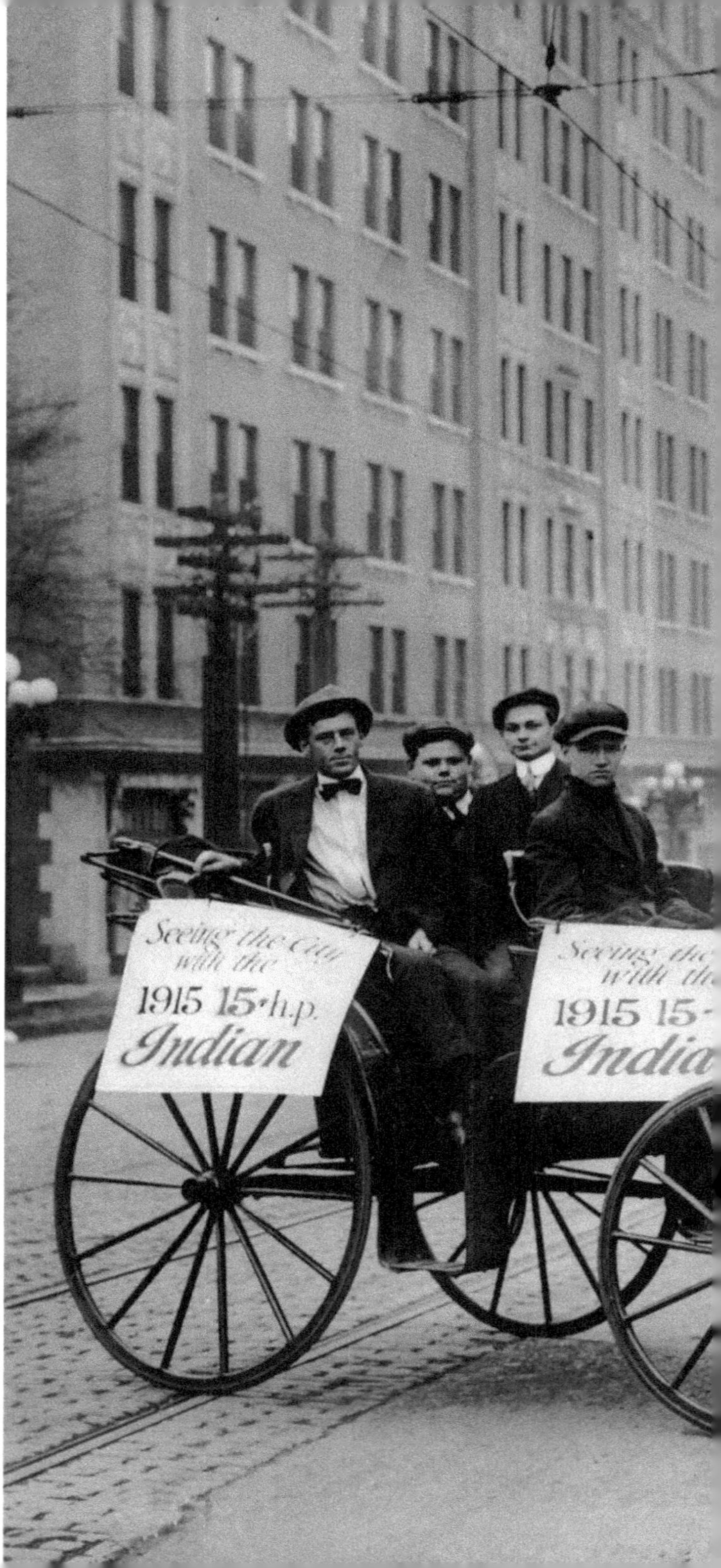

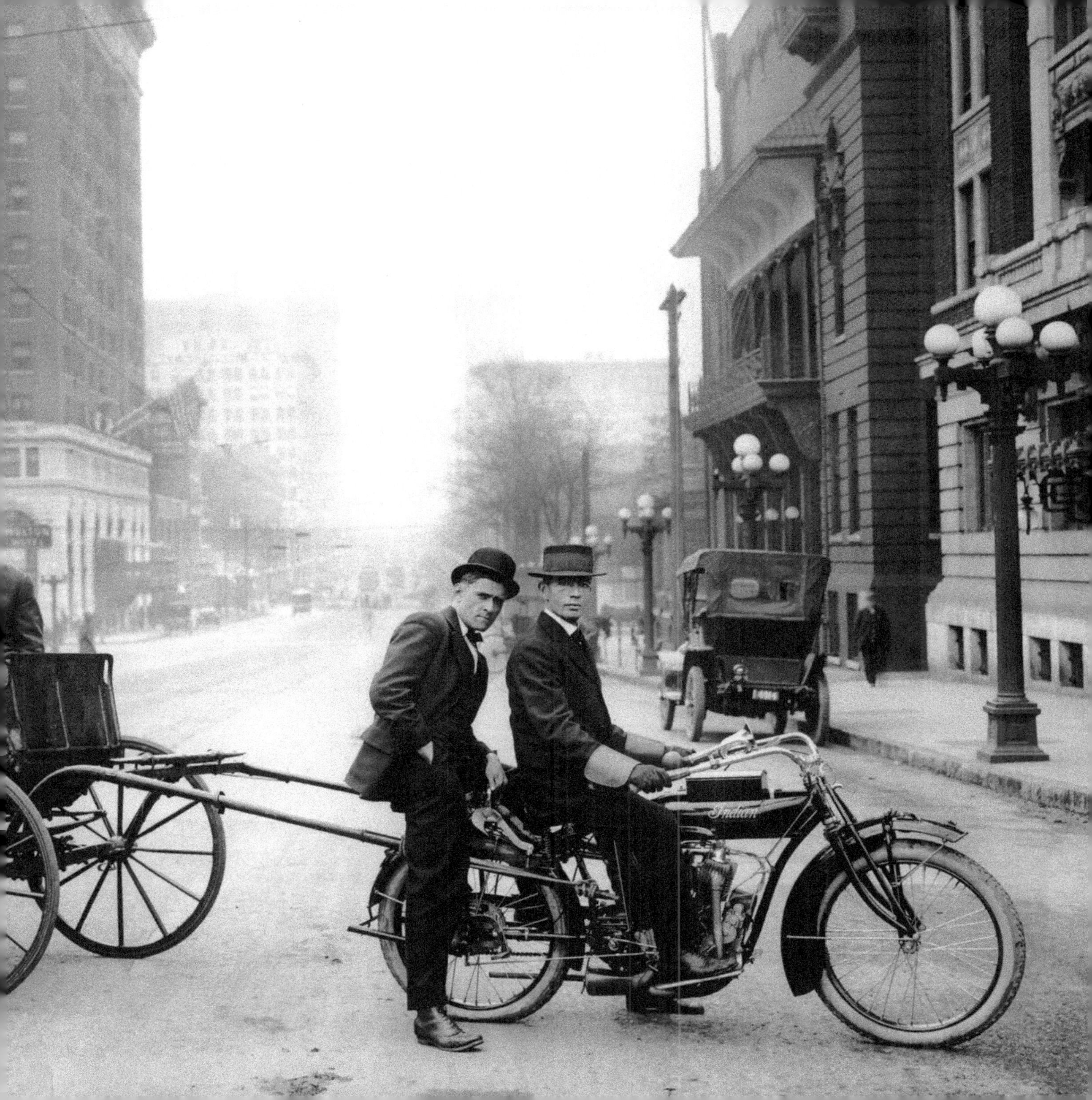
Indian

Delivery men on Harley-Davidson motorcycles. This photo was taken sometime after 1914, the first year that Harley-Davidson offered bikes with sidecars.

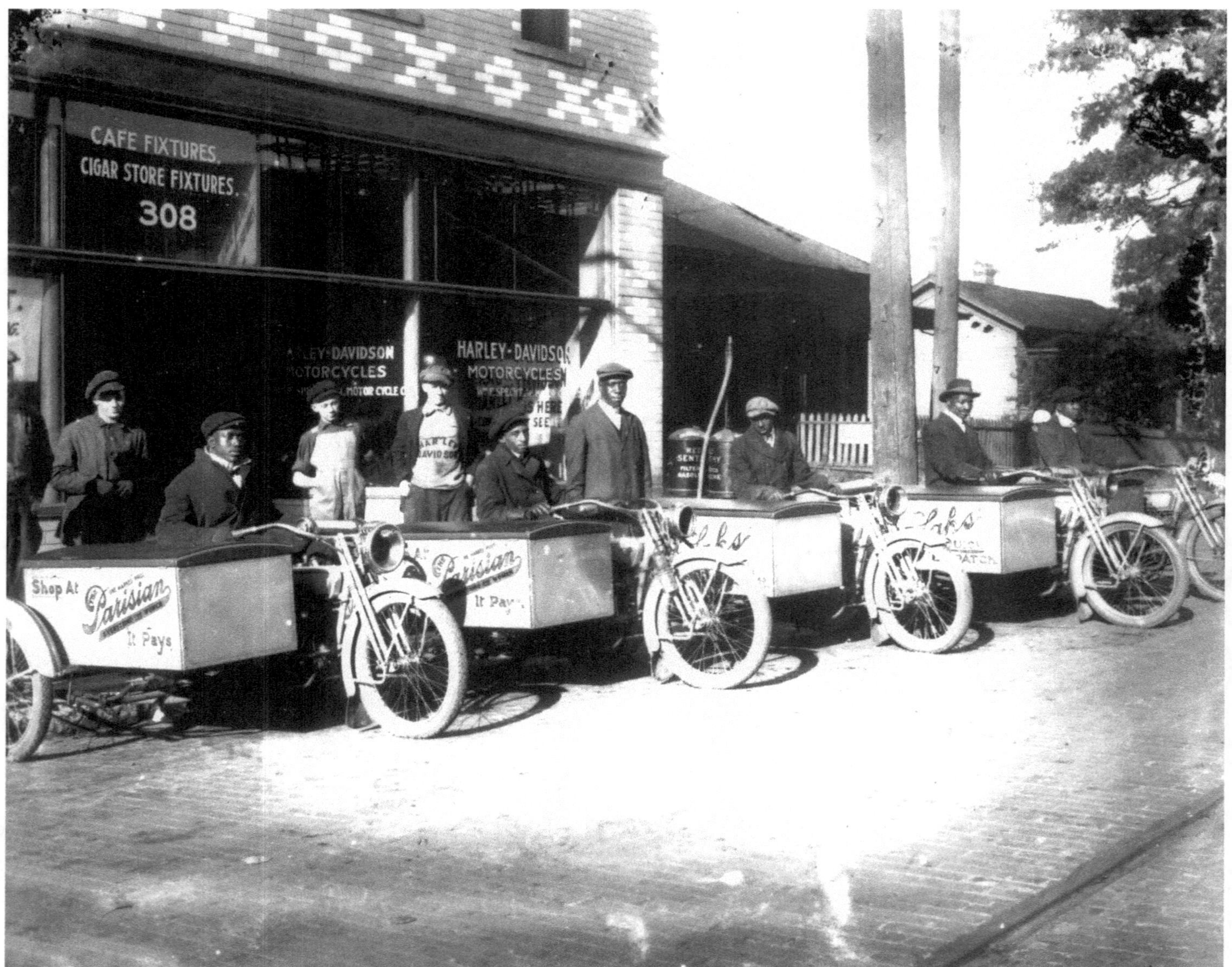

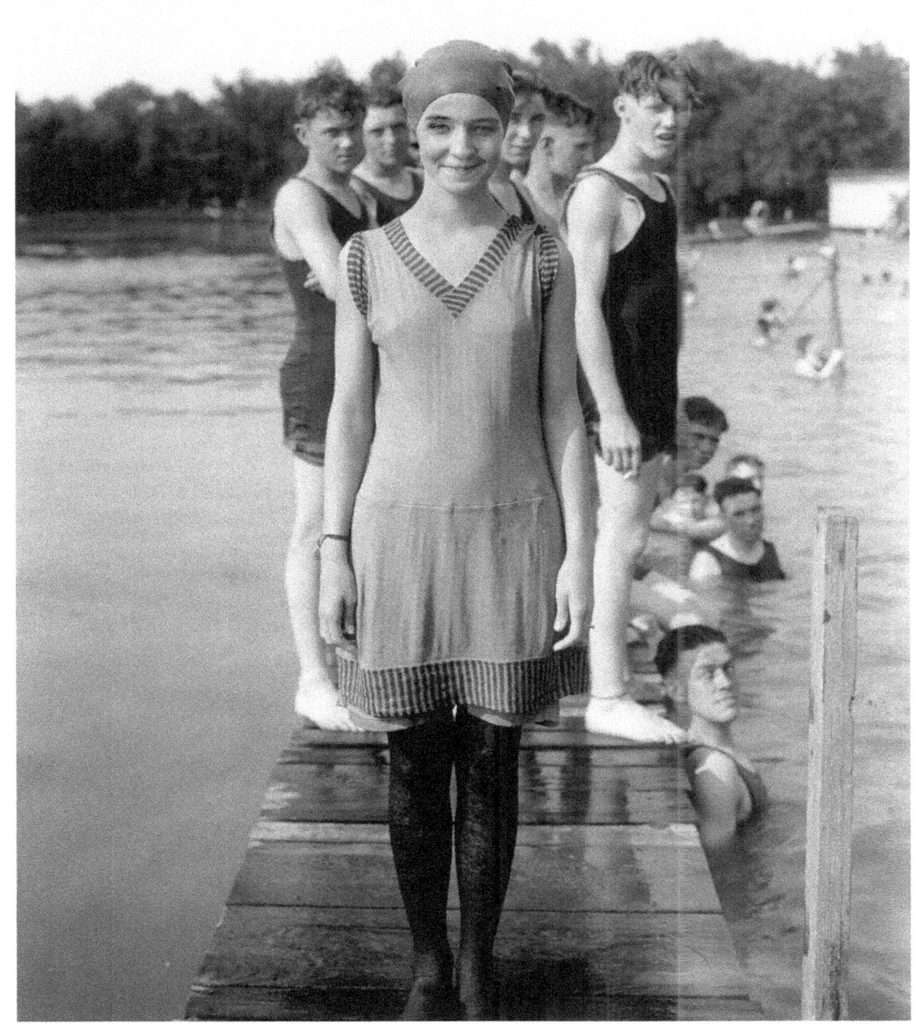

This self-assured young woman is the center of attention at East Lake, around 1915.

Motorcyclists gather, probably for a race, in front of the Birmingham Ledger Building, around 1915.

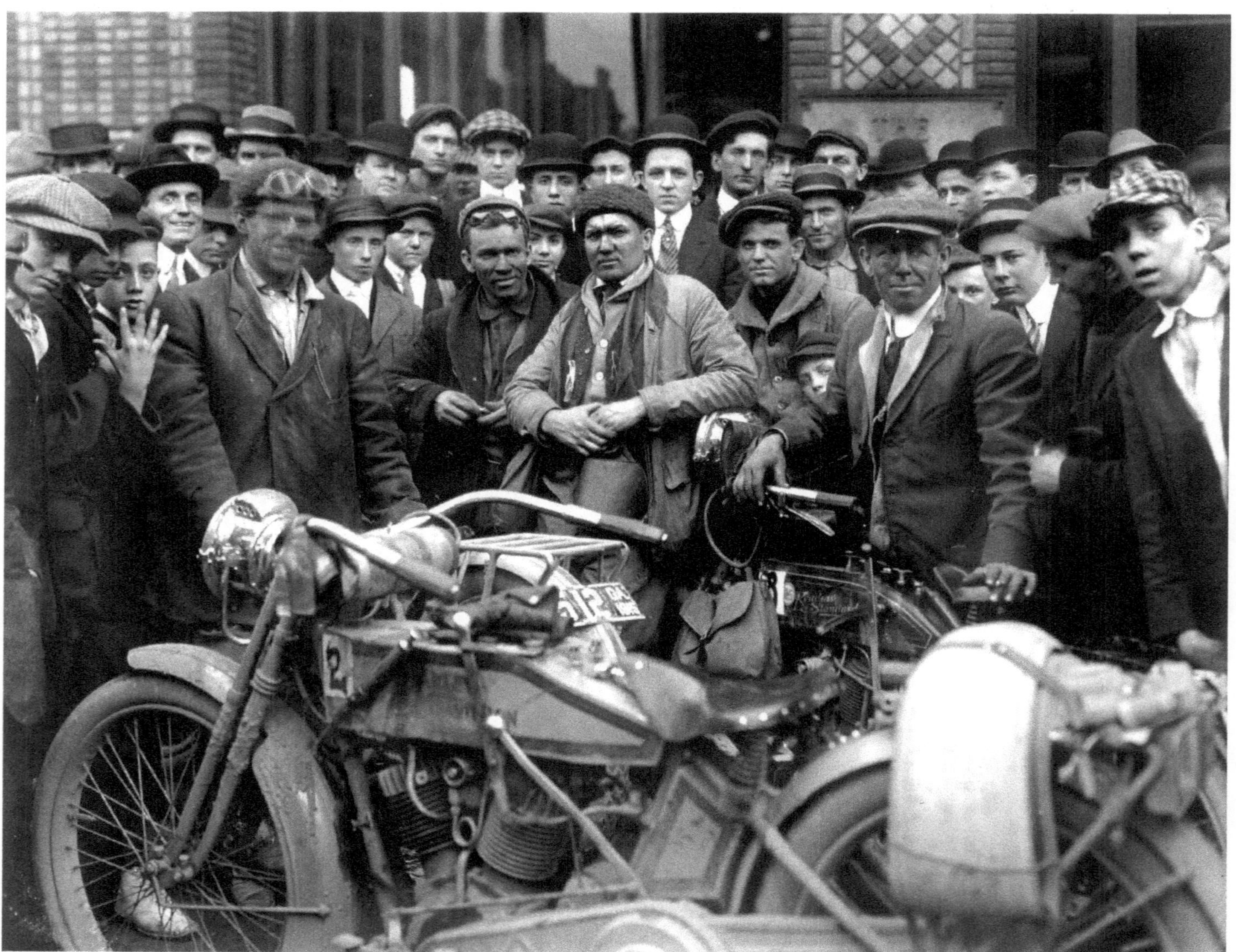

Birmingham firemen with a thoroughly modern piece of fire-fighting equipment. In 1916, the city replaced horse-drawn fire wagons with "motordrawn pumps."

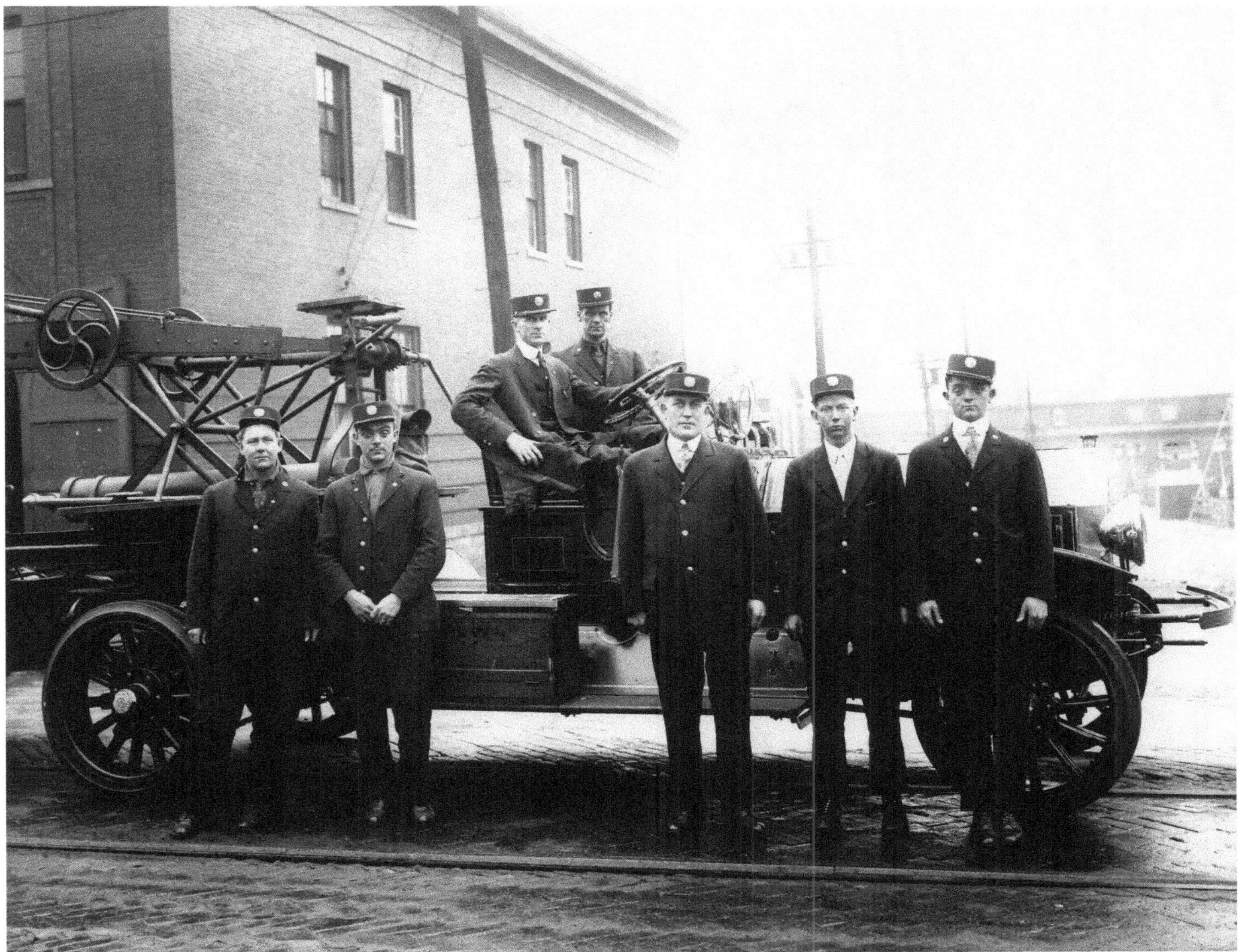

Confederate Veterans held four reunions in Birmingham in 1894, 1908, 1916, and 1926. Here in 1916, two veterans enjoy the hospitality of the White Swan Laundry.

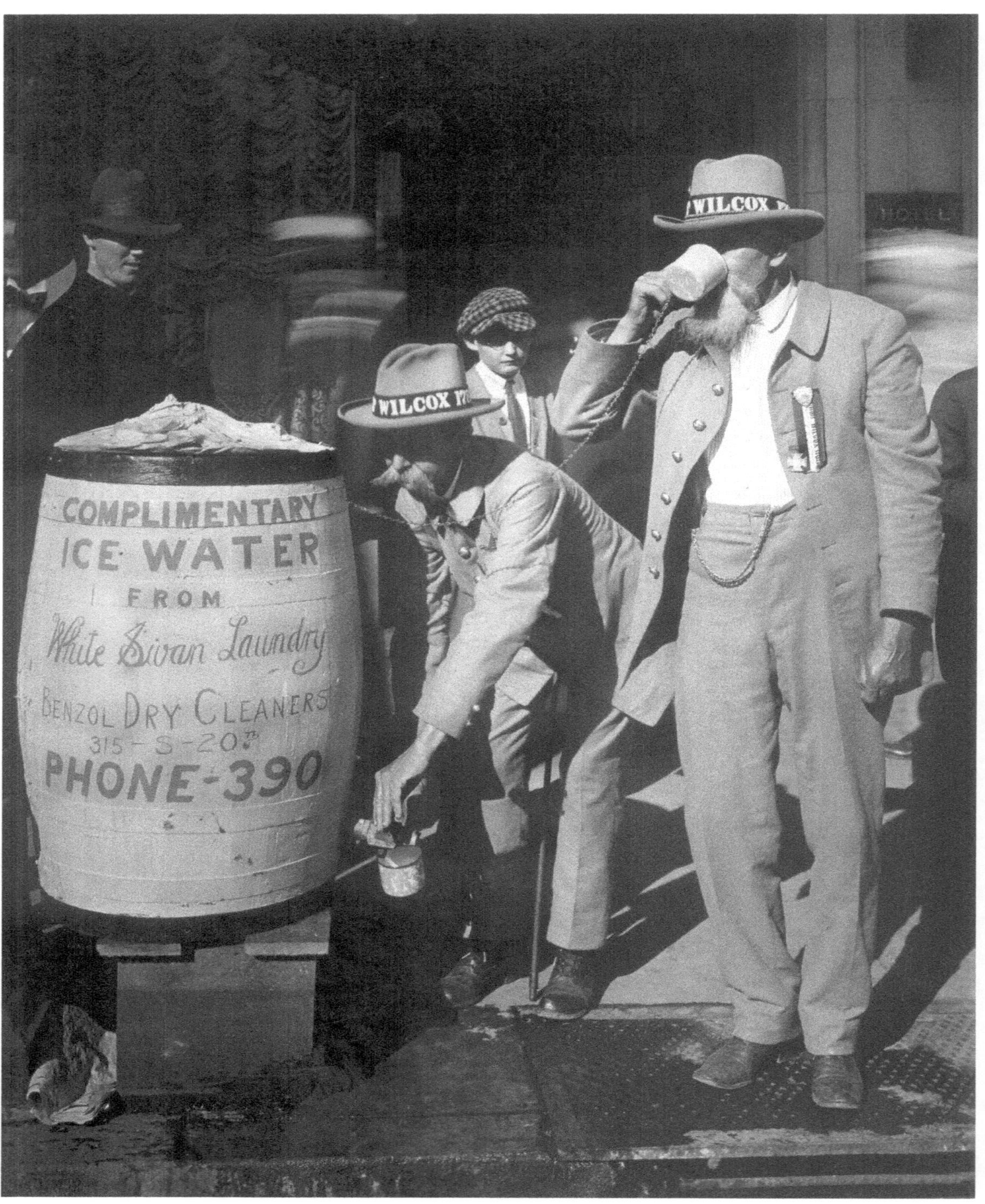

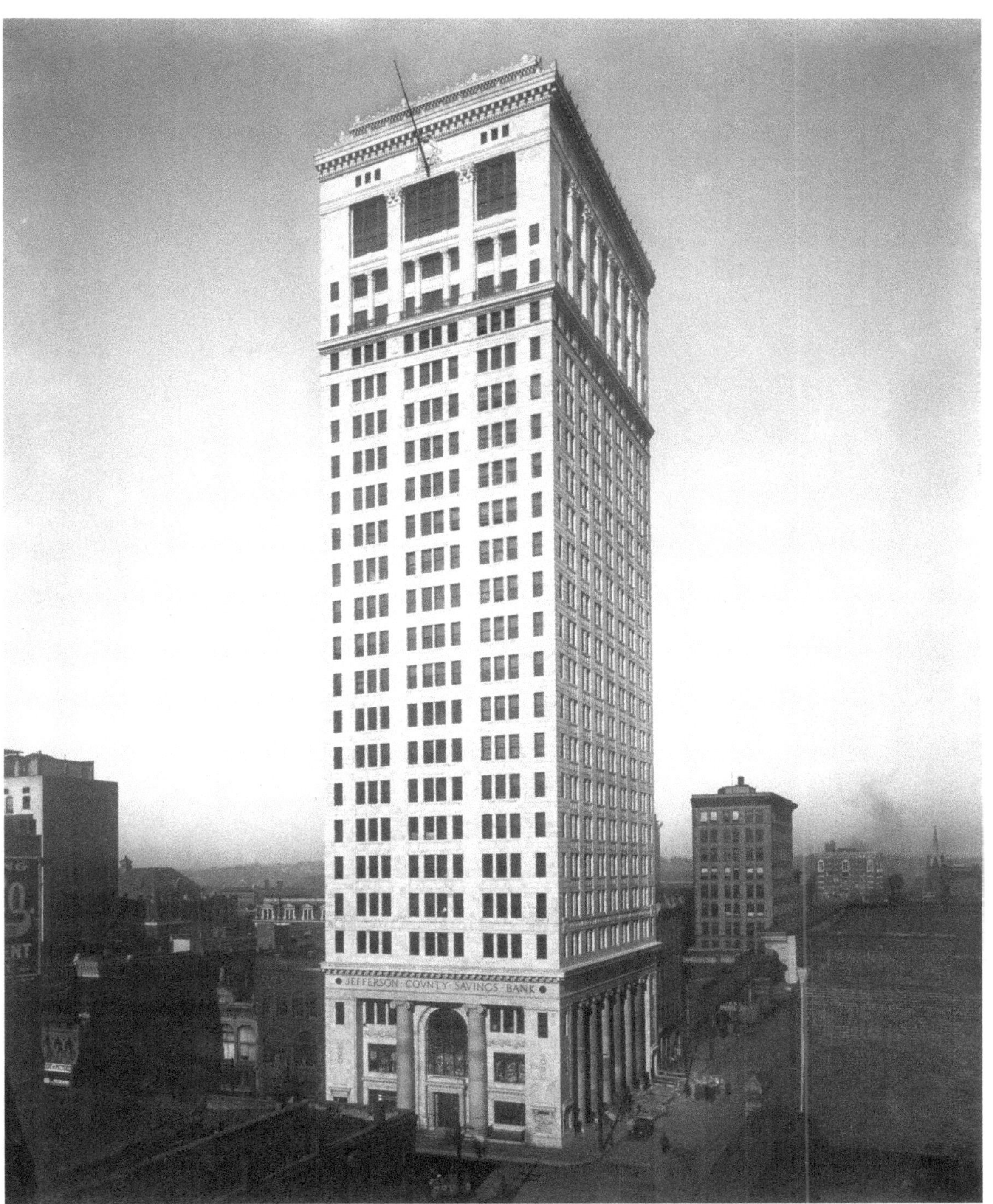

The Jefferson County Savings Bank Building, shortly after completion in 1914. Later the City Federal Building, it is now condominiums.

An early St. Vincent's medical staff: Dr. R. C. McQuiddy (standing, left), Dr. Benedict (seated left), Dr. S. L. Ledbetter (standing center), Dr. Cowls (standing right), and Dr. E. P. Solomon (seated right).

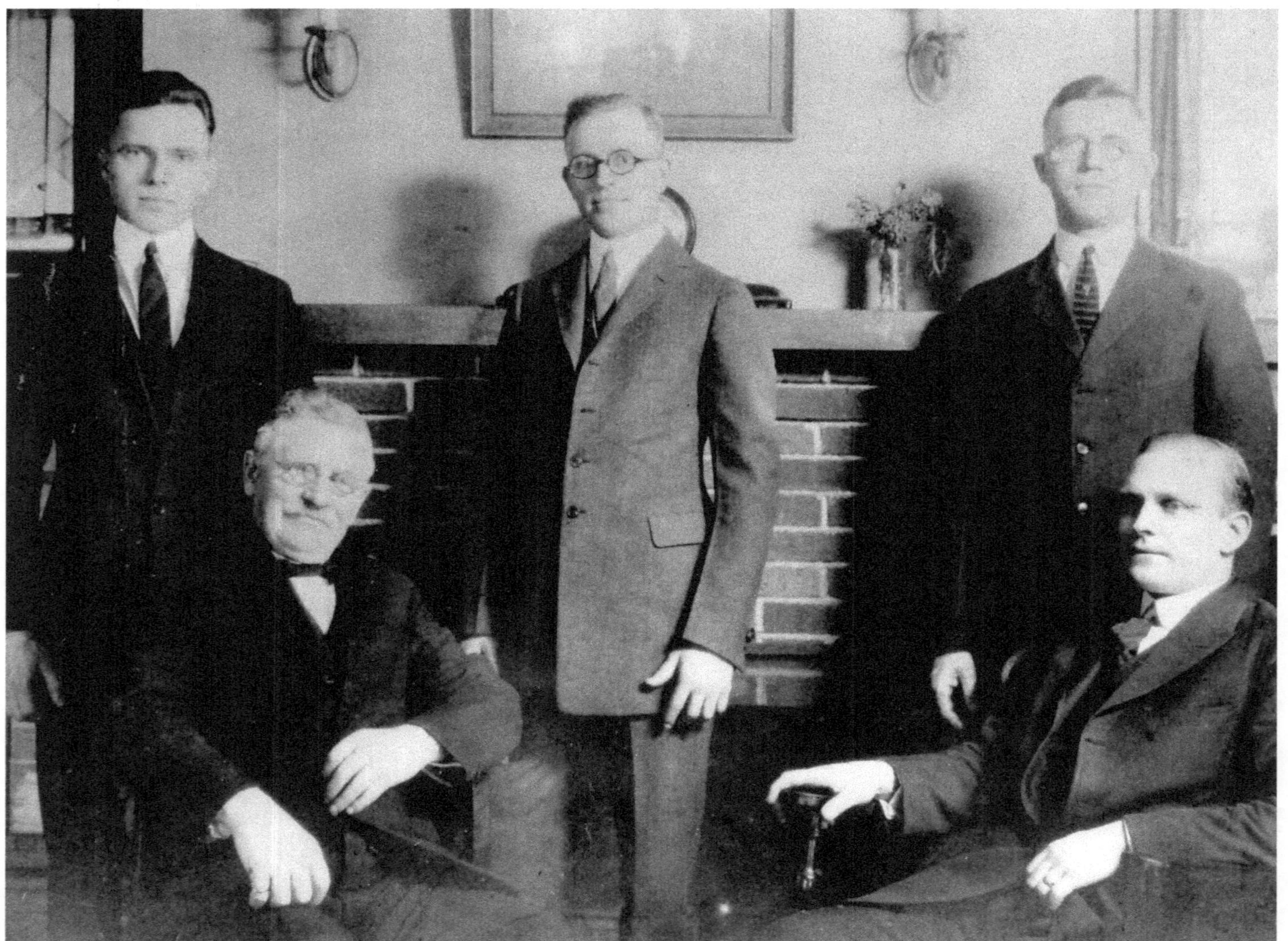

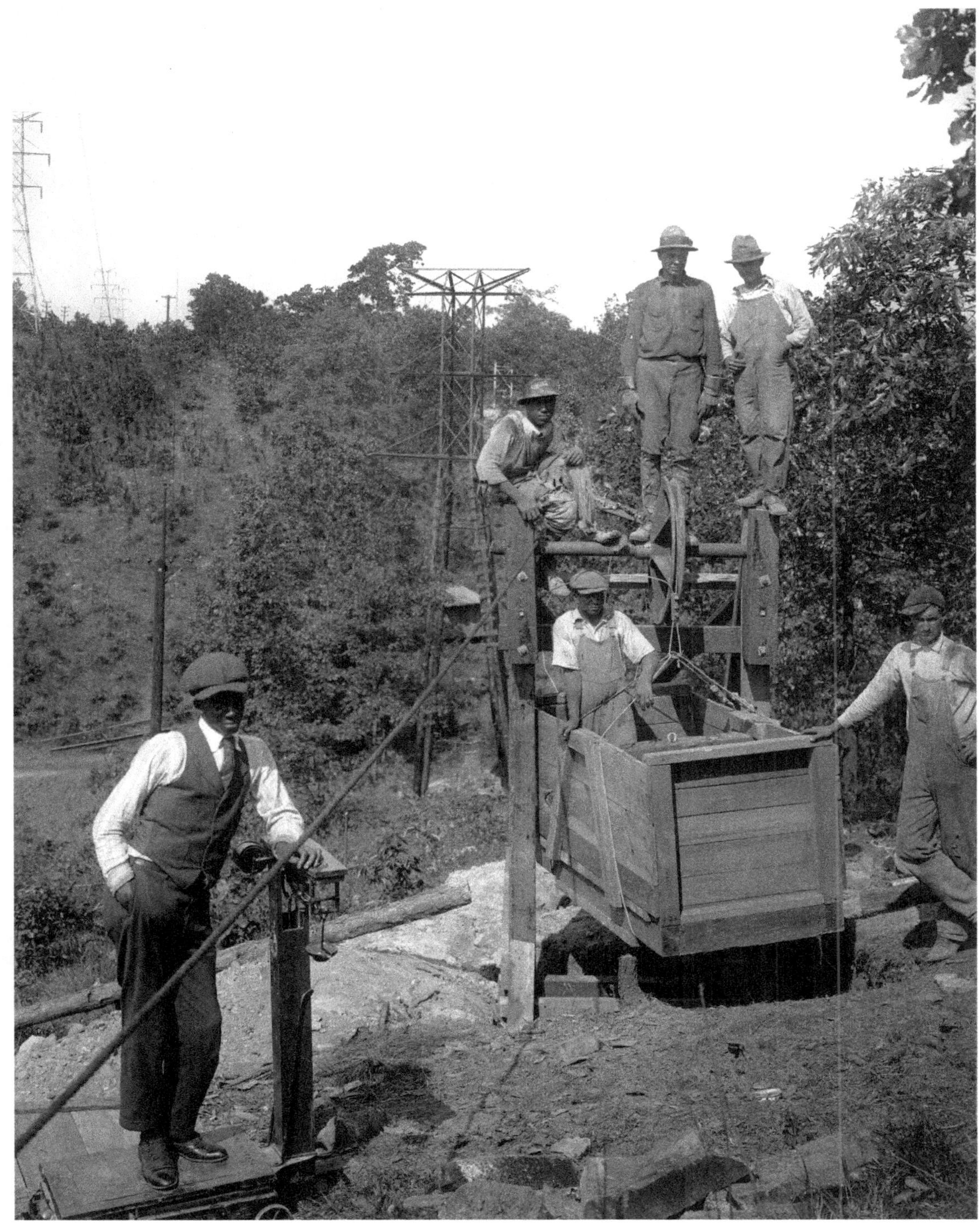

Transmission line workers of the Bessemer, Warrior line demonstrate the method of stringing electrical lines on towers, May 5, 1918. Transmission lines from Lay Dam and Gorgas Steam Plant came to substations in Bessemer and Birmingham. From the transmission substations, lines went to distribution substations throughout the area and from there to businesses, homes, and industries.

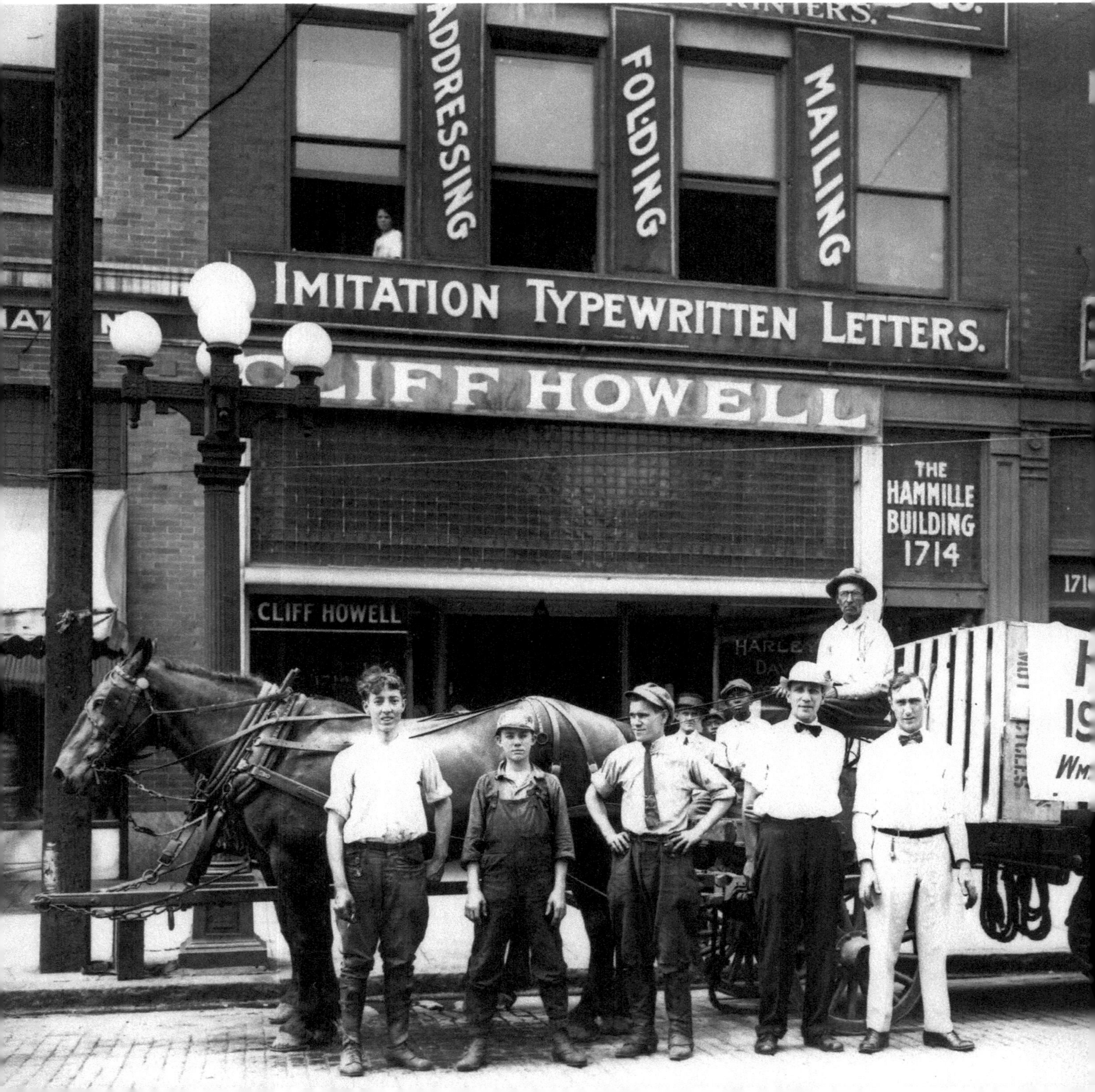

PRINTERS.
ADDRESSING
FOLDING
MAILING
IMITATION TYPEWRITTEN LETTERS.
CLIFF HOWELL
THE
HAMMILLE
BUILDING
1714
CLIFF HOWELL

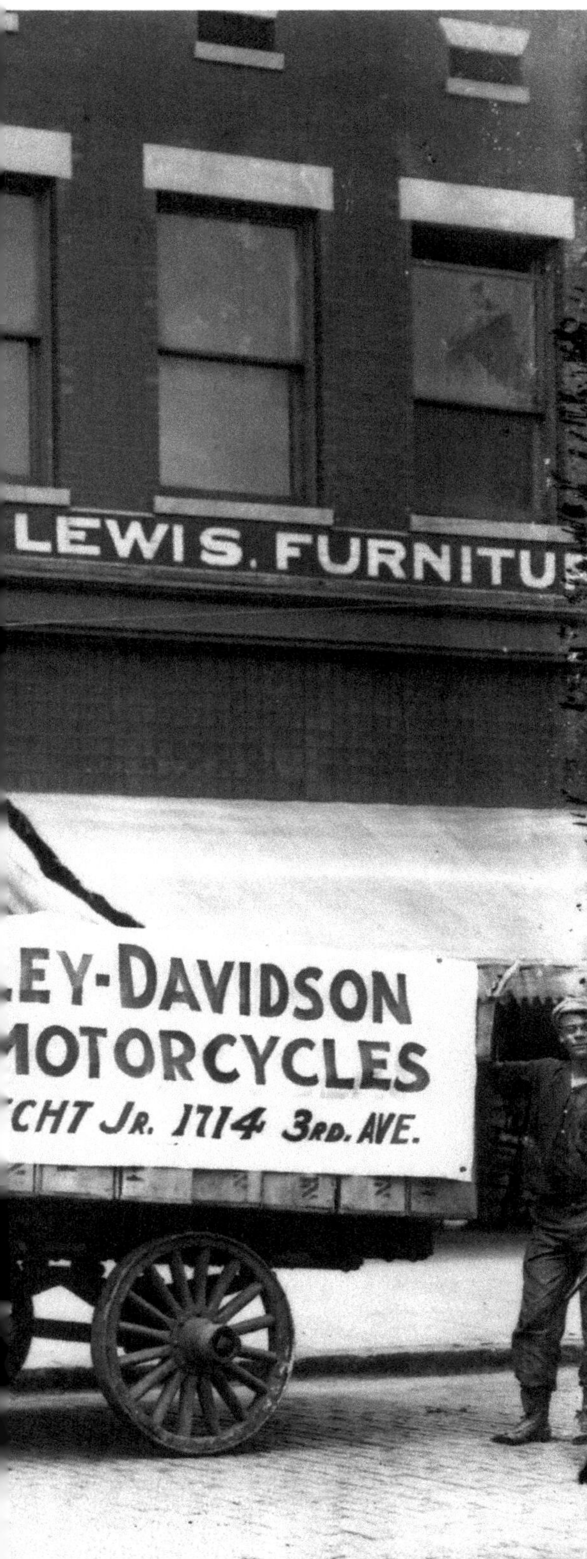

Promoting Harley-Davidson motorcycles on Third Avenue North.

U.S. Marshals stationed at Warrior Reserve (Gorgas) Steam Plant during World War I, 1918. When World War I broke out, the U.S. government contracted with Alabama Power Co. to construct a second generating unit at its Warrior Reserve Plant and build a 90-mile transmission line to Muscle Shoals to supply electricity to a nitrates plant under construction there. The nitrates plant was commissioned to manufacture munitions for the war effort.

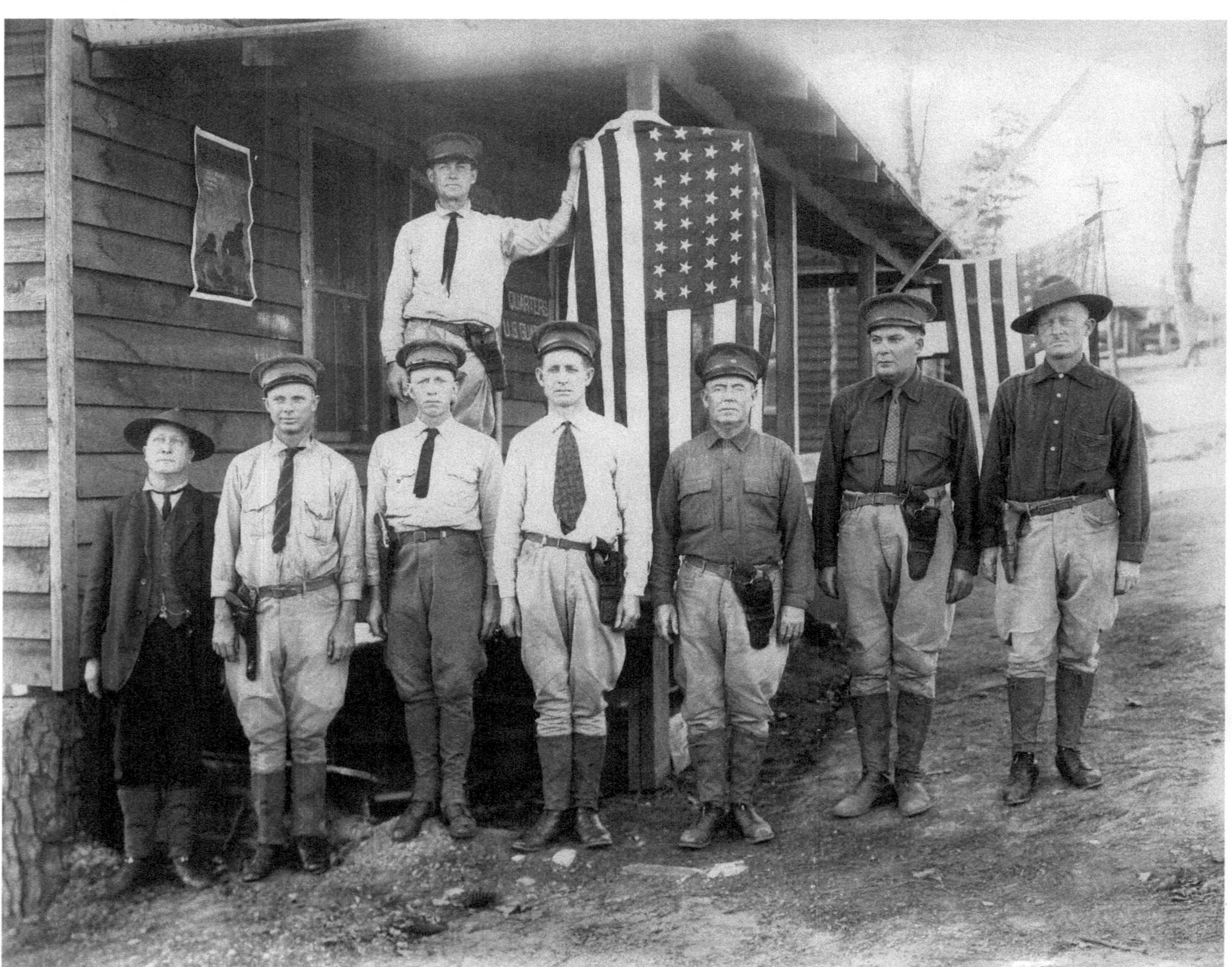

Second Avenue North at Nineteenth Street, decorated for the state fair.

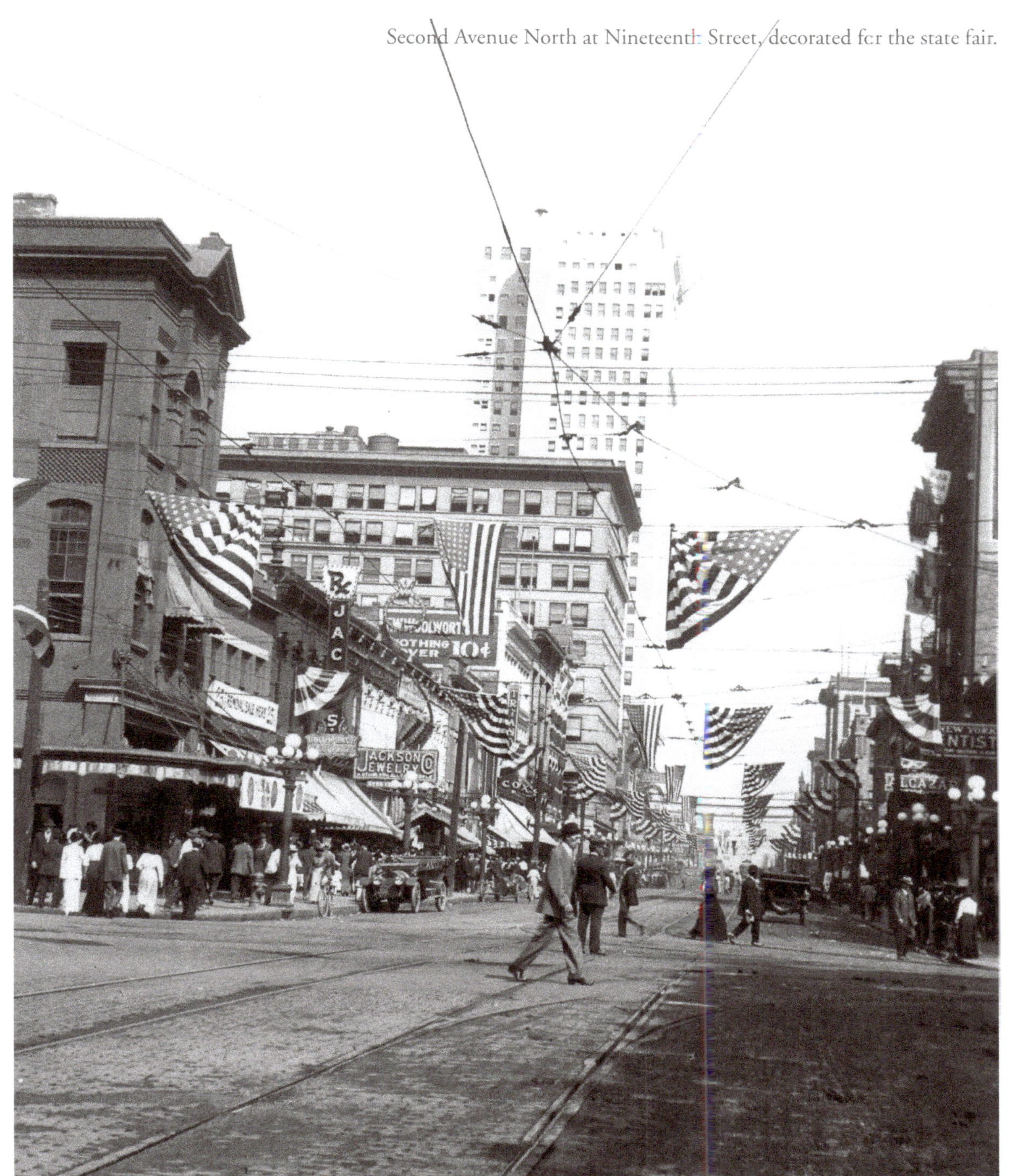

Harley-Davidson motorcycles outside Cliff Howell's bicycle repair shop, Nineteenth Street North.

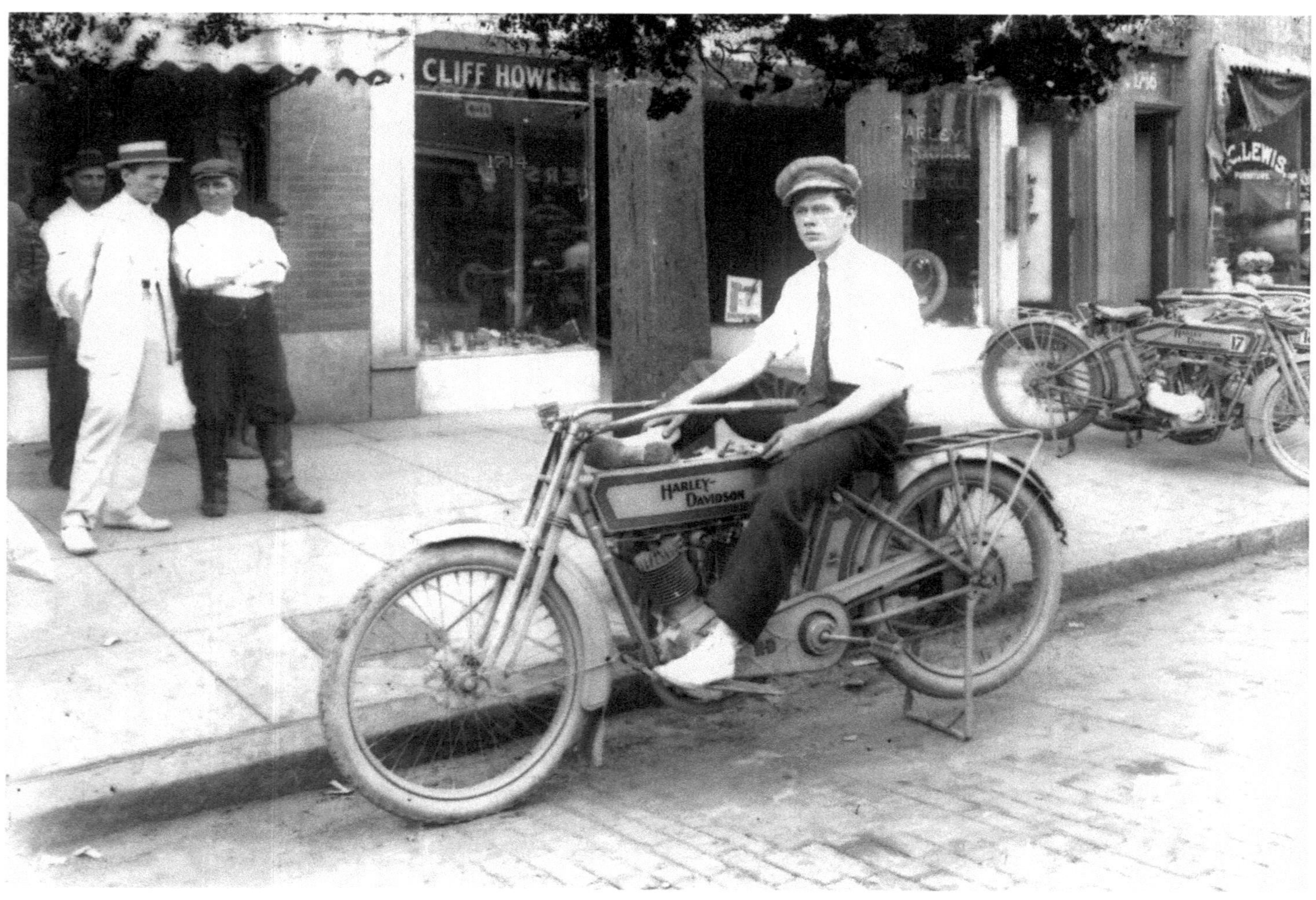

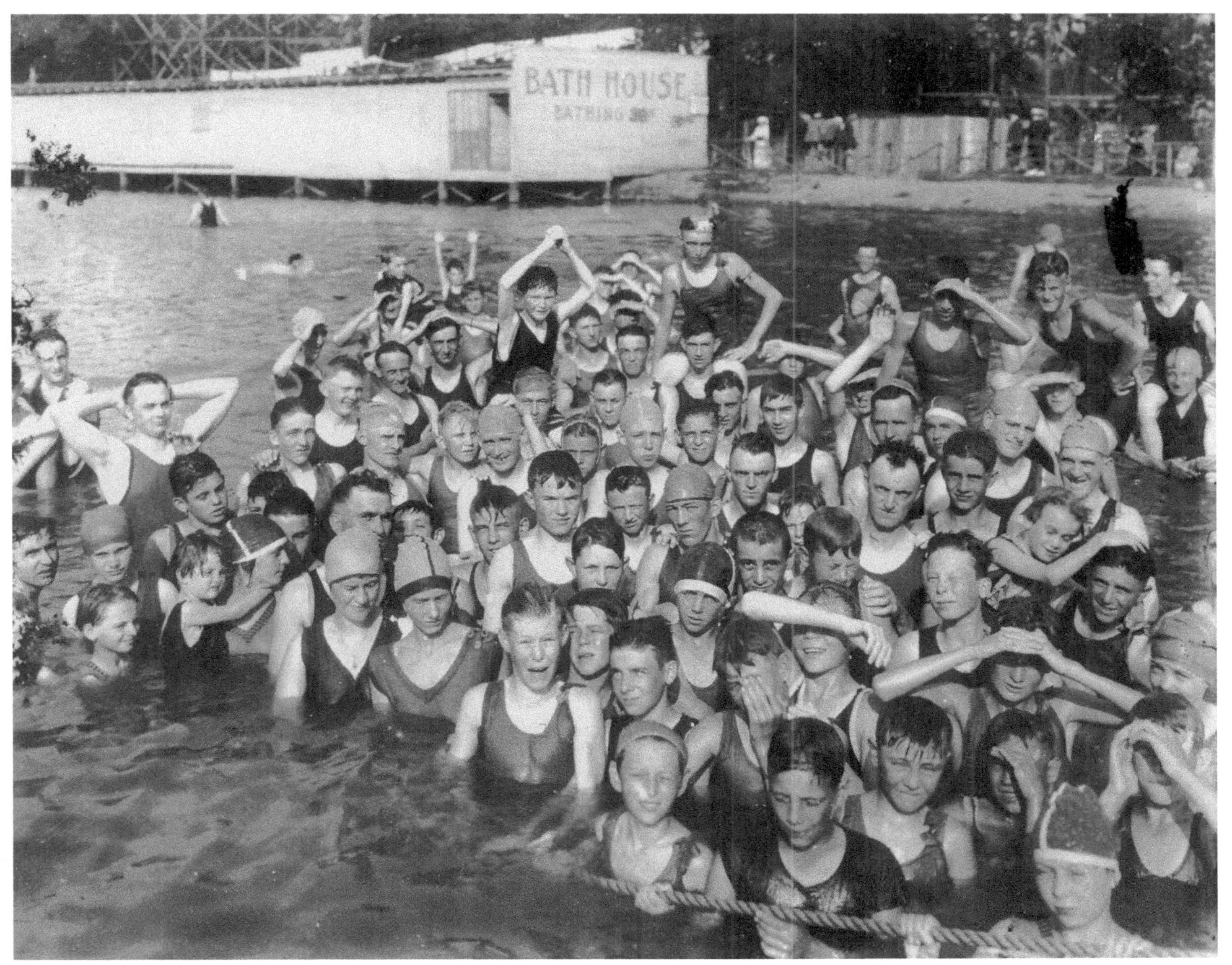

Swimming at East Lake Park.

Drivers and crew for an early auto race, 1918.

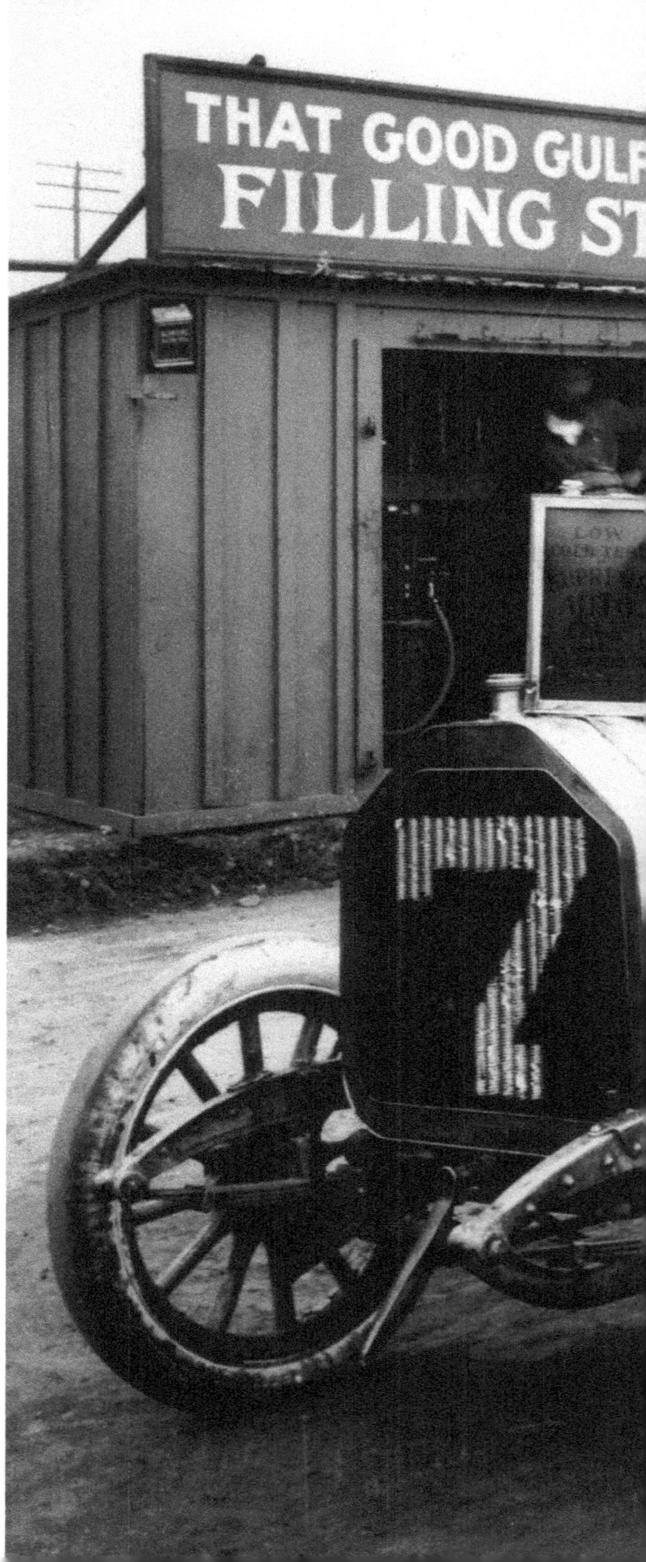

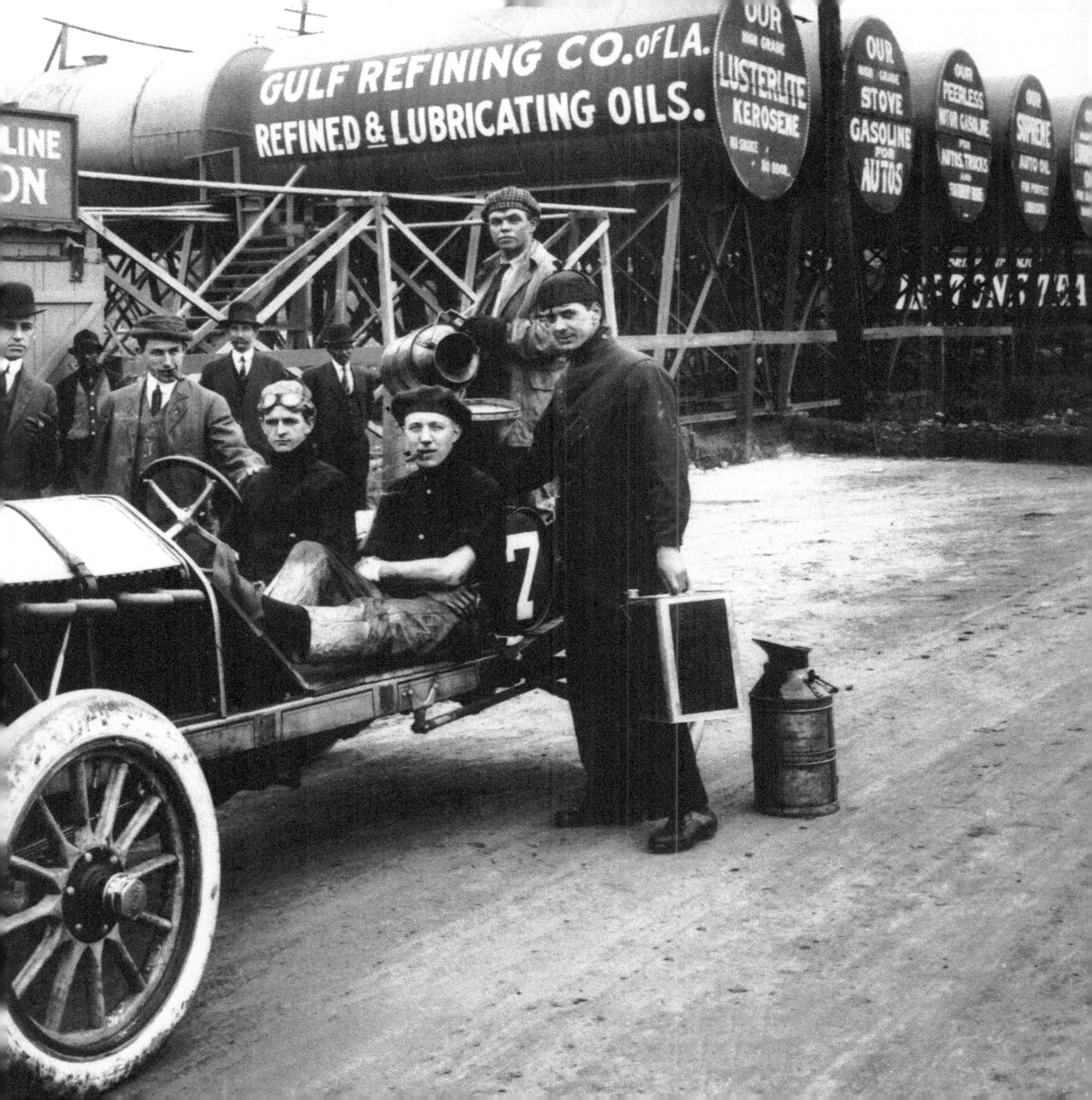

GULF REFINING CO. of L.A.
REFINED & LUBRICATING OILS.
OUR HIGH GRADE LUSTERLITE KEROSENE
OUR STOVE GASOLINE FOR AUTOS
OUR PEERLESS
OUR SUPREME AUTO OIL
7

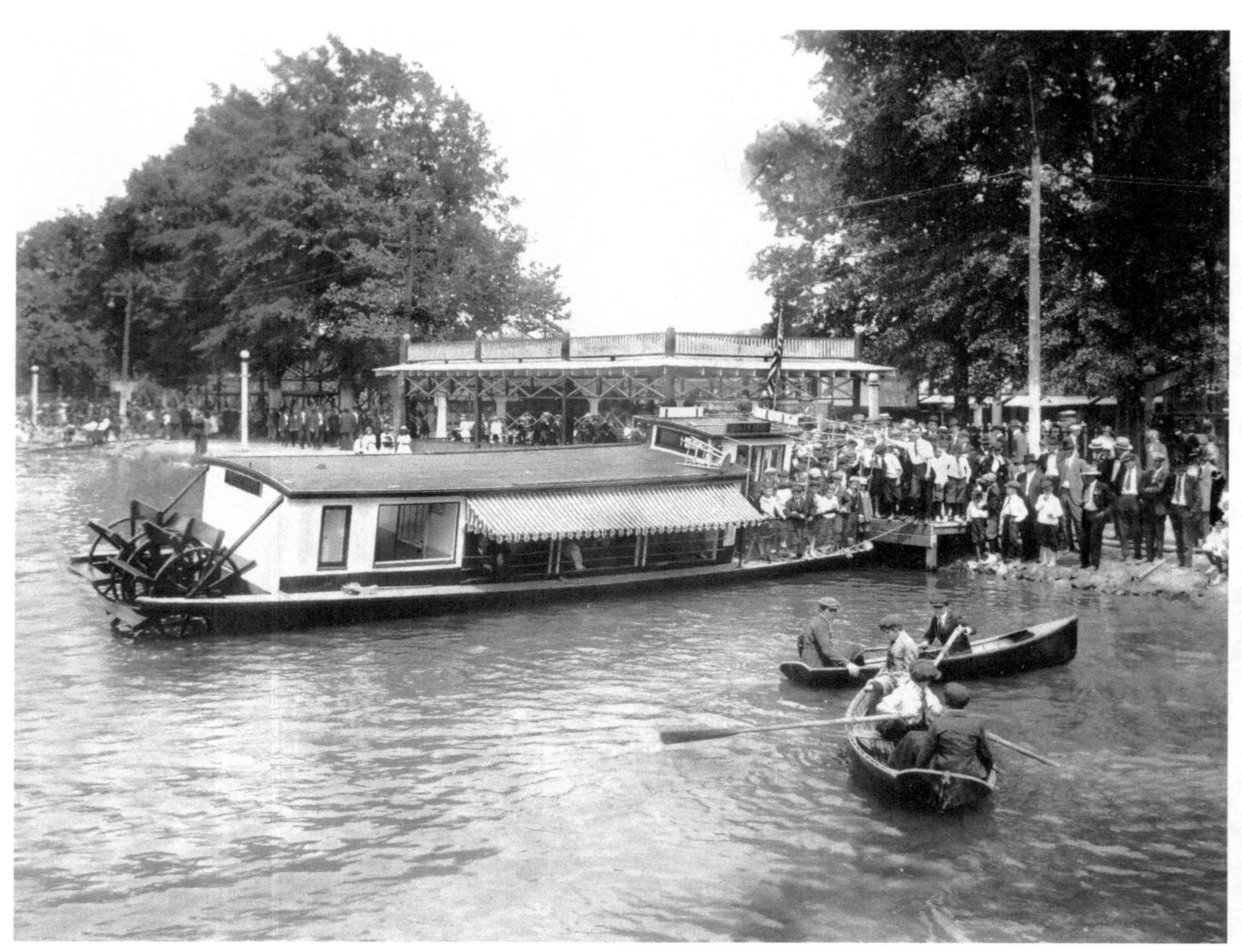

Boating at East Lake Park.

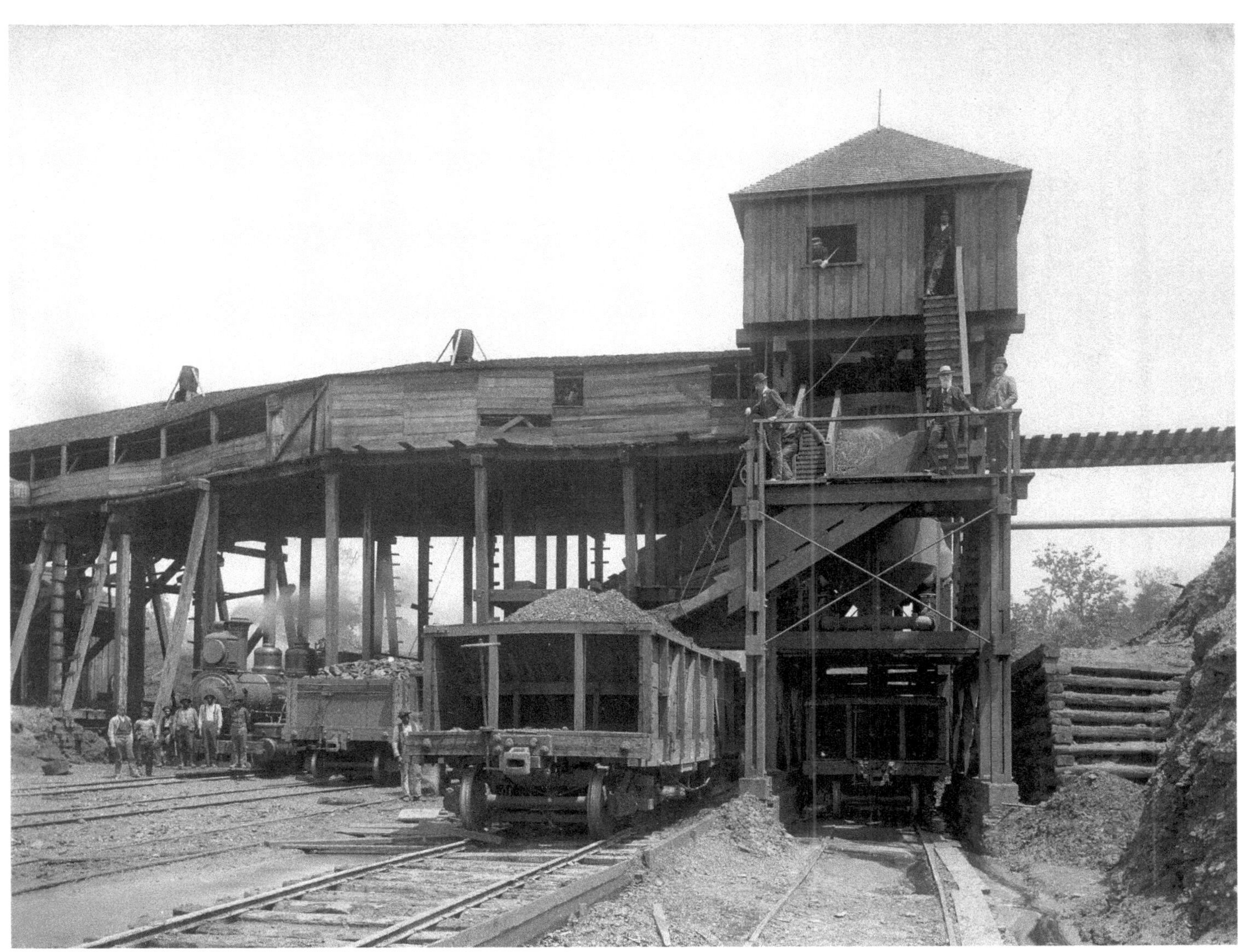

A tipple, where freight cars coming out of the mine were emptied, at the Tennessee Coal, Iron and Railroad Company's Pratt Mines.

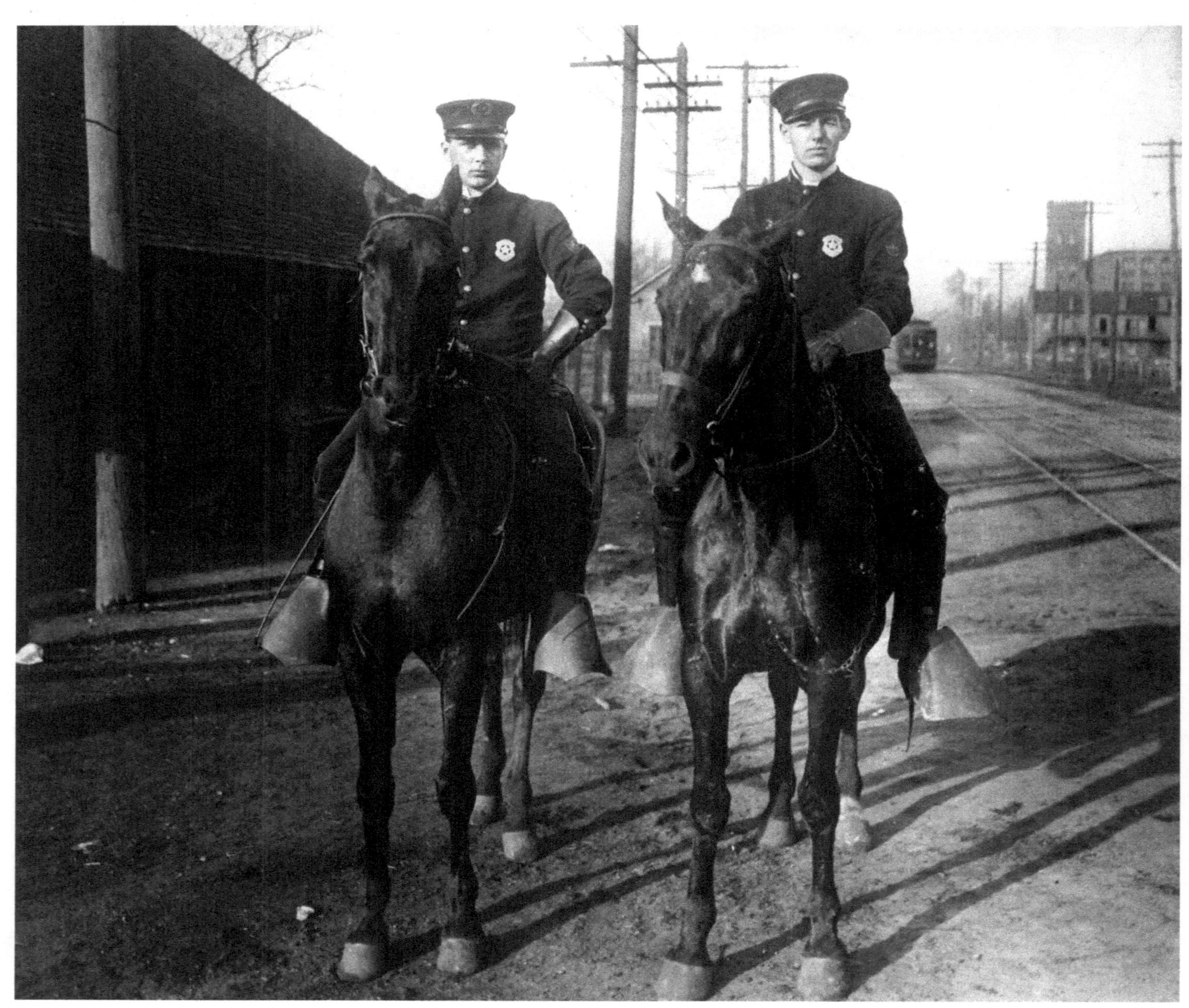

Mounted police officers on First Avenue North in Avondale. The building with the tower in the background is Avondale Mills.

The Sixteenth Street Baptist Church choir on the front steps of the church, around 1917.

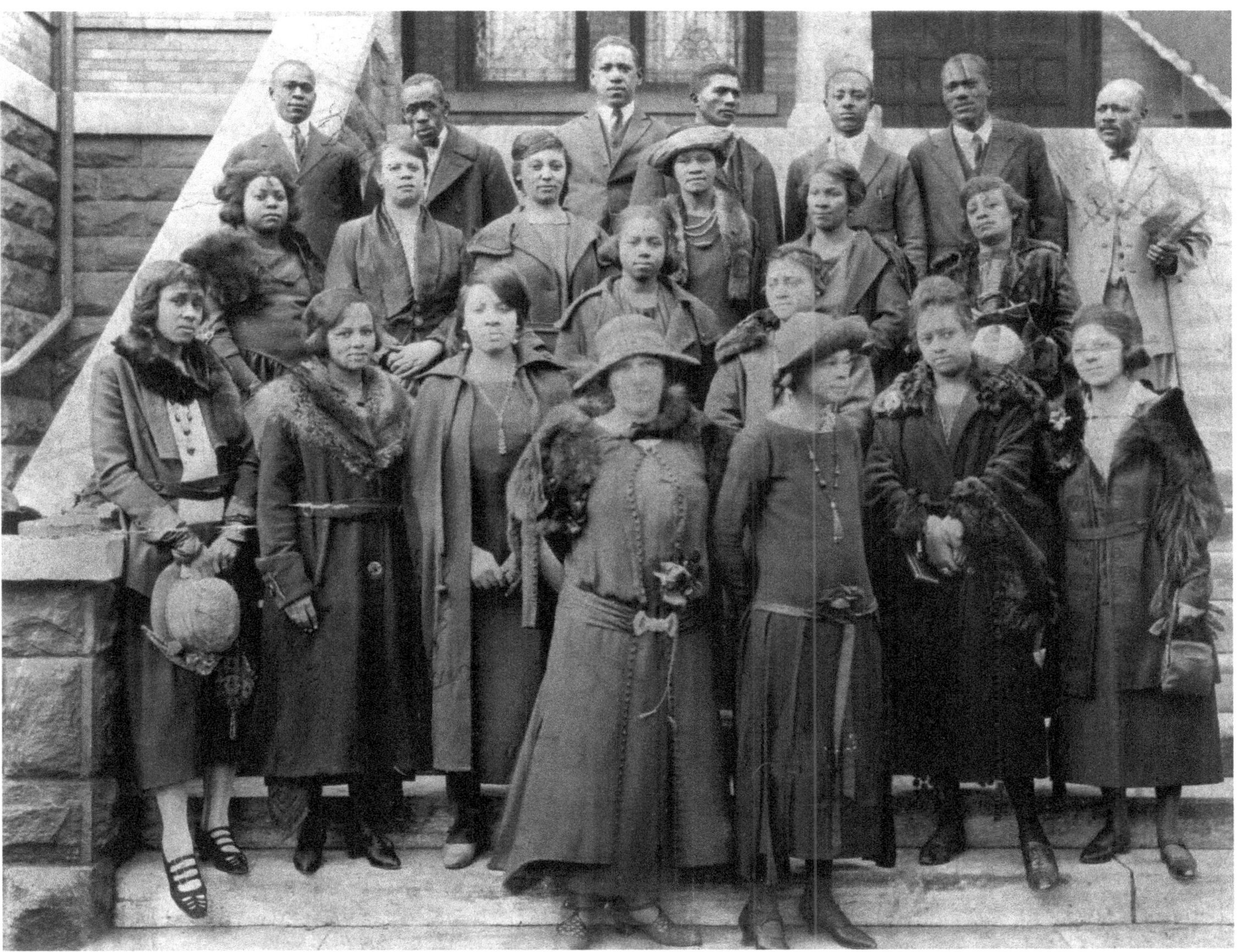

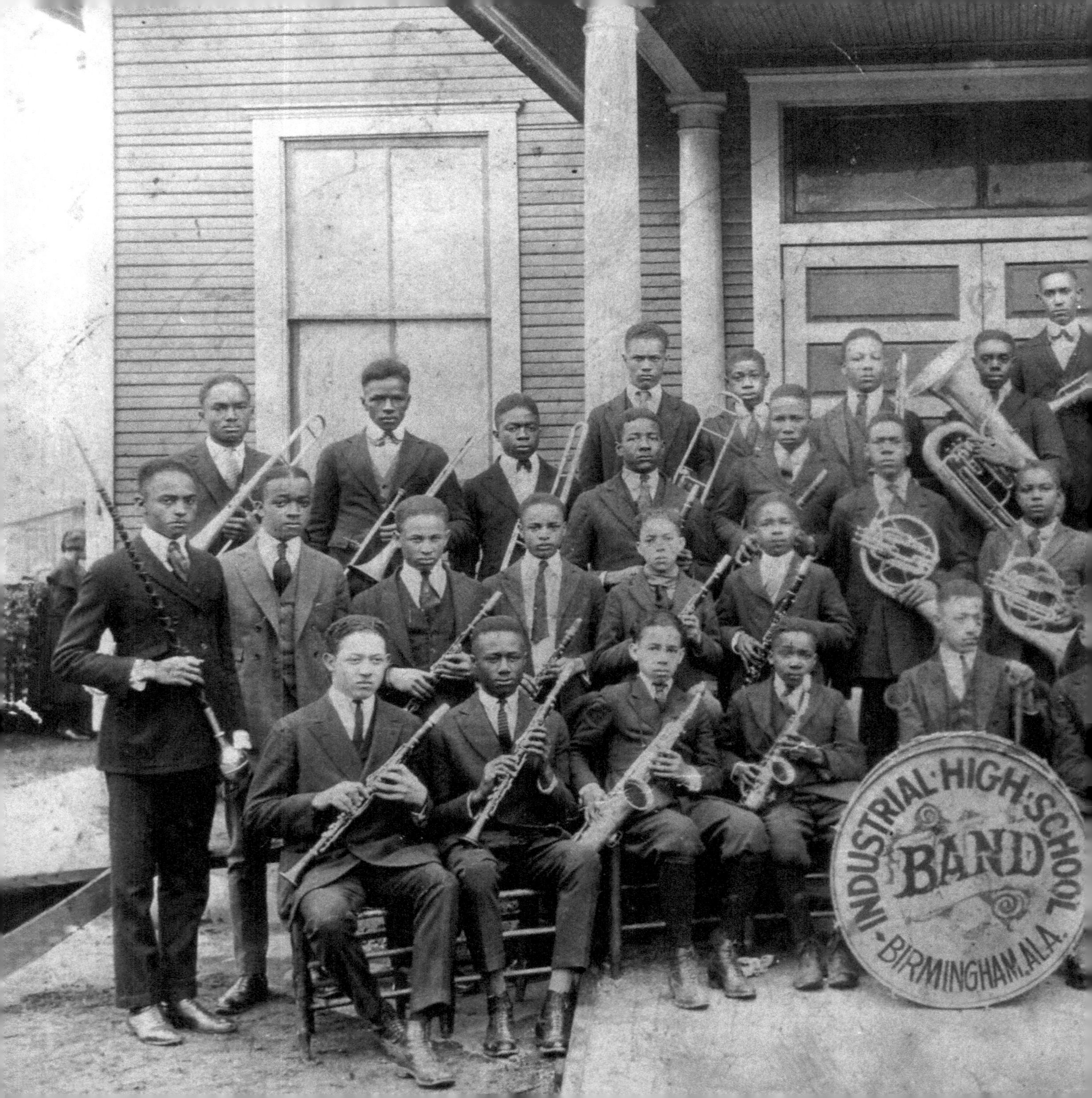
INDUSTRIAL·HIGH·SCHOOL
BAND
BIRMINGHAM, ALA.

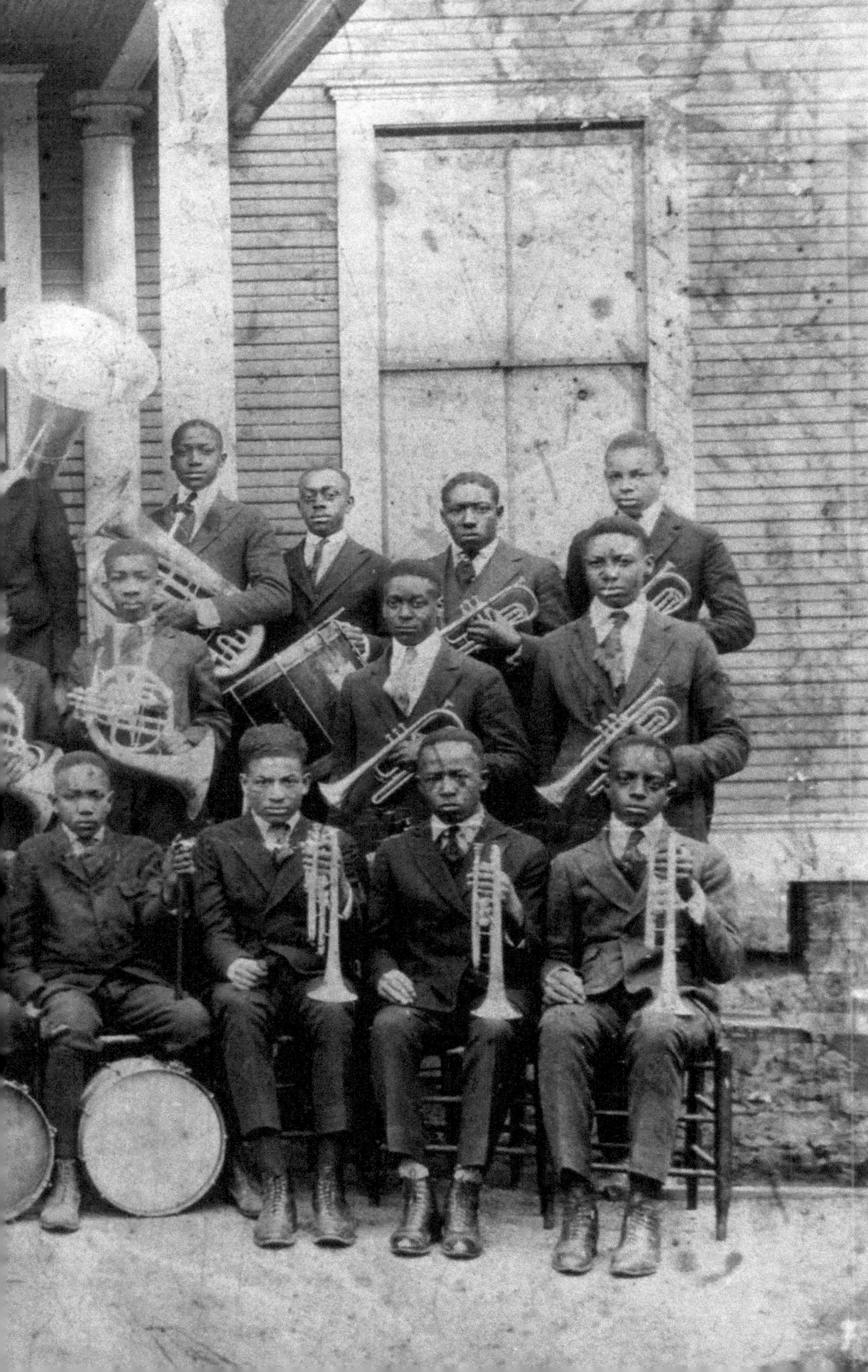

Prior to 1900, Jefferson County had no high school for African Americans. Responding to calls from parents, Industrial High was established and A. H. Parker was named its principal. Meeting first in one room, then in a series of shotgun shacks, then an old theater, the school constructed a building in 1924 on the corner of Eleventh Street and Eighth Avenue North. Later renamed to honor Dr. Parker, the institution became the largest high school for blacks in the South.

Birmingham during World War I. This is Twentieth Street looking north toward Capital Park in the distance (now Linn Park).

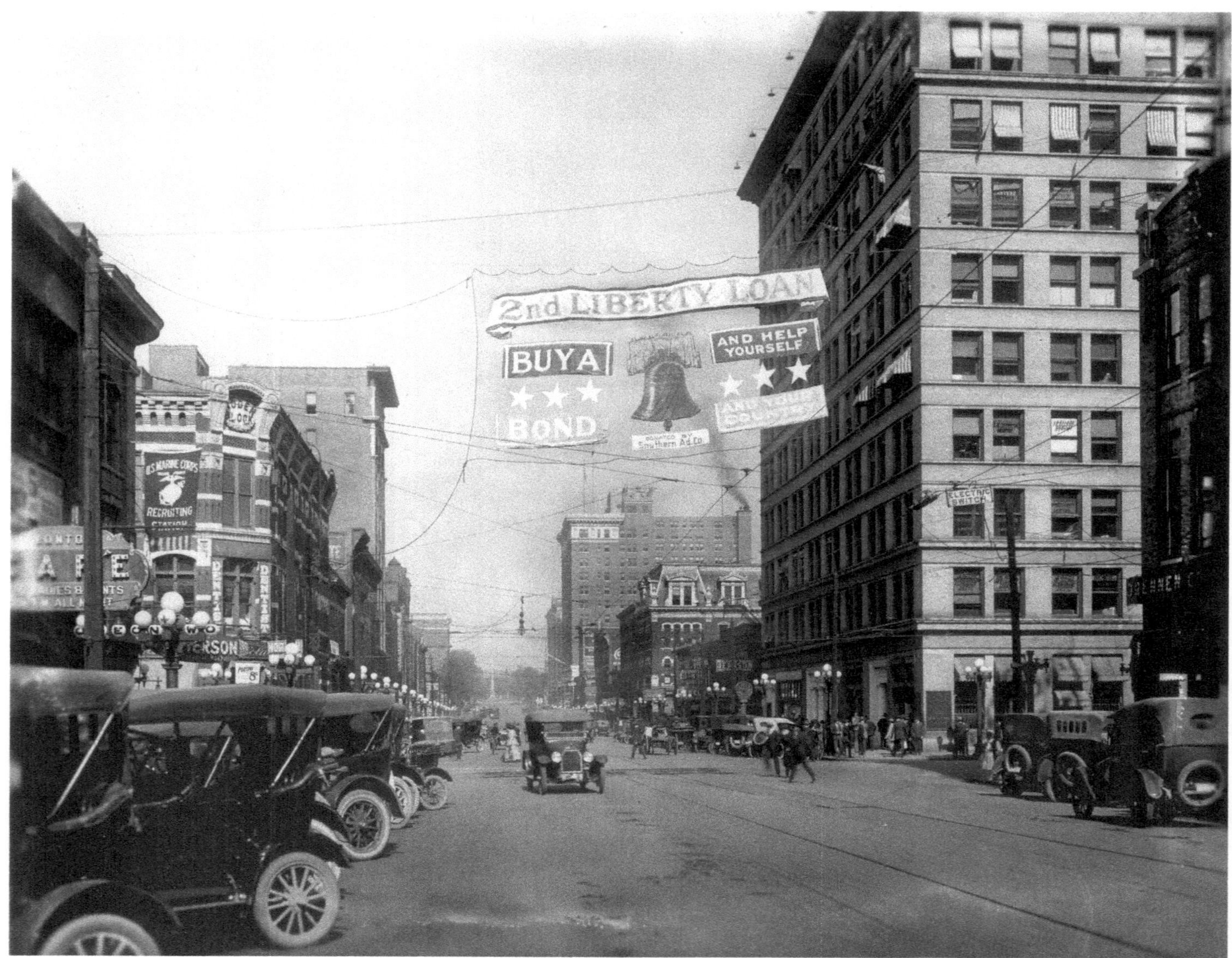

Laying of the cornerstone for the downtown post office, around 1918. This building would replace the older nineteenth-century post office on Second Avenue North, and is now used as a federal courthouse.

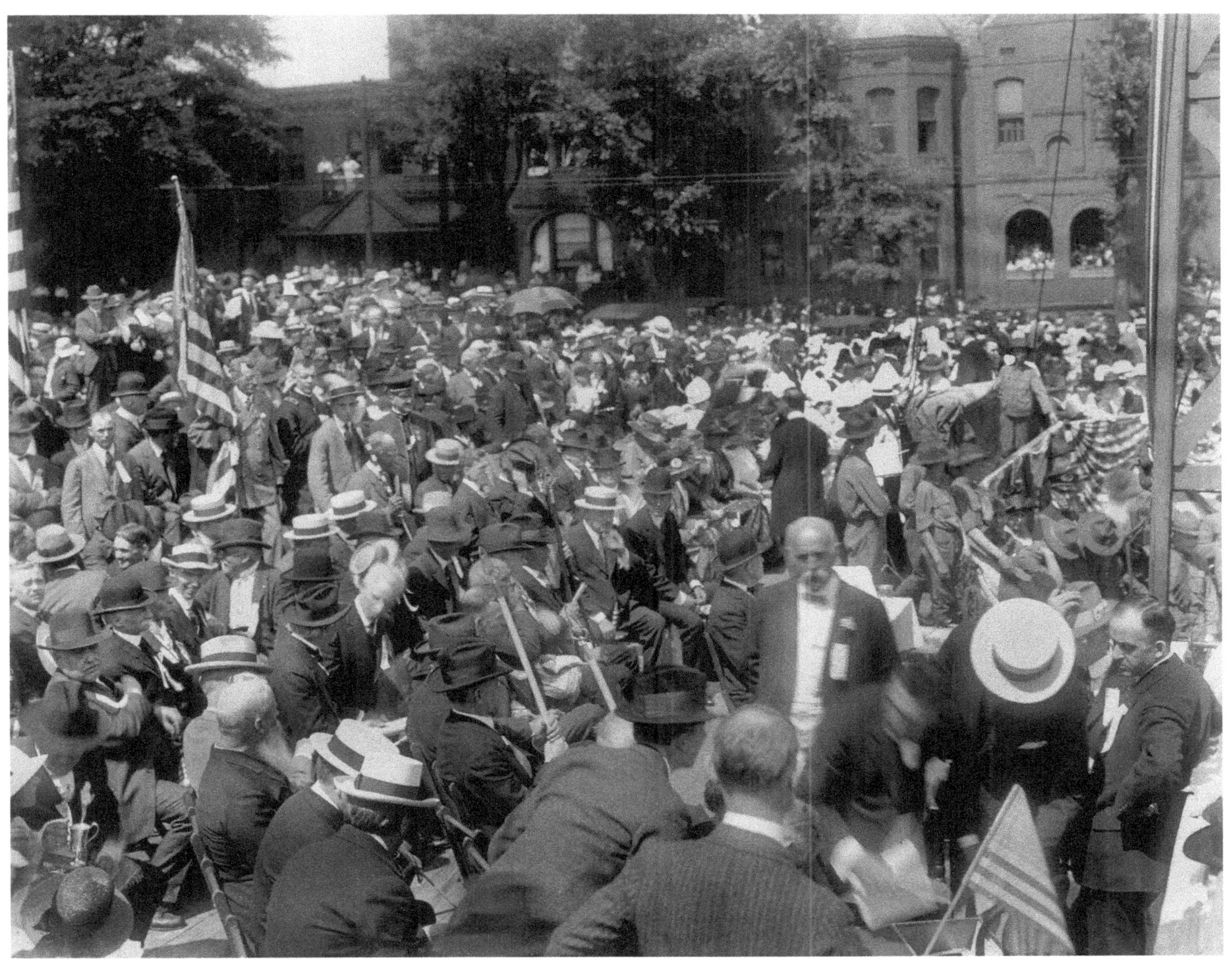

Standing on the corner of First Avenue North and Twentieth Street, the Empire Building was completed in 1909. It is shown here around 1918.

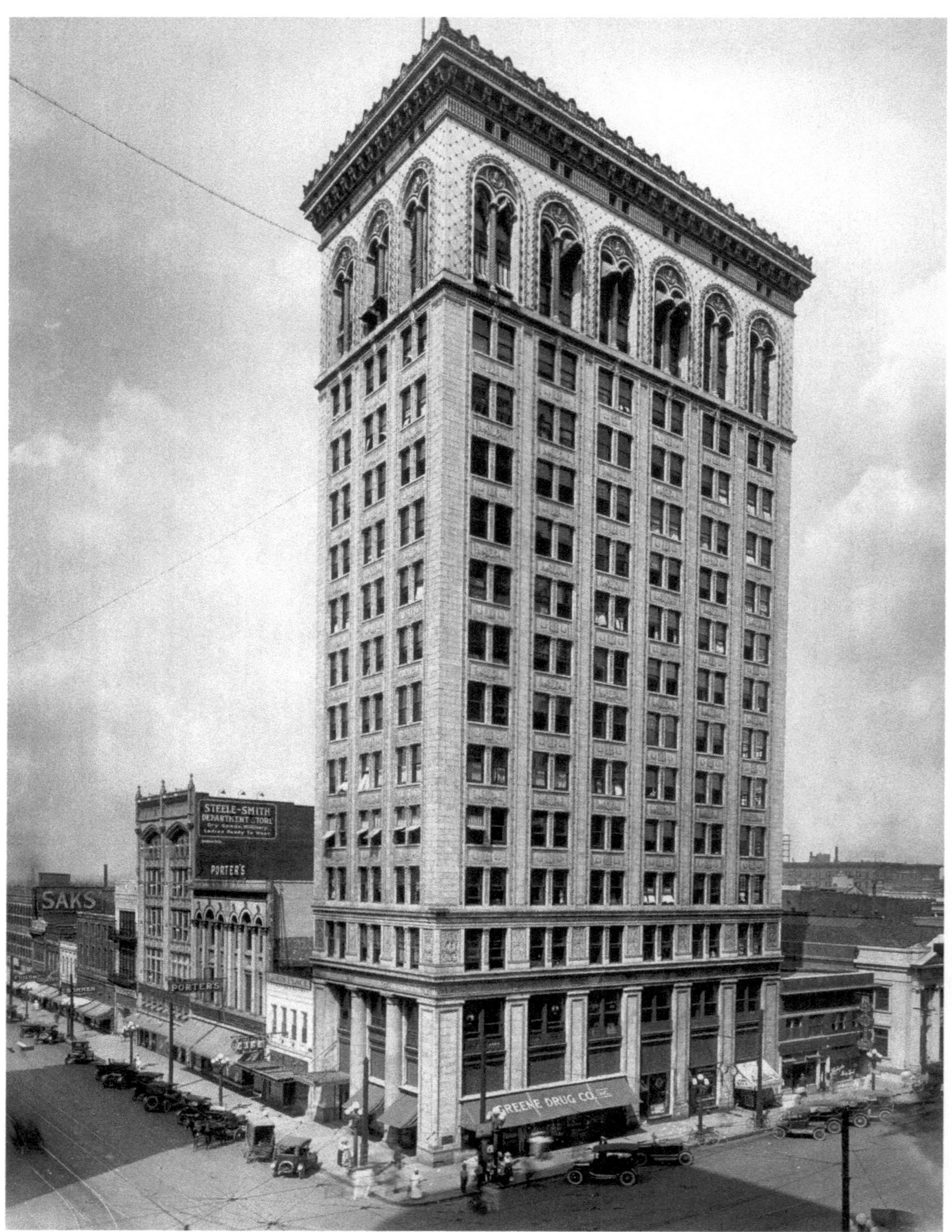

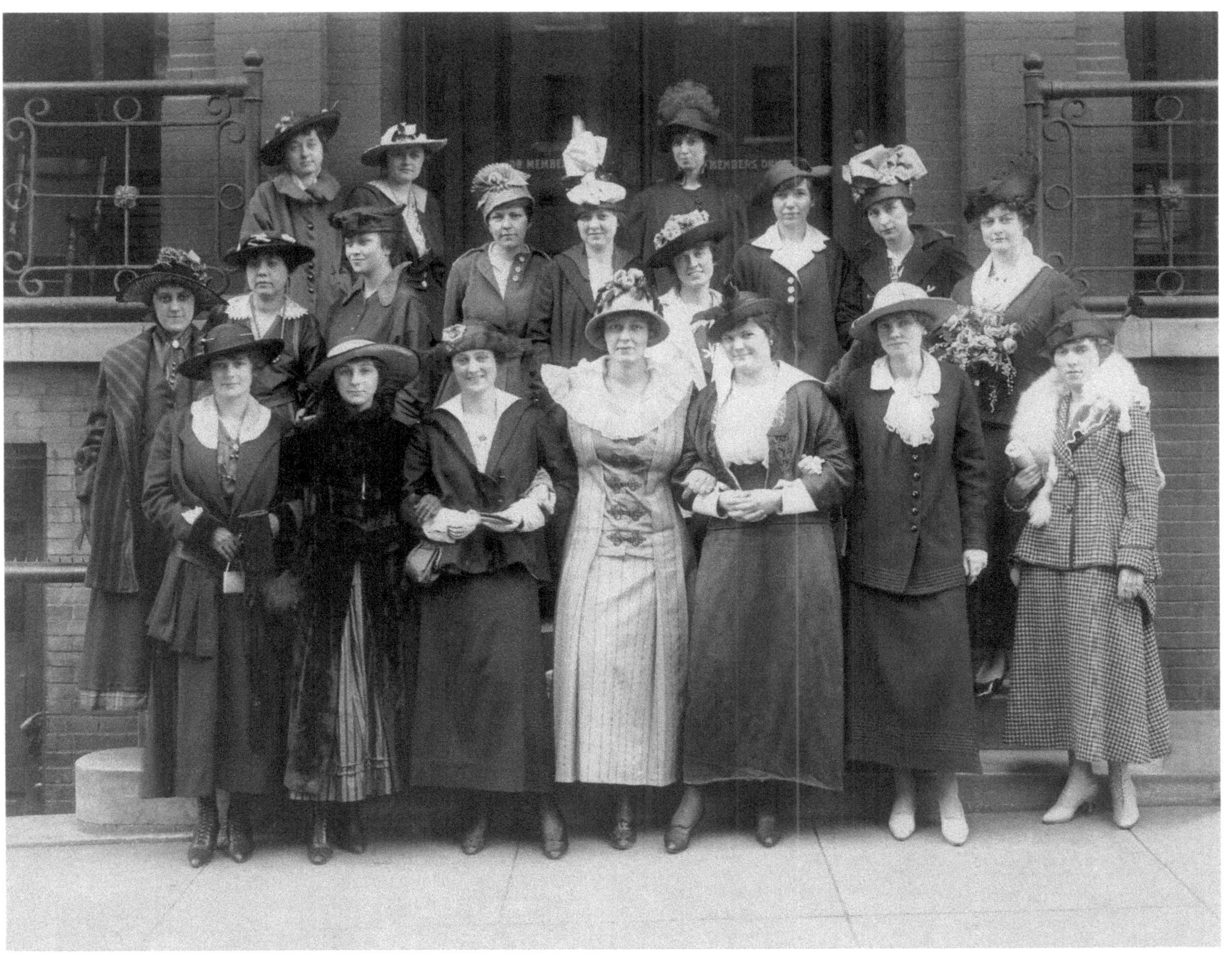

Posing on the front steps of the YWCA, around 1918. This building, located on short Twentieth Street North, facing Capital Park (now Linn Park), was demolished in the 1950s to make way for Birmingham's current city hall.

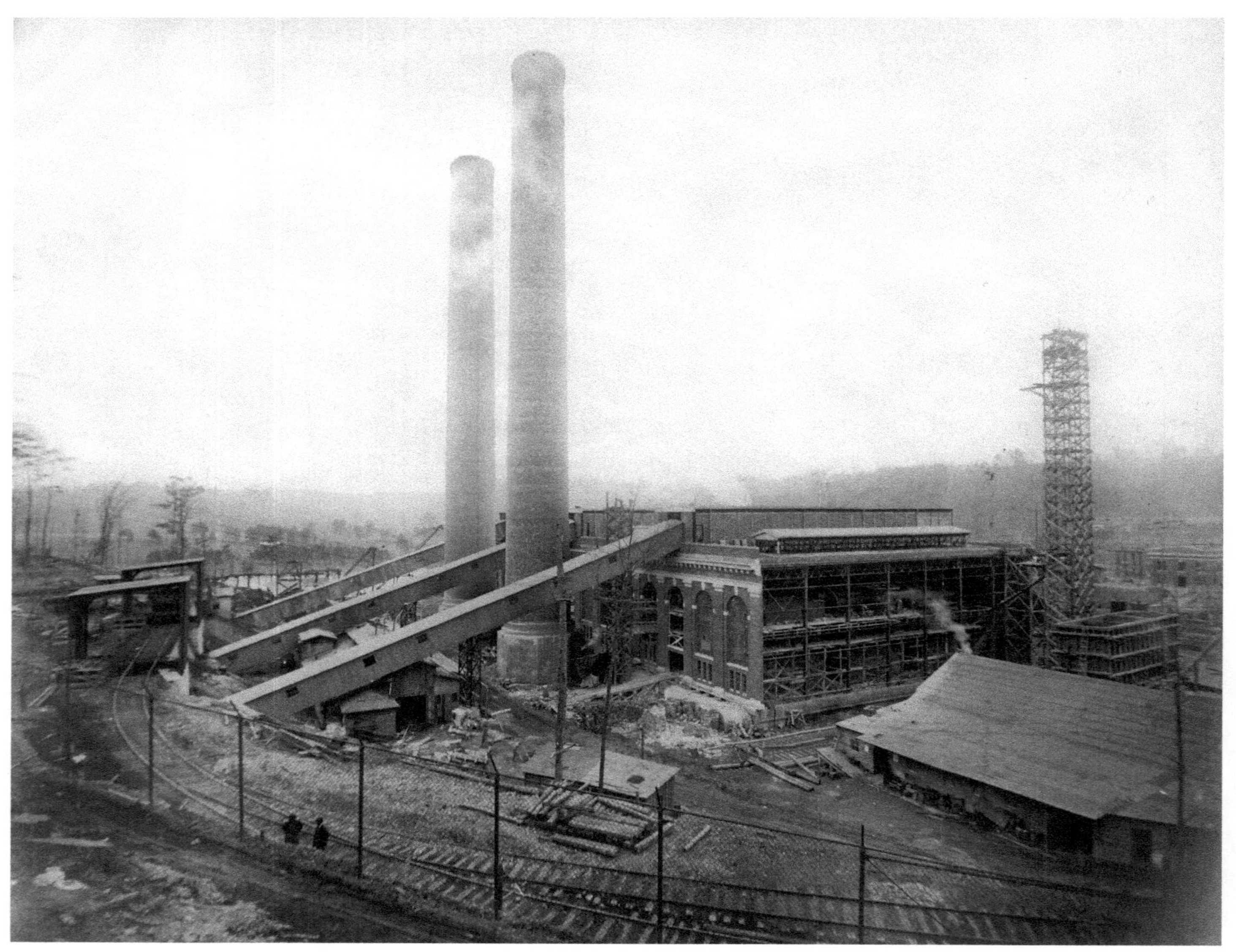

Warrior Reserve Steam Plant was later renamed in honor of William Crawford Gorgas. Located in Parrish near Birmingham, this image shows unit #2 under construction, December 10, 1918. Gorgas was the second steam plant constructed by Alabama Power Co. It was originally developed to serve as reserve or "back-up" power for the company's hydroelectric plants on the Coosa and Tallapoosa rivers. Electricity from these plants supplied wholesale power to the Birmingham Electric Co. until the two companies merged in 1952.

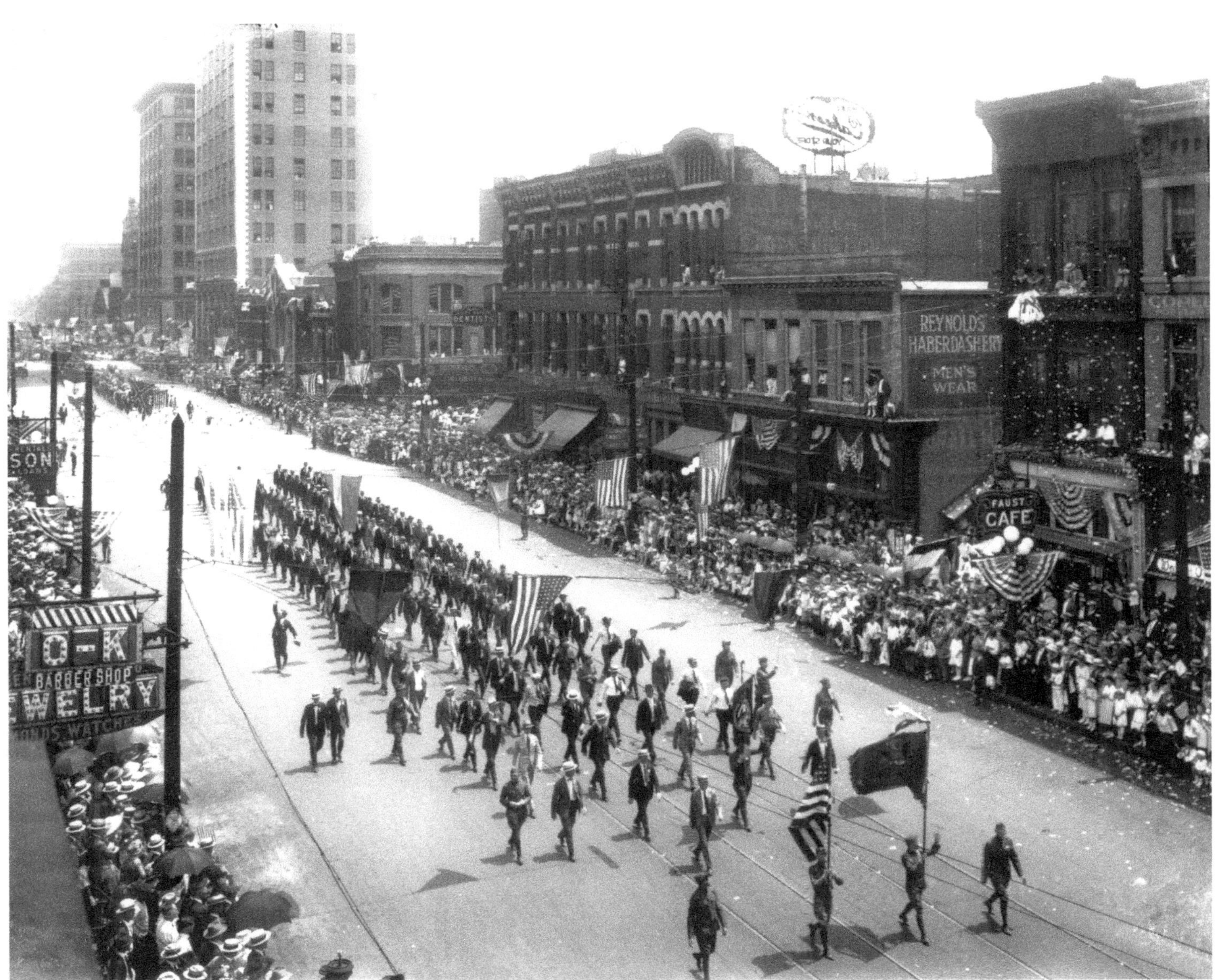

A parade down Twentieth Street honors World War I veterans of the Rainbow Division in 1919. Unlike earlier wars, in which military units were made of men from the same state or town, the Rainbow Division included men from 26 states, including Alabama, and saw extensive combat.

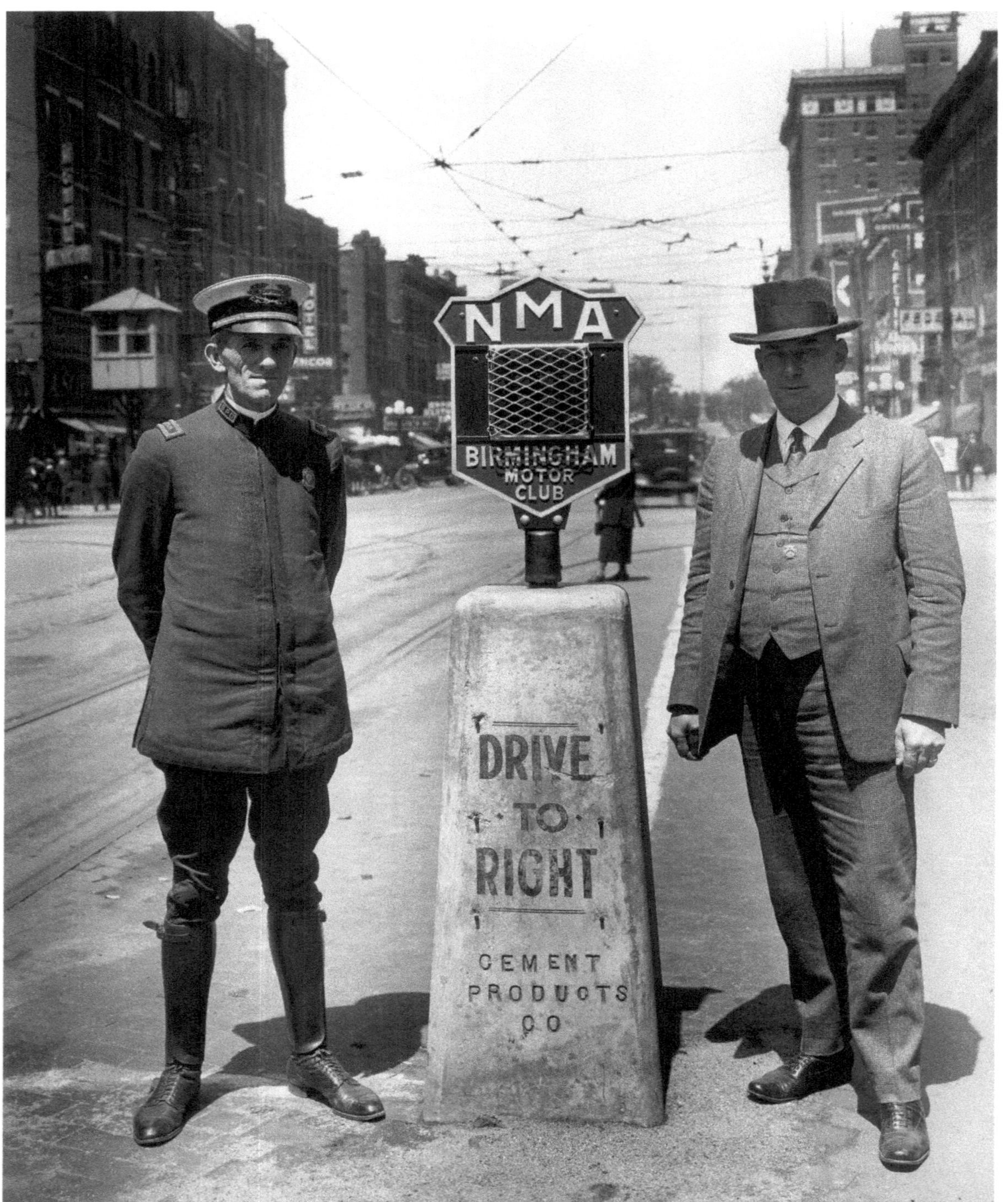

Providing drivers with some direction on Twentieth Street North in the 1920s.

A Growing Metropolis and a Great Depression

(1918–1939)

The 1920s, like the two previous decades in Birmingham, were a time of building. More skyscrapers were added to the city's skyline, including the Alabama Power Company headquarters (in 1925) and the Watts Building (in 1928). The city also dedicated impressive new places of learning in the 1920s, including Woodlawn High School, Industrial High School (later A. H. Parker), Phillips High School, and the downtown Birmingham Public Library.

The 1920s brought changes in everyday life to the people of Birmingham through technologies devised in previous decades, like the motion picture and the automobile. Dozens of new movie theaters opened, giving residents more entertainment options; and as more people bought automobiles, new suburbs sprang up farther from the city. Thousands of new cars also created new problems as traffic began to choke downtown streets. In 1921, Birmingham celebrated its semi-centennial, and the city founded in a cornfield fifty years earlier now had a population of 178,000.

The expansion and prosperity of the early 1920s was replaced by a gradual economic decline in the late 1920s, which was amplified by the economic collapse caused by the Great Depression. Factories and mines closed, government services were curtailed, and more than 100,000 people lost their jobs. Many workers and their families faced severe hardship.

Where photographs had once documented Birmingham's growth, in the 1930s they documented the city's desperate poverty. Although the area benefited from many of Franklin Roosevelt's New Deal programs, it would take a second world war to return prosperity to Birmingham.

Second Avenue North around 1920. The building with the tower is the old downtown post office on the corner of Eighteenth Street.

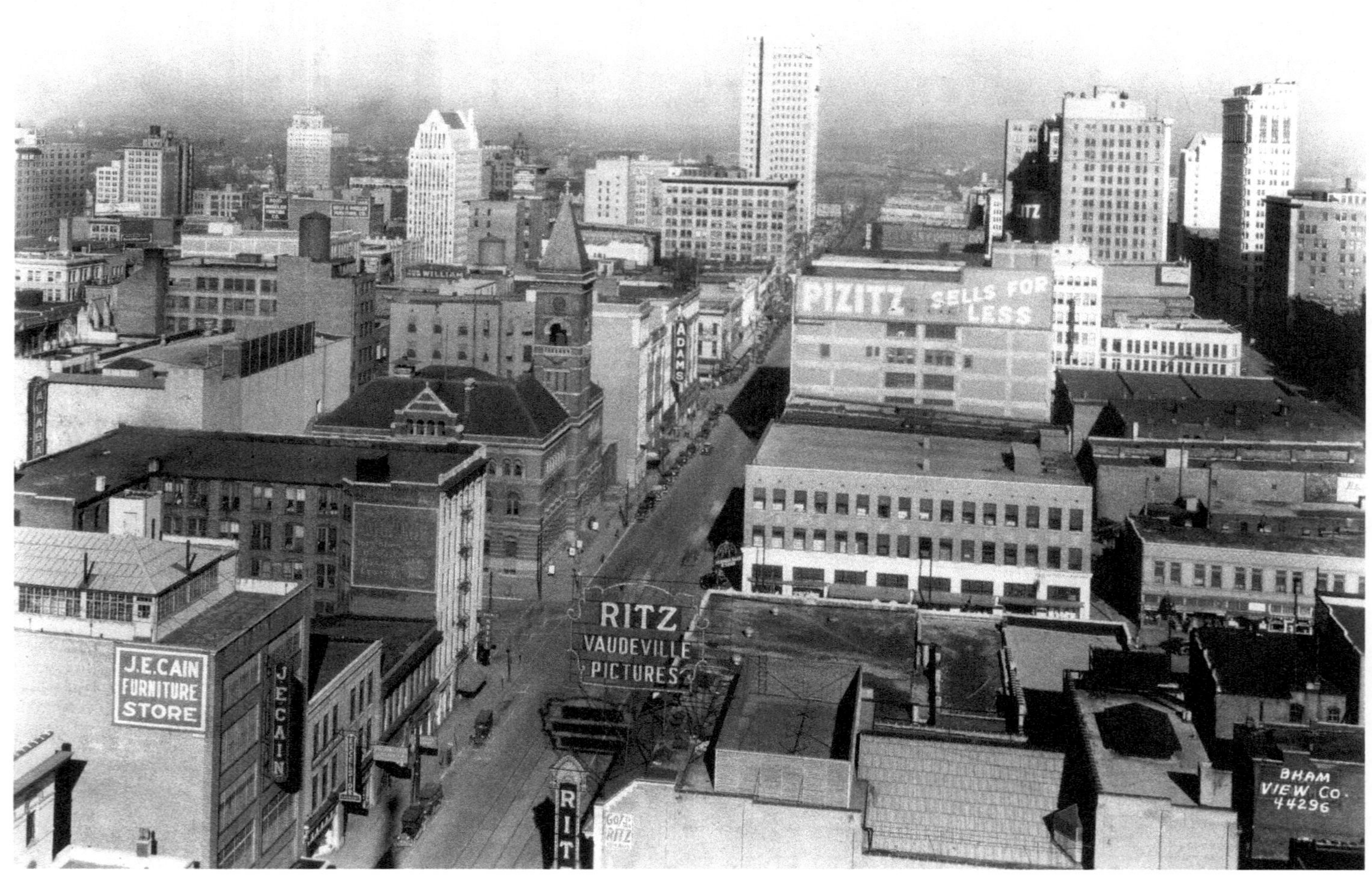

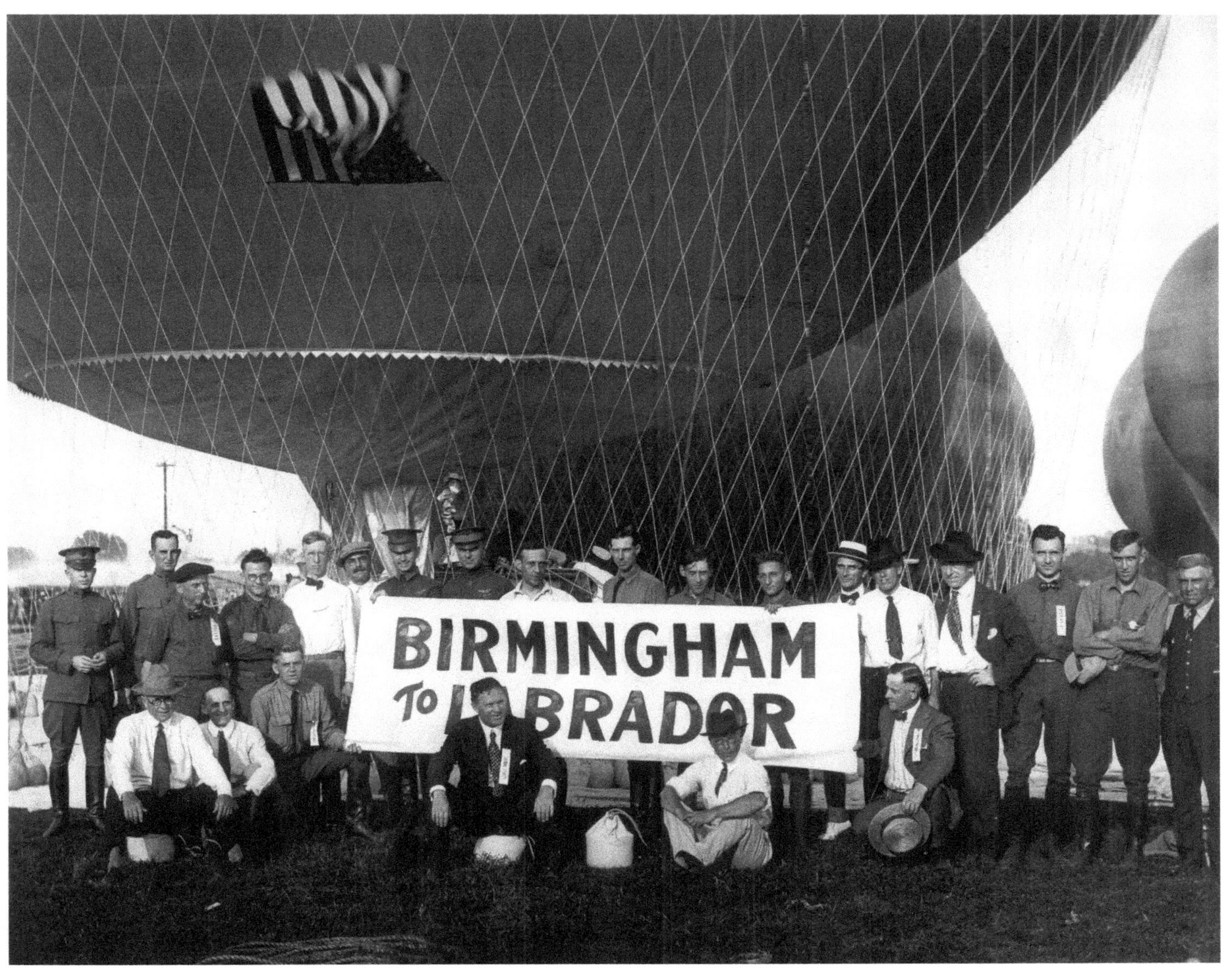

Birmingham hosted three national hot-air balloon races in 1920, 1921, and 1934. Here pilots and local sponsors pose with the line of balloons before take-off in 1920. The winner would be the balloon that made it farthest because none made it all the way to Labrador.

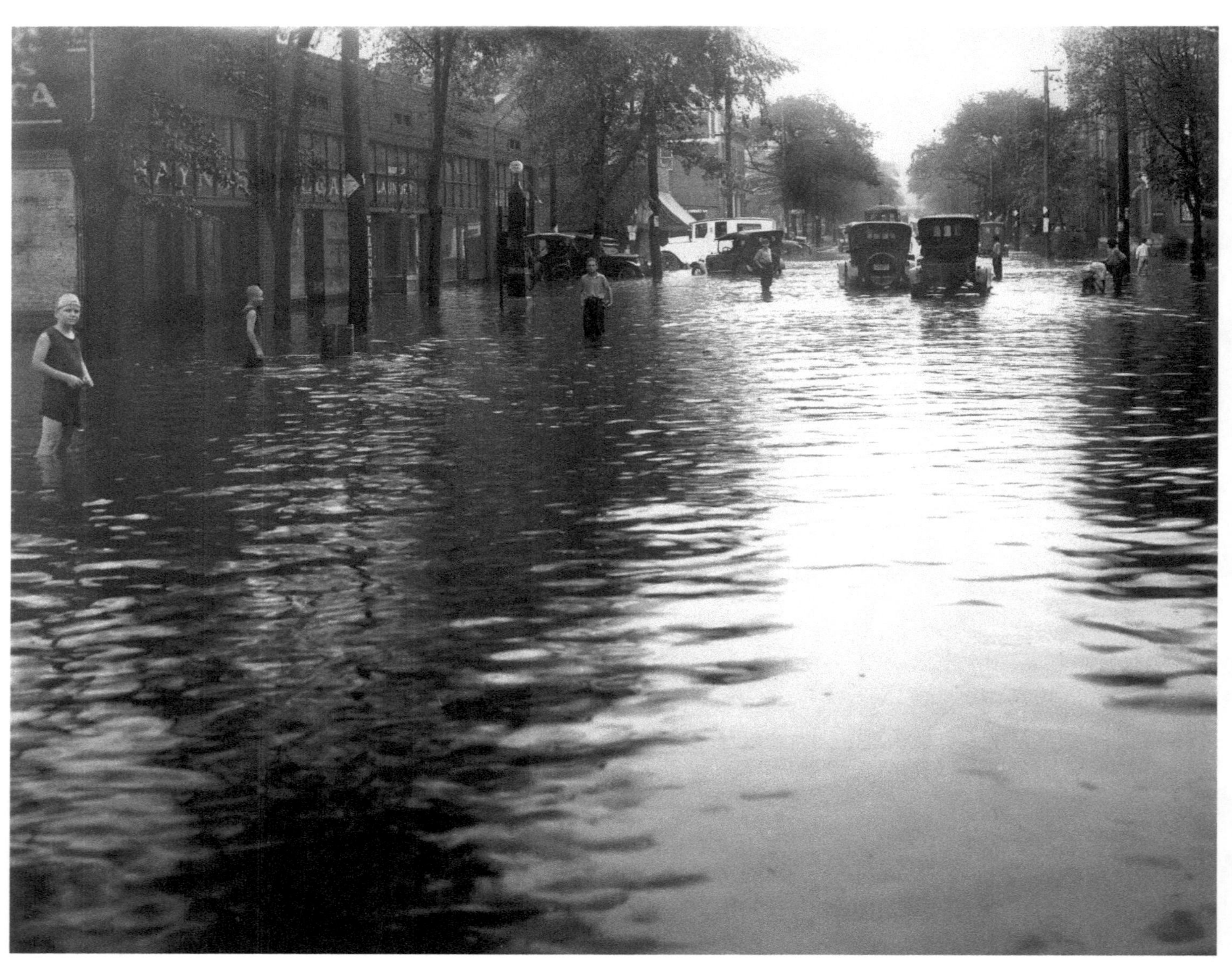

Two boys have donned their swimsuits to play in floodwaters on Fifth Avenue North.

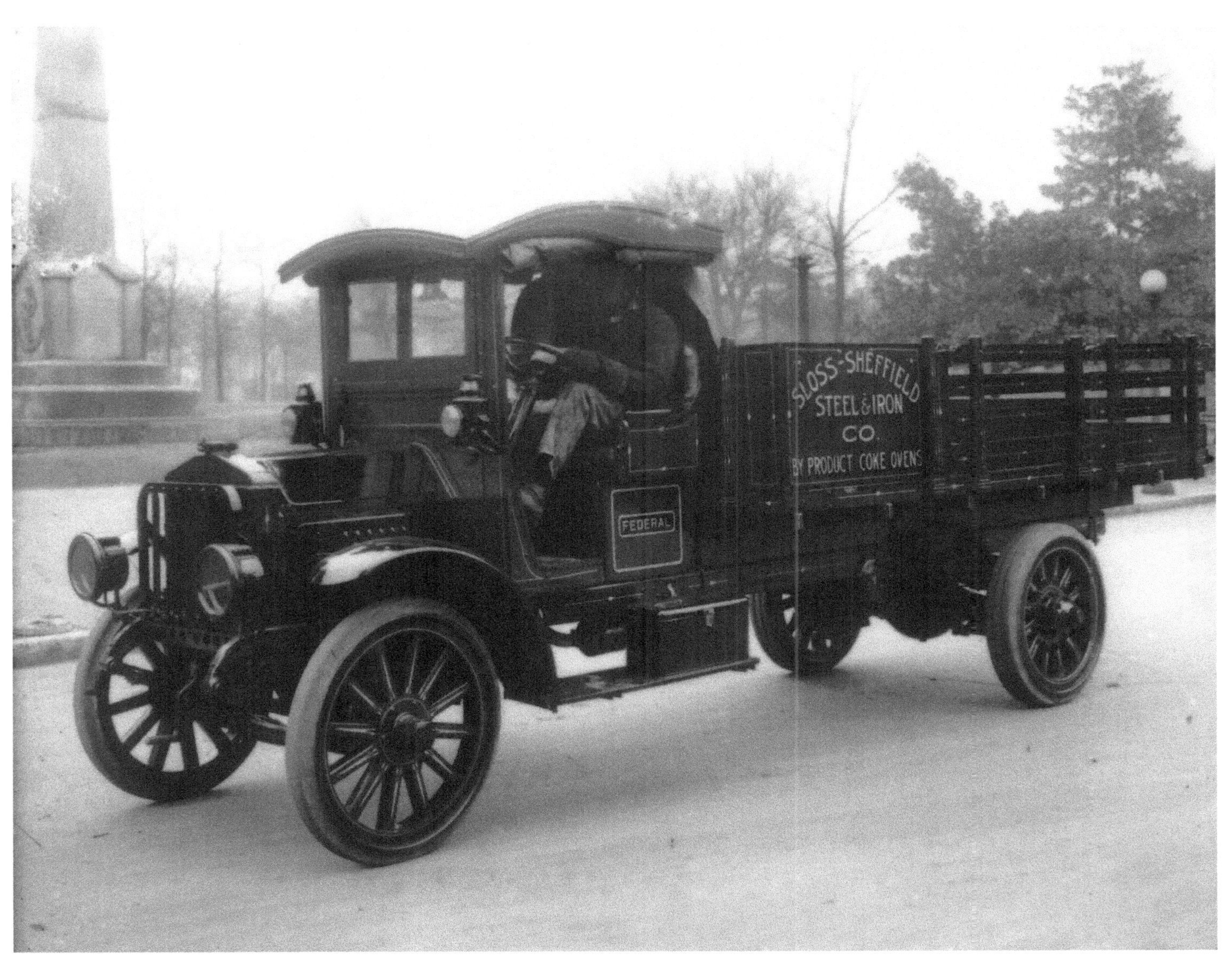

A Sloss-Sheffield truck is parked beside Woodrow Wilson Park (now Linn Park).

Looking north over the wooden Twenty-second Street overpass. Shown here in the 1920s, the bridge was built in the 1890s to carry streetcars over the railroad reservation.

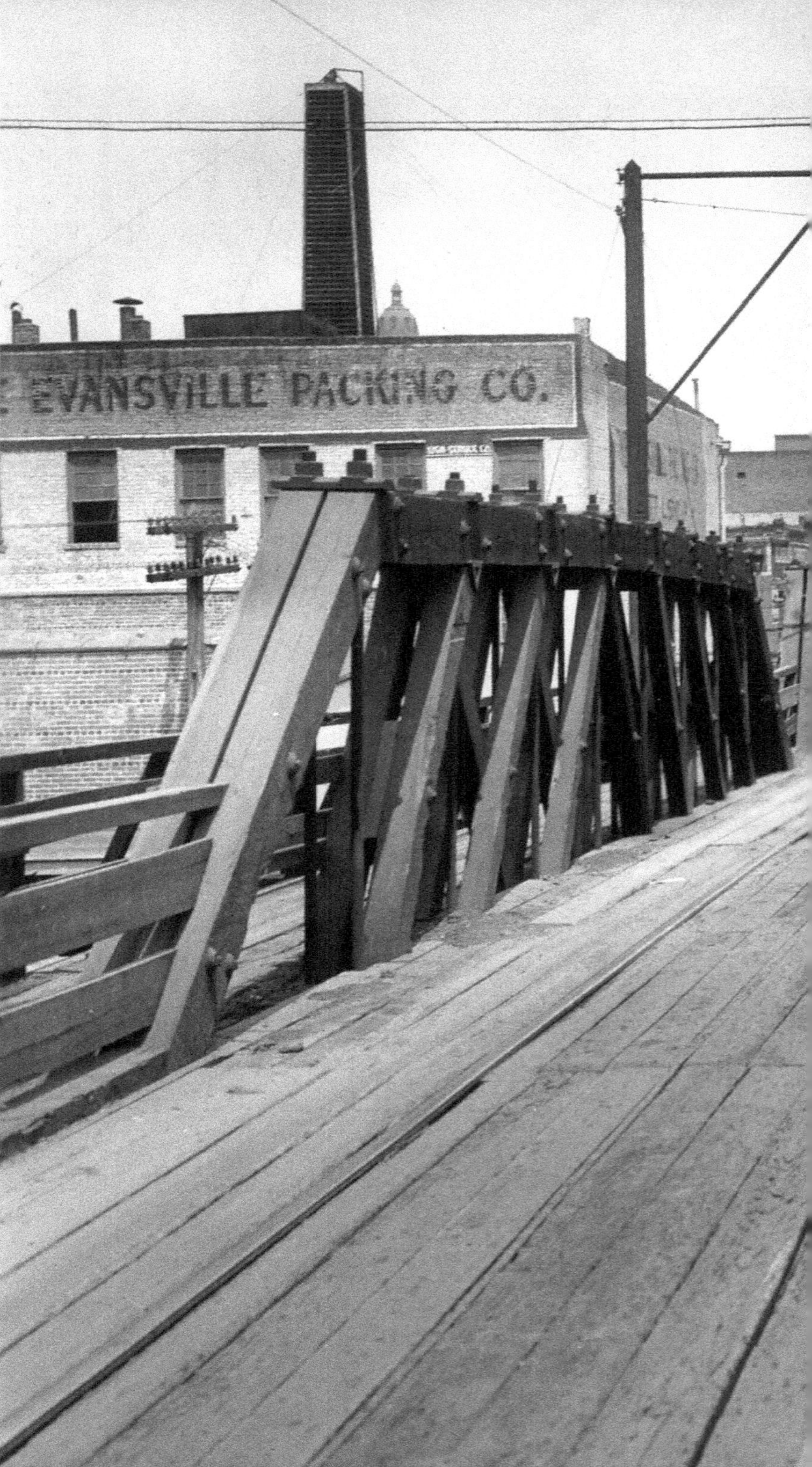

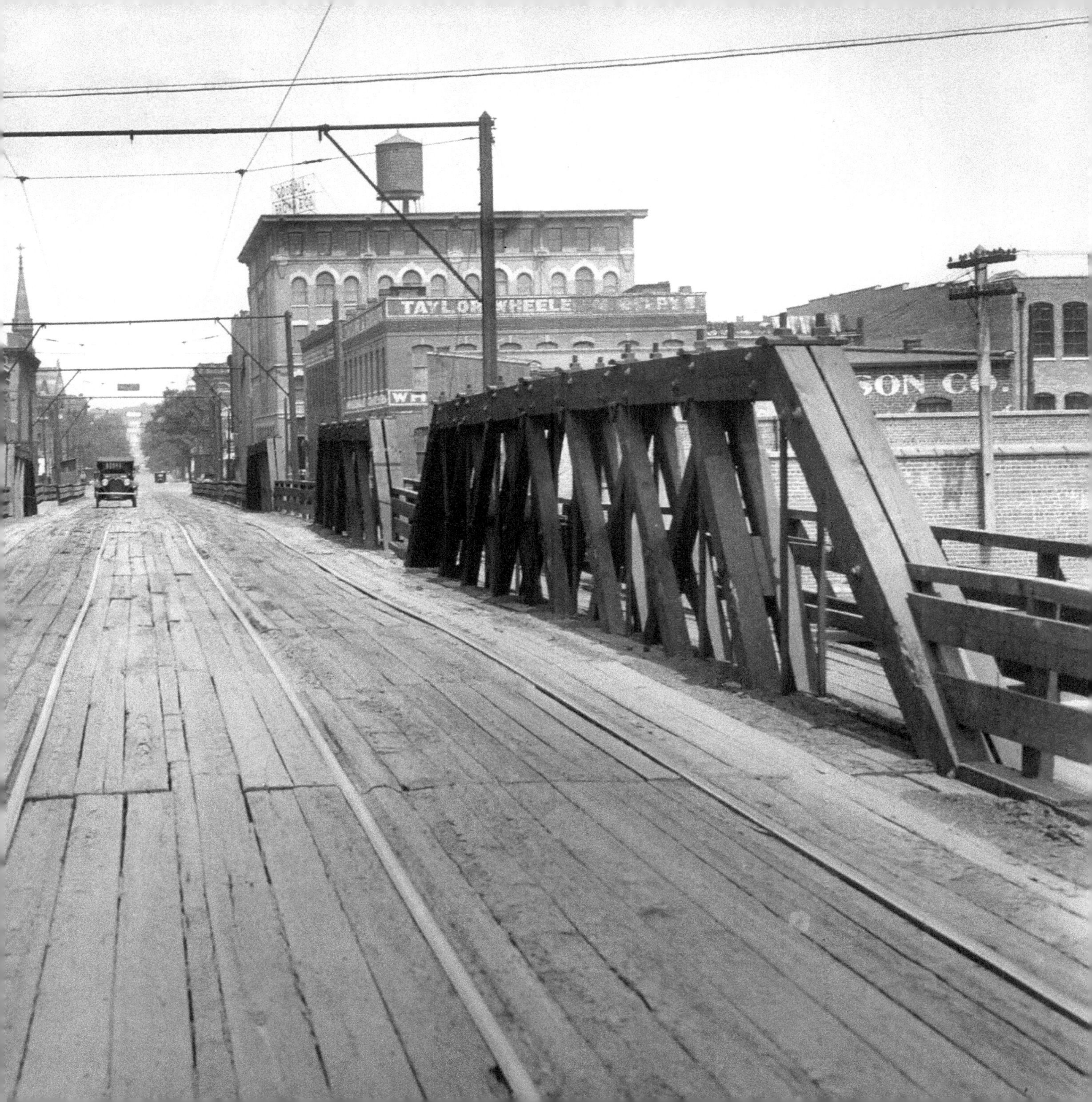
TAYLOR WHEELE
SON CO.

Lay Dam powerhouse crew, around 1920. Lay Dam was the first hydroelectric plant constructed by Alabama Power Company and was the first step in W. P. Lay's, James Mitchell's, and Thomas W. Martin's vision of creating an interconnected system of hydro and steam plants that would provide safe, reliable, and economical electricity—not only to Alabama, but to the wider Southeast.

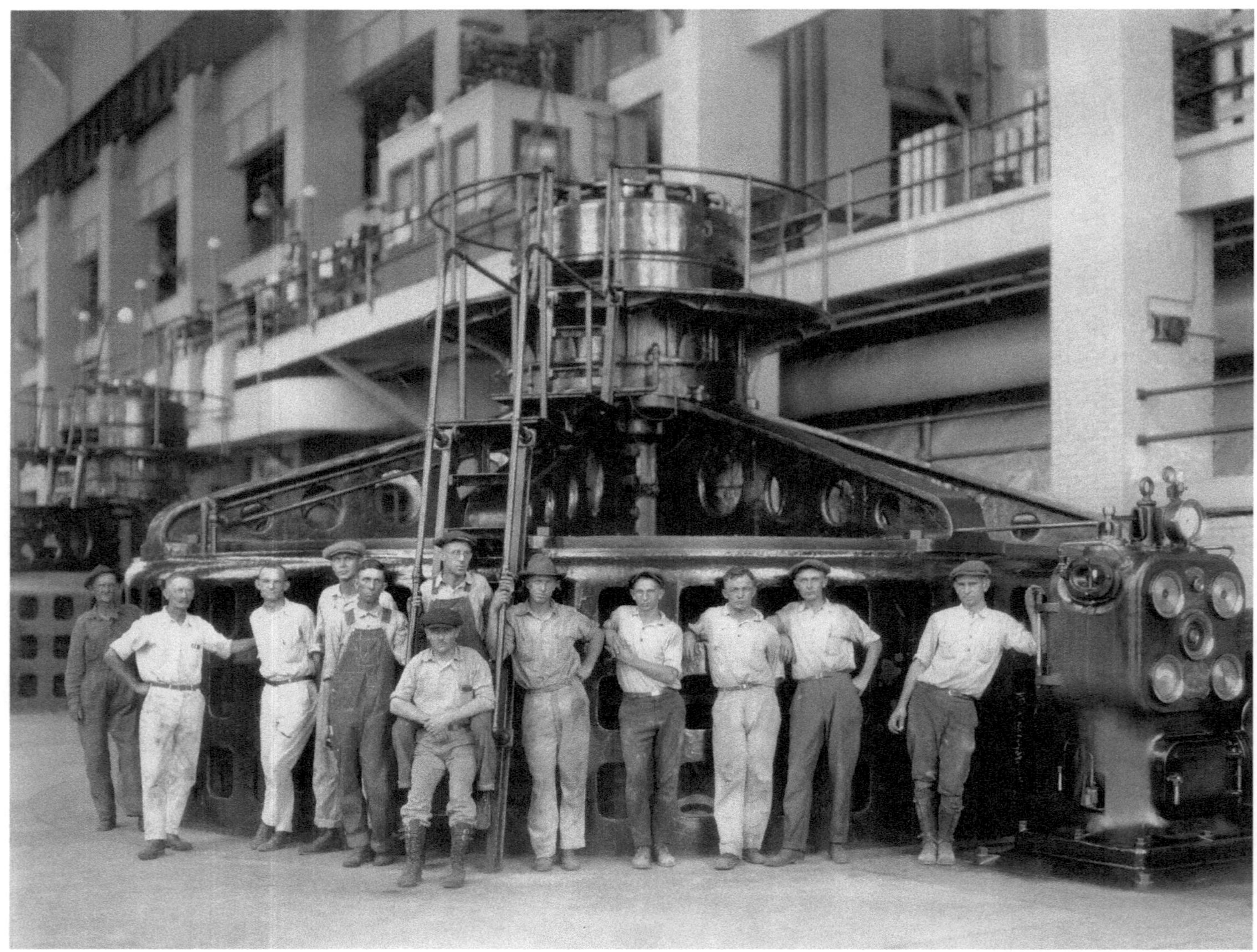

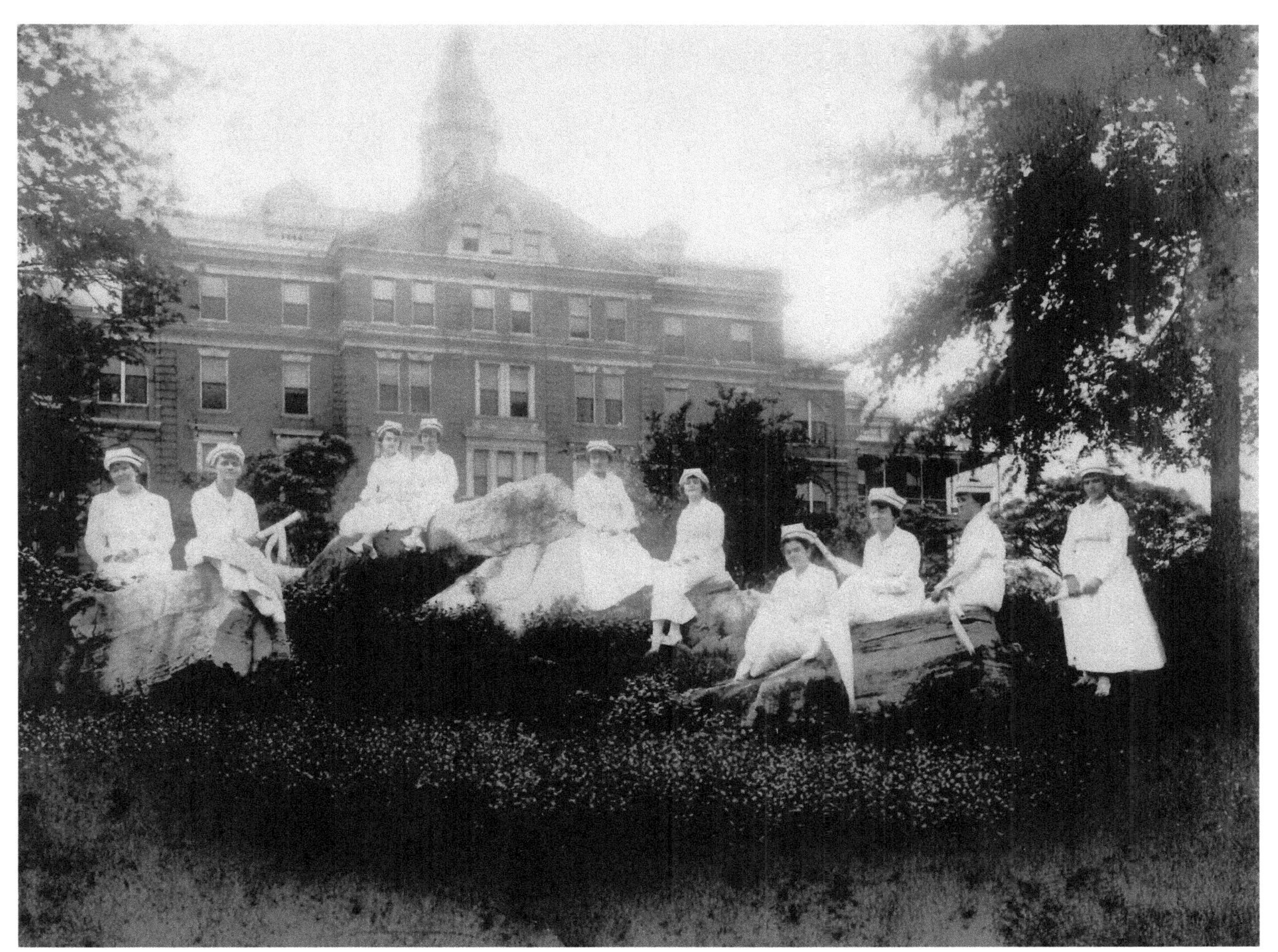

St. Vincent's Nursing School Graduating Class of 1920.

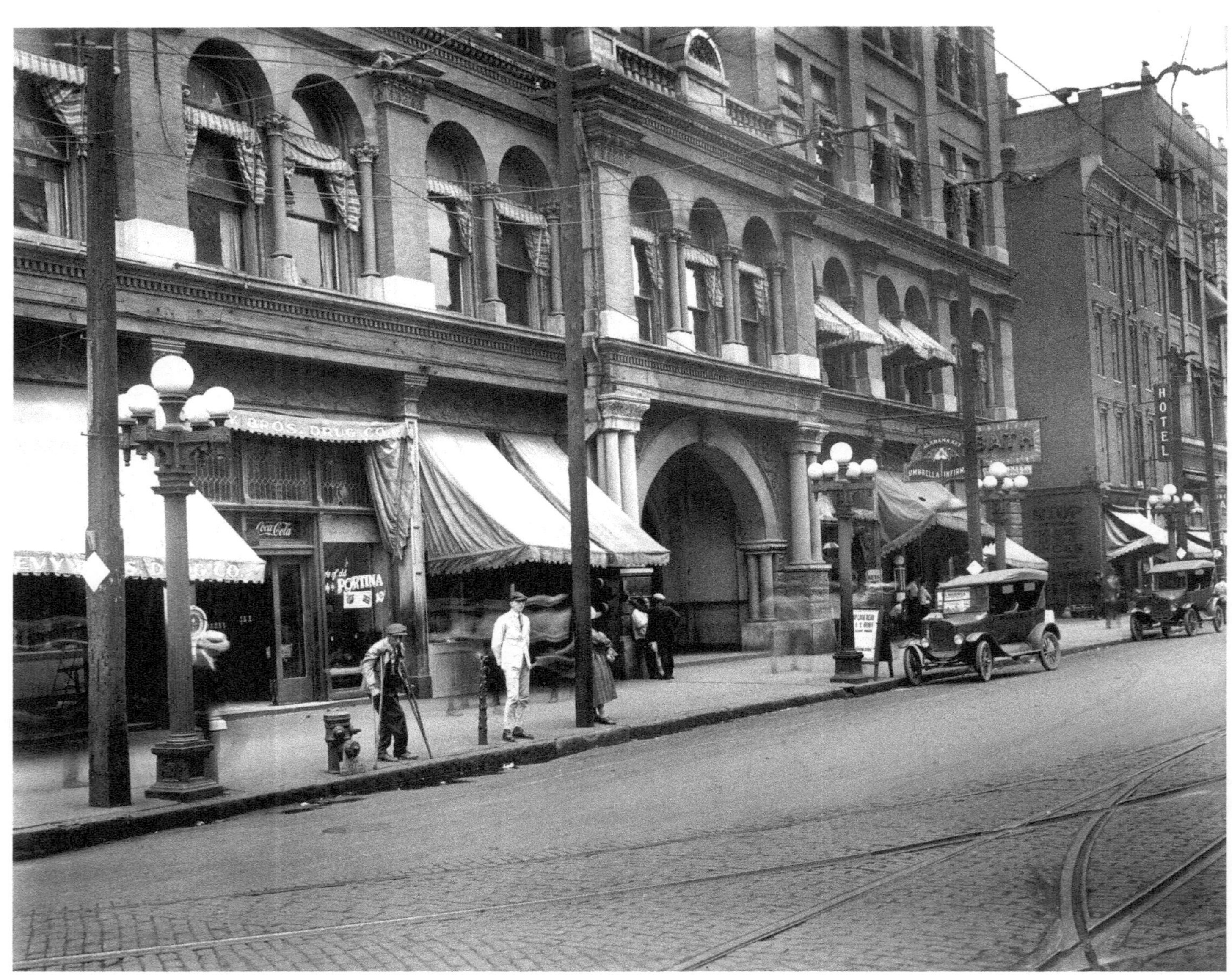

Street-level view of Birmingham's second City Hall on the corner of Fourth Avenue North and Nineteenth Street, around 1920. Much of the first floor was rented out as retail space.

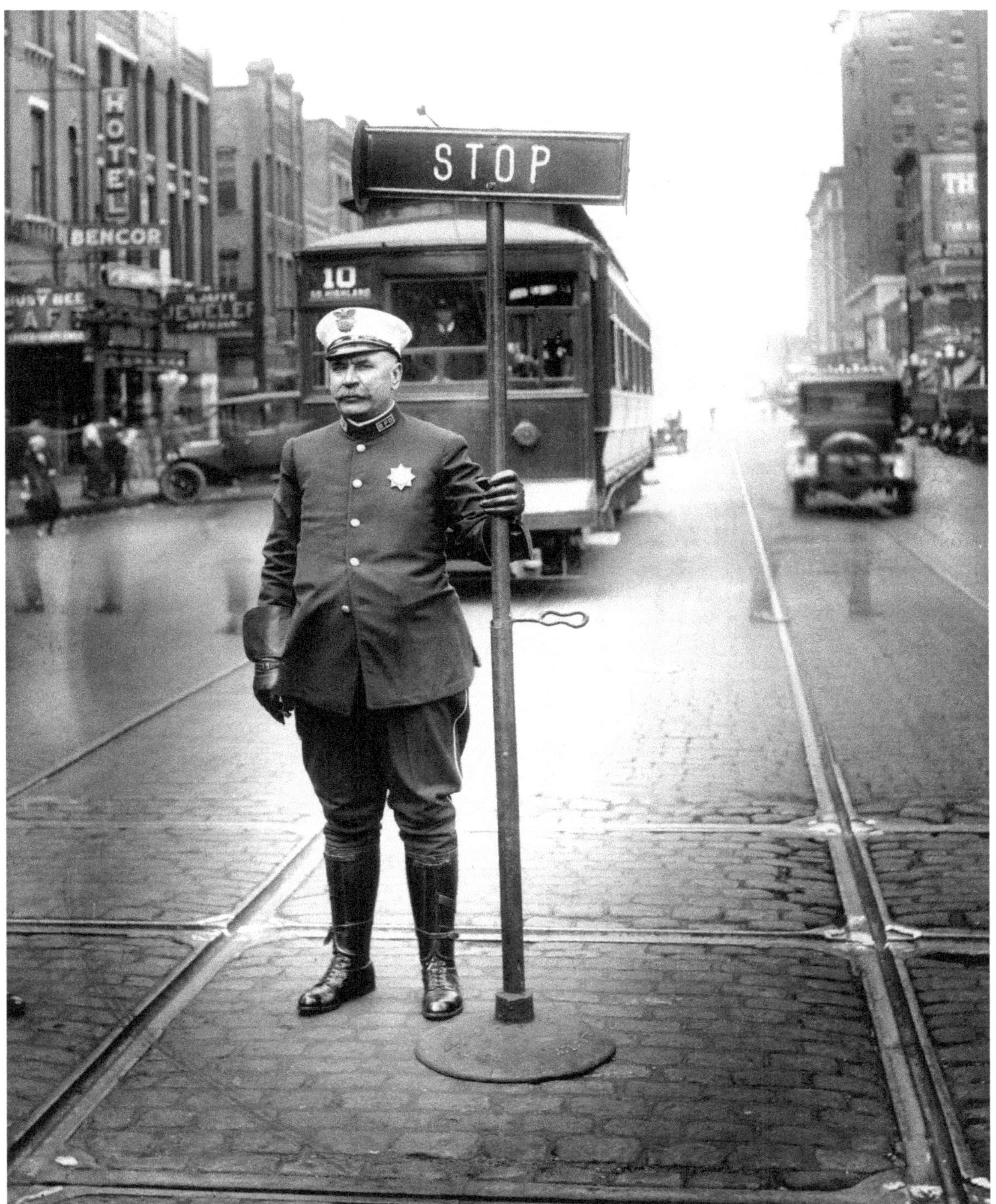

A traffic cop on Twentieth Street North. Before the installation of traffic lights in the early 1920s, police officers directed cars through downtown intersections.

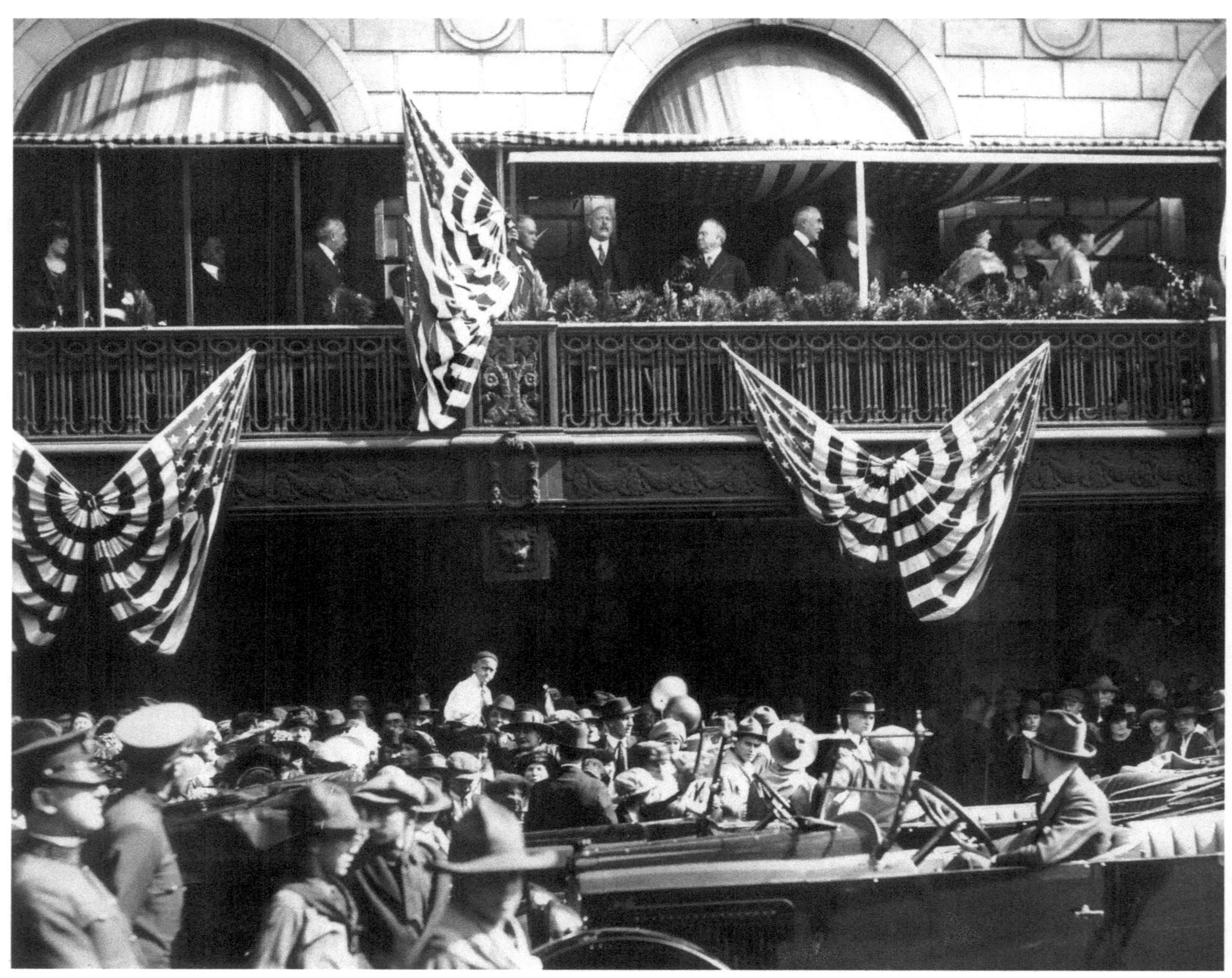

President Warren G. Harding on the balcony of the Tutwiler Hotel, October 1921. Harding visited Birmingham as part of the city's semi-centennial celebration.

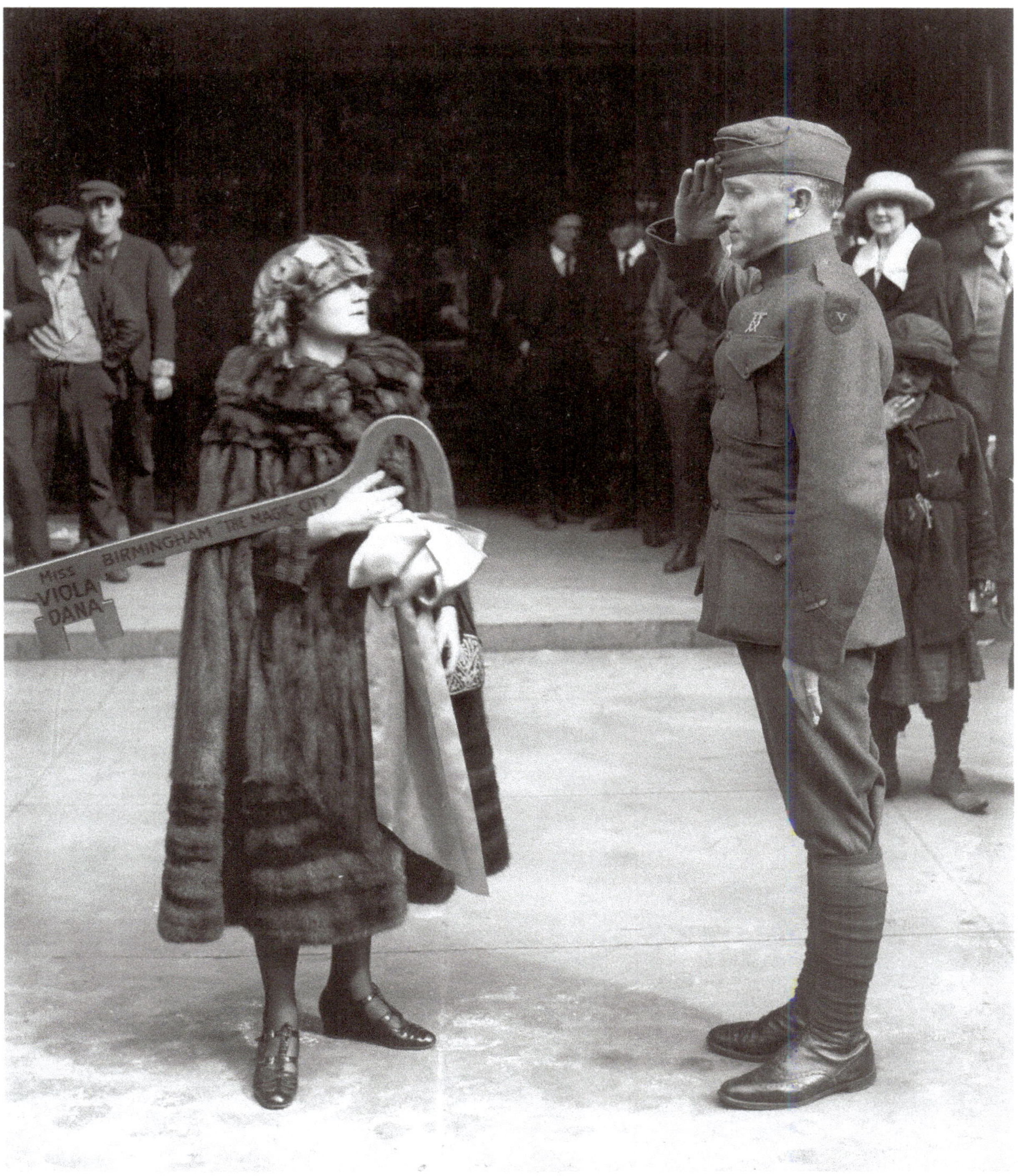

Silent-film star Viola Dana receives a key to the city during her visit to Birmingham in the early 1920s.

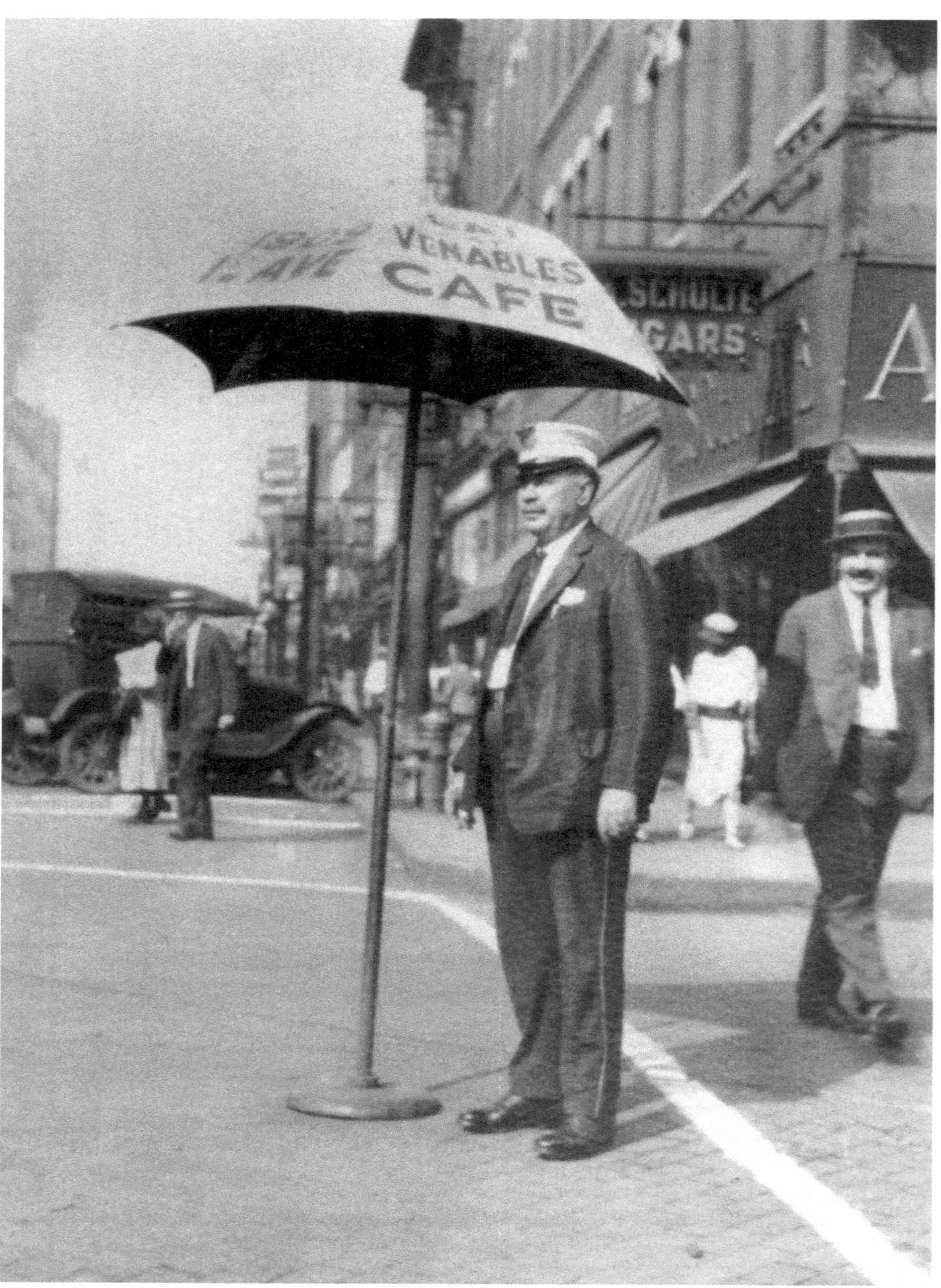

In exchange for advertising space, in 1923 Birmingham merchants provided umbrellas for downtown traffic cops.

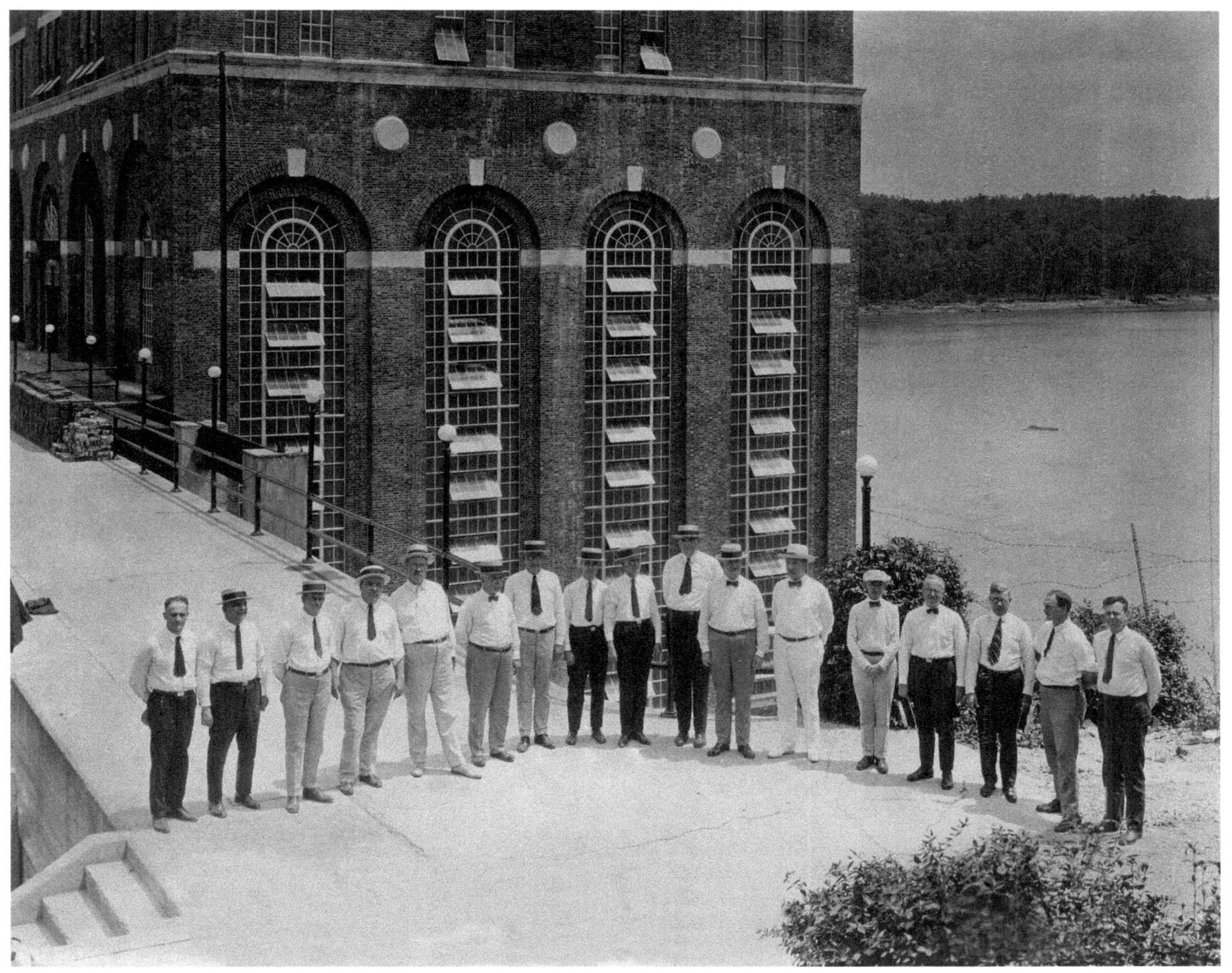

Alabama Power Company board of directors visit Lay Dam, August 18, 1923. Lock 12, later named Lay Dam in honor of Alabama Power founder W. P. Lay, was the first hydroelectric plant constructed by the company. It went into service April 12, 1914. From left to right are J. M. Barry, Thomas Bragg, W. J. Henderson, O. G. Thurlow, W. H. Weatherly, W. H. Hassinger, Frank M. Moody, J. A. Debus, E. C. Melvin, E. A. Yates, R. A. Mitchell, S. Z. Mitchell, Thomas W. Martin, H. G. Abell, Richard M. Hobbie, W. E. Mitchell, and F. P. Cummings.

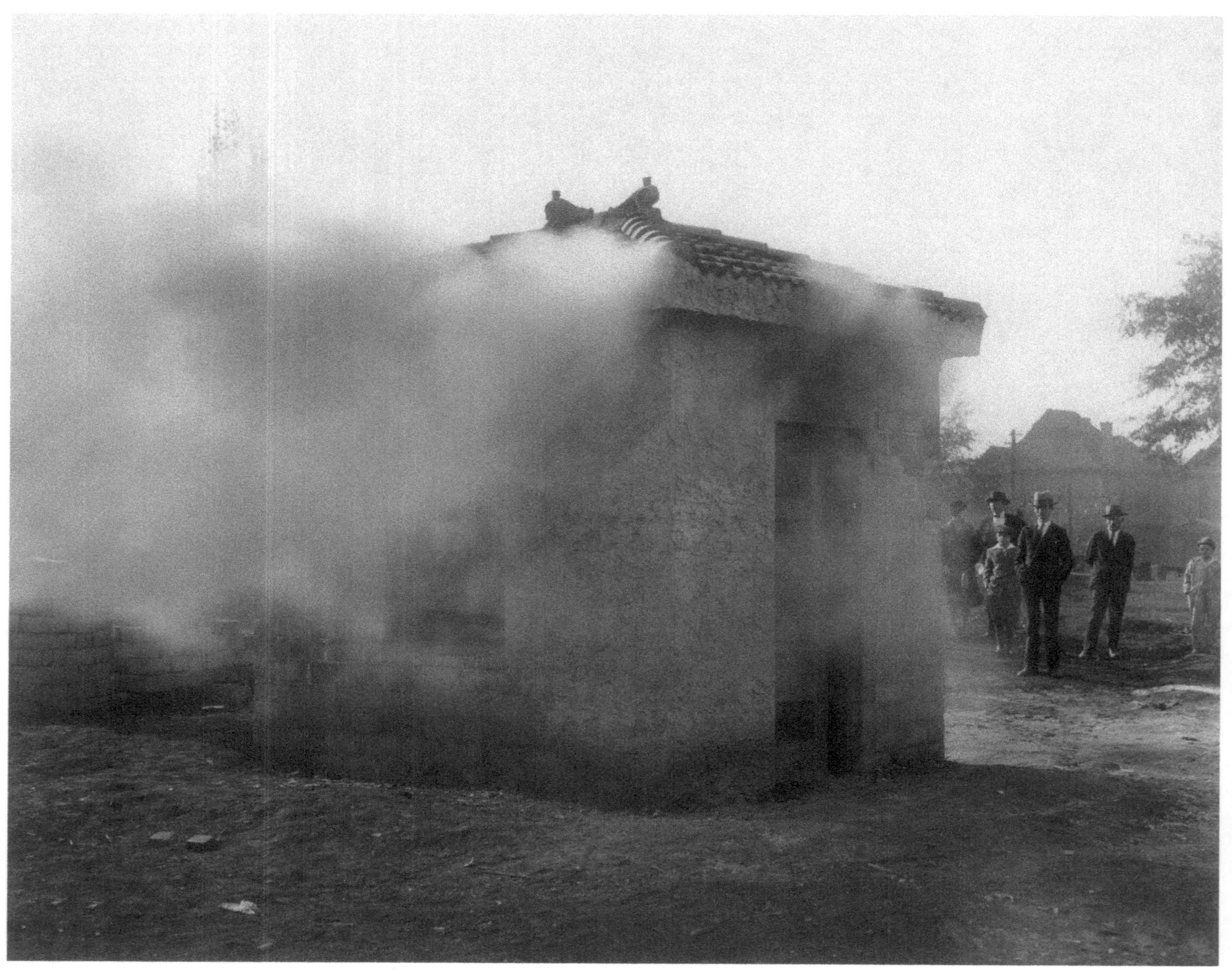

A small, house-like structure built of concrete block, portions of which were covered with stucco, is being used as a demonstration project. The roof tiles may also have been concrete. The interior contents of the building were set on fire to prove that a concrete structure could survive a fire intact.

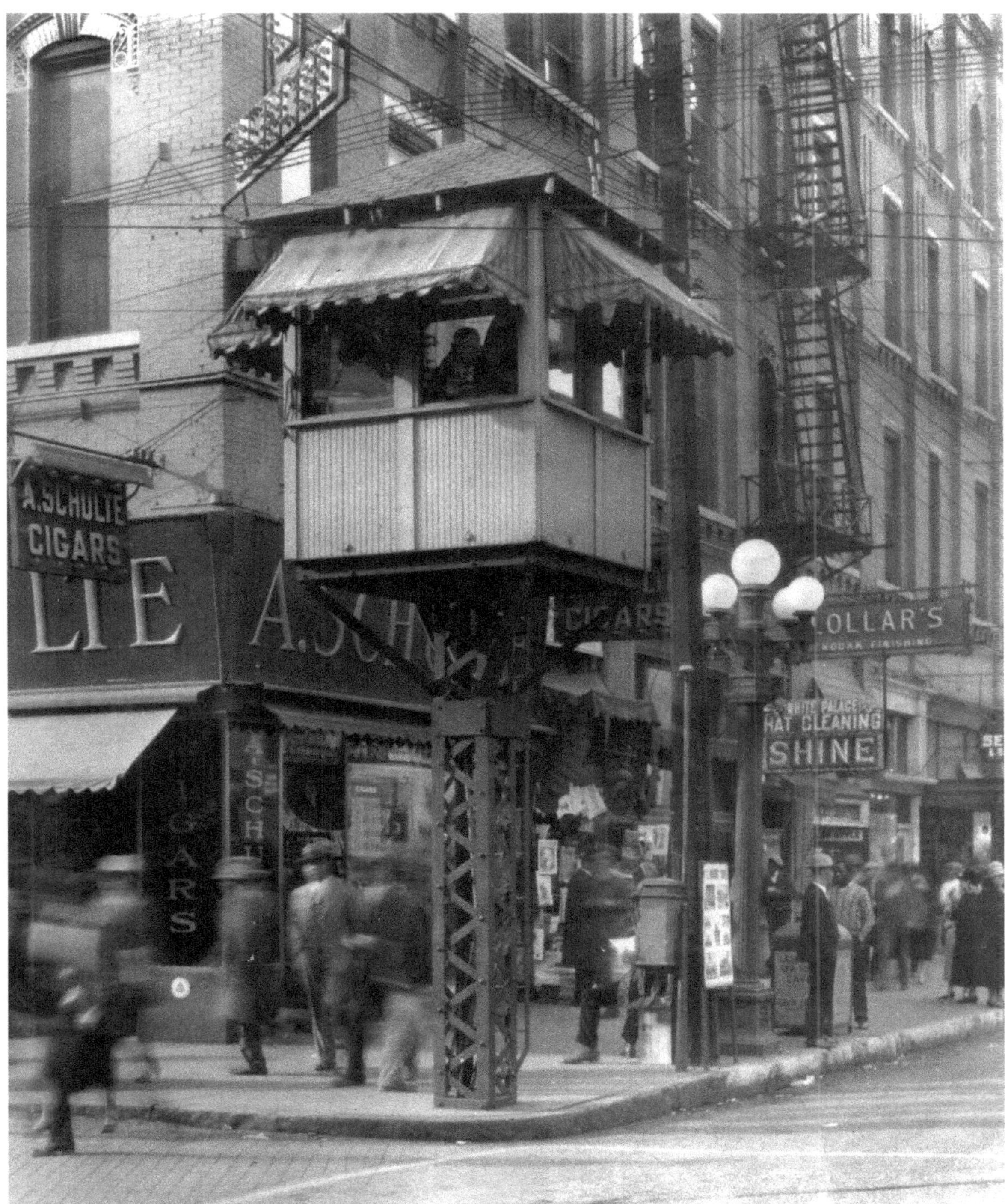

Birmingham entered the era of modern traffic control with the 1924 installation of this tower at the corner of Third Avenue North and Twentieth Street. As the *Birmingham News* reported, a worker in the tower manually controlled new "amber, green, and red" traffic lights mounted at downtown intersections.

Celebrating Casey Jones outside the Lyric Theatre, 1928.

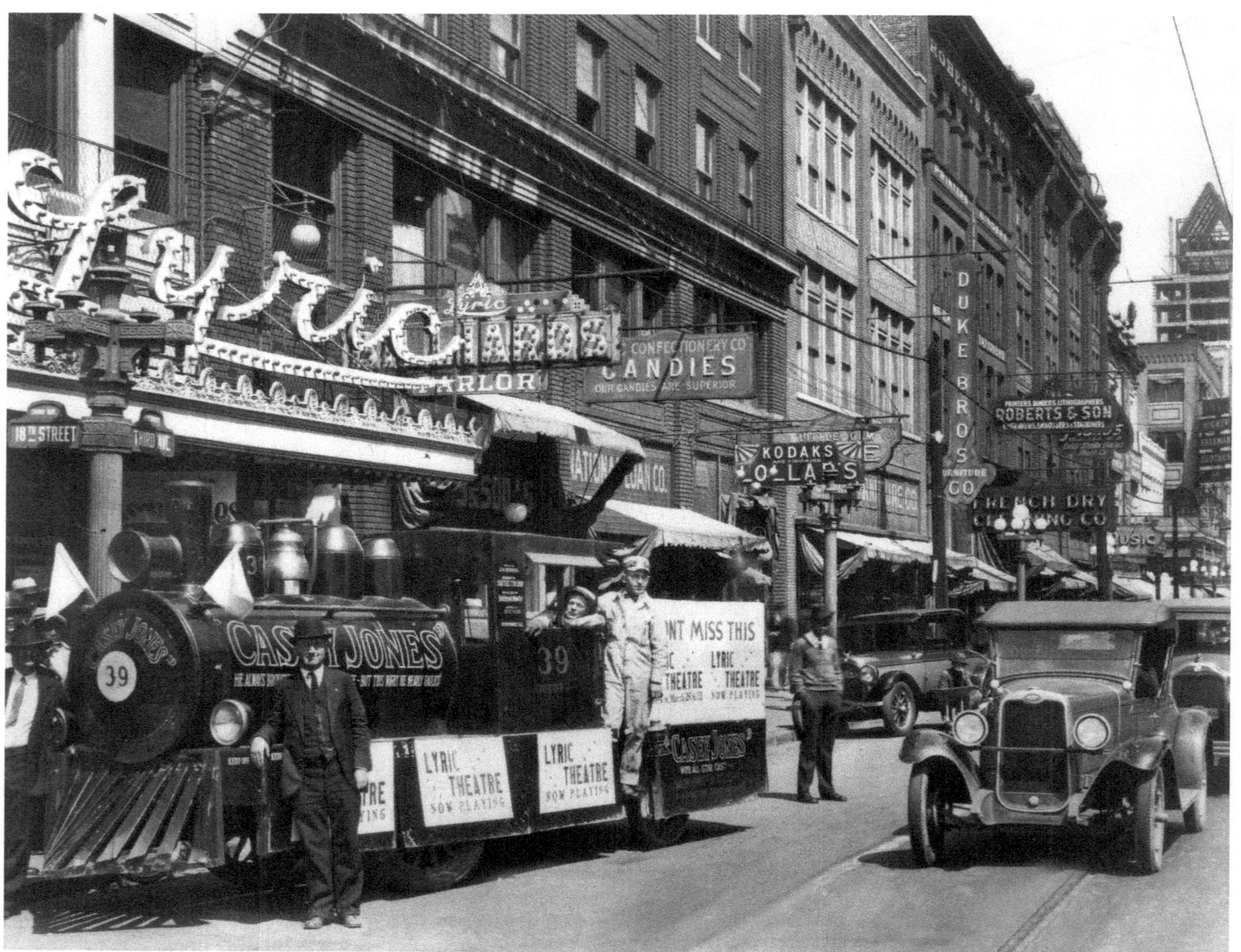

The elegant Morris Hotel on the corner of First Avenue North and Nineteenth Street. Seen here in the 1920s, the Morris was constructed in 1888 as an office building, but then converted to a hotel.

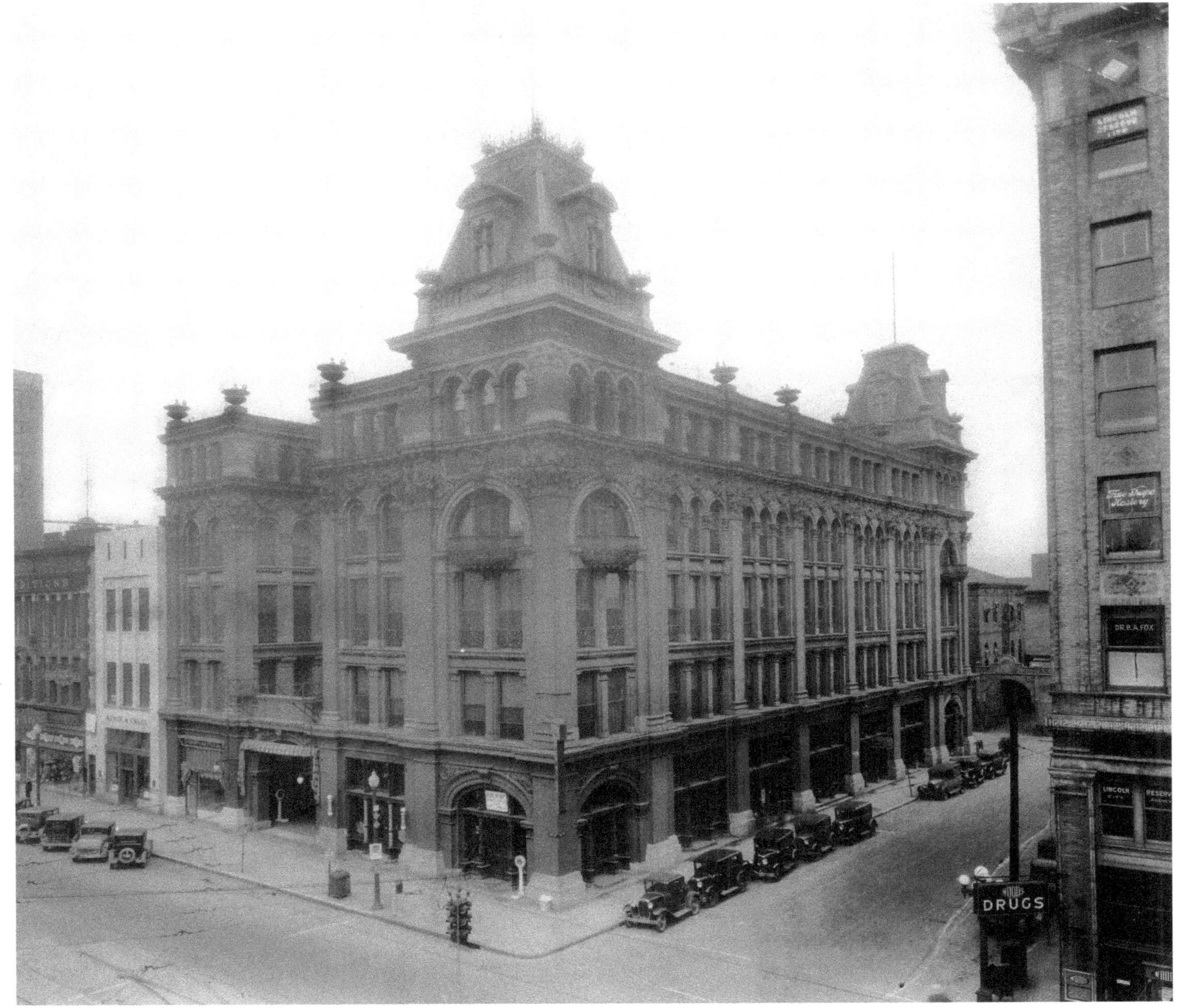

The Spirit of St. Louis over Birmingham. In October 1927, five months after becoming the first person to fly solo across the Atlantic Ocean, Charles Lindbergh visited Birmingham as part of a nationwide tour.

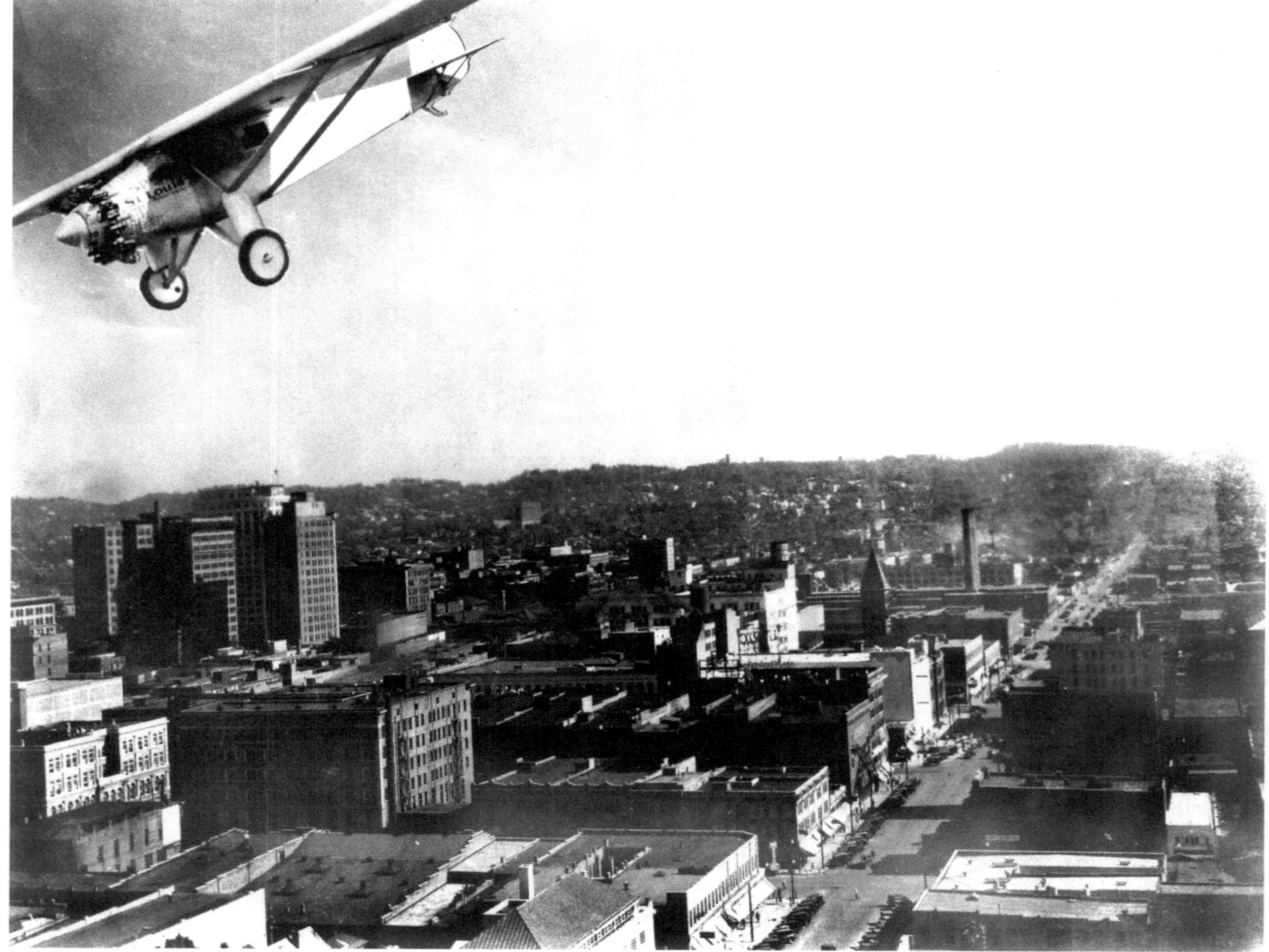

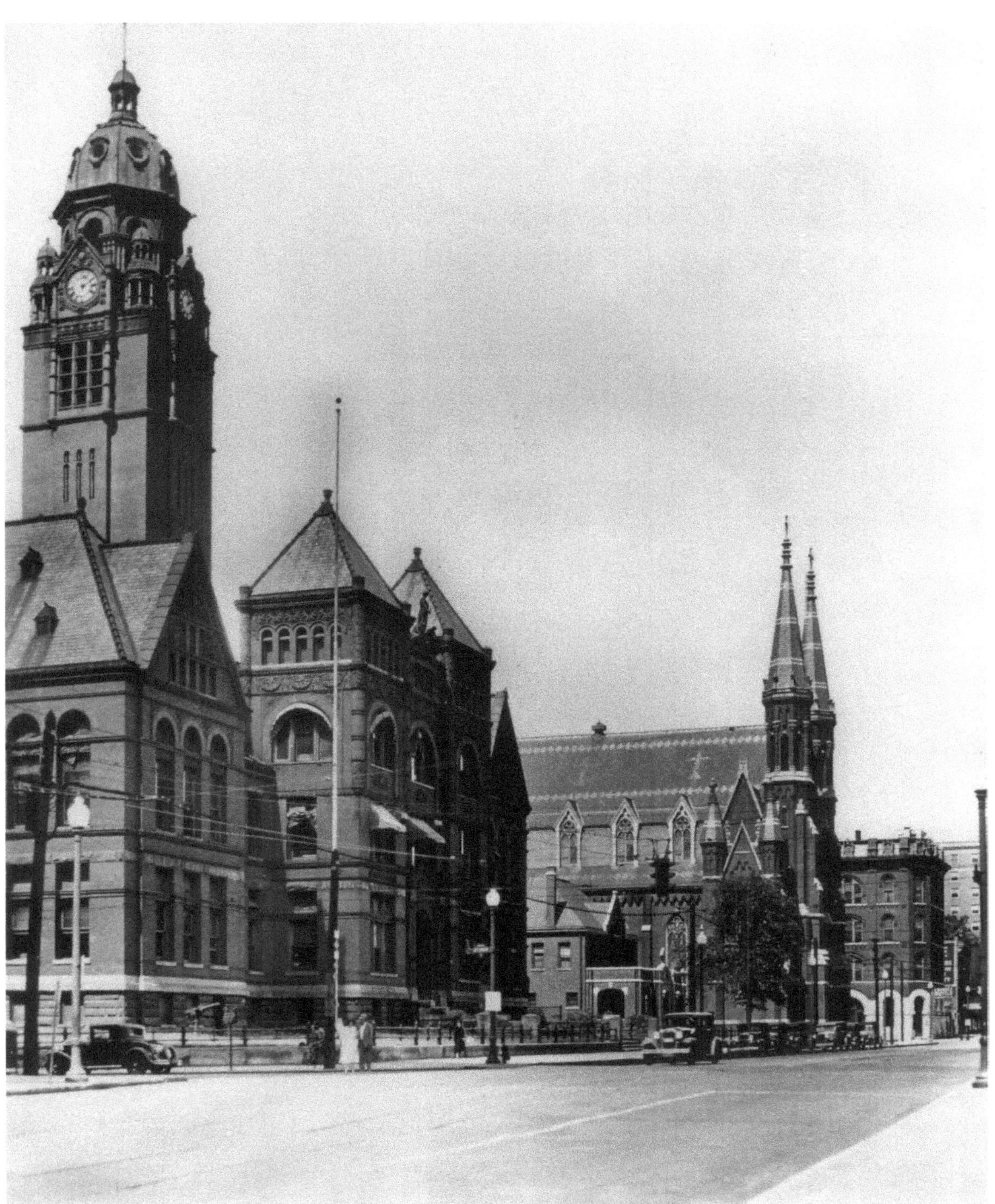

The Jefferson County Courthouse on Third Avenue North, with St. Paul's Catholic Church just beyond, in the 1920s.

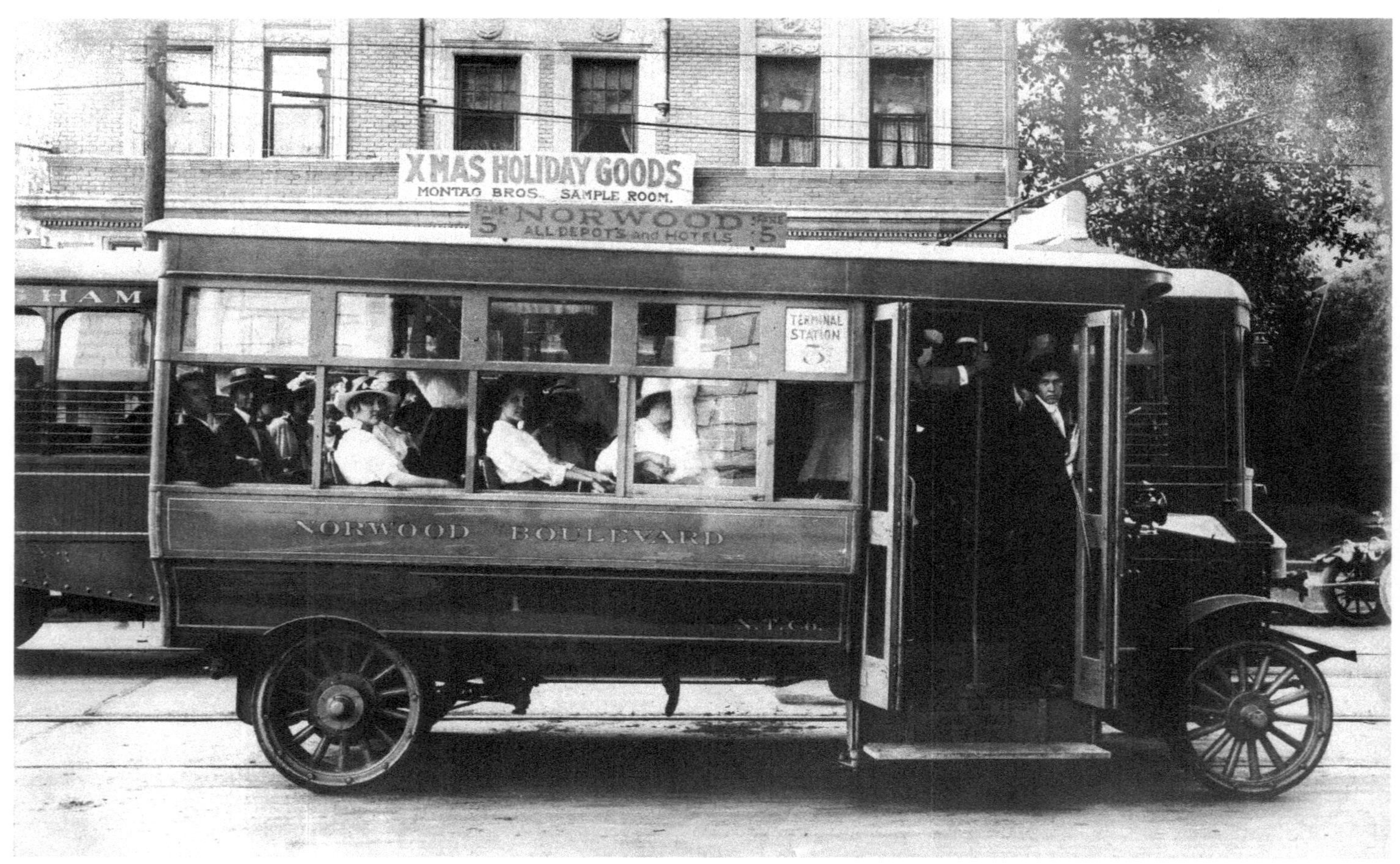

One of Birmingham's "notorious jitneys." In 1923, Birmingham citizens voted overwhelmingly to outlaw these private taxis, which competed with the city's streetcars and whose drivers had been deemed dangerous and irresponsible by the City Commission.

The H. J. Heinz Company on Morris Avenue, 1920s.

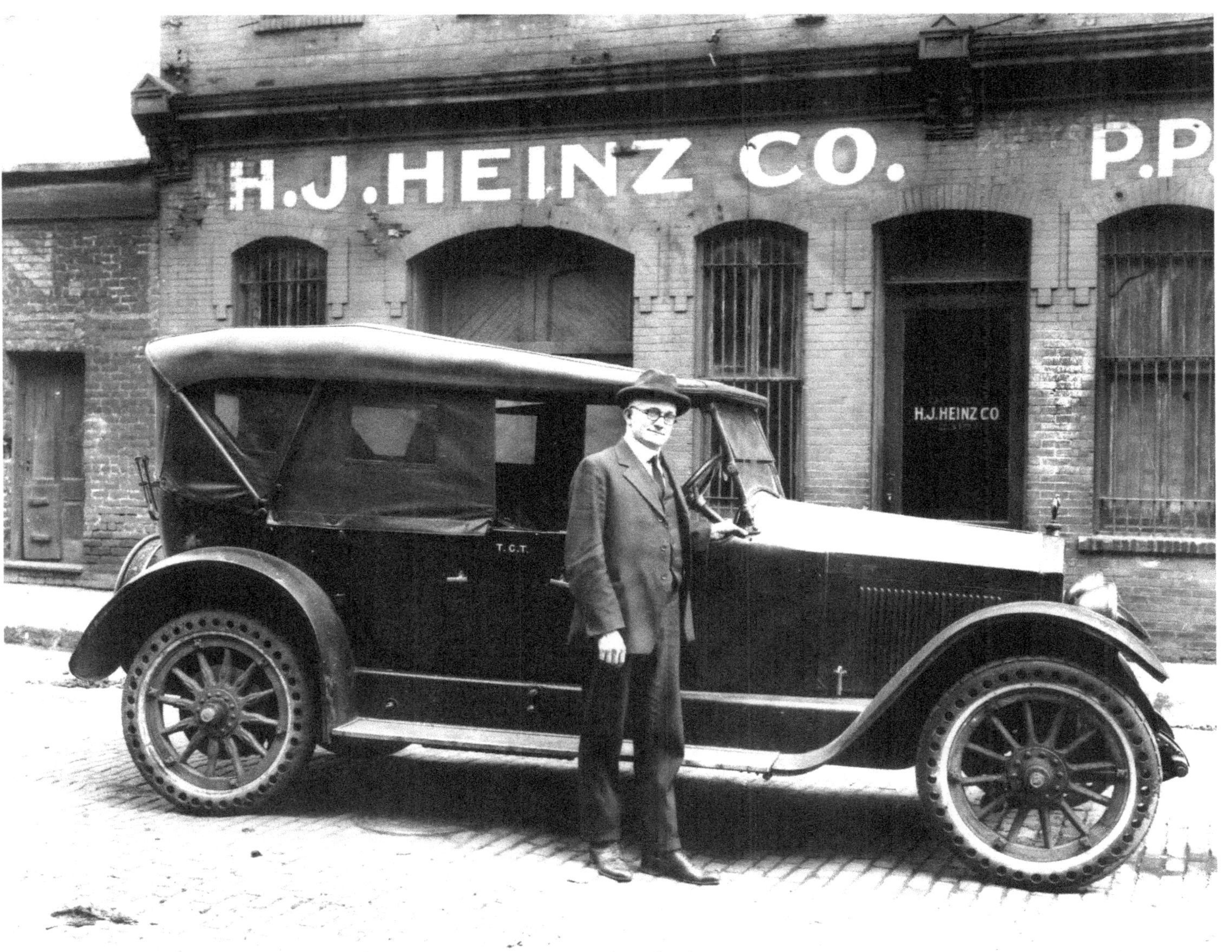

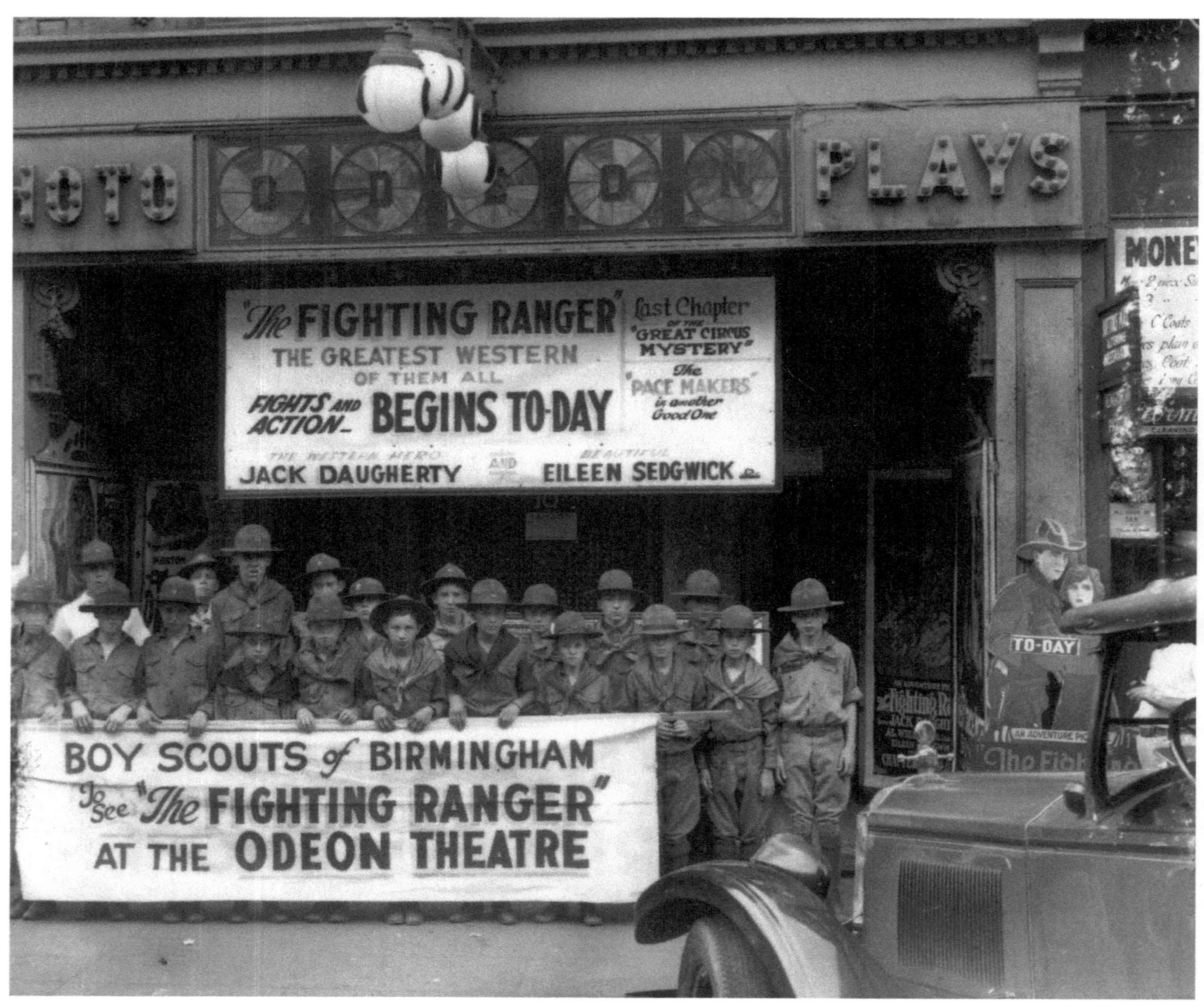

Boy Scouts about to take in the 1925 movie *The Fighting Ranger* at the Odeon Theatre on Second Avenue North.

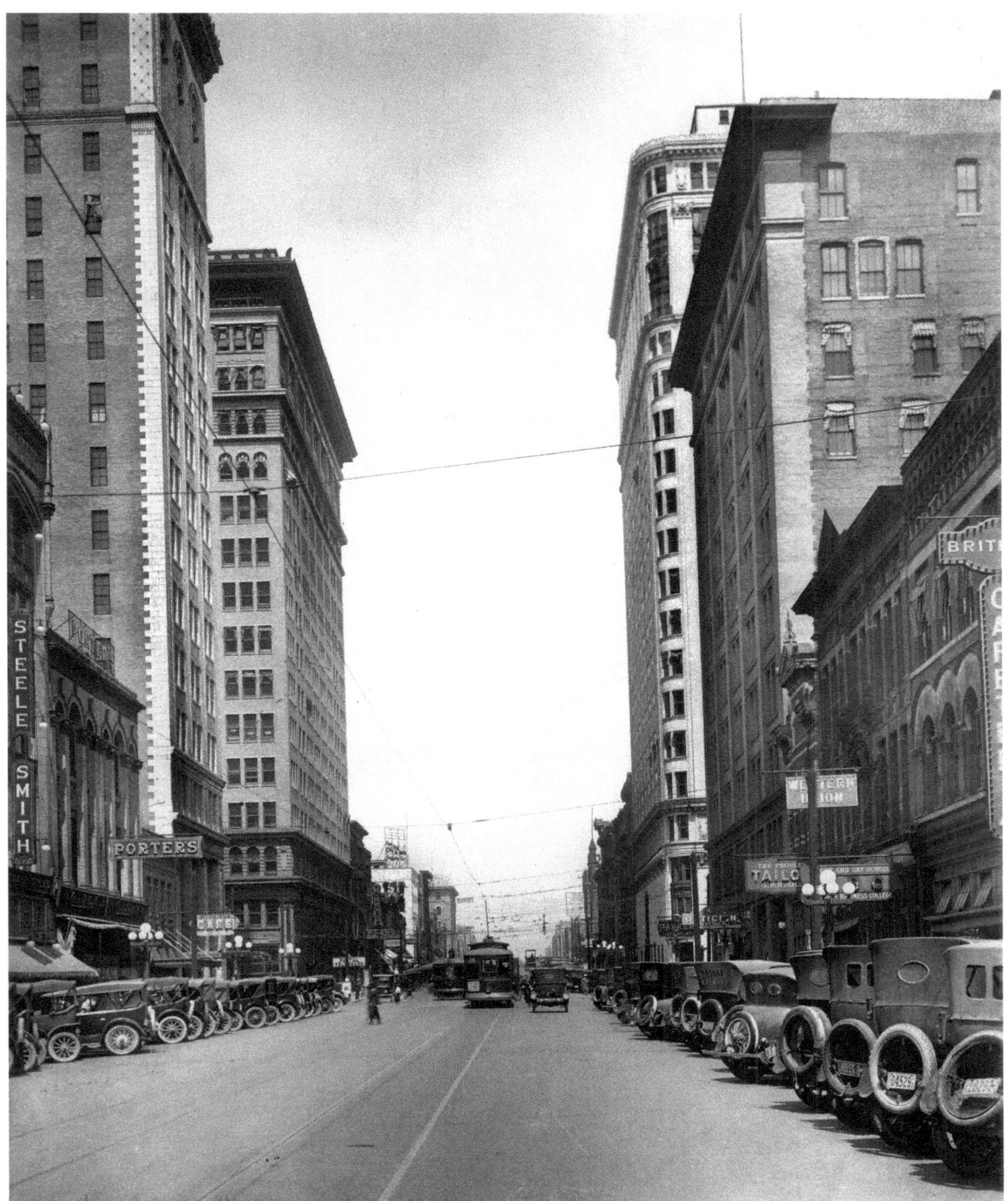

First Avenue North lined with cars.

Located in what was then the northwest edge of the Birmingham business district, the Alabama Power General Office building was constructed in just over one year. This view from the southeast shows the progress of brickwork on May 1, 1925.

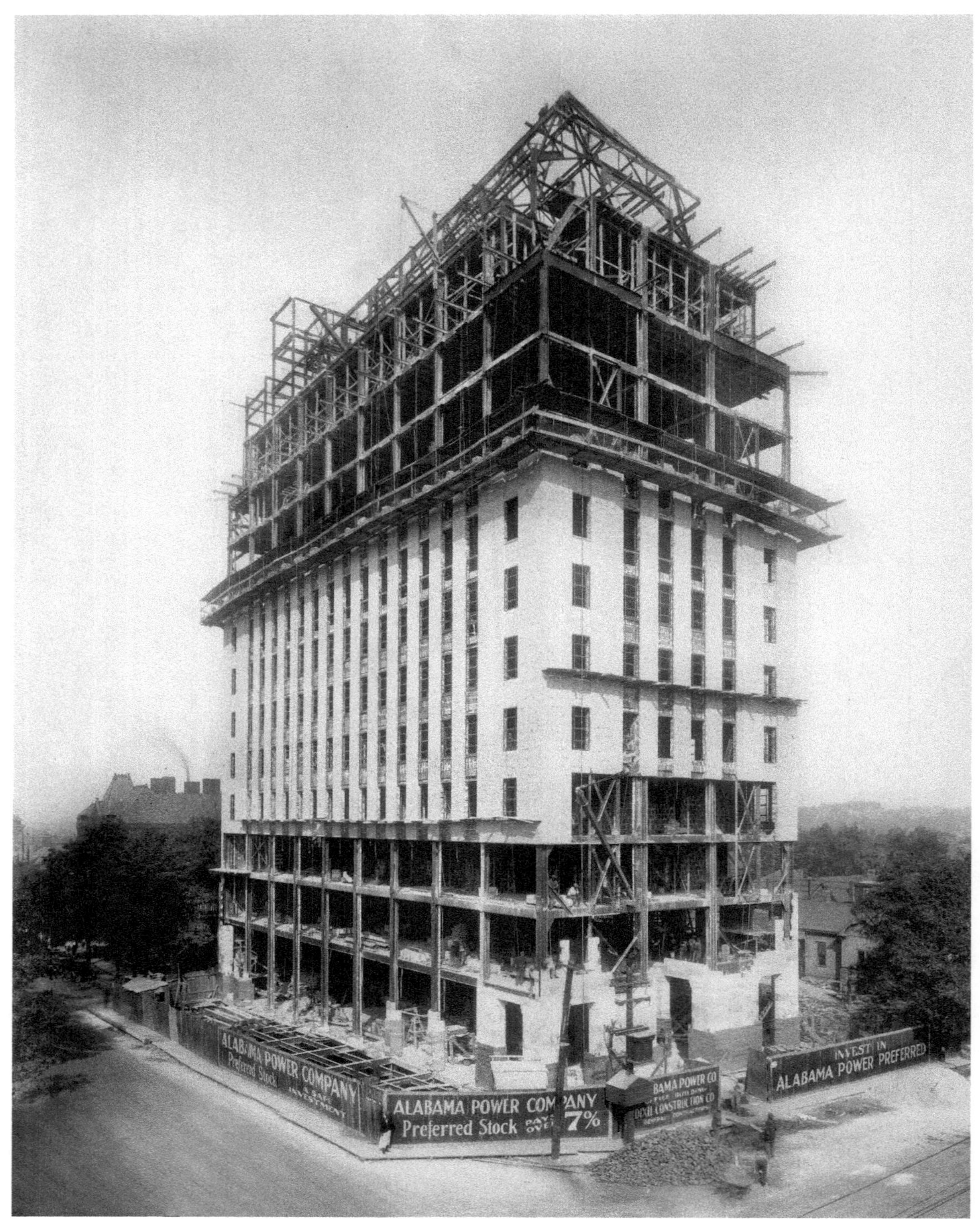

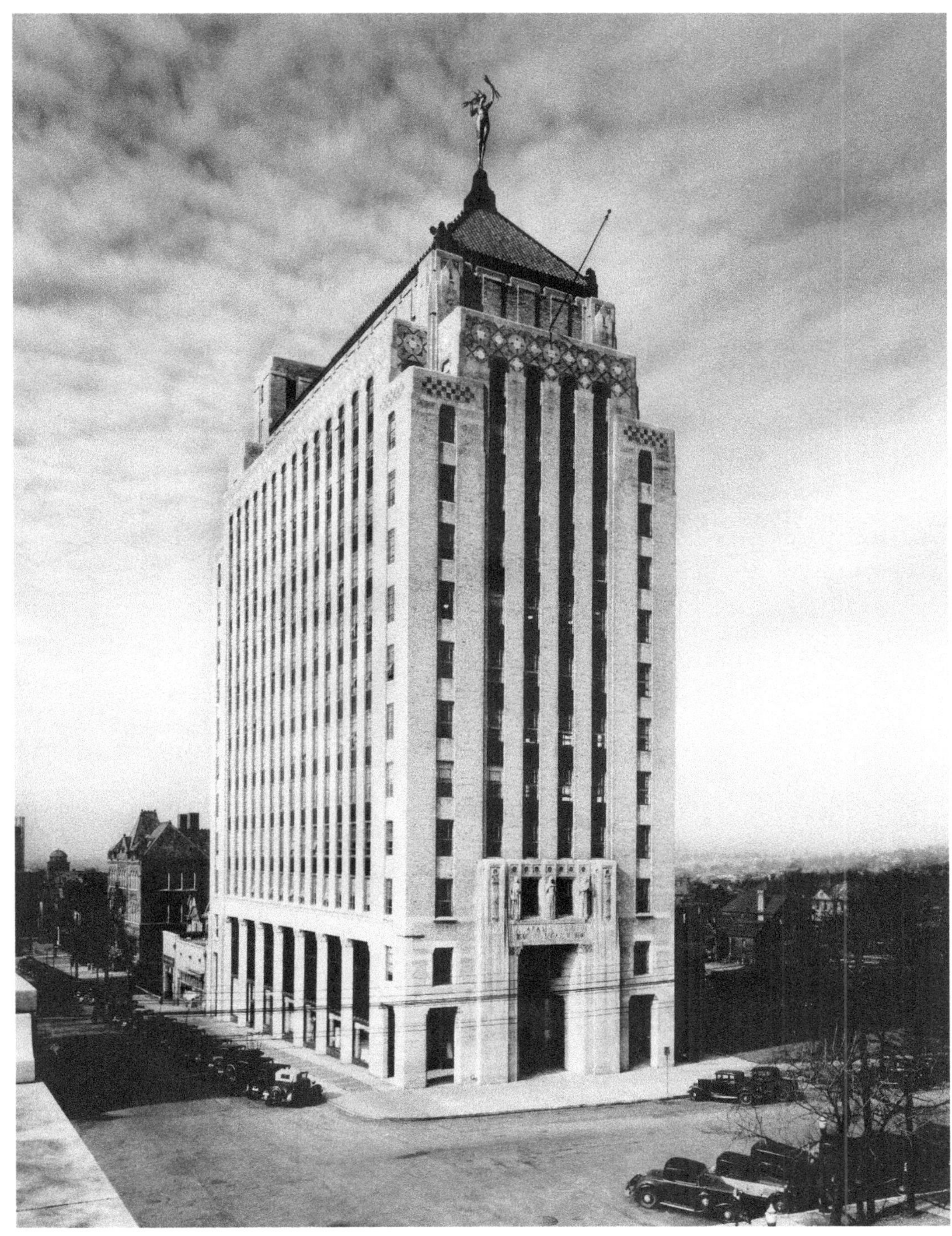

In 1924 the Alabama Power Company board of directors decided to consolidate company operations and strengthen its corporate identity by building a new corporate headquarters. Completed in 1925, the building was the first example of art deco design in Birmingham. Standing above the entrance are three eight-foot-tall figures—Power, Heat, and Light. Surmounting the peak of the building's sloped roof stands the statue *Electra,* who holds lightning bolts in both her hands with lightning bolts projecting from her hair. In describing the statue, sculptor Edward Field Sanford said it was his intent to create a symbol of "the State of Alabama rising triumphantly in her electrical progress." In 1926, the *London Daily Express* selected the Alabama Power building as the most beautiful utility building in the United States.

View of the General Office building from the northwest, November 15, 1925. The General Office building was constructed in an area that was still largely residential.

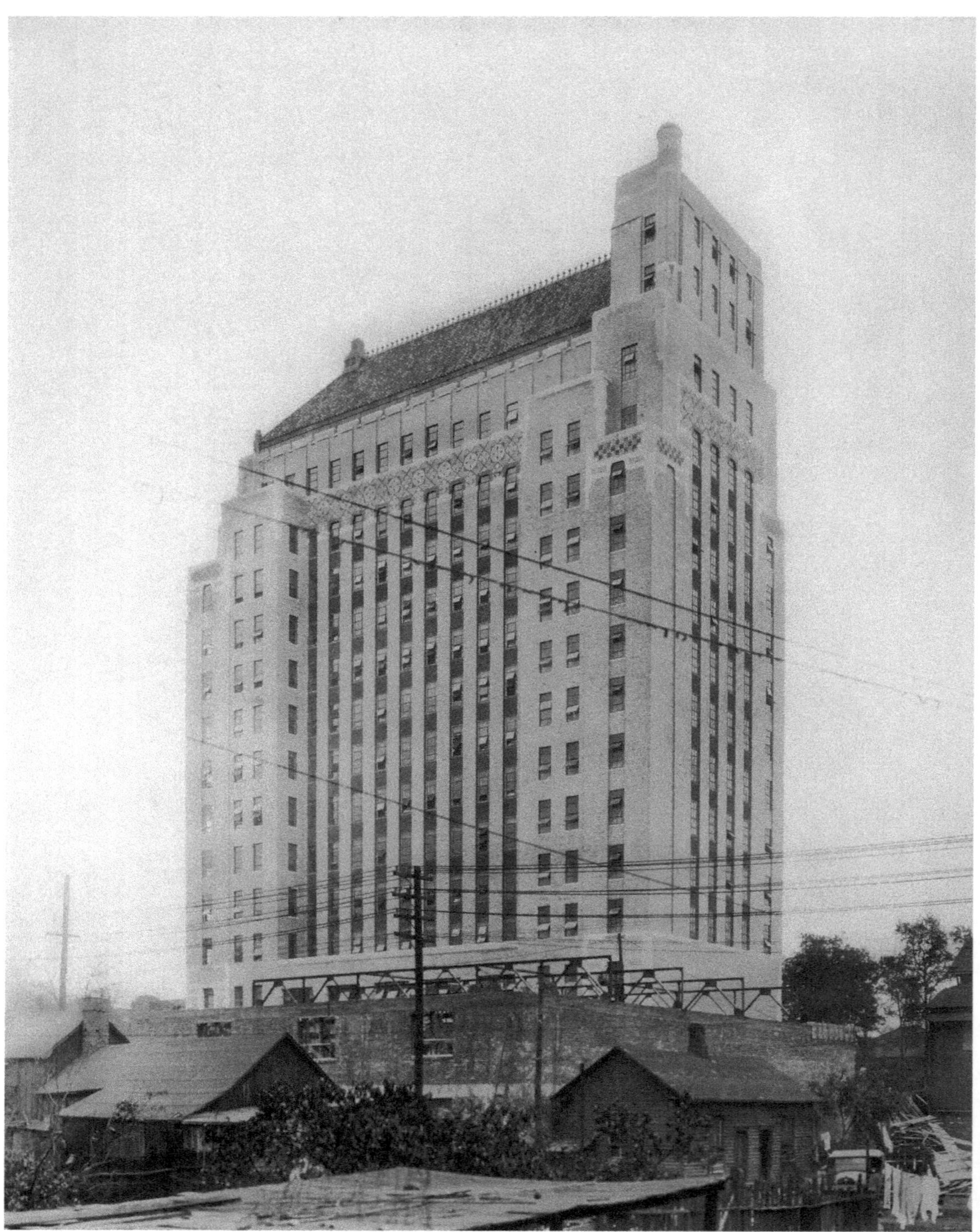

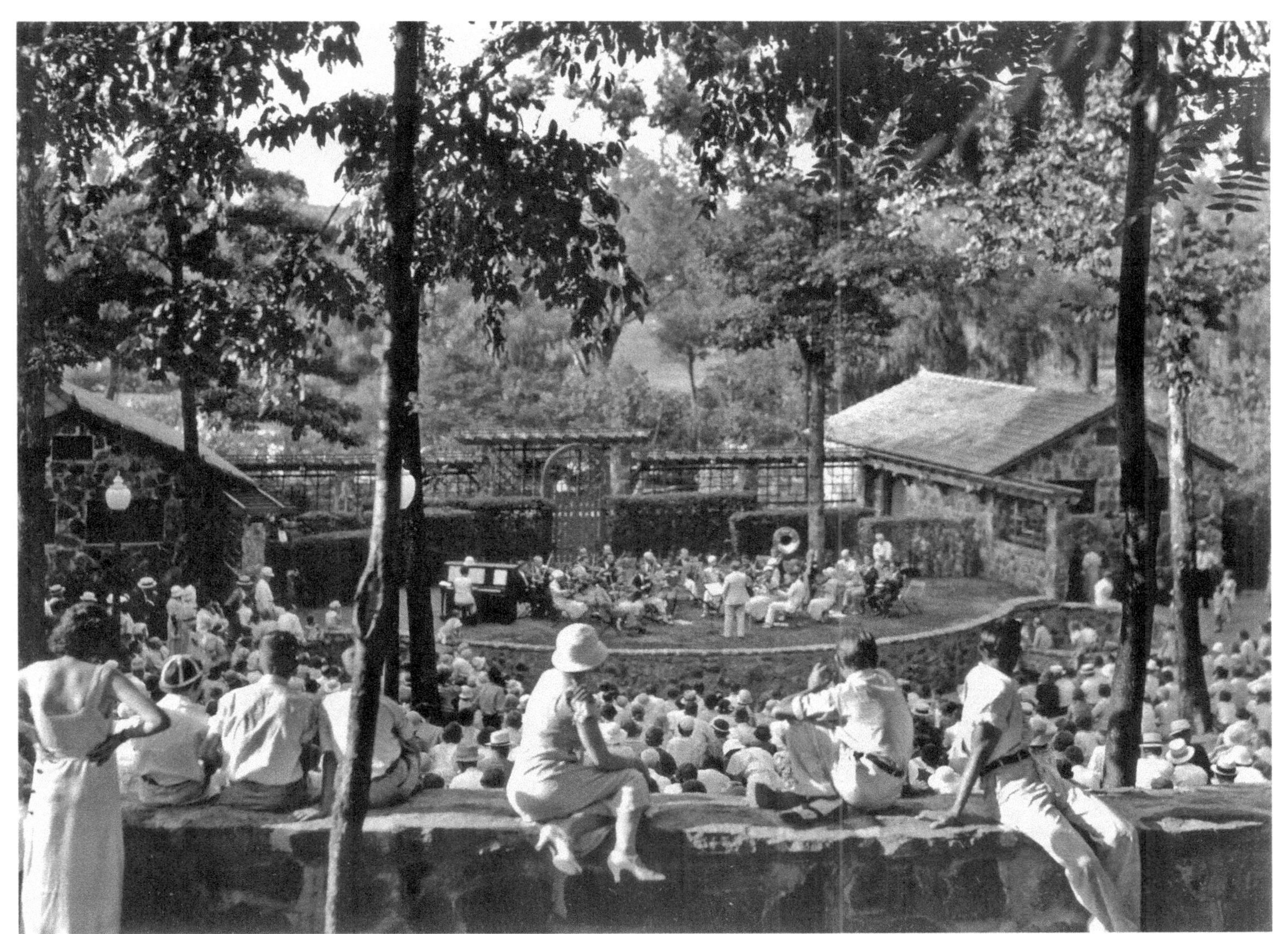

Enjoying a concert in Avondale Park.

Six decades after Appomattox, a few aging Confederate veterans meet in Birmingham for the last time.

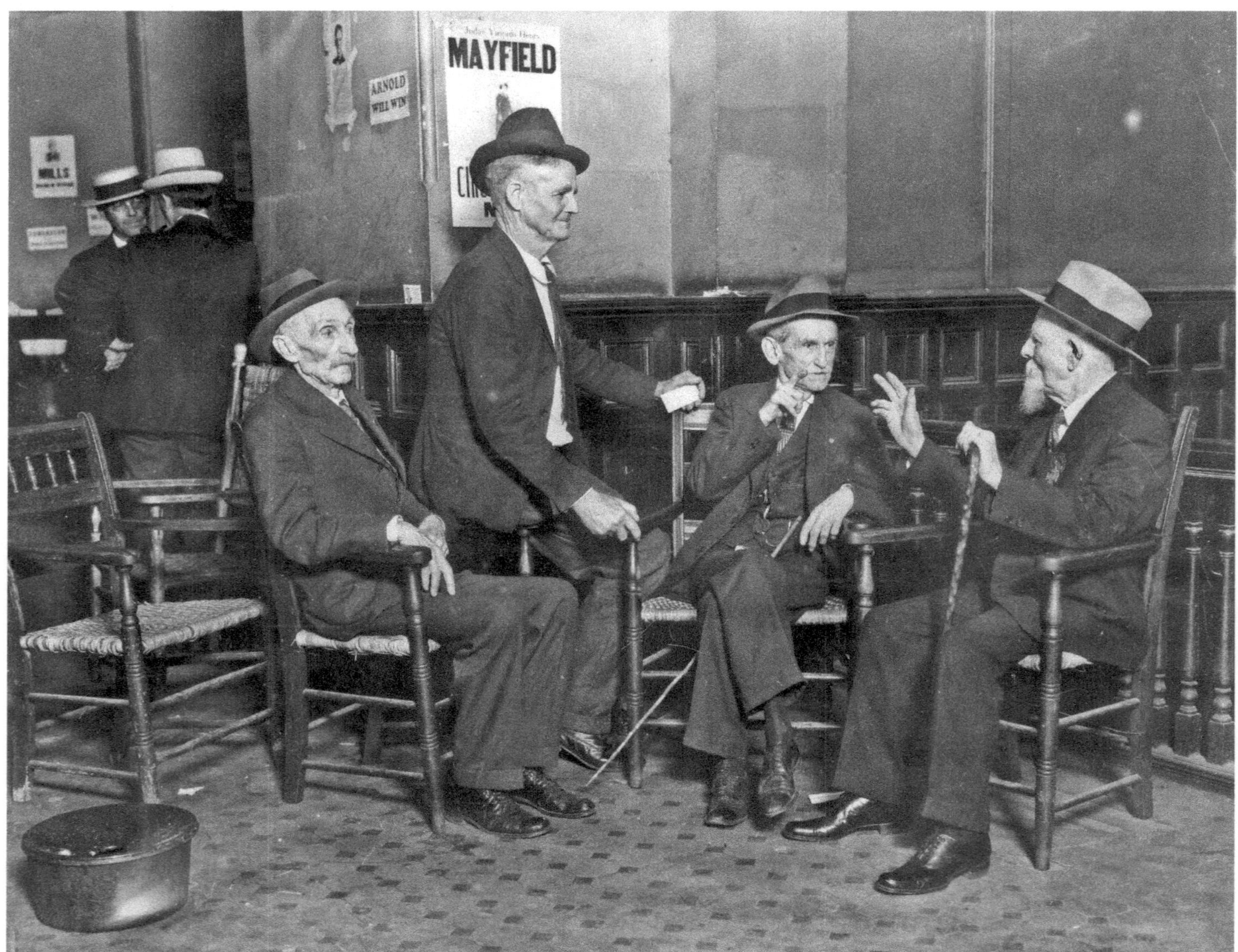

Once a post office, this building on the corner of Fifth Avenue North and Nineteenth Street is now part of the federal courthouse. Today's First United Methodist Church is visible on the right. One Federal Place is now located directly across Fifth.

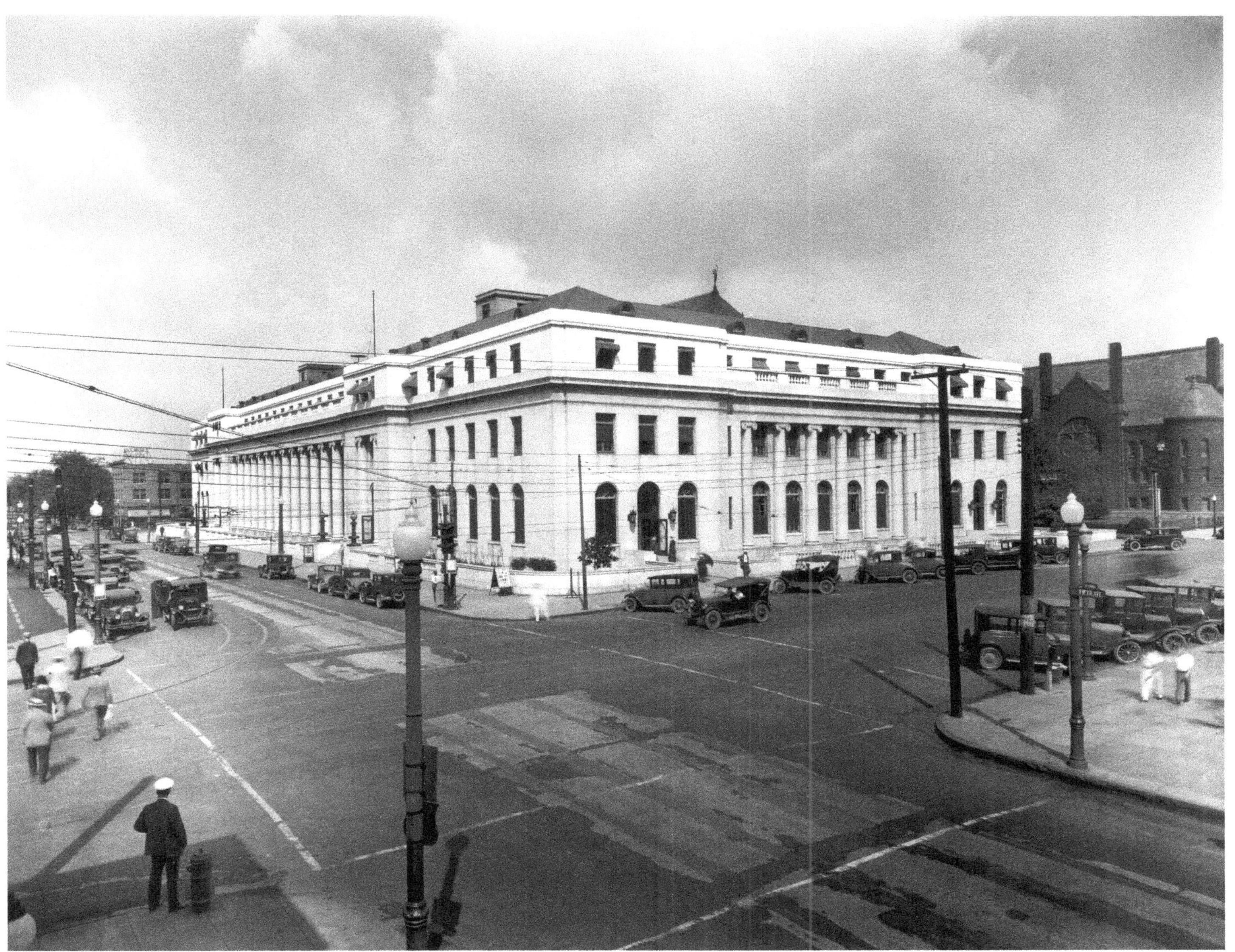

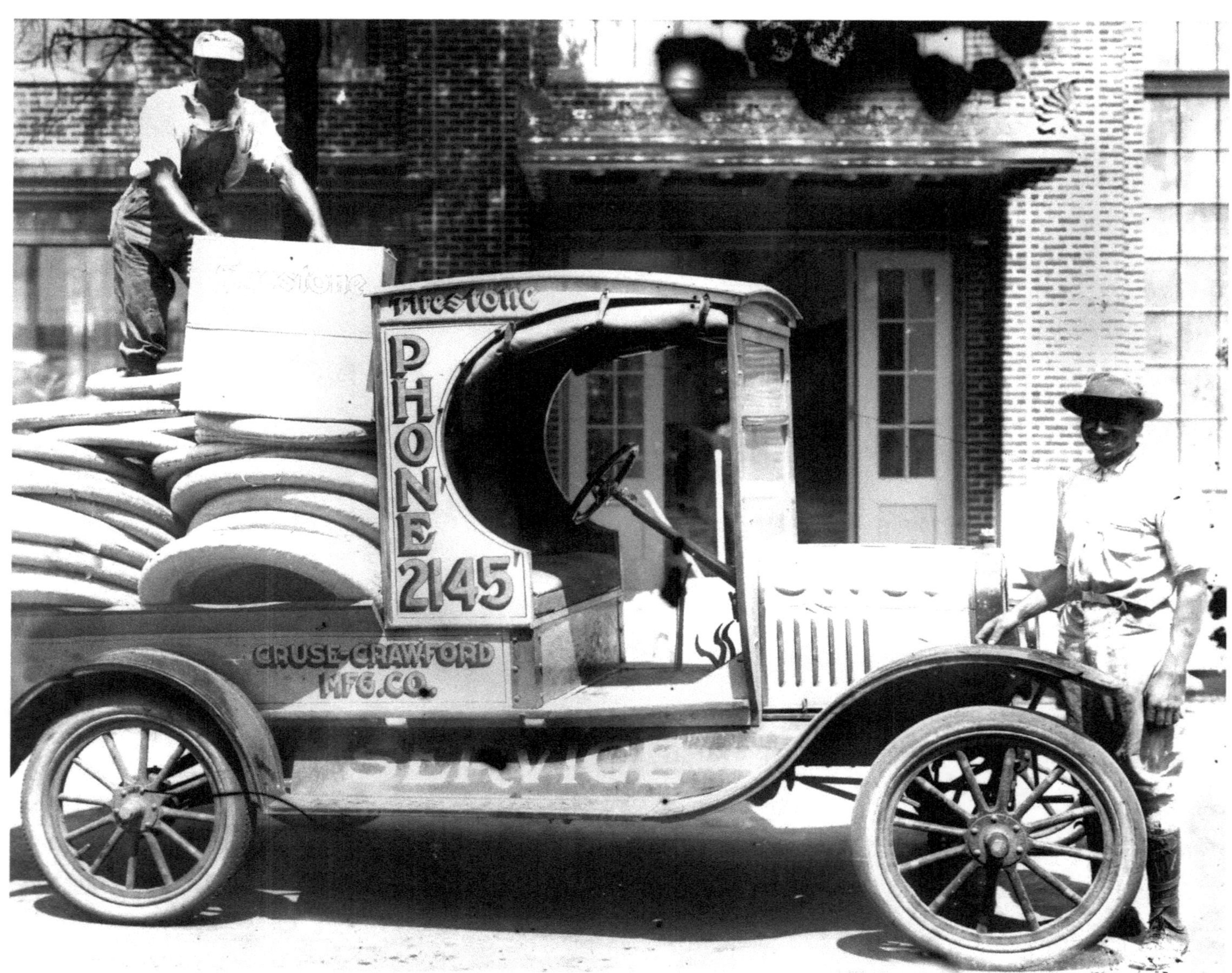

Firestone tires are loaded and ready for delivery.

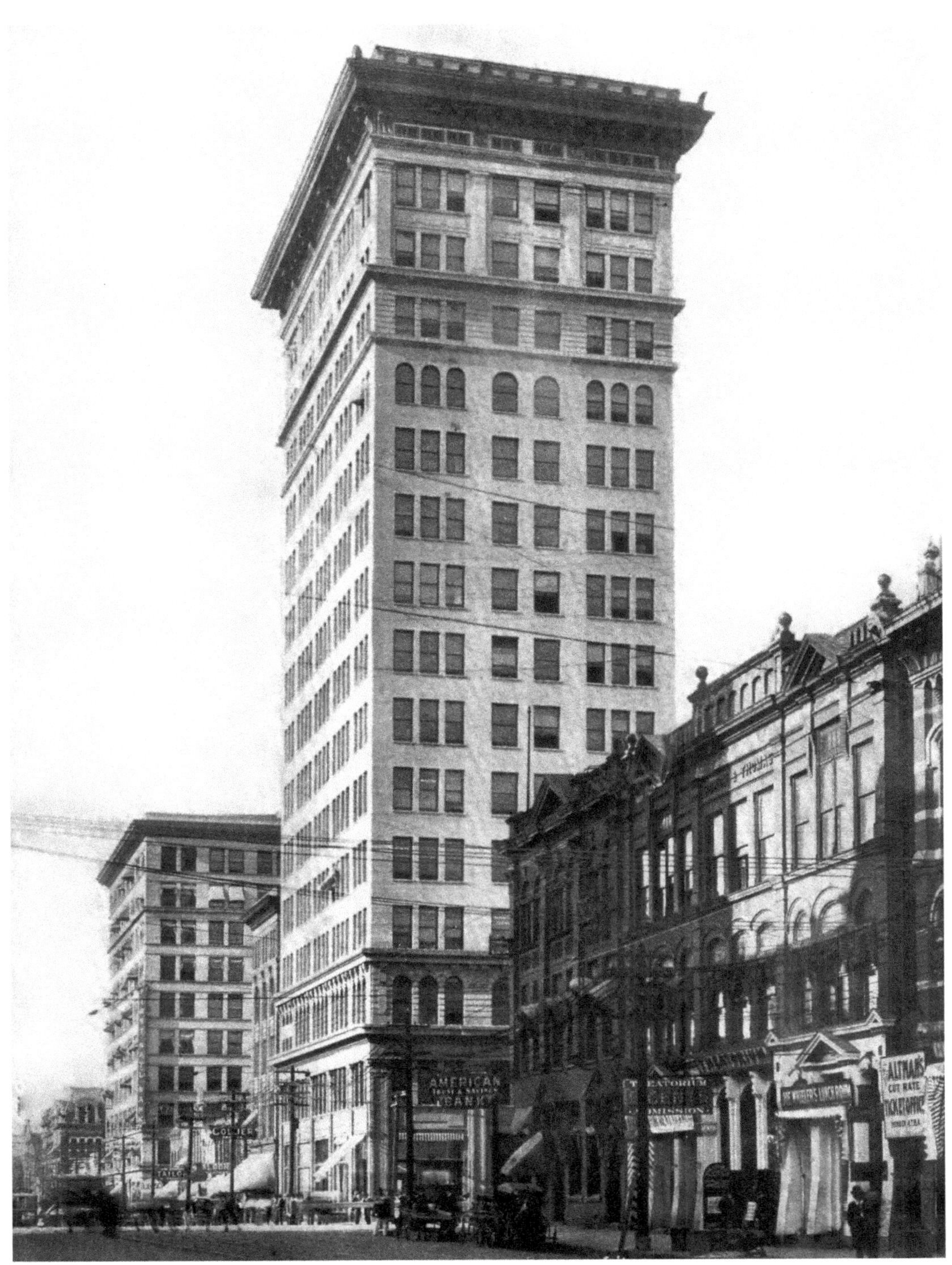

The Brown-Marx Building, at the corner of First Avenue North and Twentieth Street. The skyscraper towers over the older three-story Victorian buildings in the foreground.

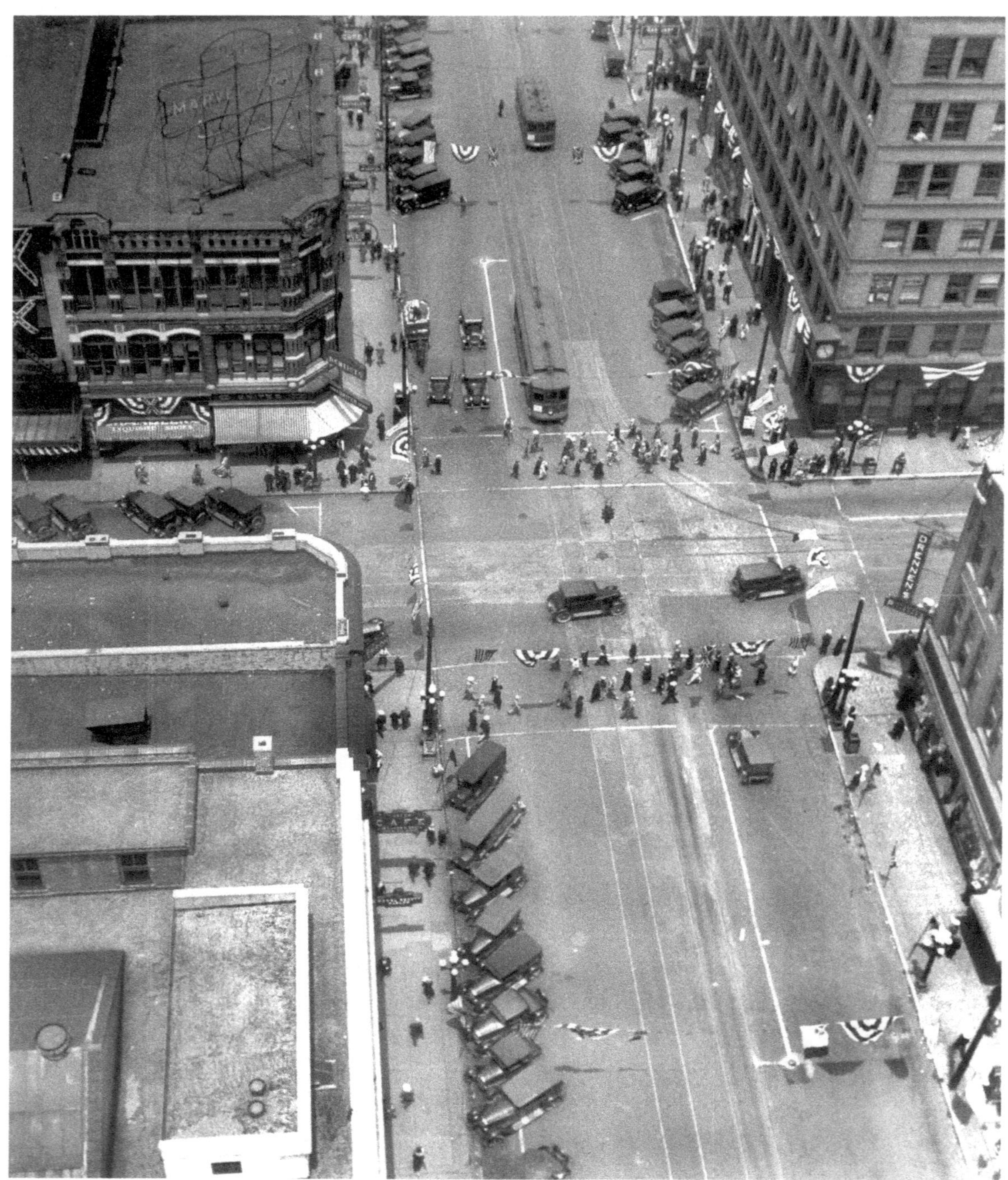

Looking down on the intersection of Twentieth Street and Second Avenue North, 1926.

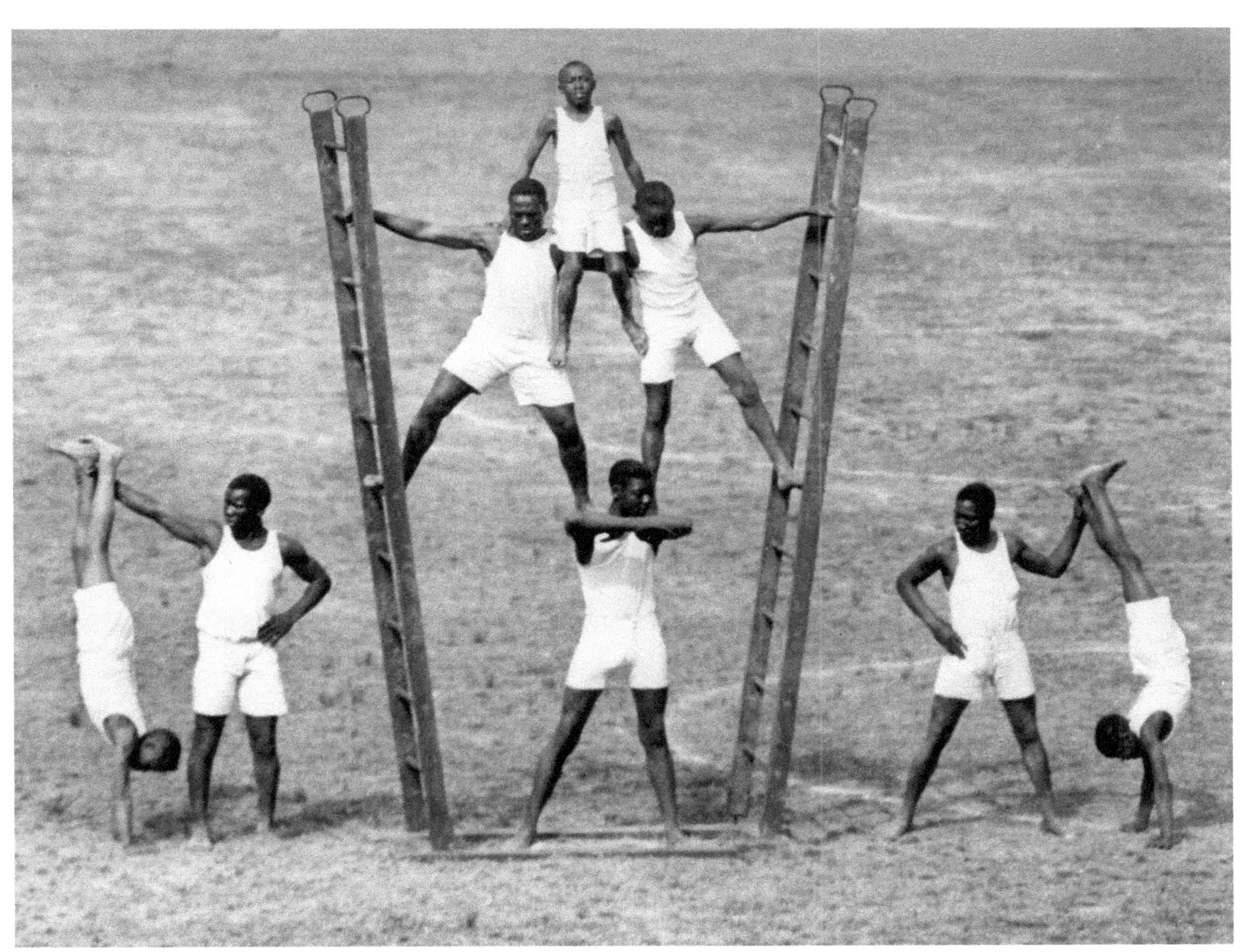

Children of employees show off their athletic skills at the 1928 Tennessee Coal, Iron and Railroad Company's Spring Festival.

In 1929, the Birmingham Barons, champions of the Southern Association, played the Texas League champions Dallas Steers for the Dixie Series championship. The Barons took the series, 4 games to 2.

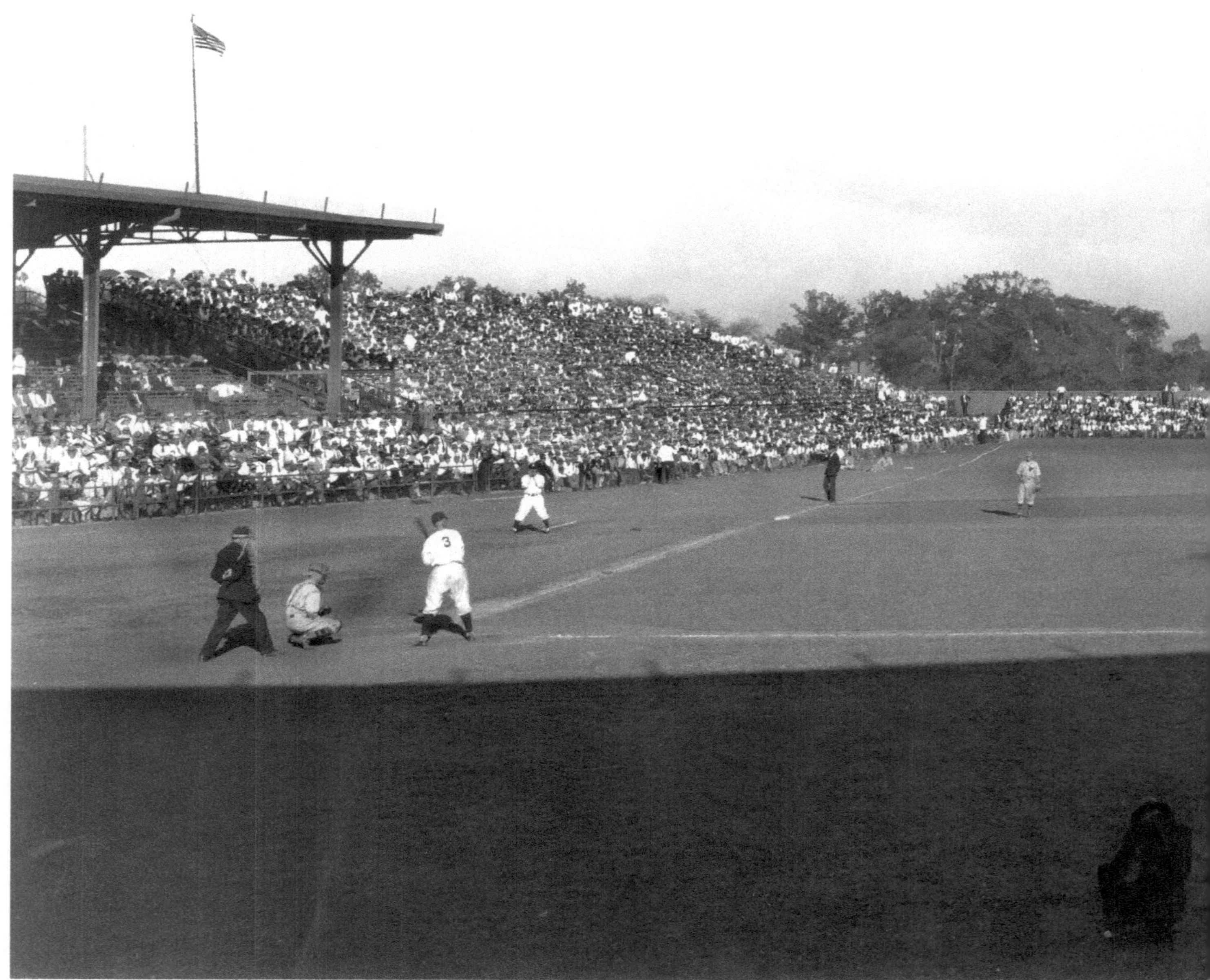

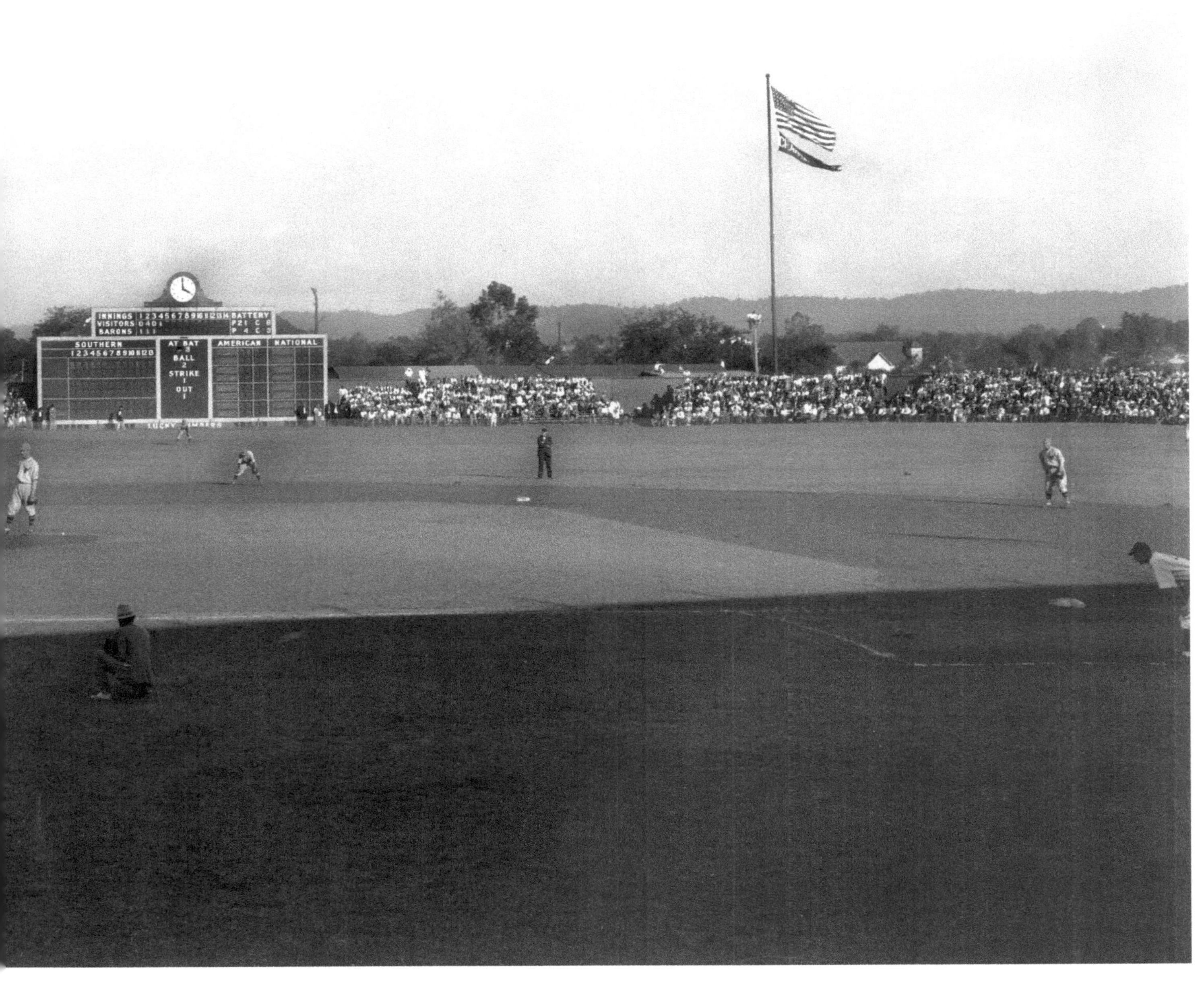
INNINGS
BATTERY
VISITORS
BARONS
SOUTHERN
AT BAT
BALL
2
STRIKE
1
OUT
1
AMERICAN
NATIONAL

Aeriel view of the Birmingham business district facing north from First Avenue South down Twentieth Street showing the L&N Depot and the Twentieth Street underpass, April 23, 1933. The Alabama Power Company building can be seen in the upper left-hand corner.

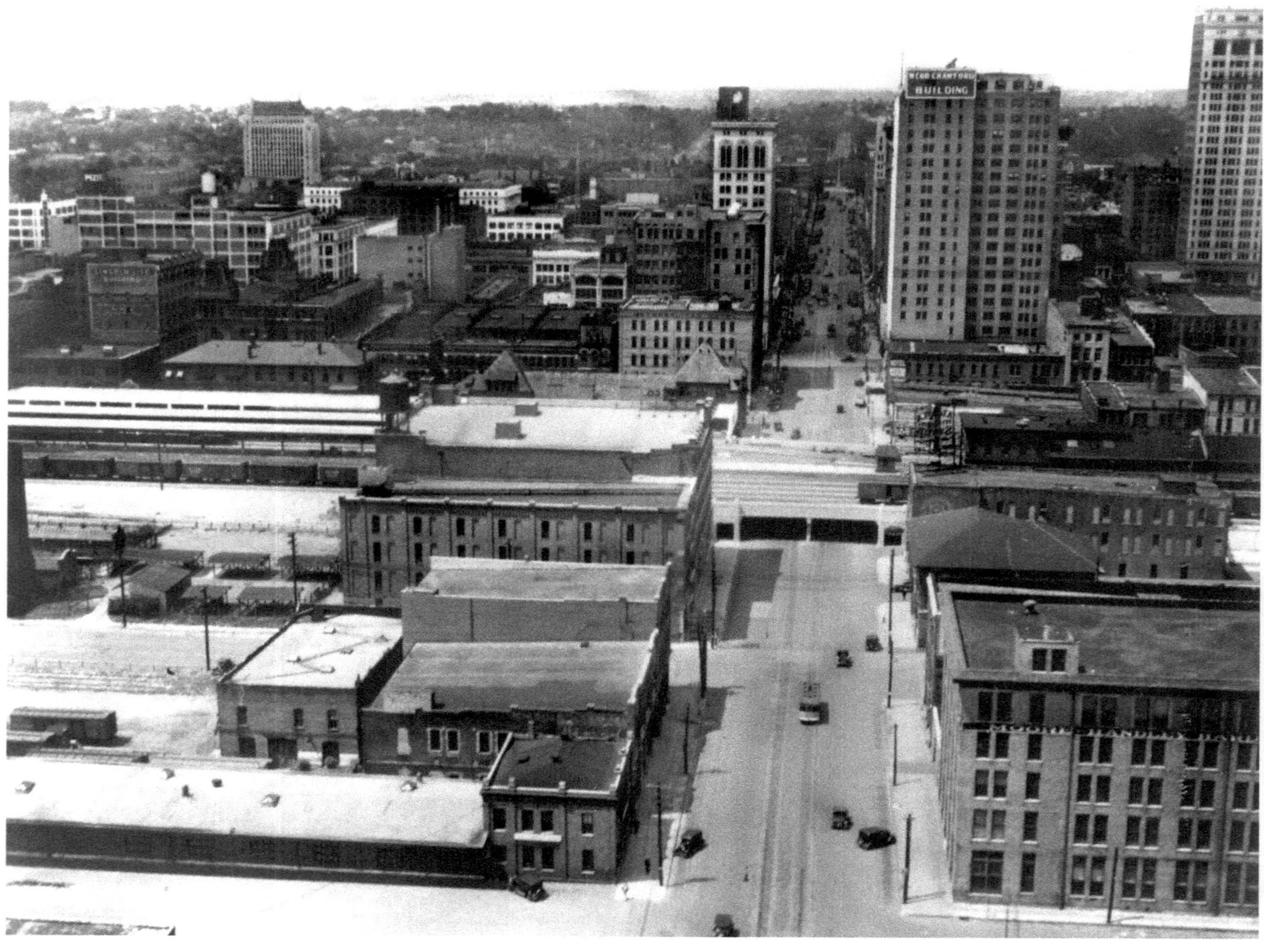

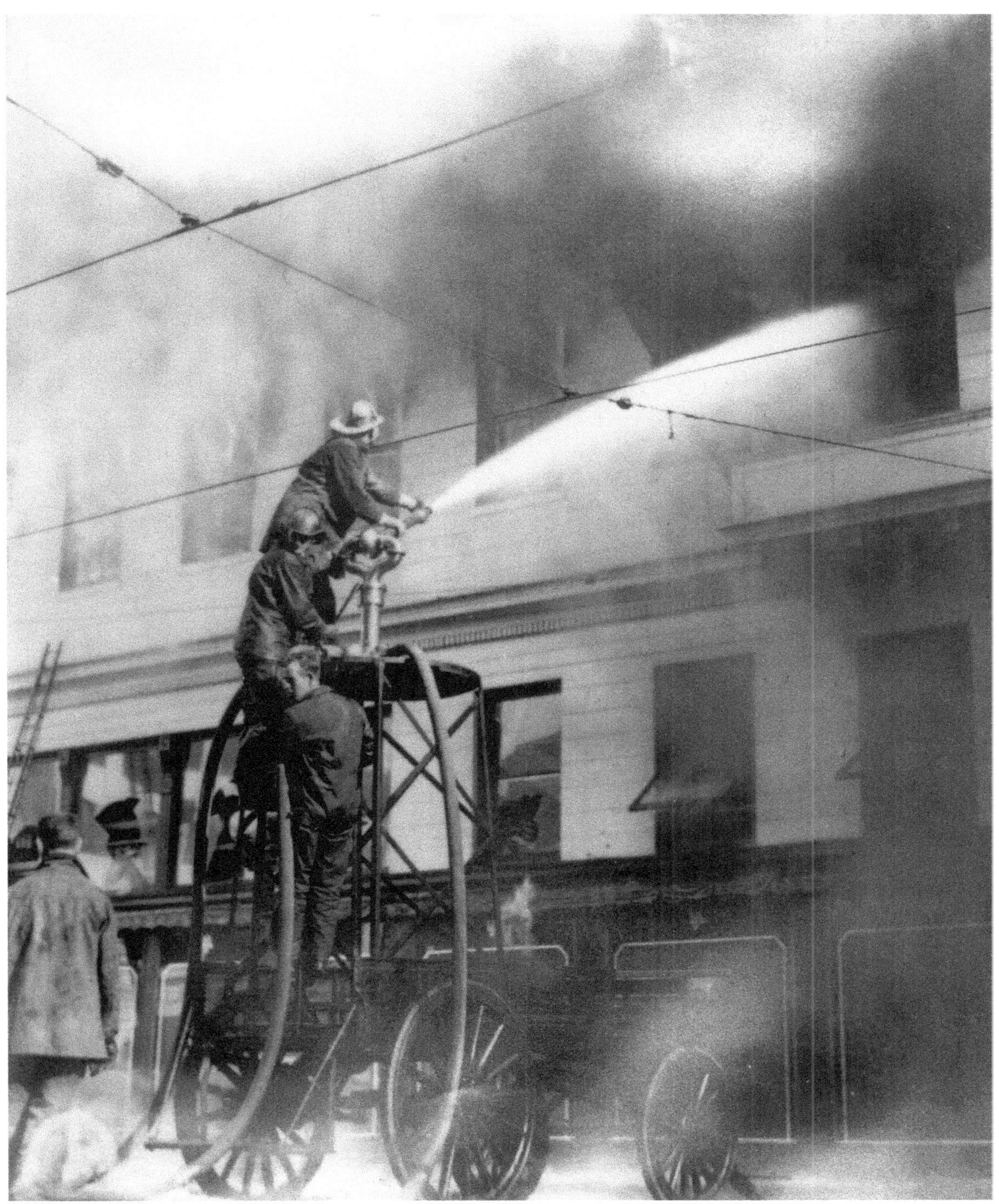

Birmingham fire fighters battle the blaze that destroyed Loveman's Department Store in 1934. Afterward, many local civic leaders complained that the fire department was ill-equipped to handle a fire of this magnitude.

Bystanders watch from rooftops as men from the Birmingham Fire Department extinguish the last embers of the Loveman's fire.

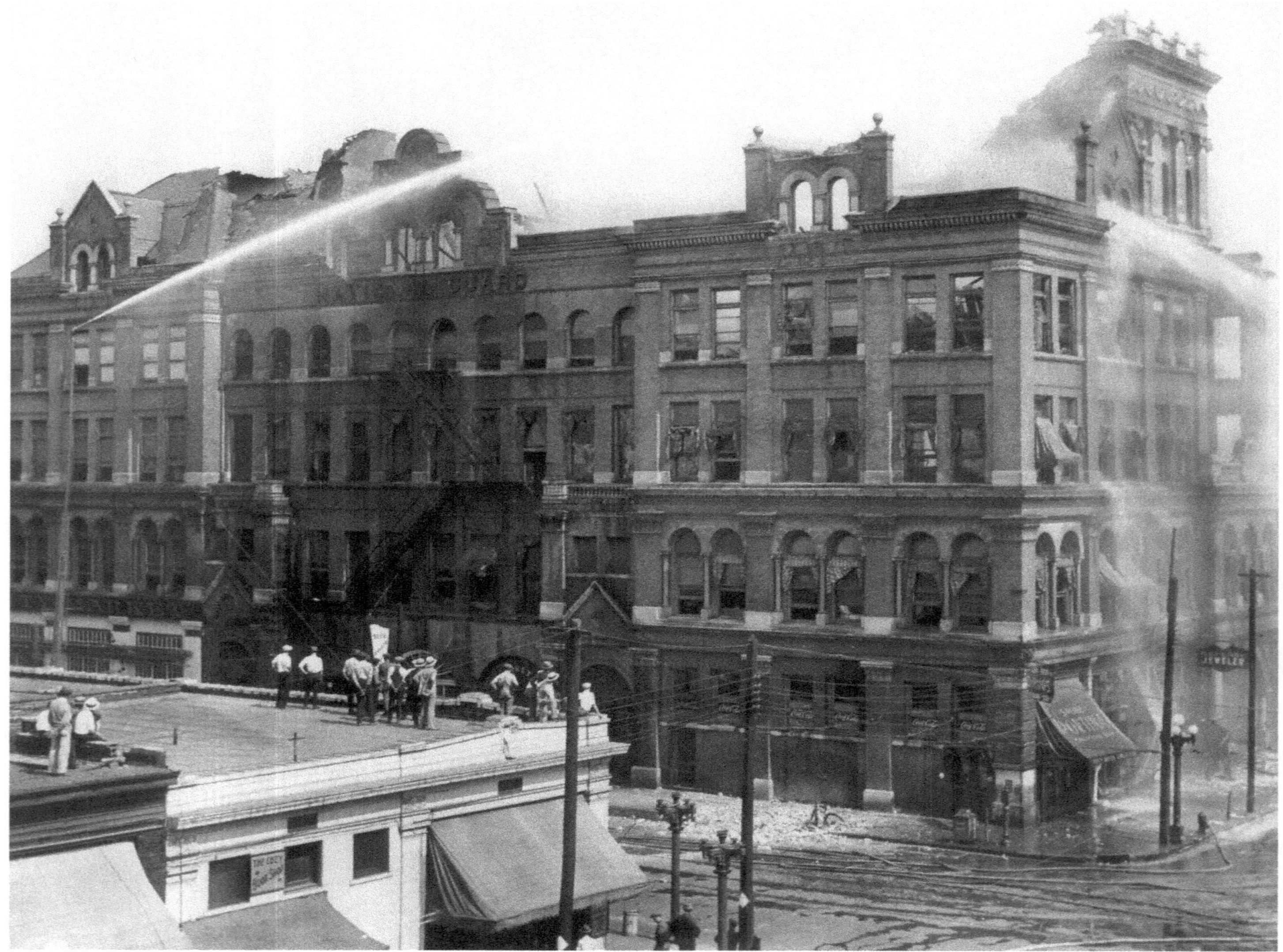

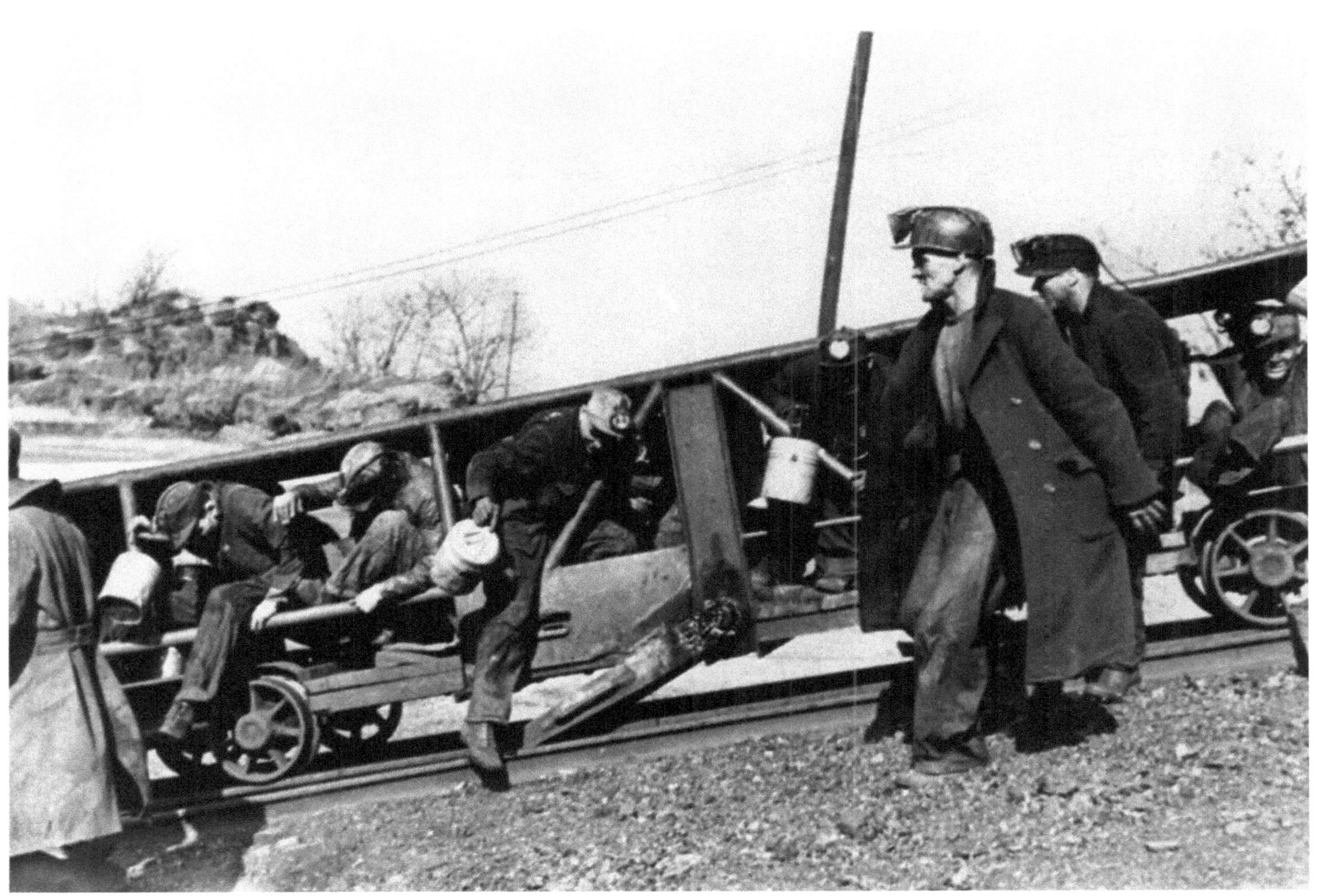

Birmingham area coal miners ending their shift, 1937.

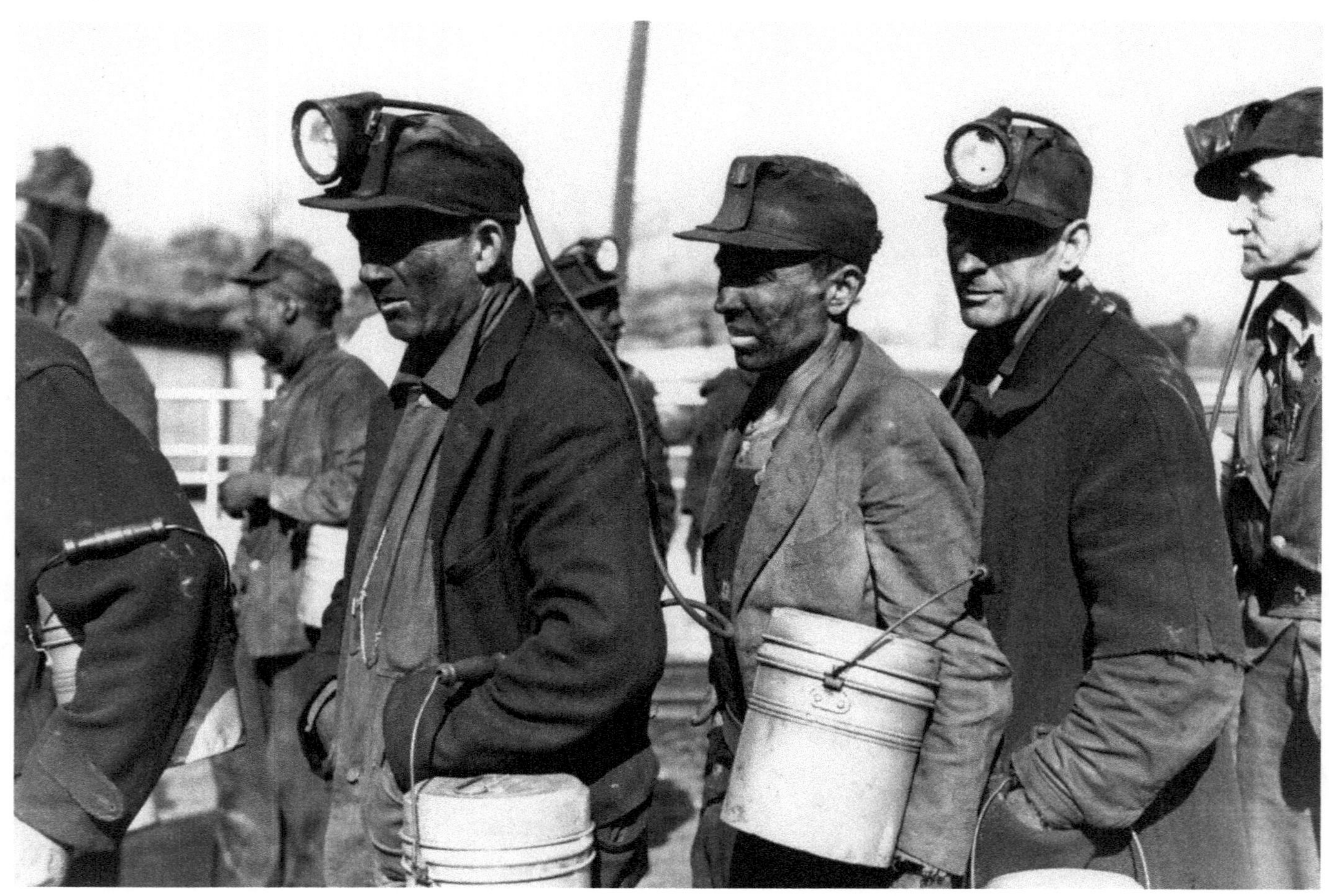

Miners head for home, their faces covered in dust and their lunch pails over their arms, 1937.

In the first half of the twentieth century, many Birmingham area companies offered housing, medical care, education, and other social services to their workers. But these companies also took great pains to prevent their workers from unionizing or striking. Here a company guard watches over a worker village in 1937.

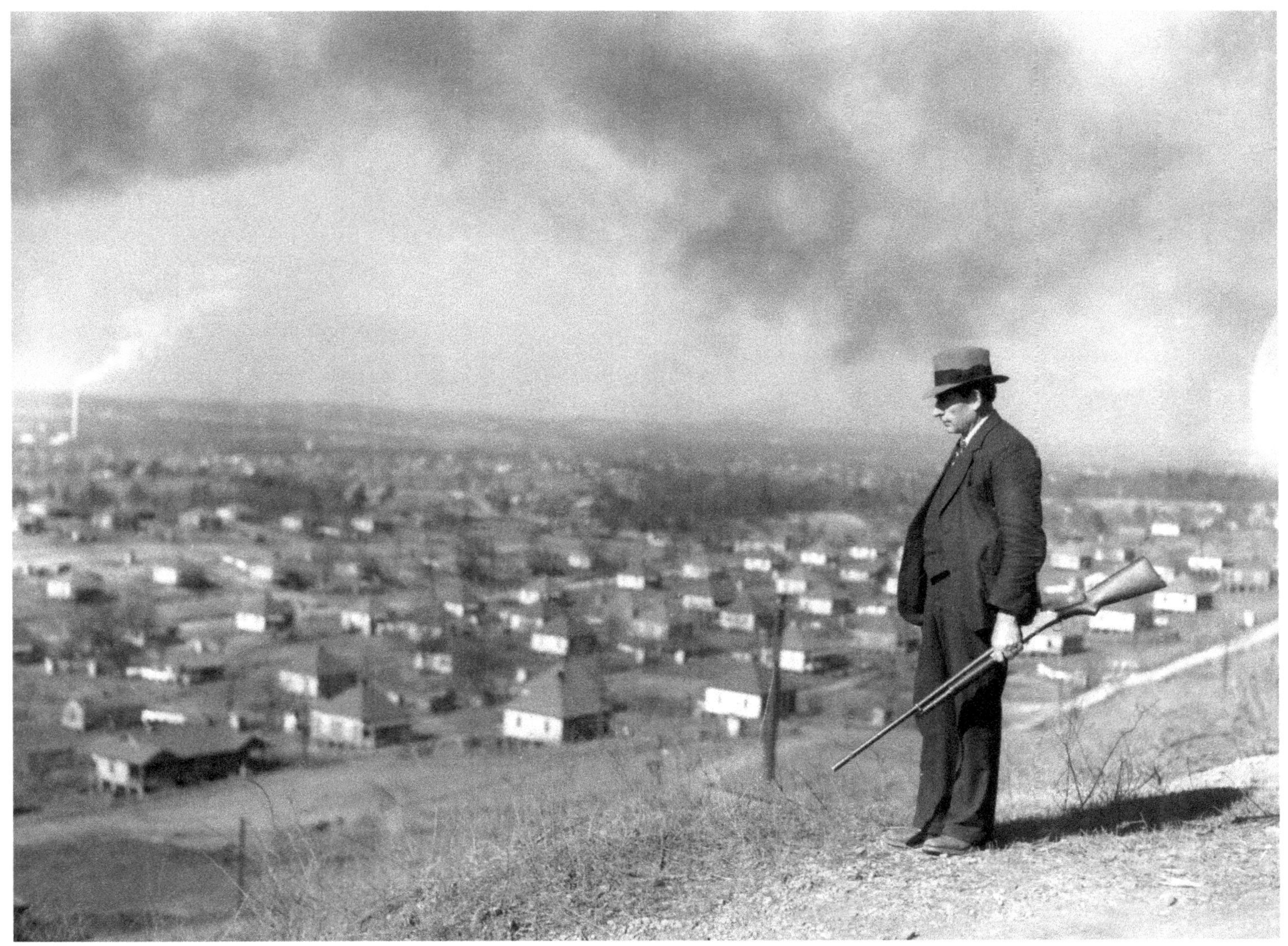

Shopping along Second Avenue North in the 1930s. Kress five-and-ten stores were a fixture in many American cities in the era.

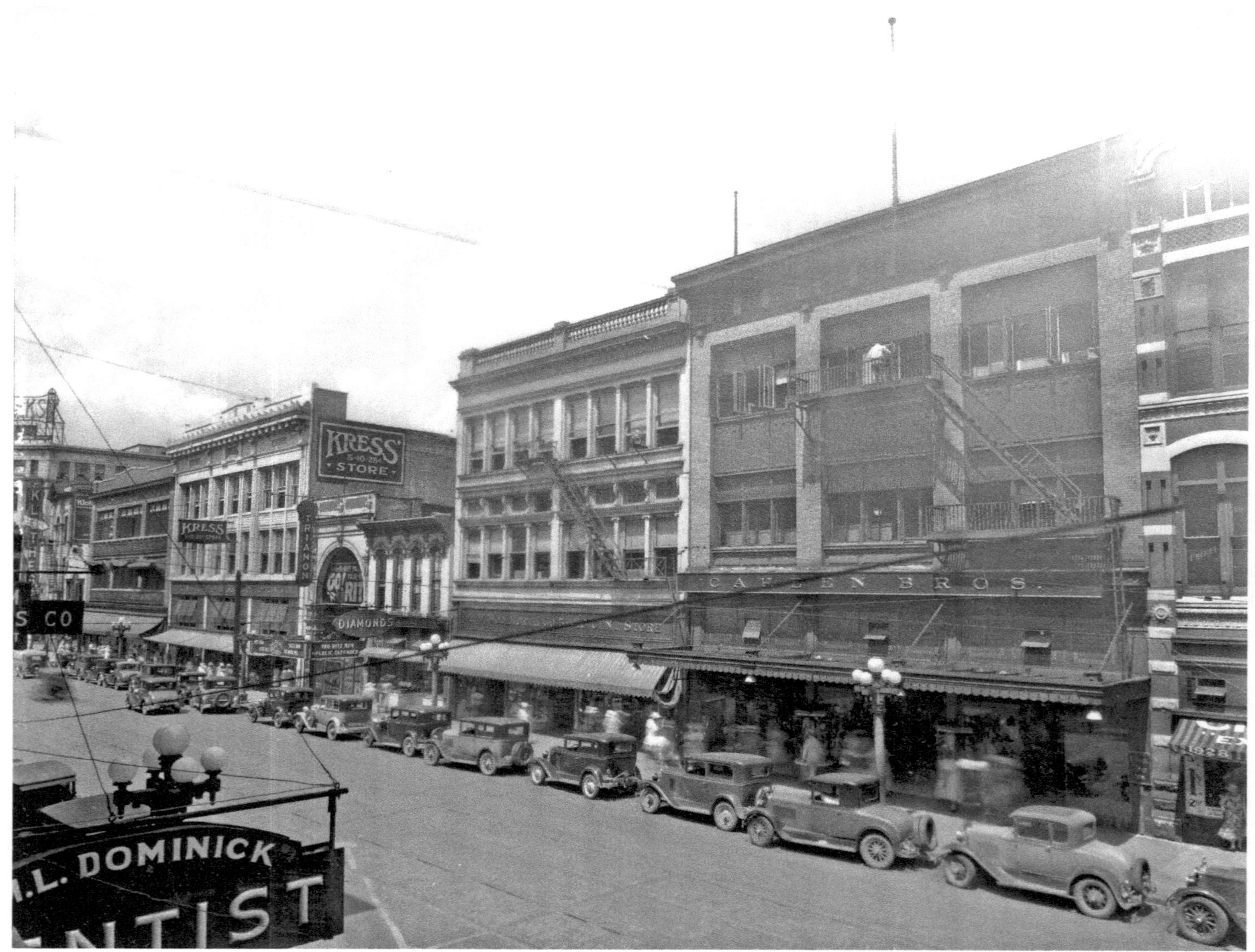

The business district of Ensley, Avenue F and Nineteenth Street, in the 1930s.

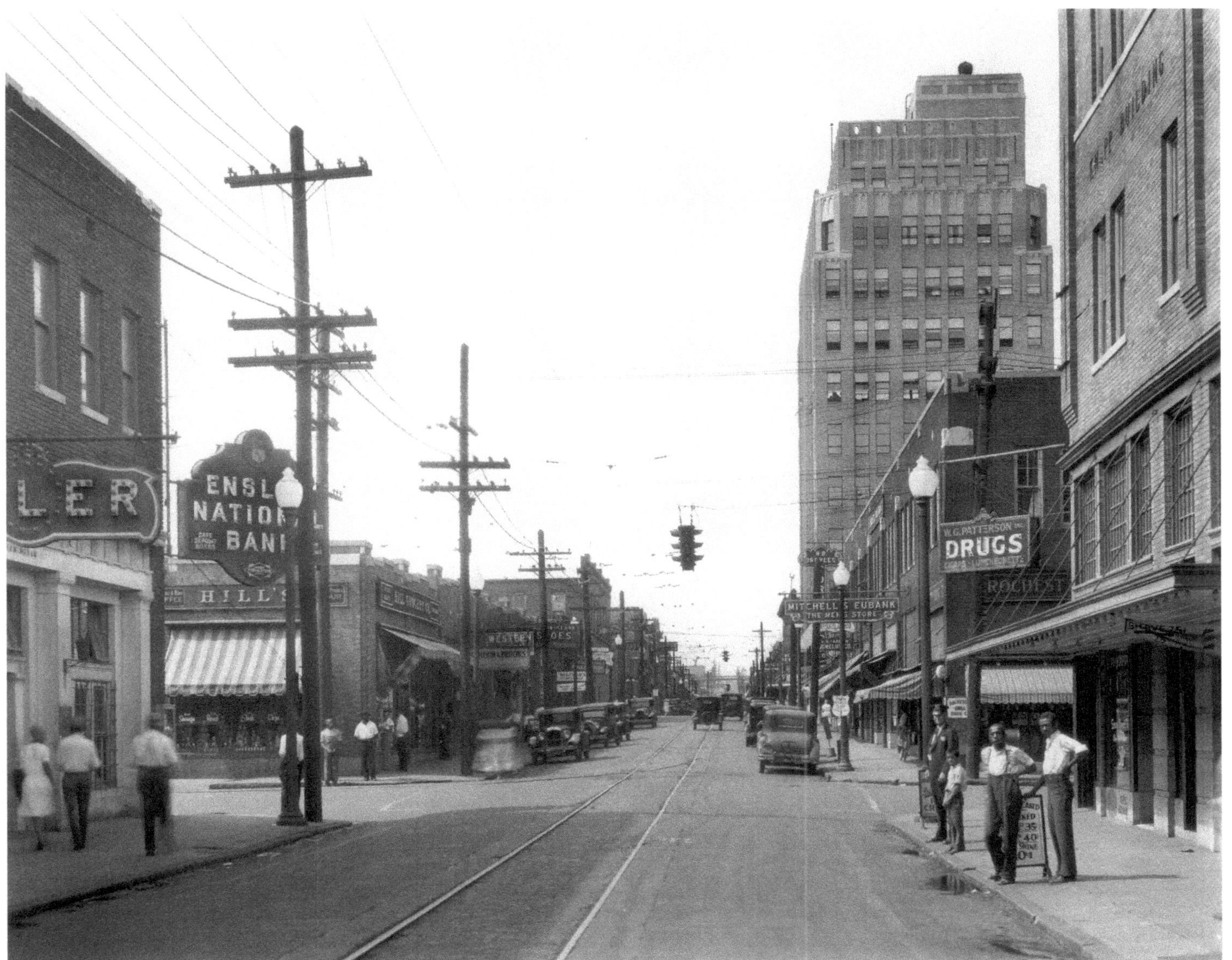

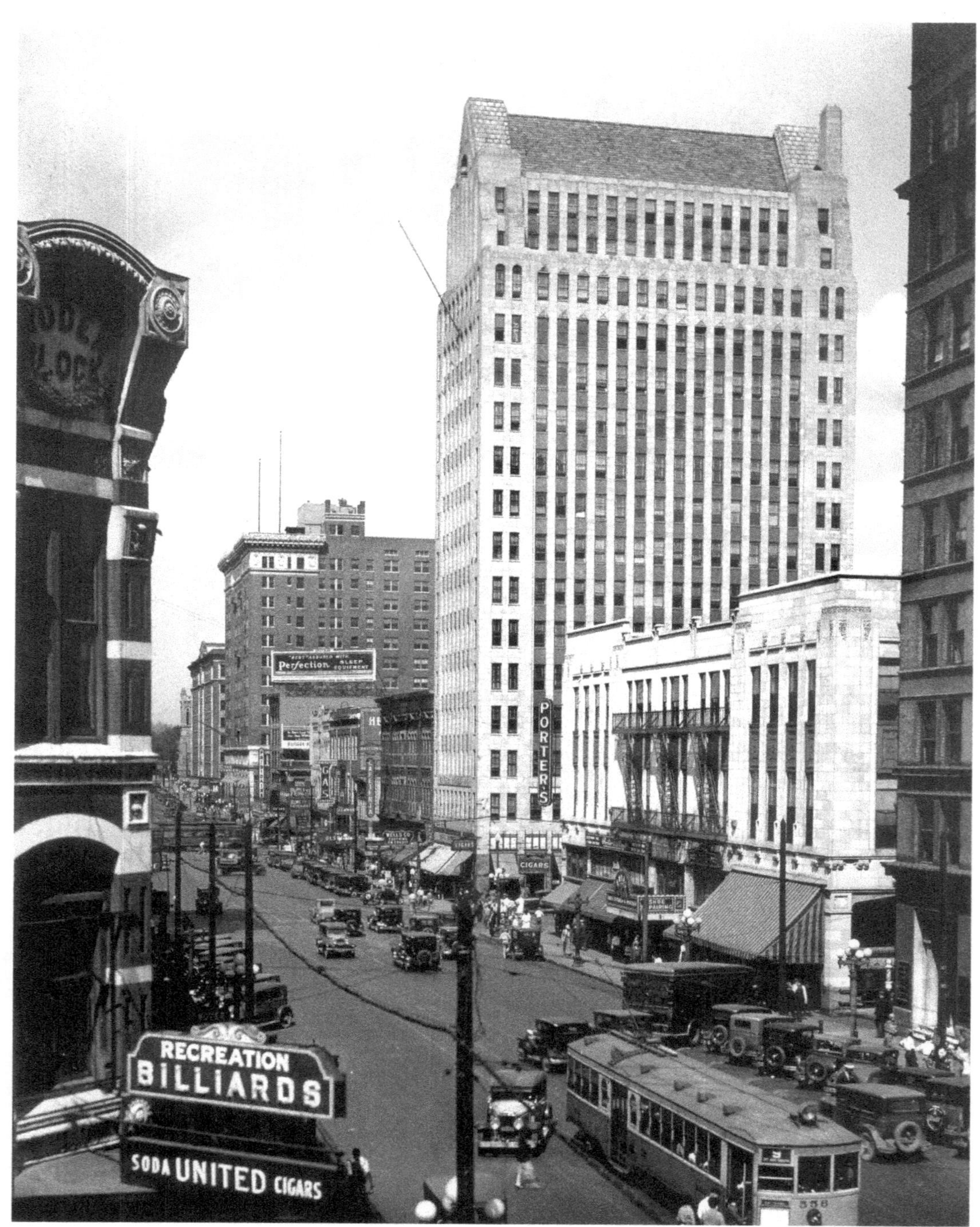

Twentieth Street at Second Avenue North in the 1930s. The tall building in the center is the Watts Building.

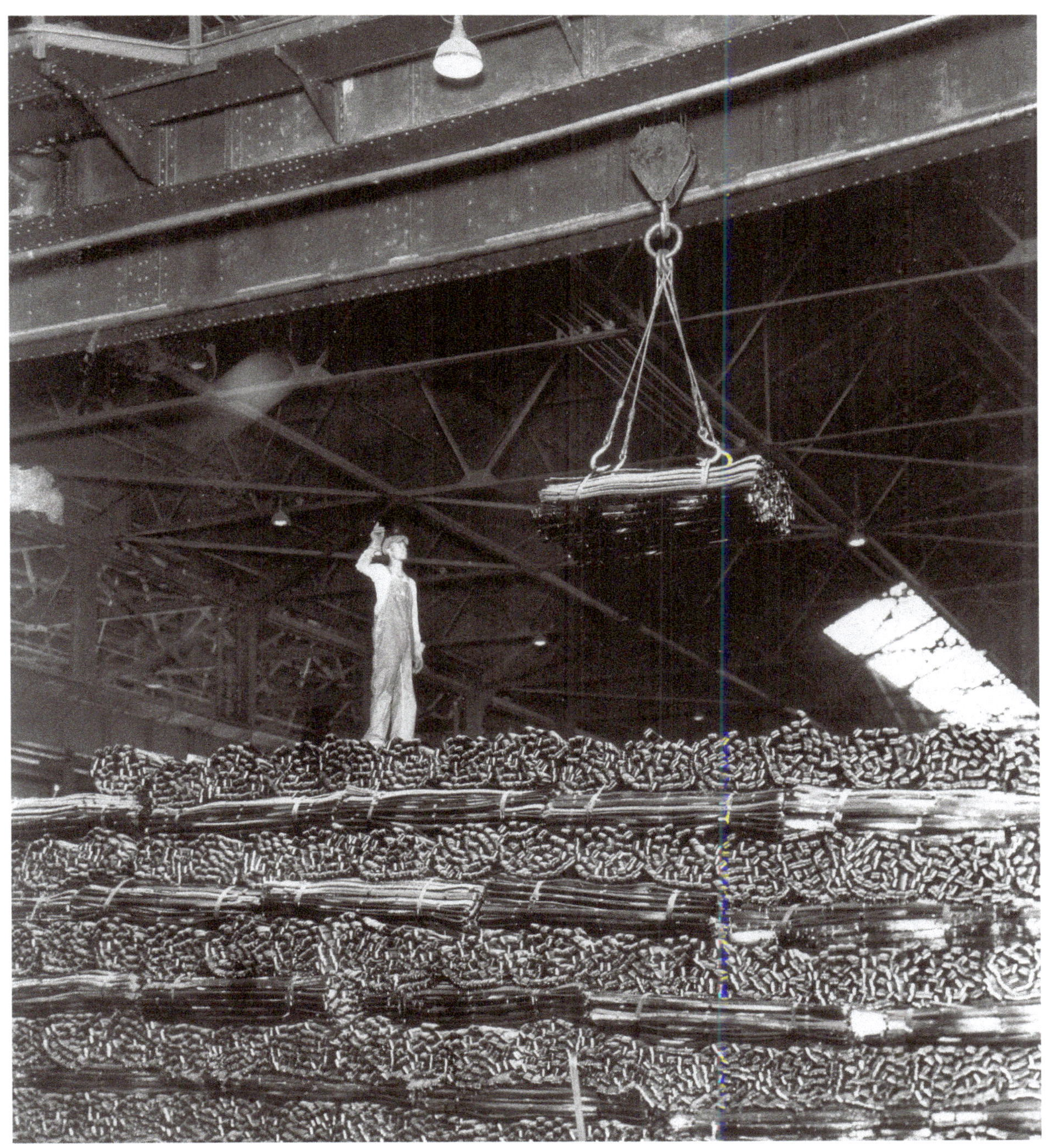

Cotton ties being warehoused. Ties for cotton bales were manufactured year-round and stored until cotton was harvested in the late summer and fall.

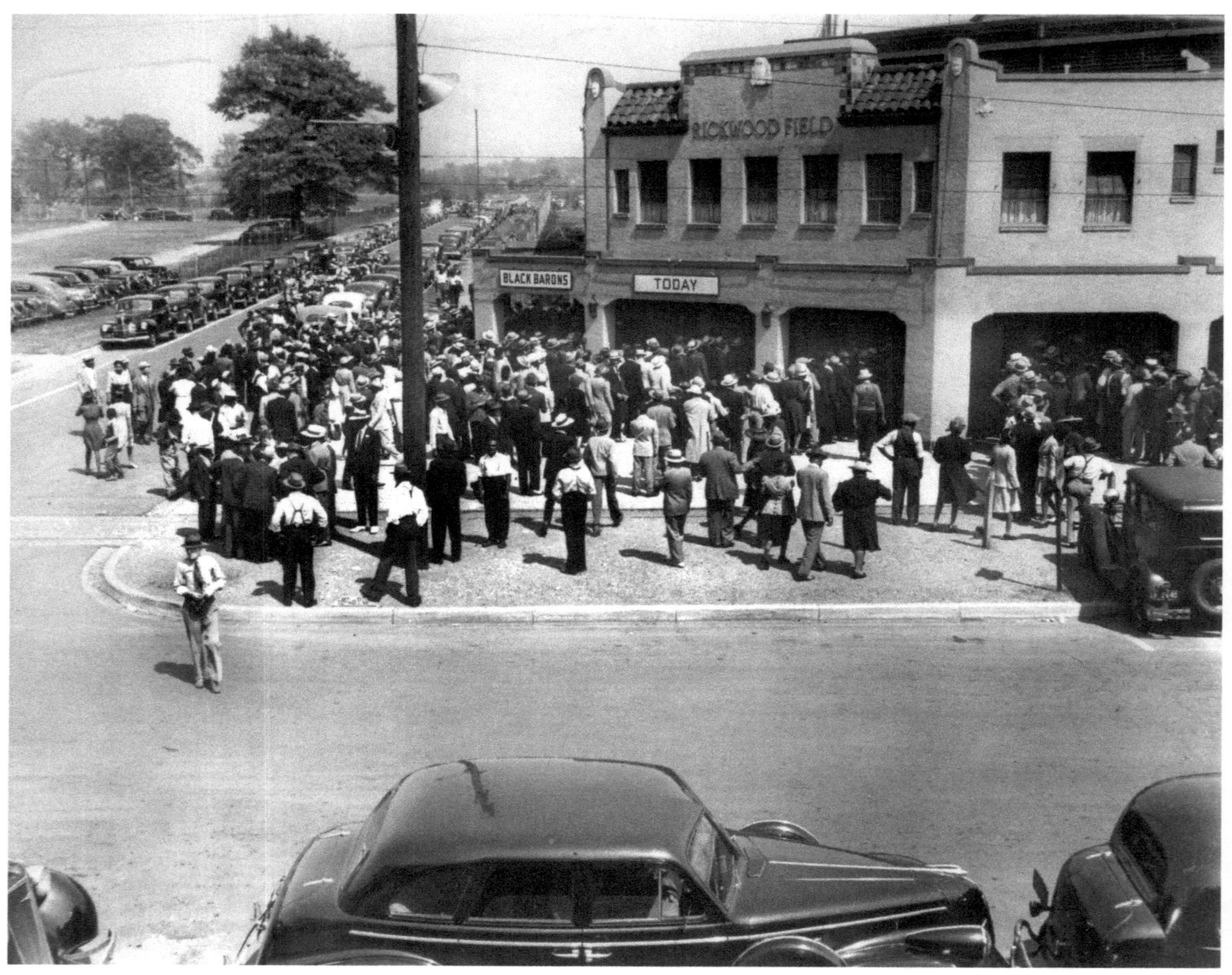

Like so much of life in the early twentieth century, sports were racially segregated, and Birmingham, like many other cities, hosted two professional baseball teams. The white Birmingham Barons and the Birmingham Black Barons shared Rickwood Field. When the white Barons played, white spectators sat in the grandstand and black spectators in the bleachers. When the Black Barons played, the seating was reversed.

The downtown Birmingham Public Library in the snow, 1936. Built in the 1920s as Birmingham's first free-standing central library, this building now houses one of the finest genealogical and local history collections in the United States and Alabama's first municipal archives.

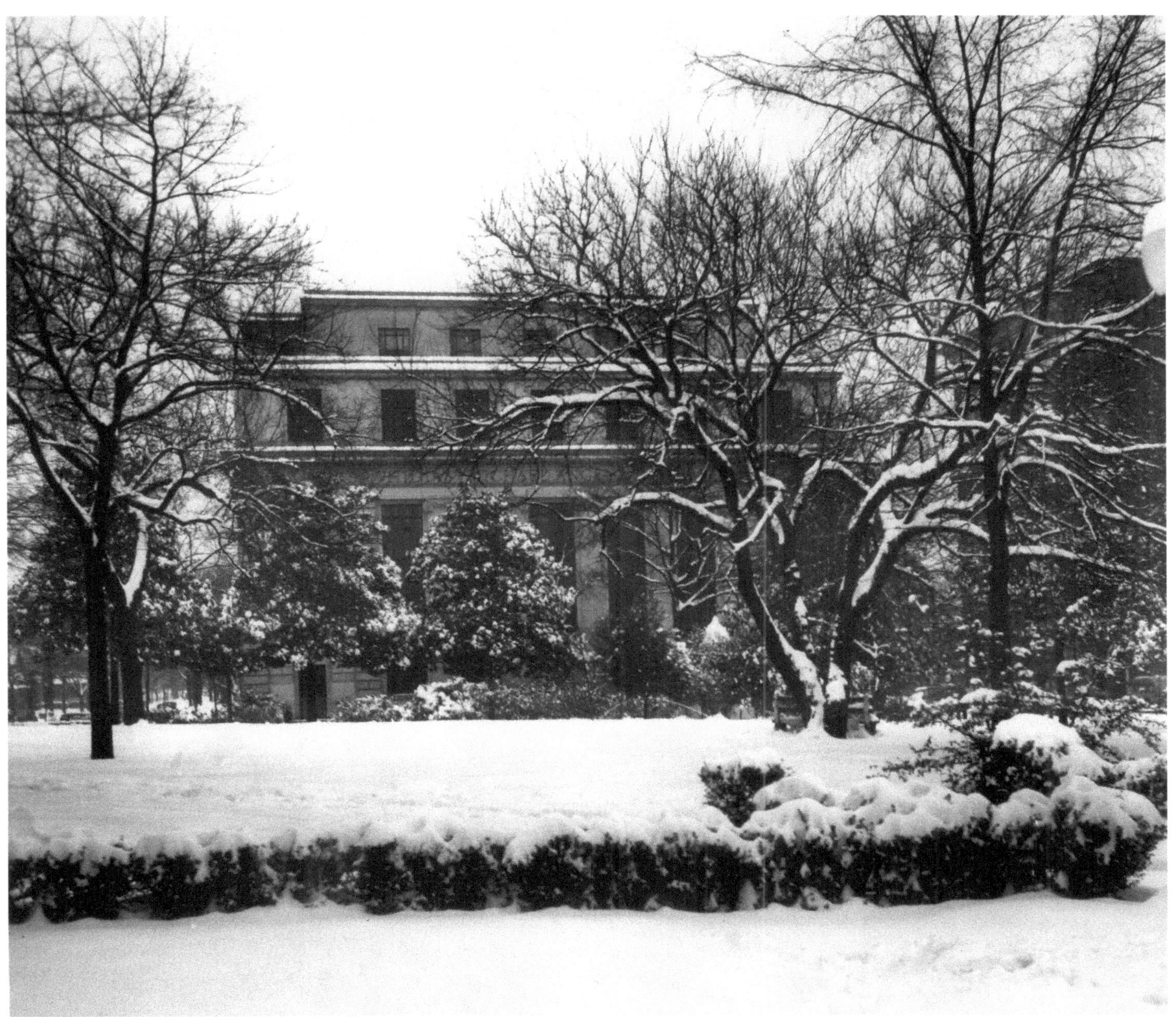

Birmingham City Hall and the Jefferson County Courthouse in the 1950s.

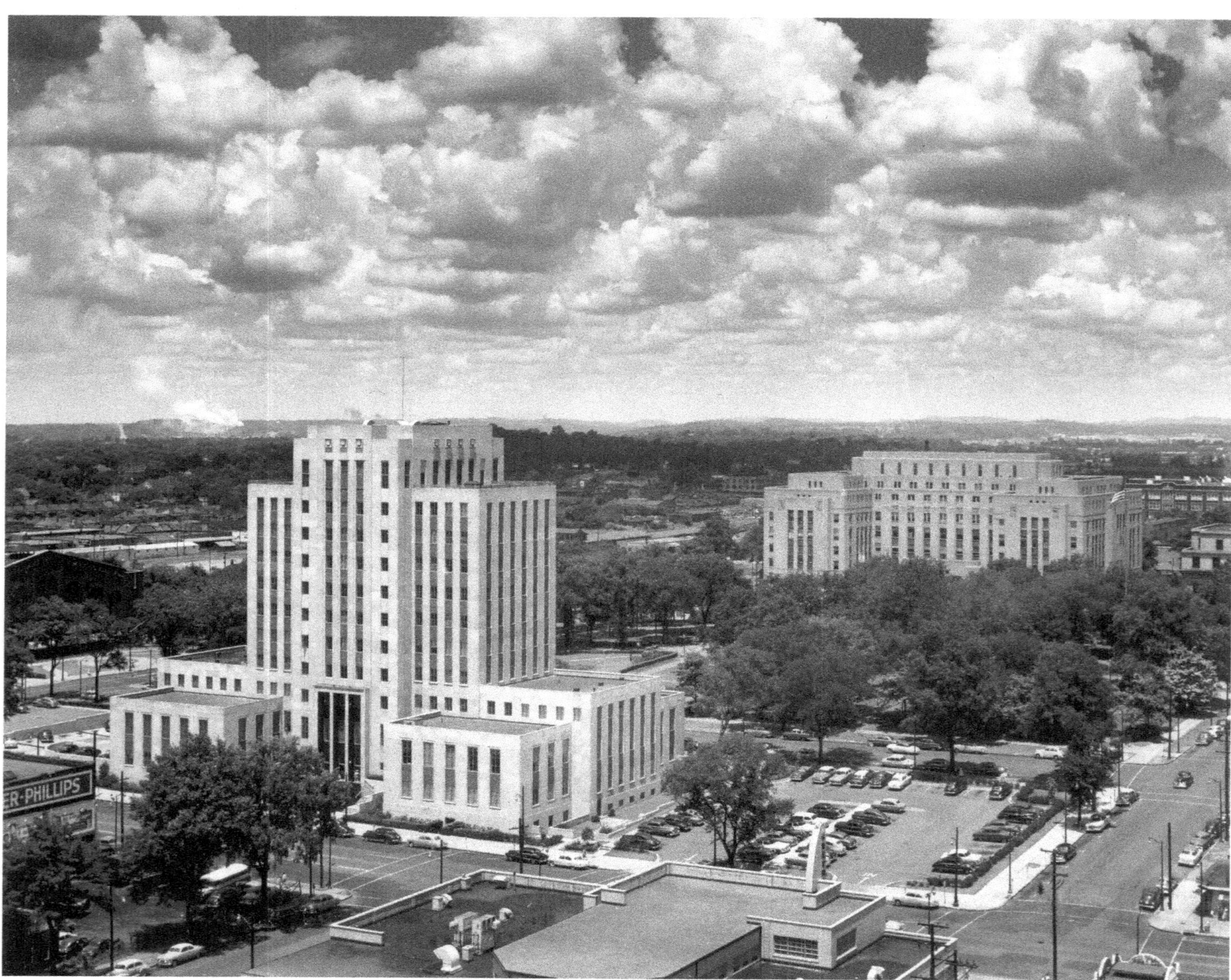

Difficult Days and Changing Times

(1940–1990)

During the five decades between 1940 and 1990, Birmingham was transformed by three of the most significant upheavals of the twentieth century—World War II, the civil rights movement, and the decline of America's industrial economy.

The industrial demands of the Second World War ended the hard economic times of the Great Depression. Factories that had been nearly idle now ran three shifts a day, and many women entered the work force for the first time. The city's population swelled with new migrants.

The experiences of war and the possibilities of postwar prosperity intensified African American resistance to the restraints and injustices of racial segregation. Black protests were often met with vigilante violence and official repression. Because of its convulsive civil rights history, Birmingham is now remembered around the world as a symbol of both racial intolerance and racial reconciliation.

The 1970s and 1980s saw another wave of downtown construction with the completion of the South Central Bell building, First National Bank (now AmSouth) building, First Alabama Bank building (on the site of the old Tutwiler Hotel), AmSouth-Harbert Plaza, and SouthTrust Tower (now Wachovia Bank). As manufacturing moved to cheaper overseas markets, Birmingham's steel mills and ore mines closed. These skyscrapers, along with the expanding campus of the University of Alabama at Birmingham, illustrate the transformation of Birmingham from a place reliant on heavy industry to a center of finance and medical research.

Looking south on Twentieth Street, 1940s.

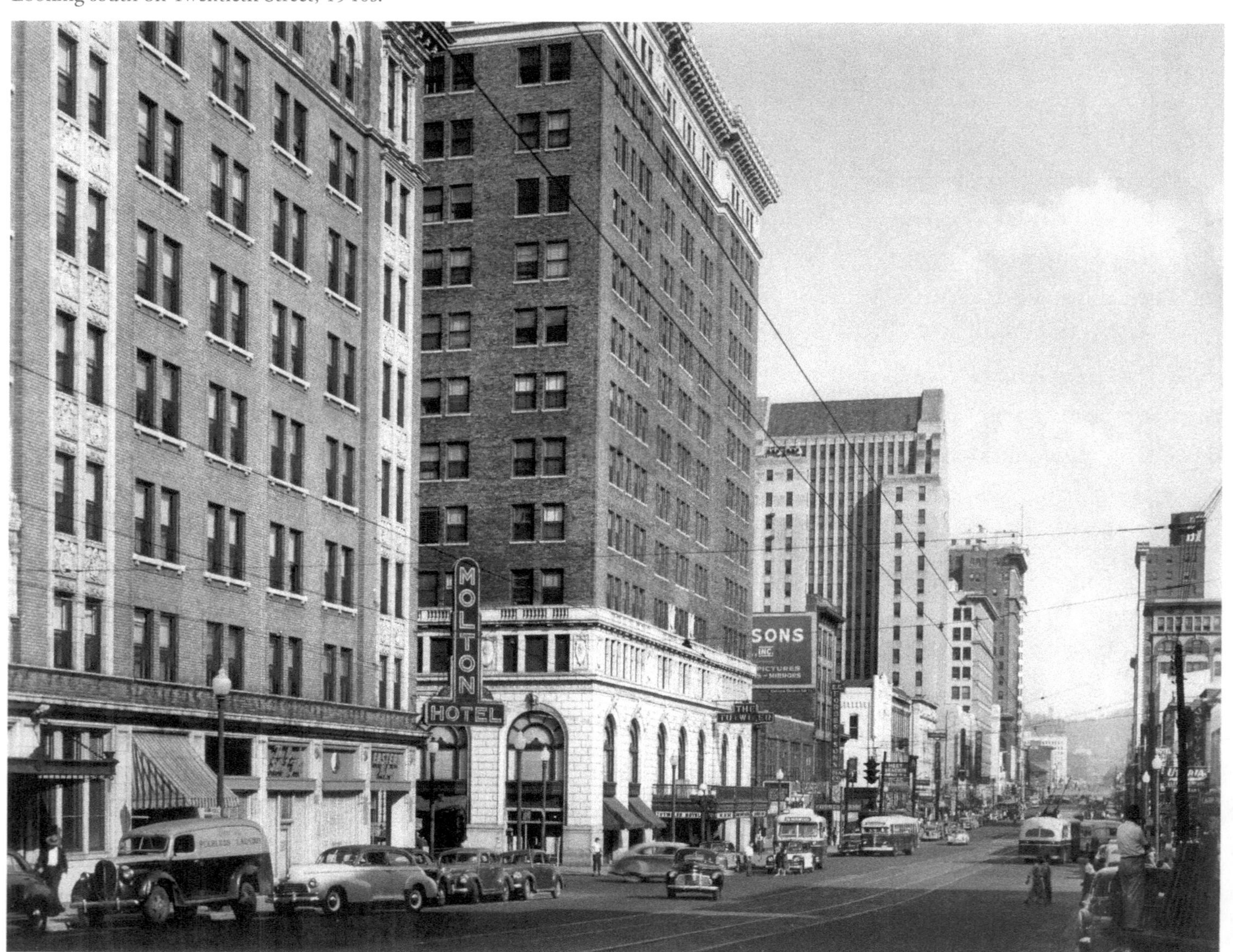

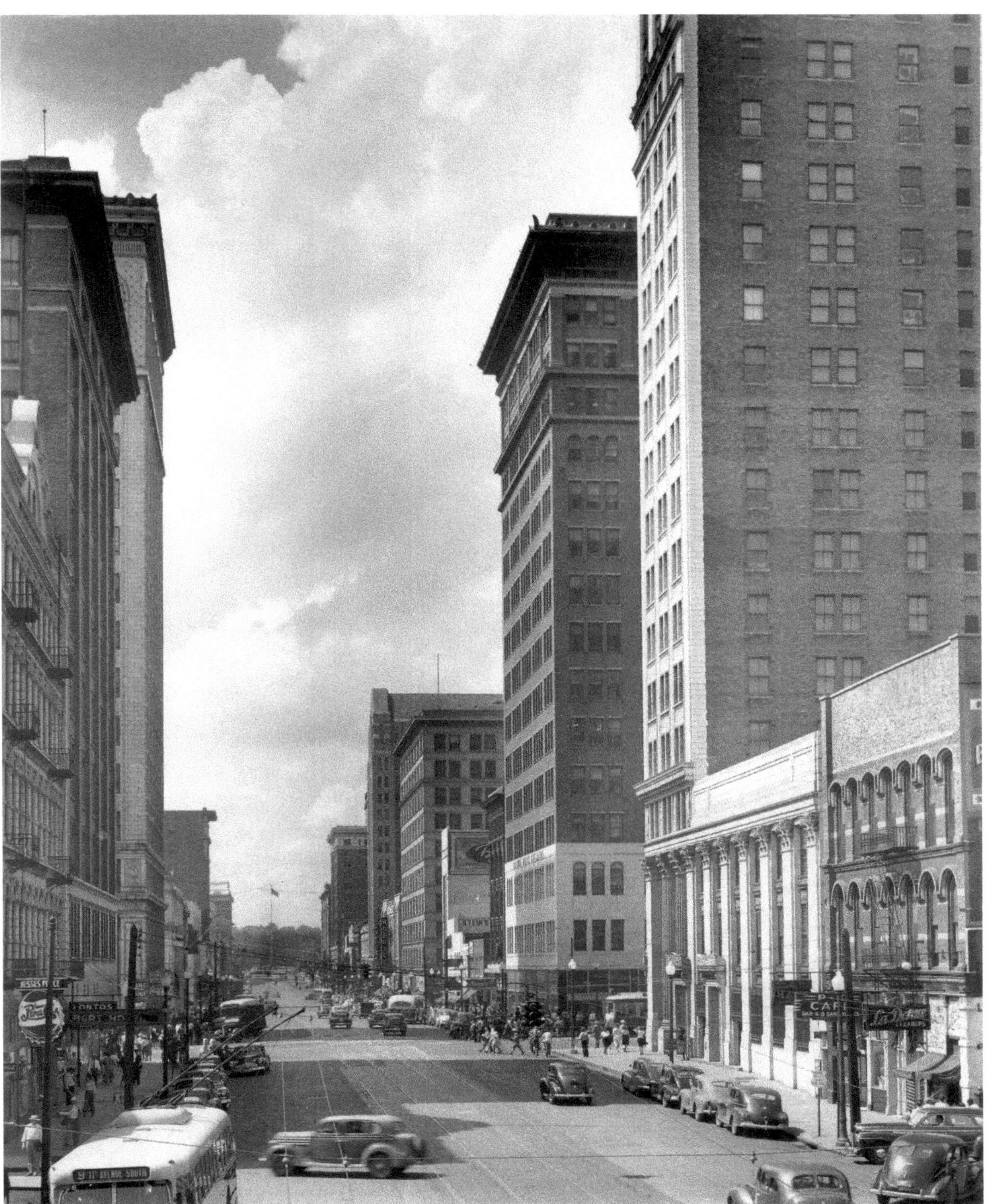

Looking north on Twentieth Street from Morris Avenue, 1940s.

One of Birmingham's oldest churches, First Presbyterian, is shown here as it appeared in the 1940s.

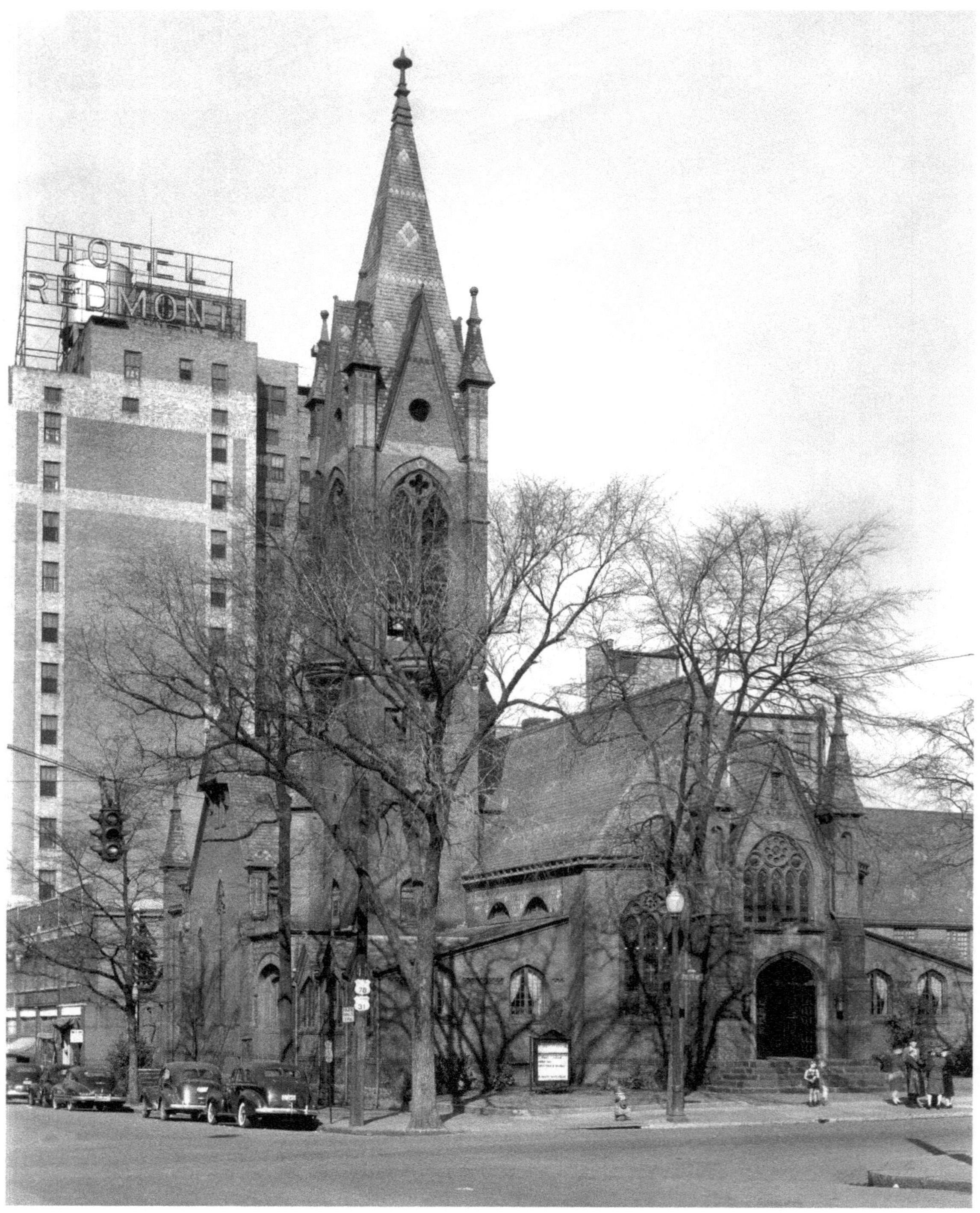

Easter egg hunt at Avondale Park, late 1940s.

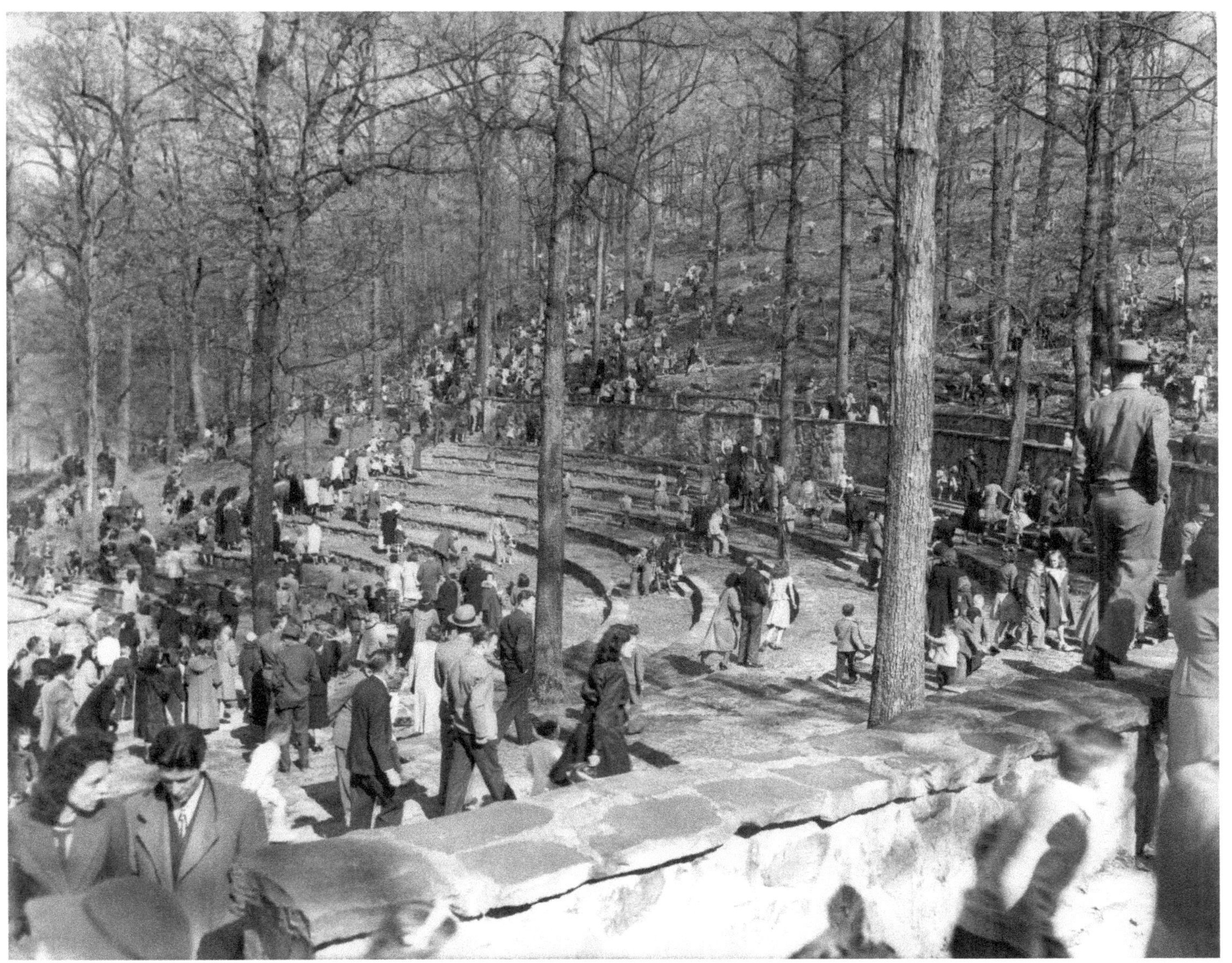

During the era of racial segregation, many white-owned businesses in Birmingham did not serve African American customers. To provide for the black community, black-owned businesses like Tom's Real Shine, the Famous Theater, and others operated on and around Fourth Avenue North. This area, now known as the Black Business District, is listed on the National Register of Historic Places.

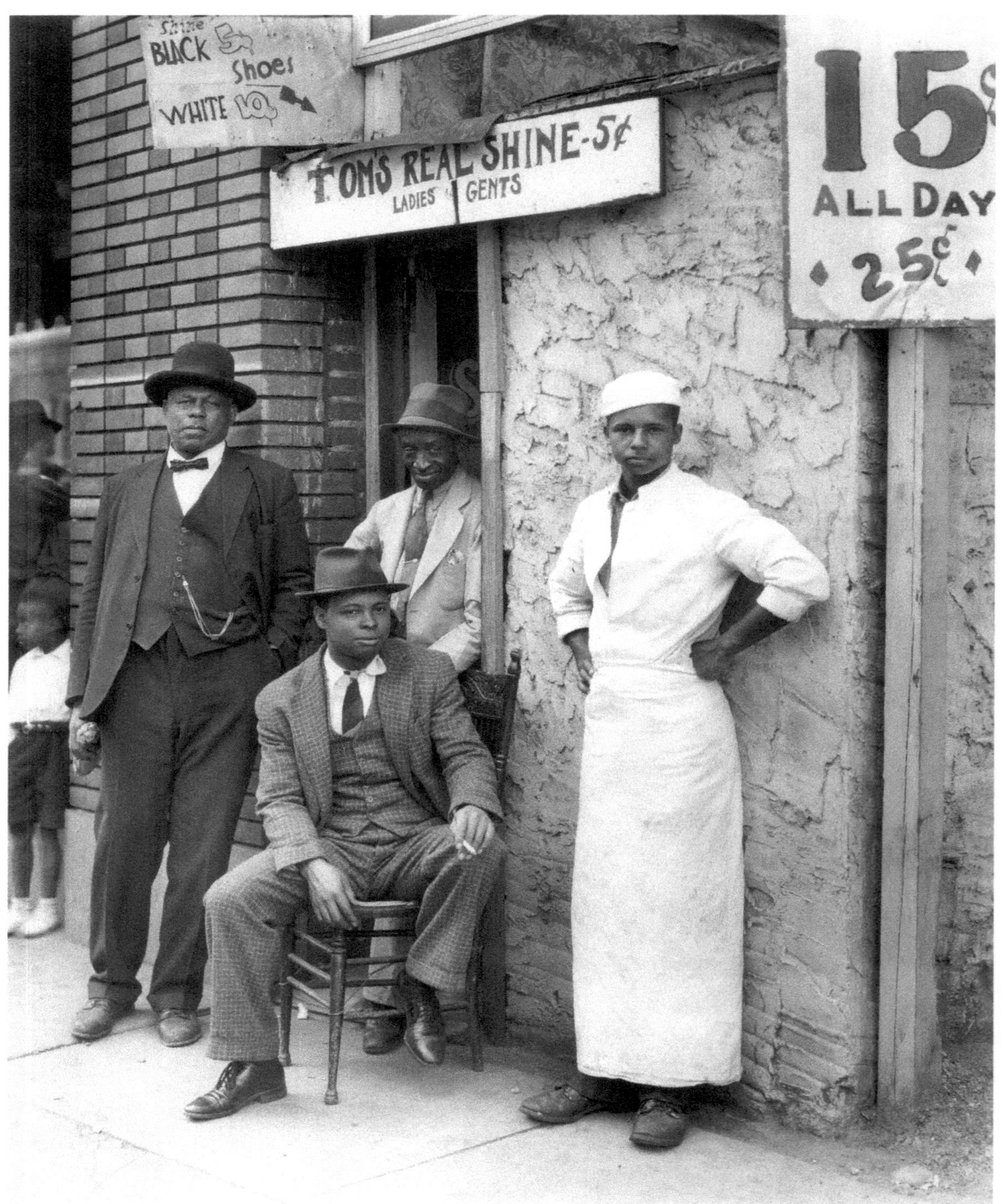

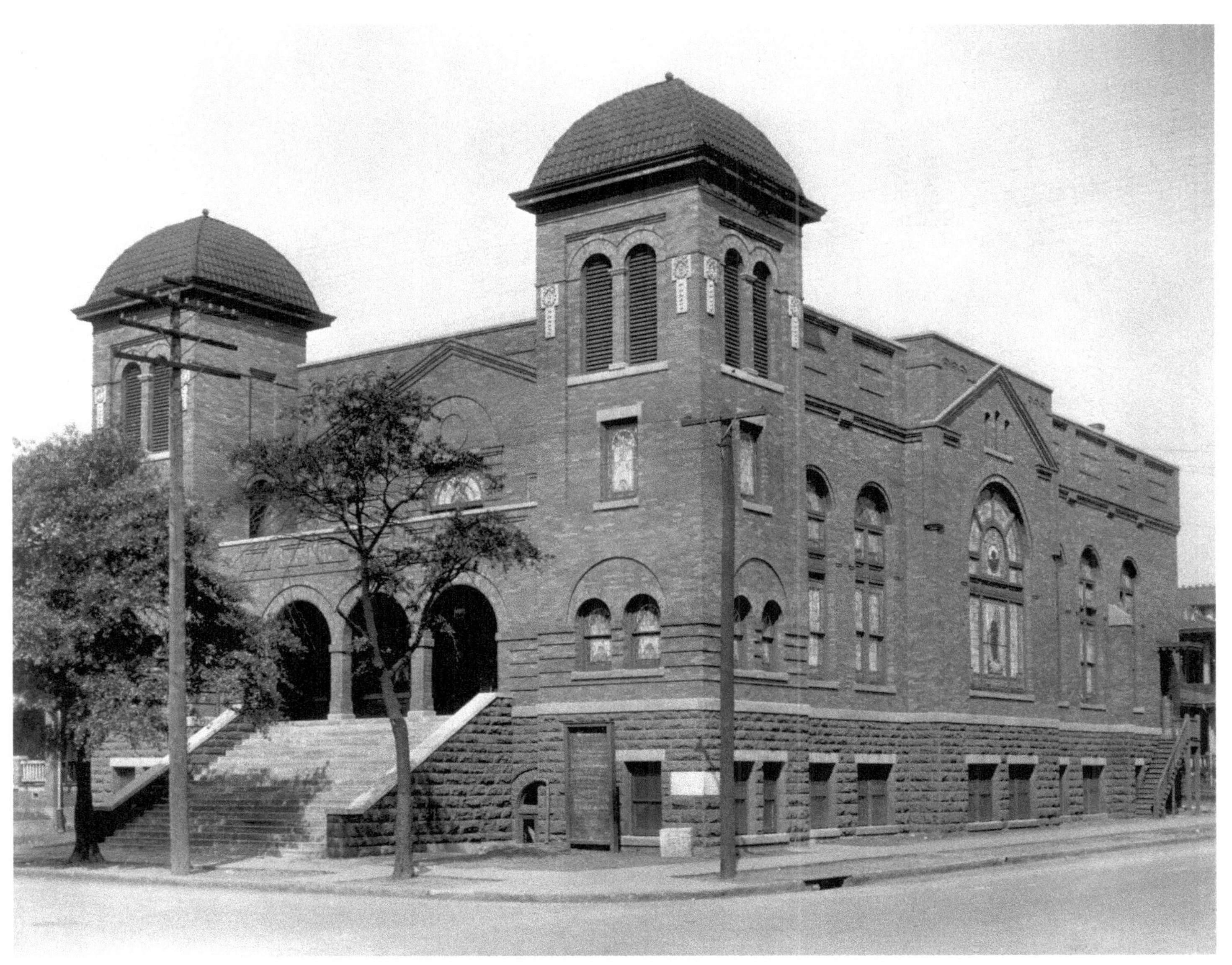

Sixteenth Street Baptist Church, one of Birmingham's oldest African American congregations.

Bob Hope and Doris Day at the Birmingham airport, April 1949. In town for one night, the Bob Hope Show treated a packed audience at the Municipal Auditorium to music and comedy.

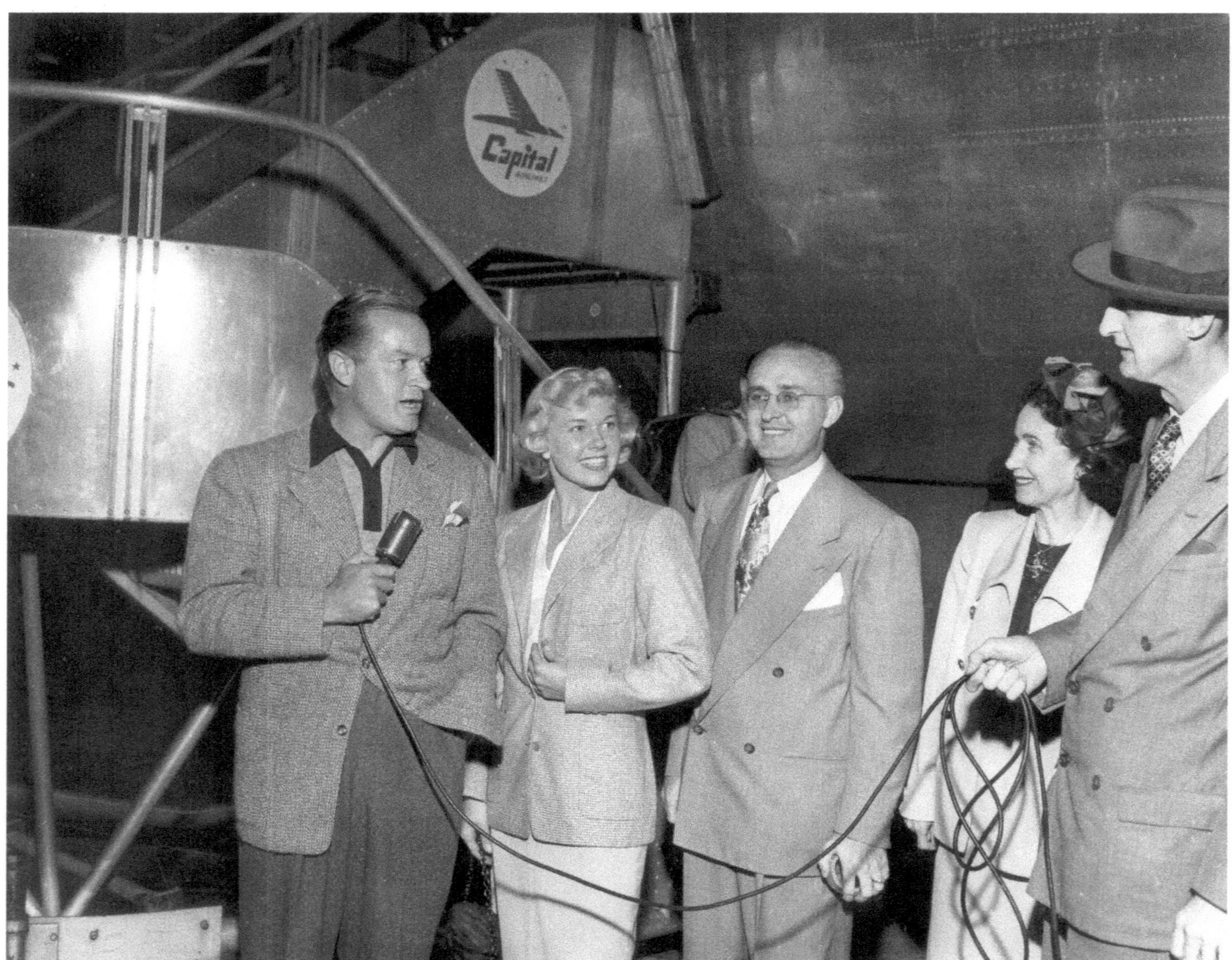

Employees of the Birmingham Mop Manufacturing Company on Fifth Avenue South, 1949.

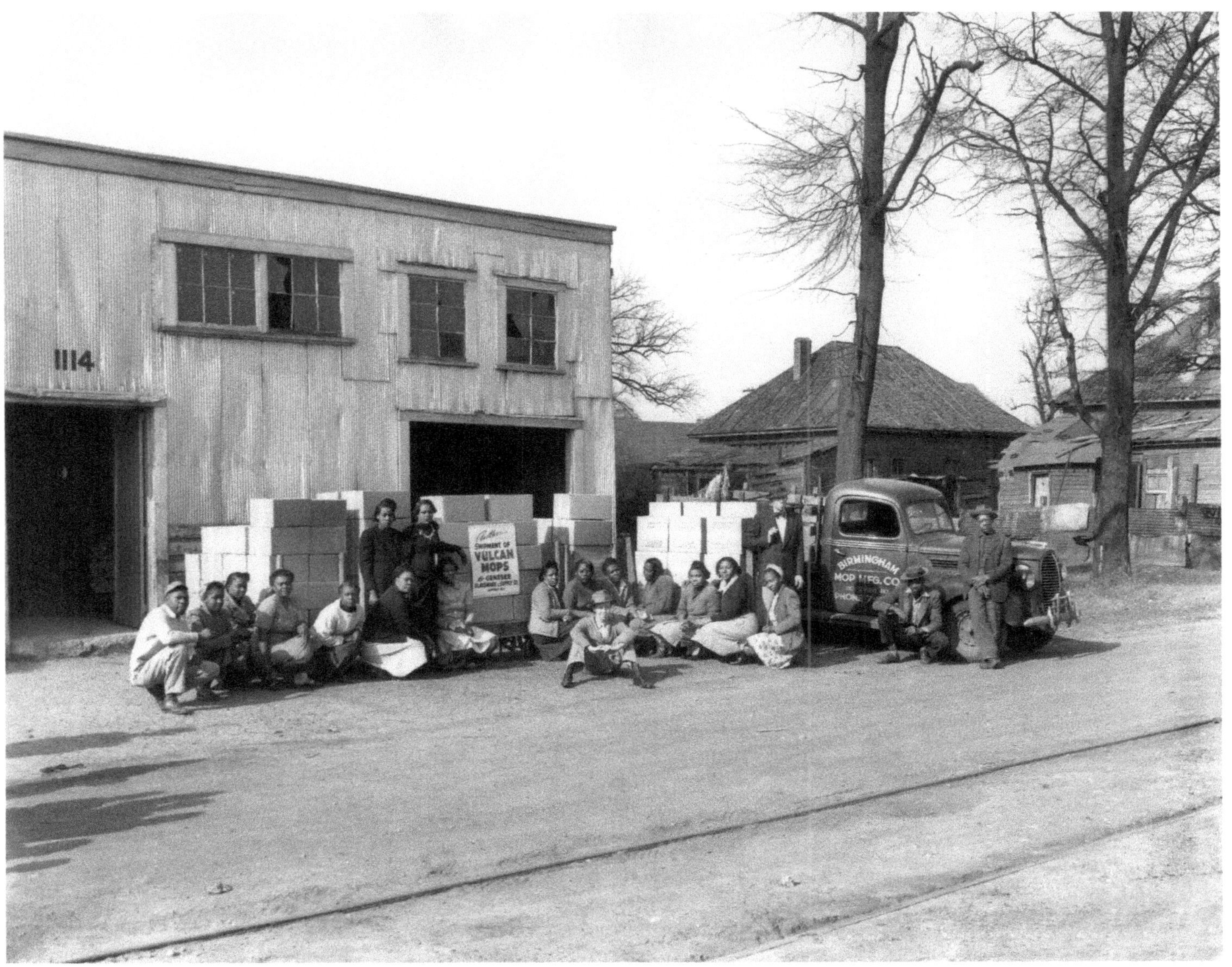

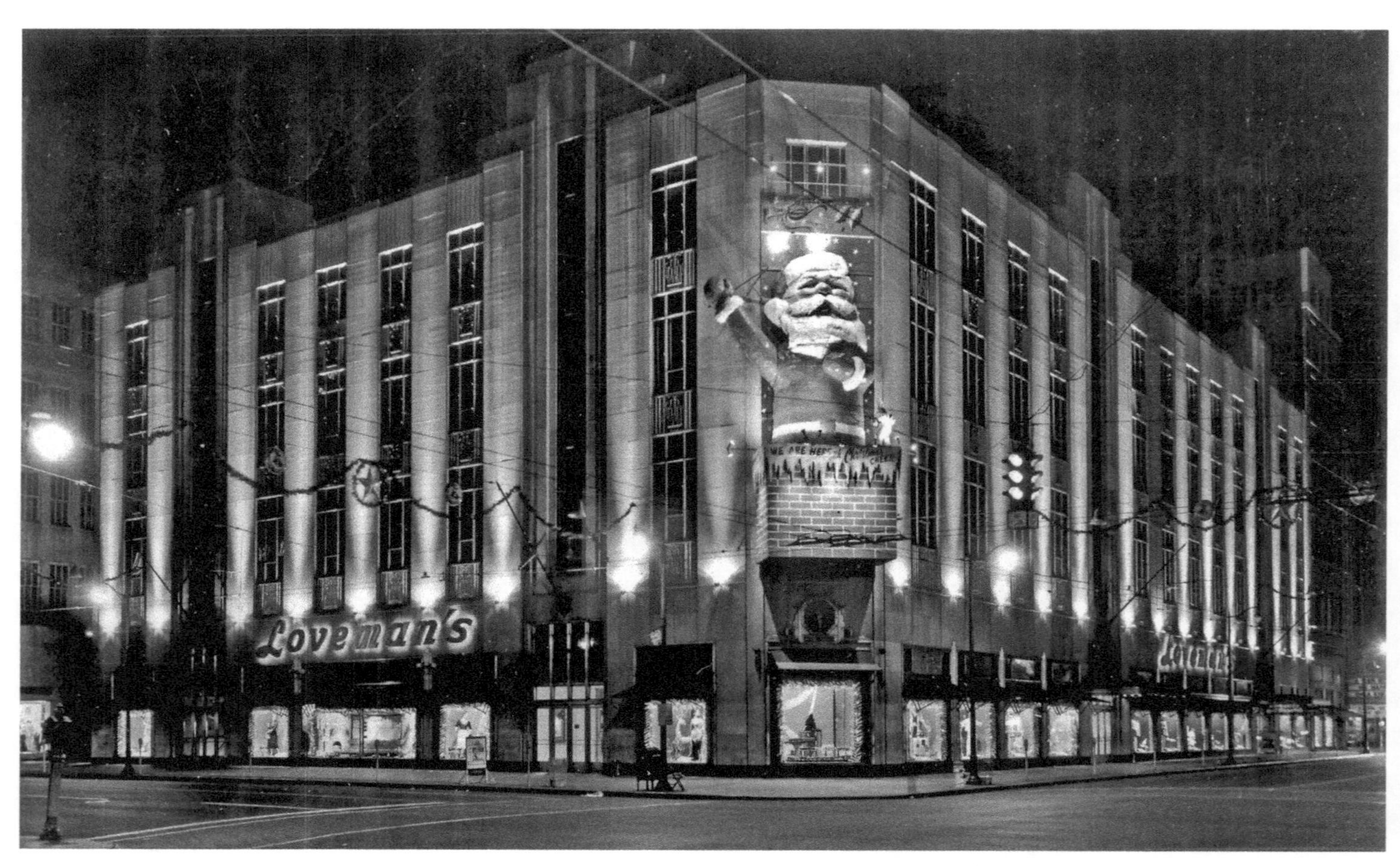

Loveman's department store, decorated for Christmas.

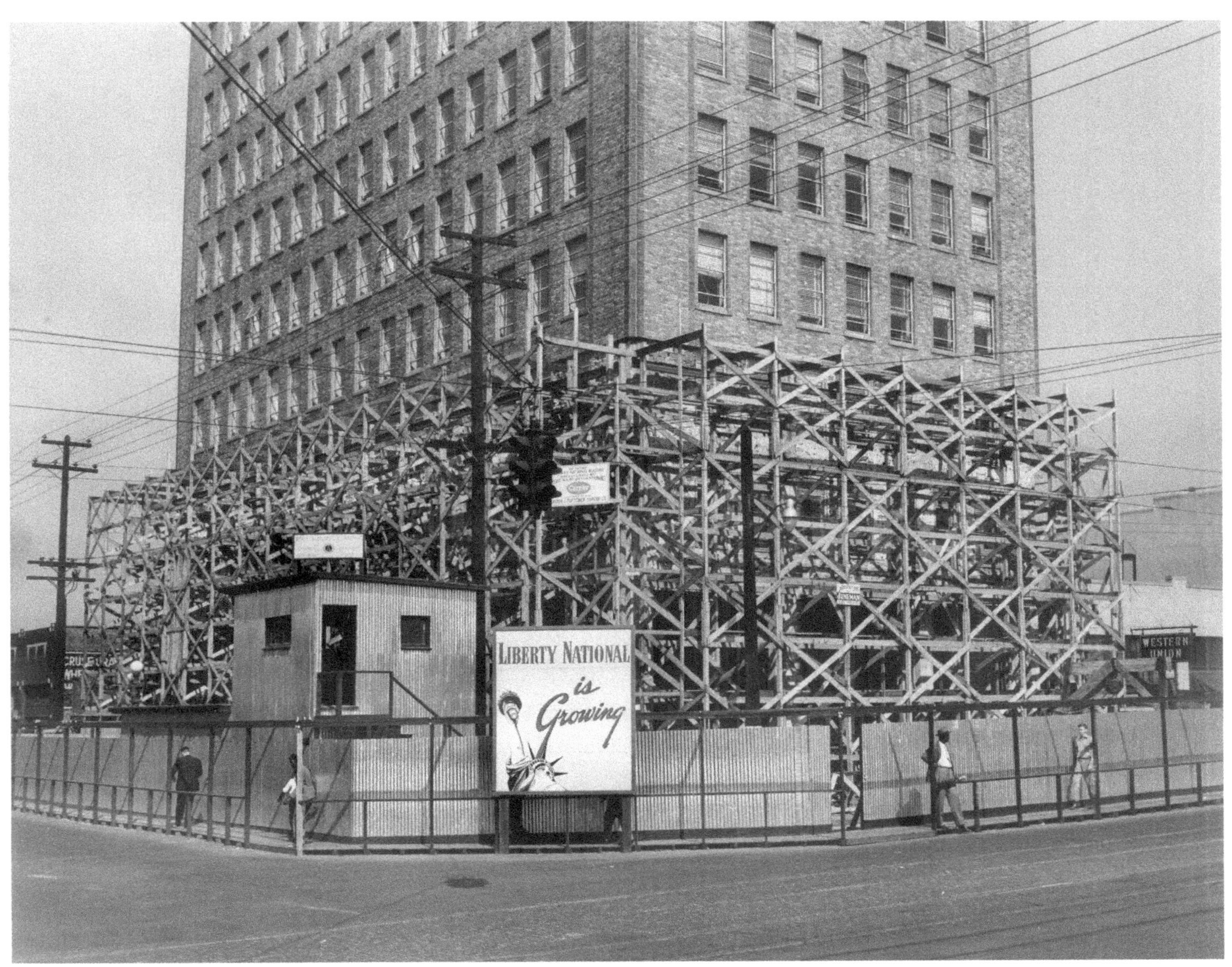

Liberty National Life Insurance Company is growing, 1946. Brice Building Company renovated the original ten-story building built around 1923.

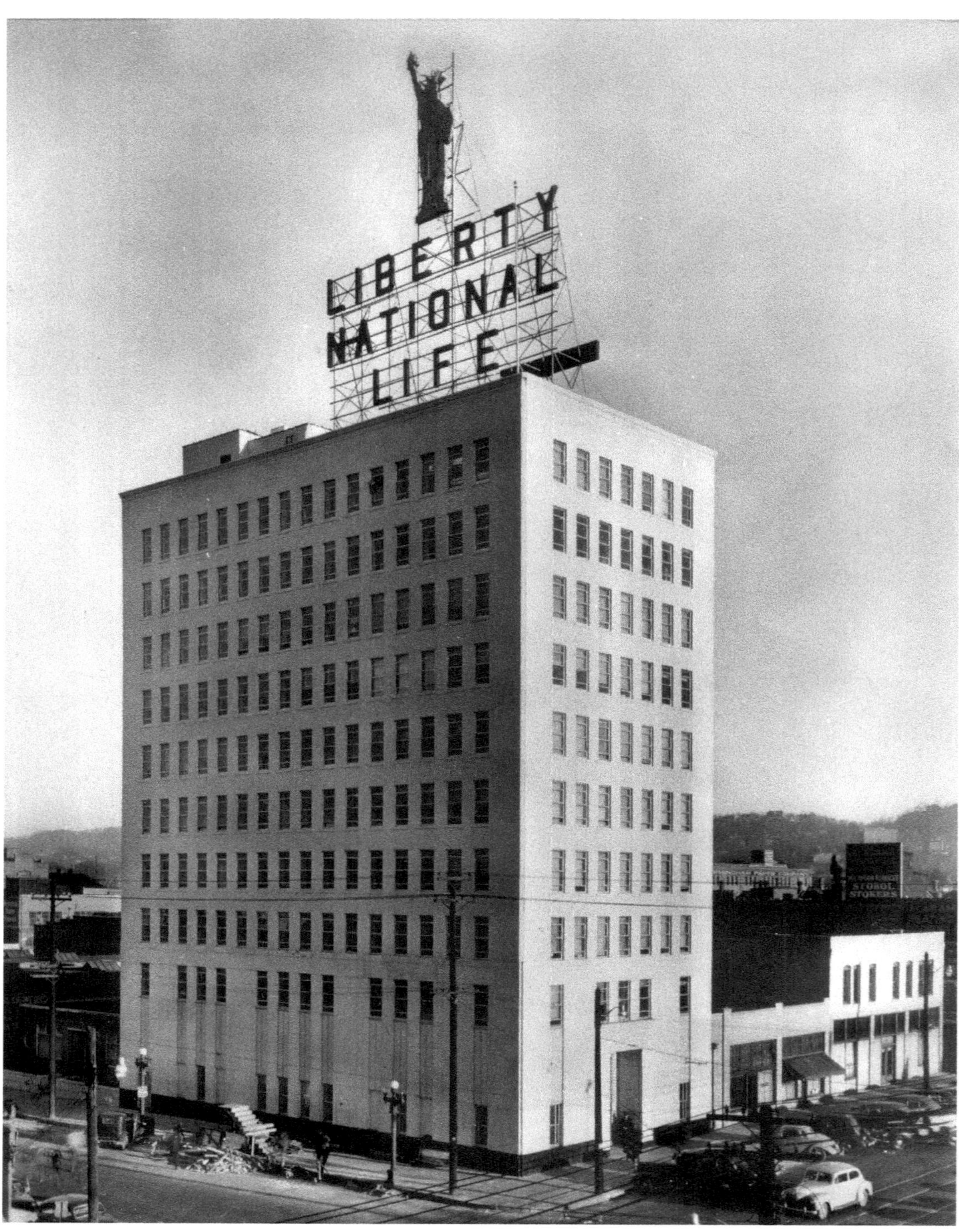

Liberty National Life Insurance Company in 1947, with renovations complete inside and out.

McWane Cast Iron Pipe Company, 1946. Producers of cast-iron pipe for water and gas service of all popular sizes at the time, McWane was the world's largest producer of two-inch cast-iron pipe. This new foundry was completed by Brice Building Company in 1947.

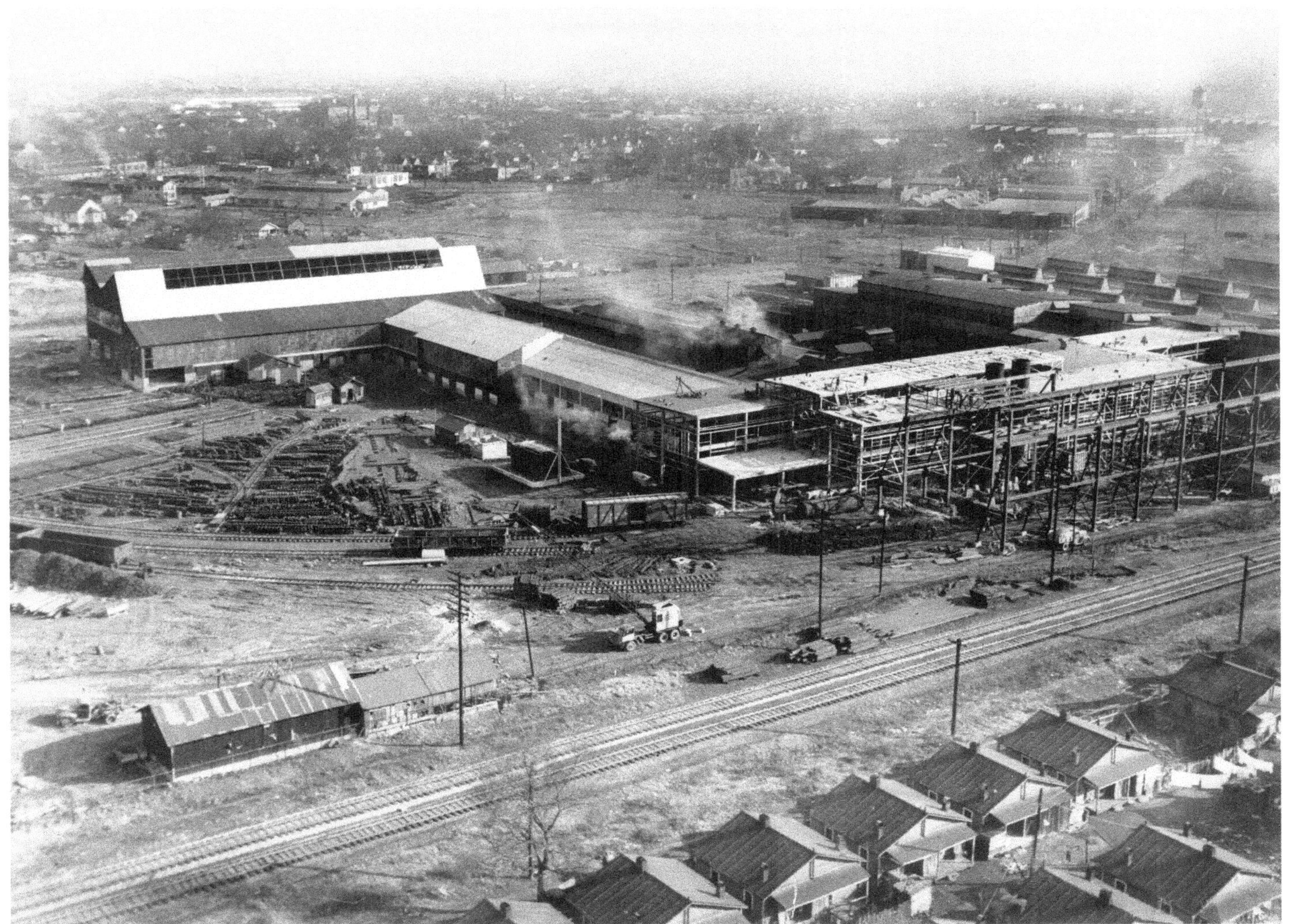

Popular Birmingham radio personality Joe Rumore, in 1948, appears to be interviewing a fowl either short on clucks or slow to crow.

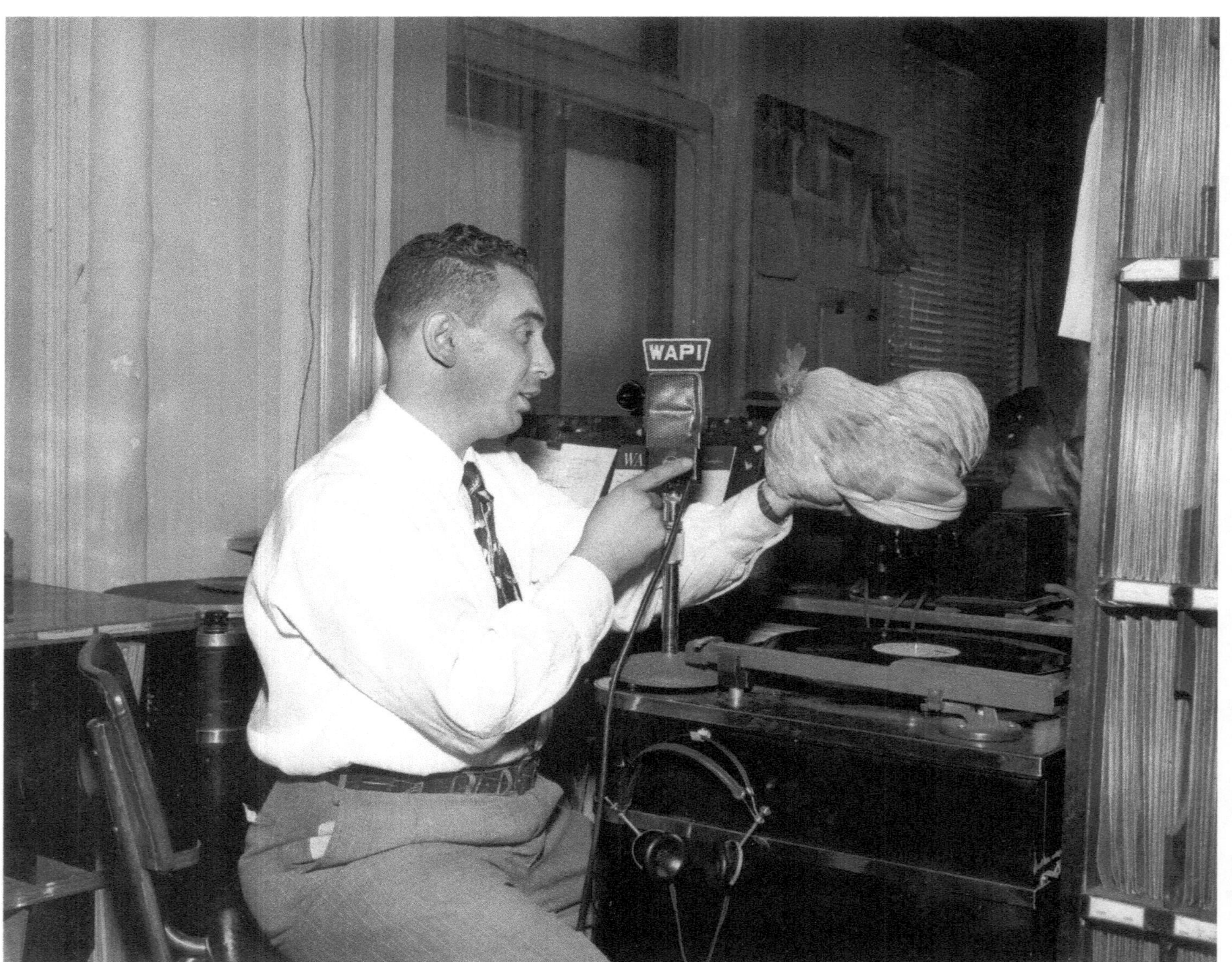

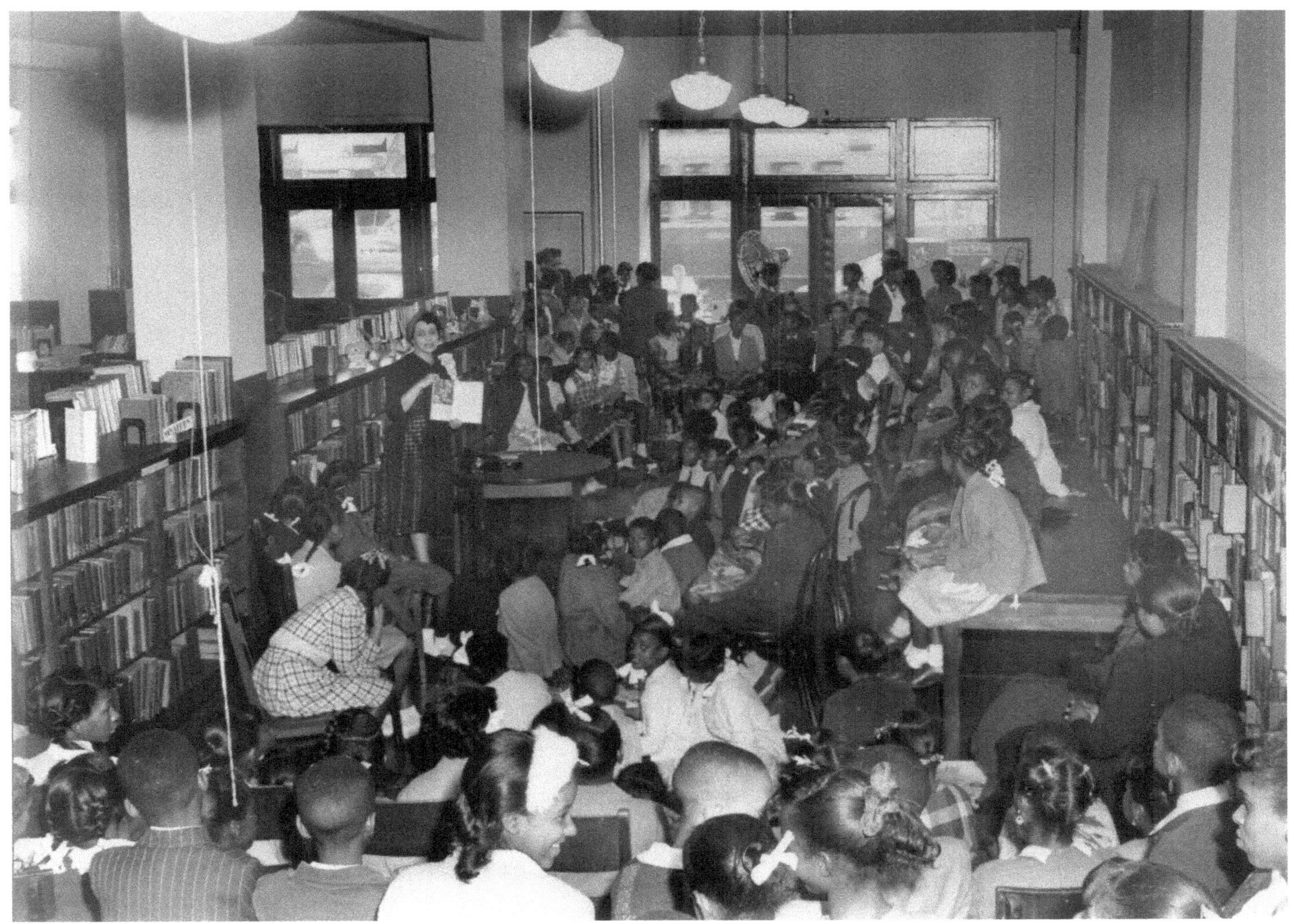

Prior to 1963, Birmingham operated a segregated library system with a Central Library and branches for whites and separate branch libraries for blacks. Birmingham's Booker T. Washington Branch opened in 1918 as Alabama's first such library for African Americans. Here, Birmingham author Ellen Tarry conducts a story time for children, around 1950.

Following Spread: Known during his lifetime as "Mr. Birmingham," Robert Jemison, Jr., developed many of the area's buildings and communities, from Fairfield to Mountain Book. Here the Jemison Company headquarters is shown on Twenty-first Street North.

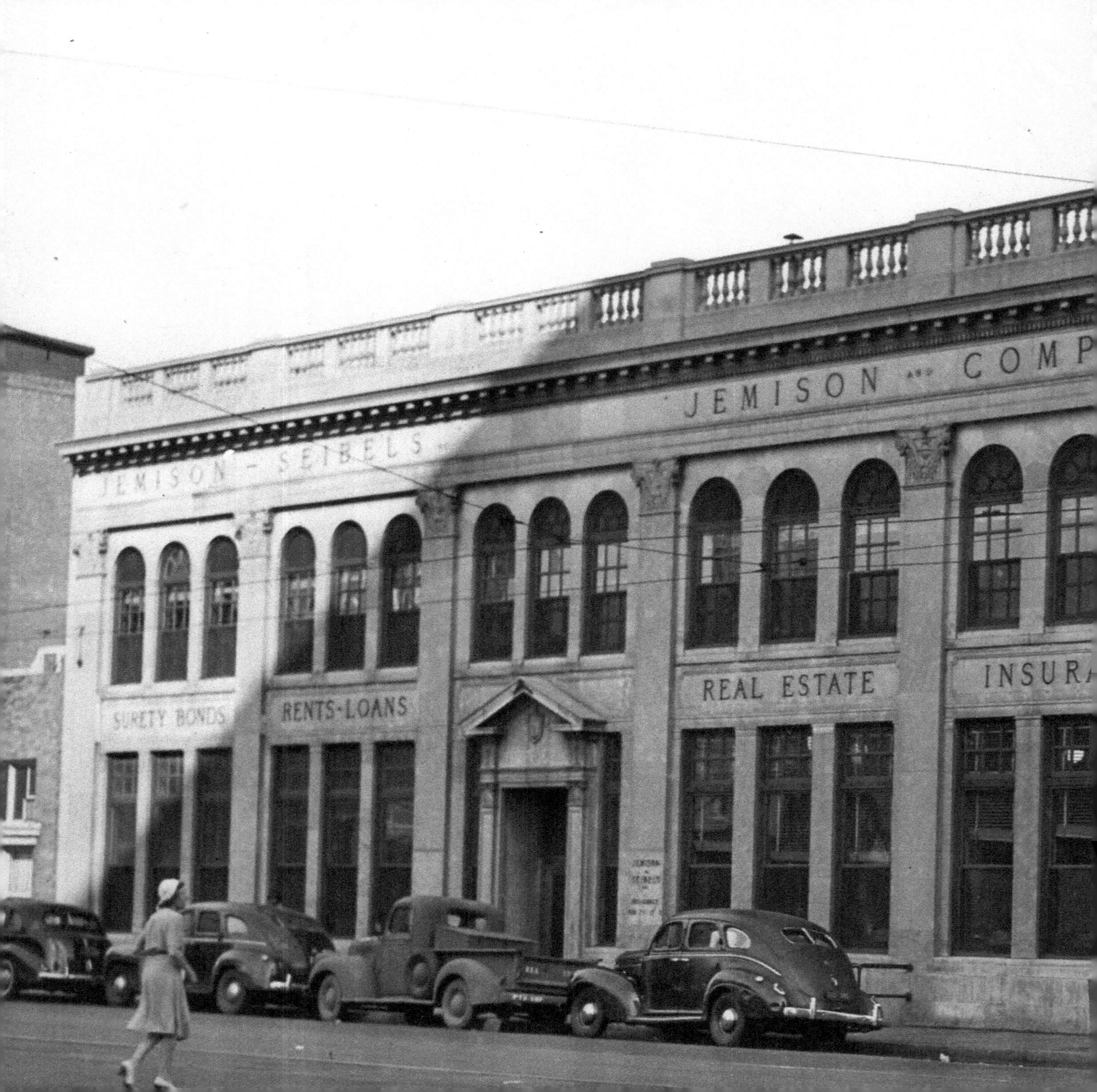
JEMISON - SEIBELS
JEMISON AND COMP
SURETY BONDS
RENTS-LOANS
REAL ESTATE
INSURA

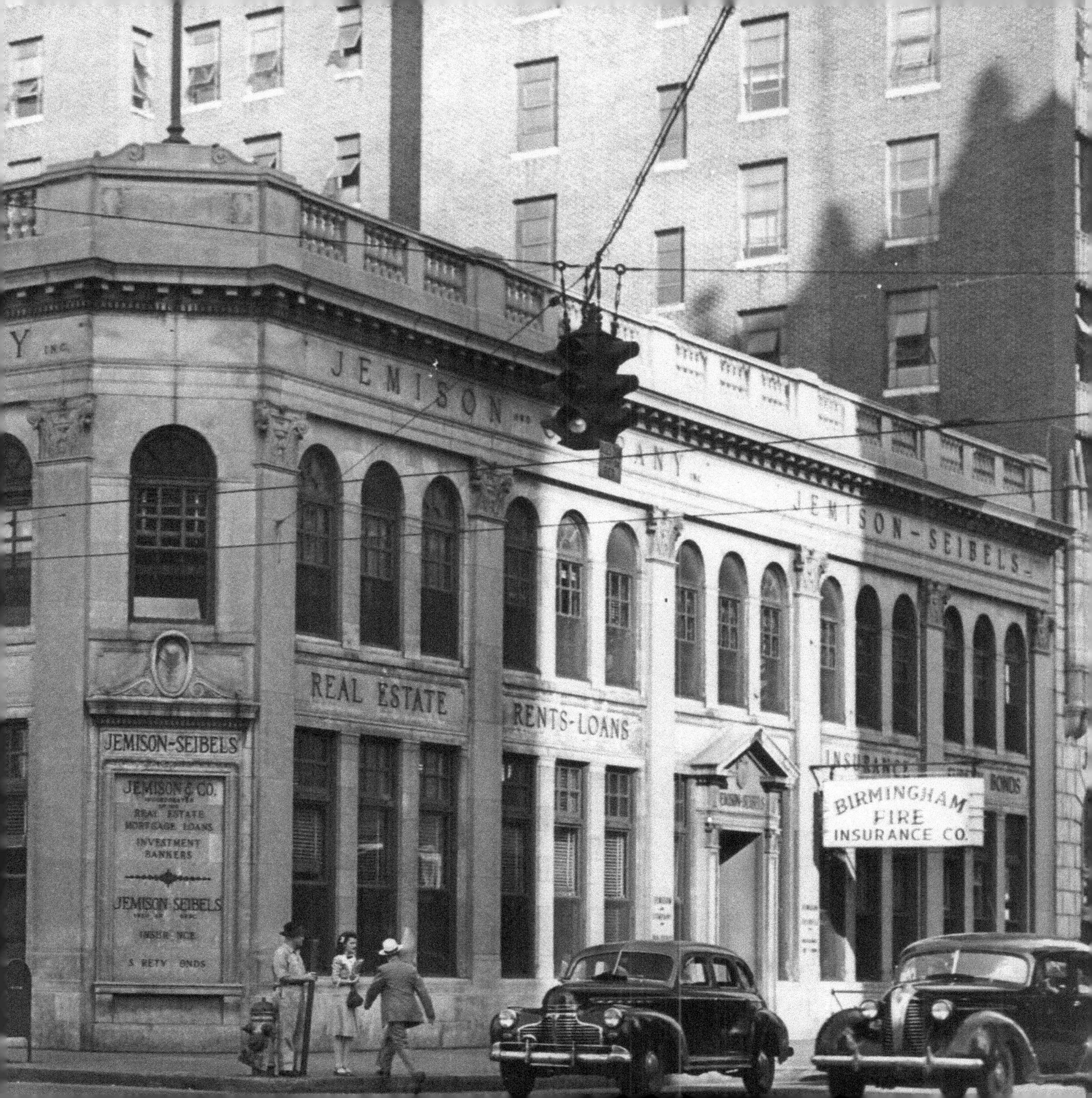
JEMISON
JEMISON-SEIBELS
REAL ESTATE
RENTS-LOANS
JEMISON-SEIBELS
JEMISON & CO.
REAL ESTATE
MORTGAGE LOANS
INVESTMENT
BANKERS
JEMISON-SEIBELS
BIRMINGHAM
FIRE
INSURANCE CO.
BONDS

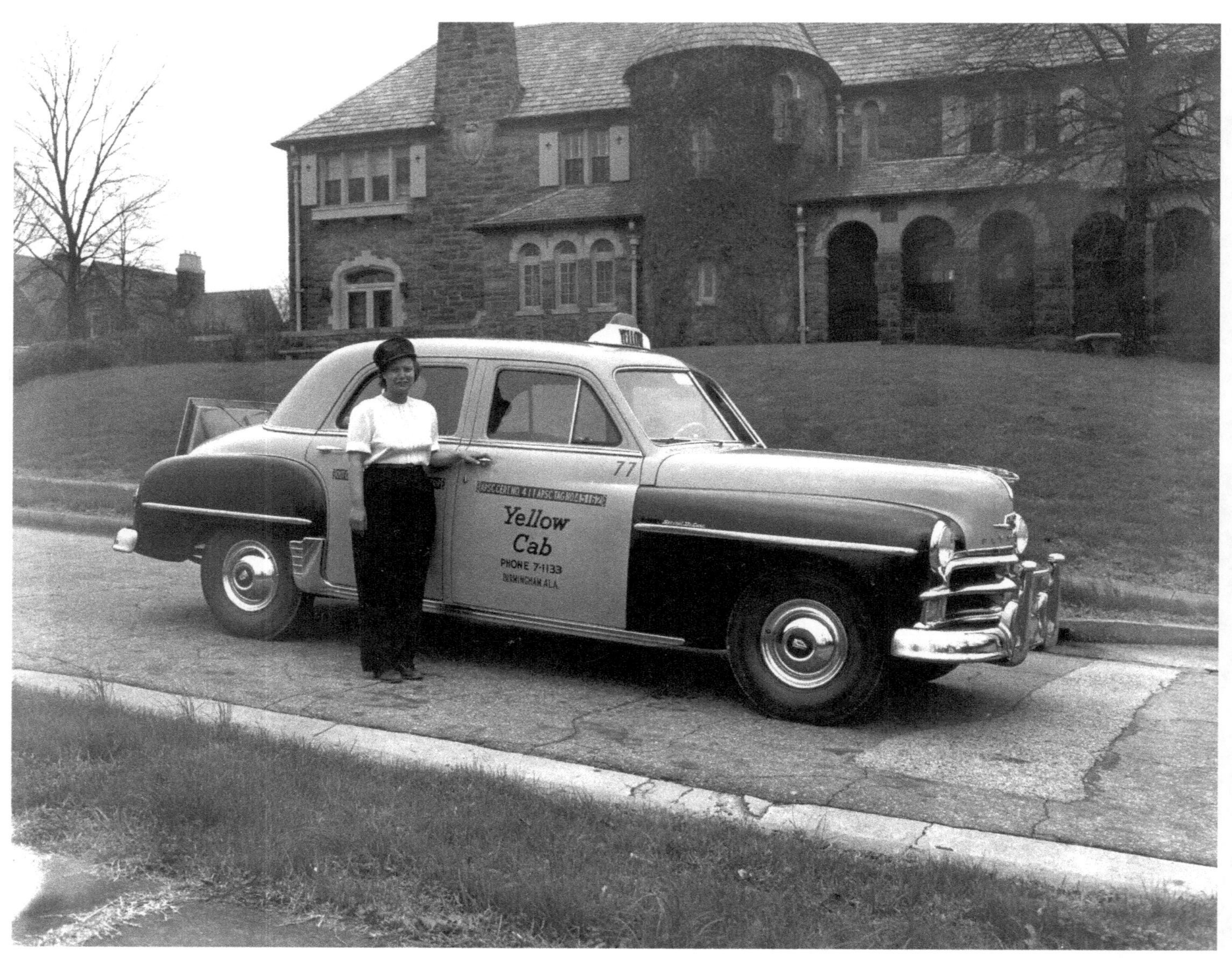

An early taxi, driven by a woman, poses for the camera on Stratford Road about 1950.

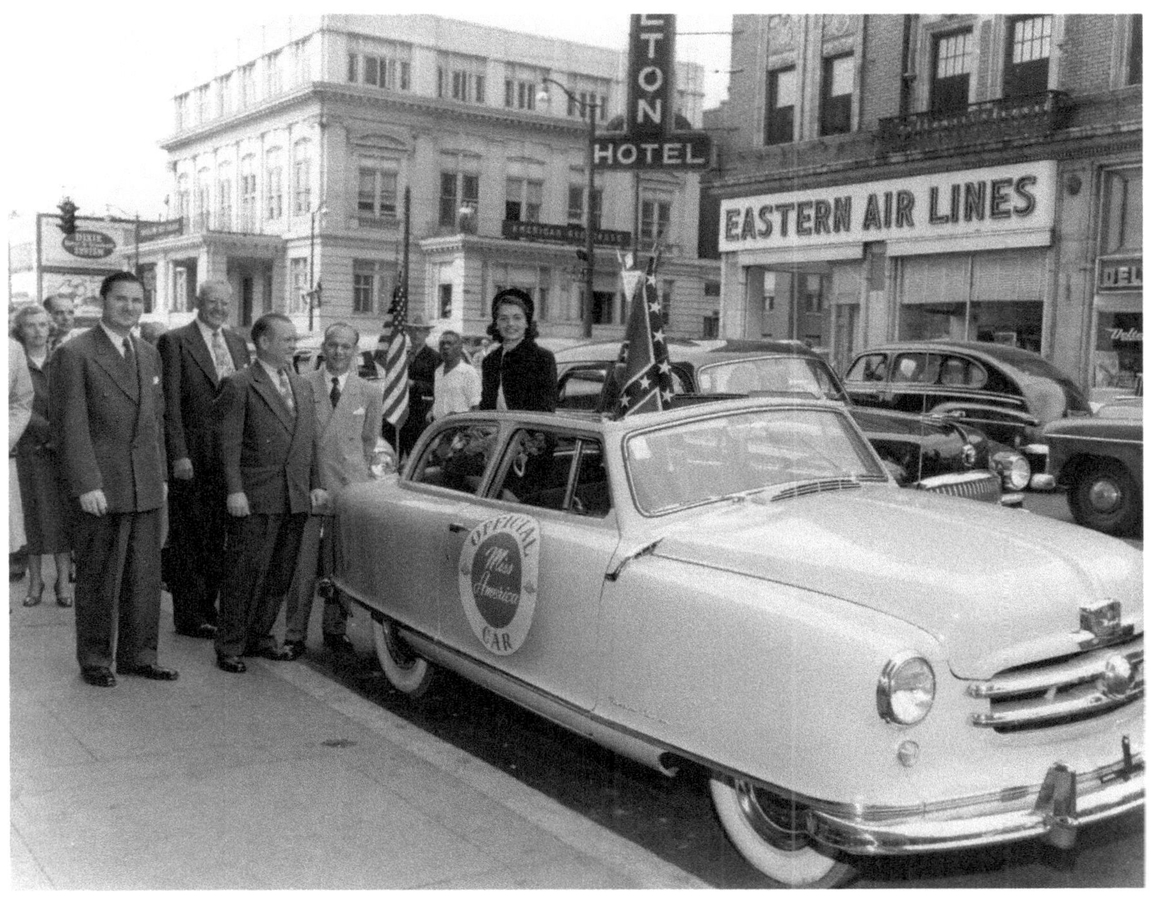

Yolanda Betbeze, the first Miss Alabama to be selected Miss America, attends a parade in her honor in downtown Birmingham in 1951. In later years, Betbeze took part in civil rights demonstrations and sit-ins.

WBRC television broadcast the returns for the 1952 presidential election, in which Republican Dwight Eisenhower and Democrat Adlai Stevenson were running for the office.

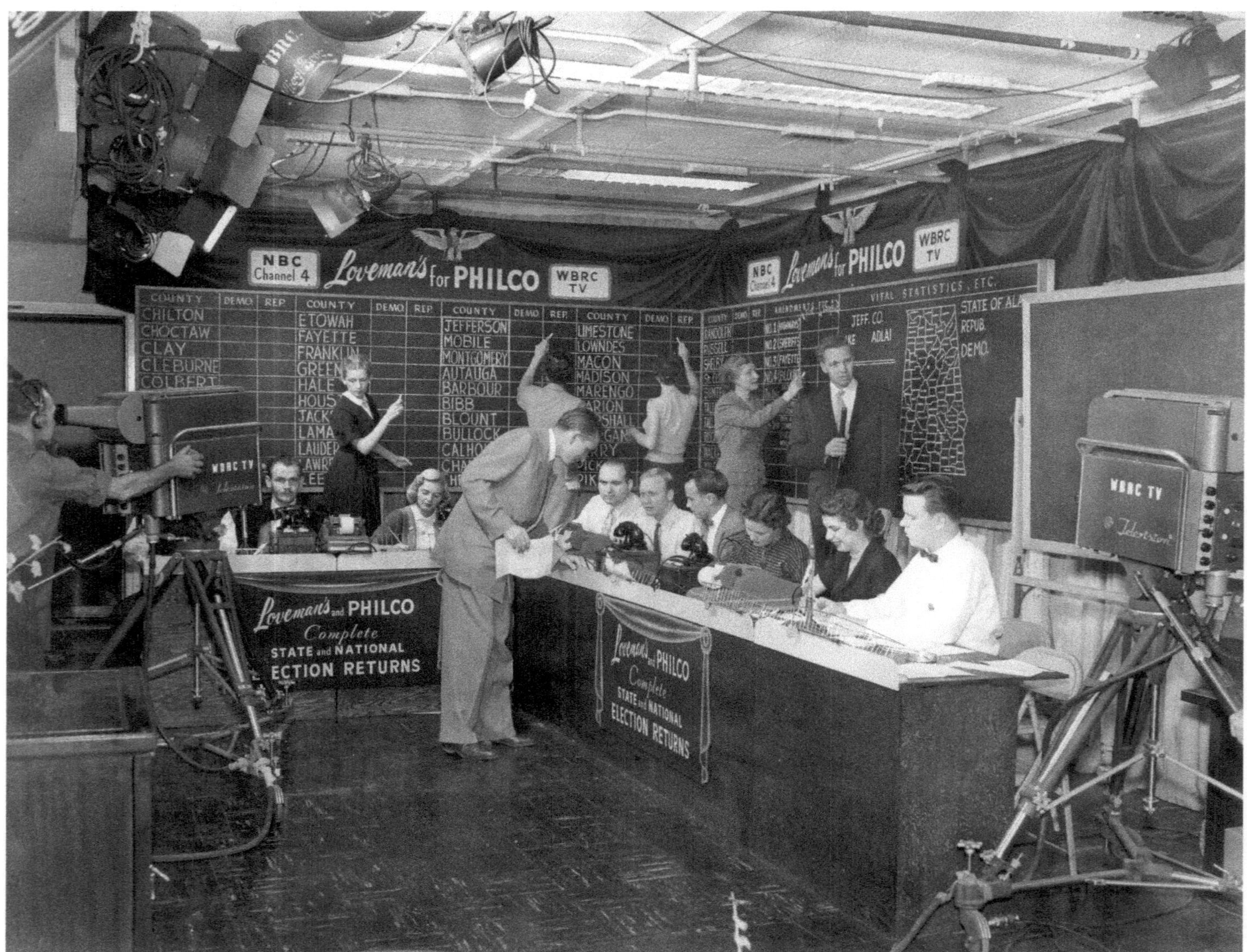

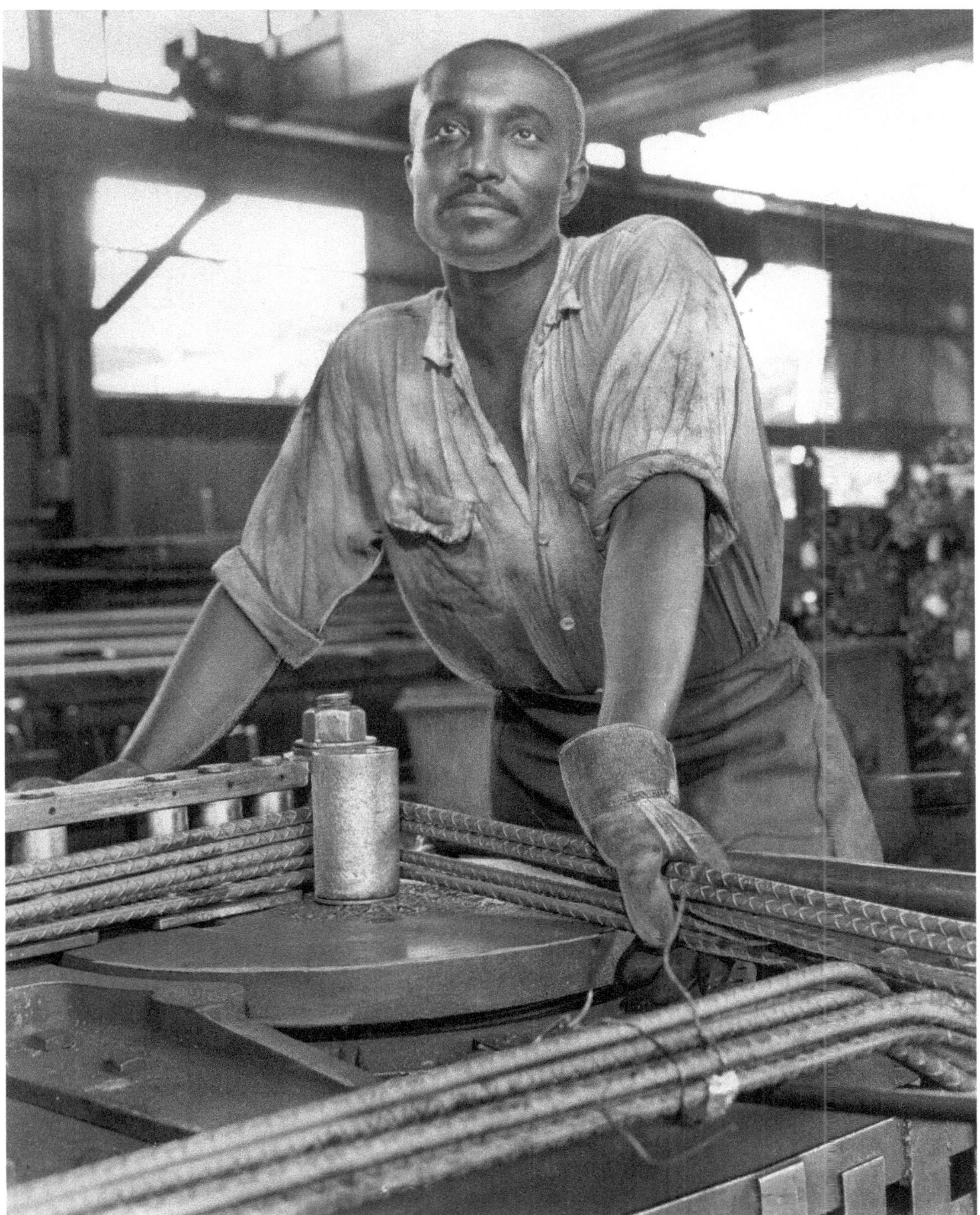

At Connors Steel Company in 1952, Willie B. Smith operates a machine that bends steel bars to be used in reinforced concrete.

Aerial view of Woodrow Wilson Park (now Linn Park), with Birmingham City Hall to the left and the Jefferson County Courthouse and Birmingham Public Library to the right, 1952.

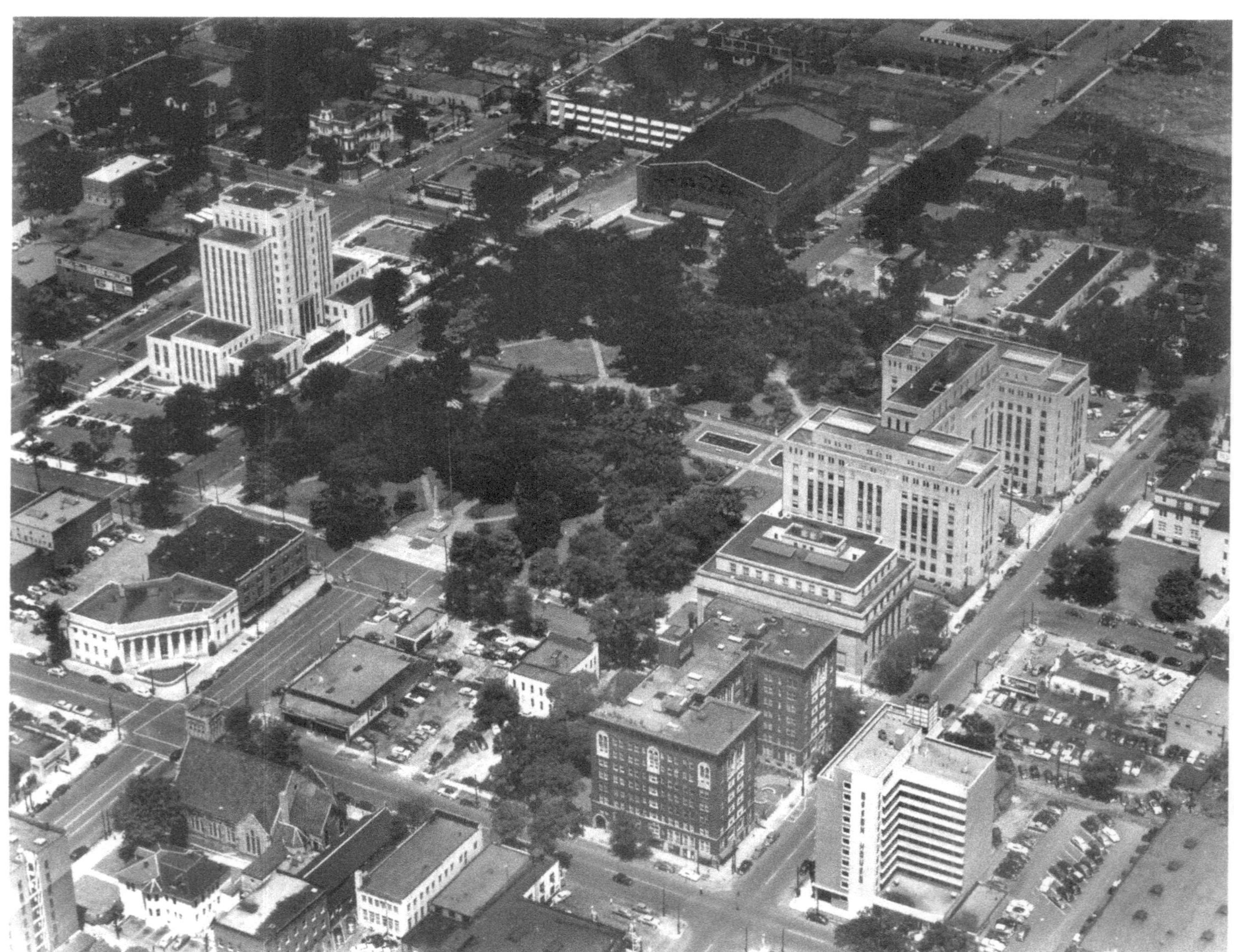

For decades, people in rural areas looked forward to the visits from the Birmingham Public Library's bookmobile. Shown here in the 1950s, this bookmobile was called a "traveling branch."

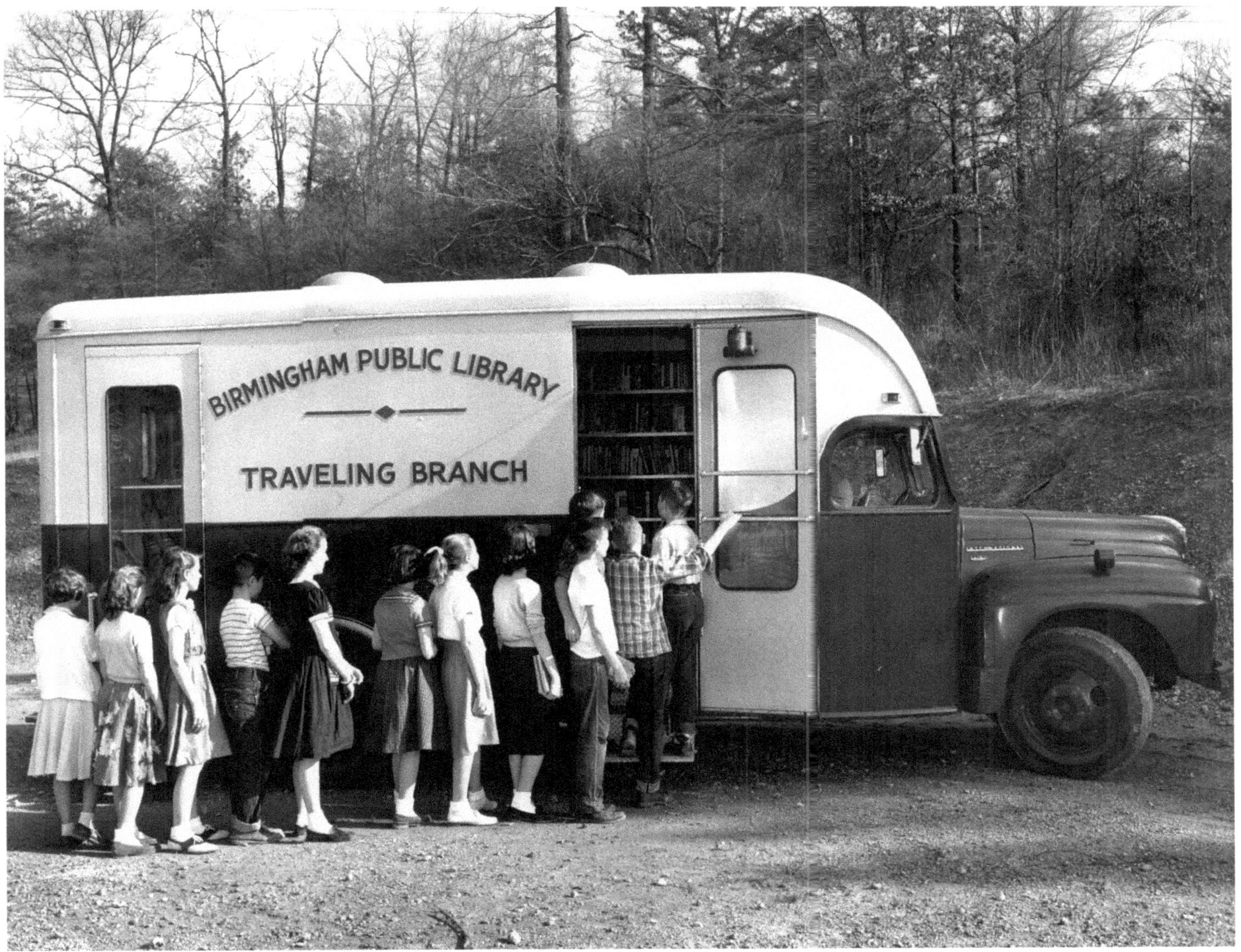

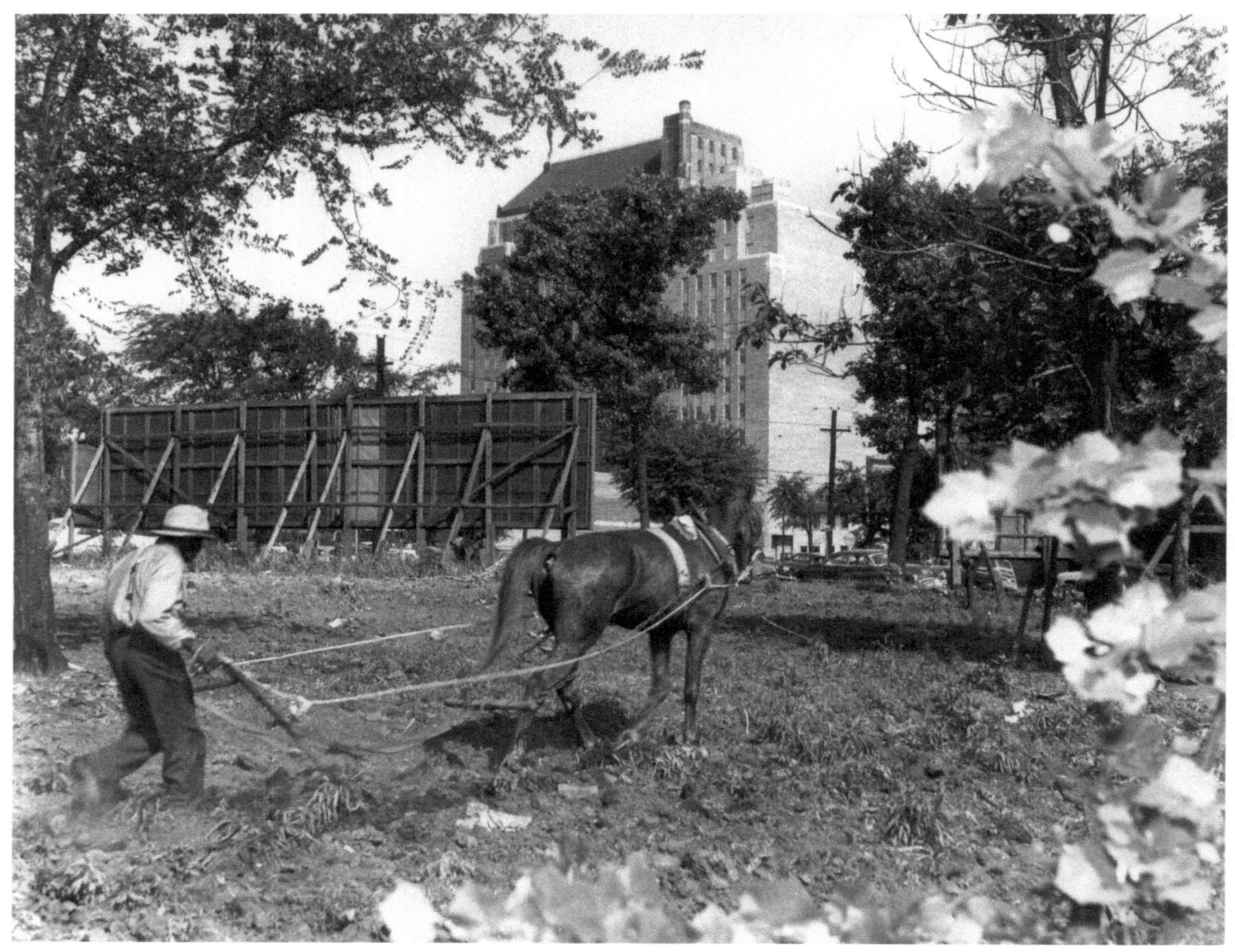

In the spring of 1953, sixty-eight-years-old Ed Burton plows the lot behind his Seventeenth Street North home. Burton grew vegetables to sell and hauled fertilizer for other "city farmers." The tall building in the background is the Alabama Power Company headquarters.

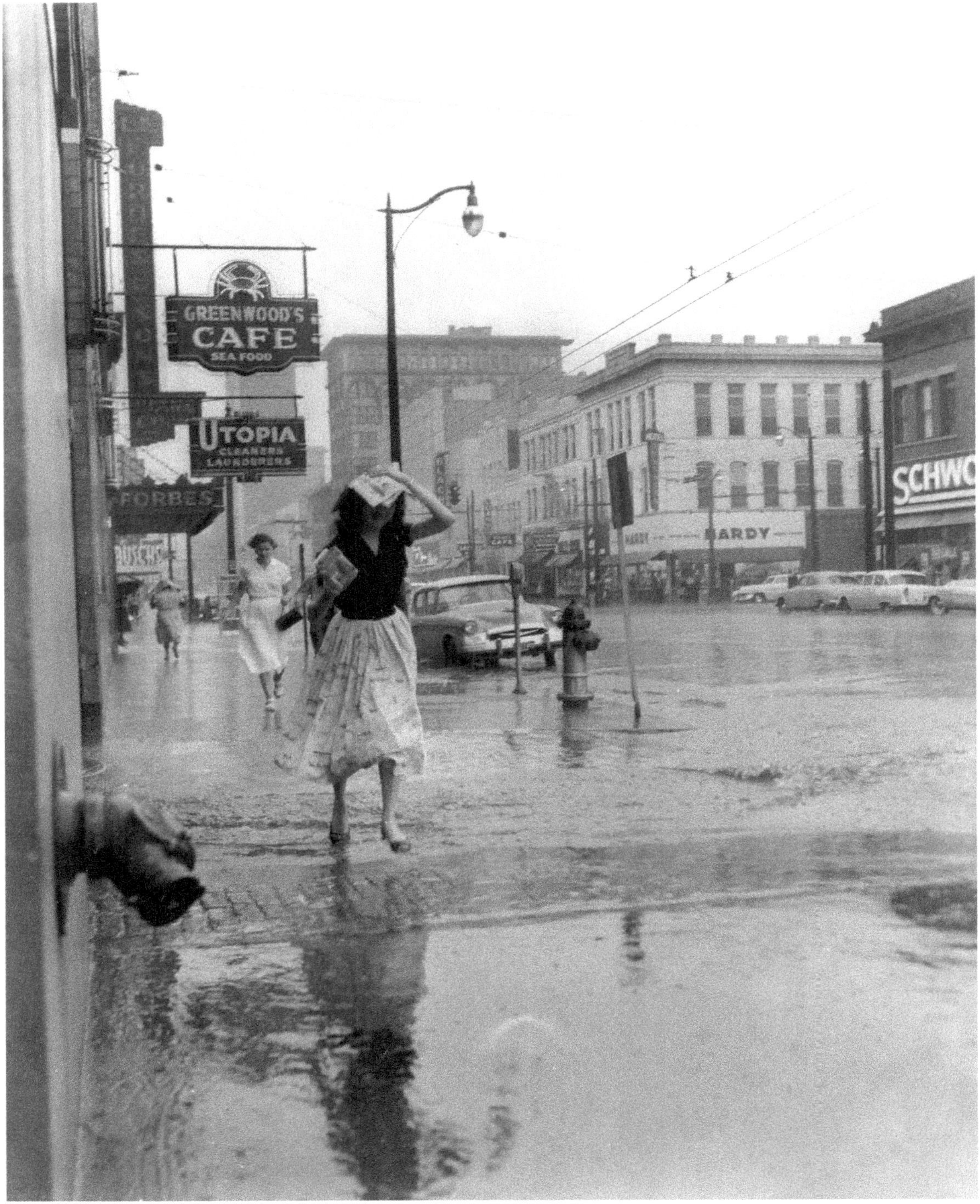

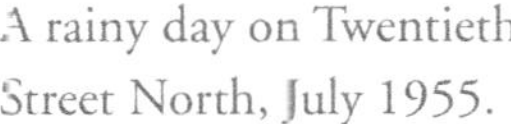

A rainy day on Twentieth Street North, July 1955.

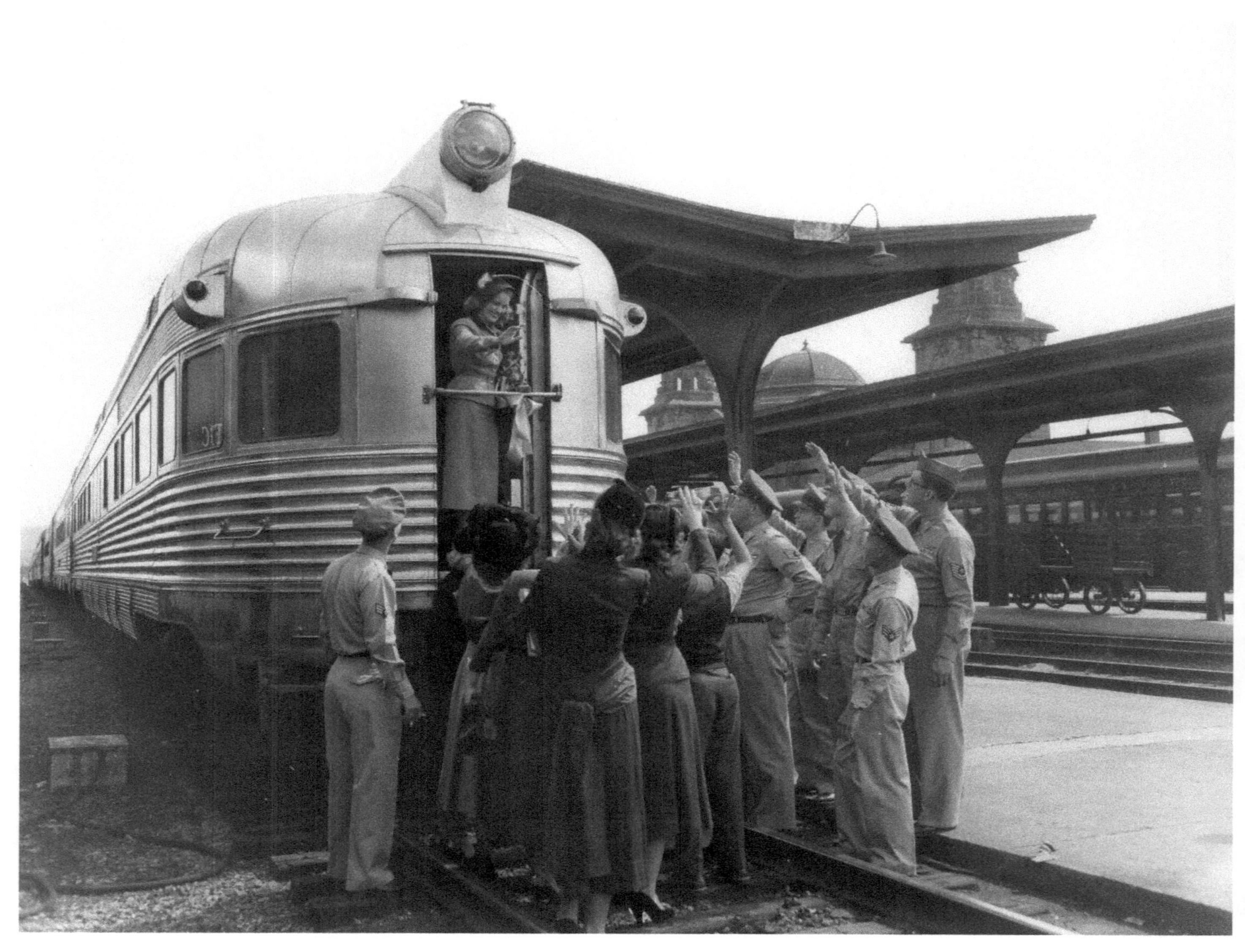

Miss Alabama Gwen Harmon leaves Terminal Station in 1952.

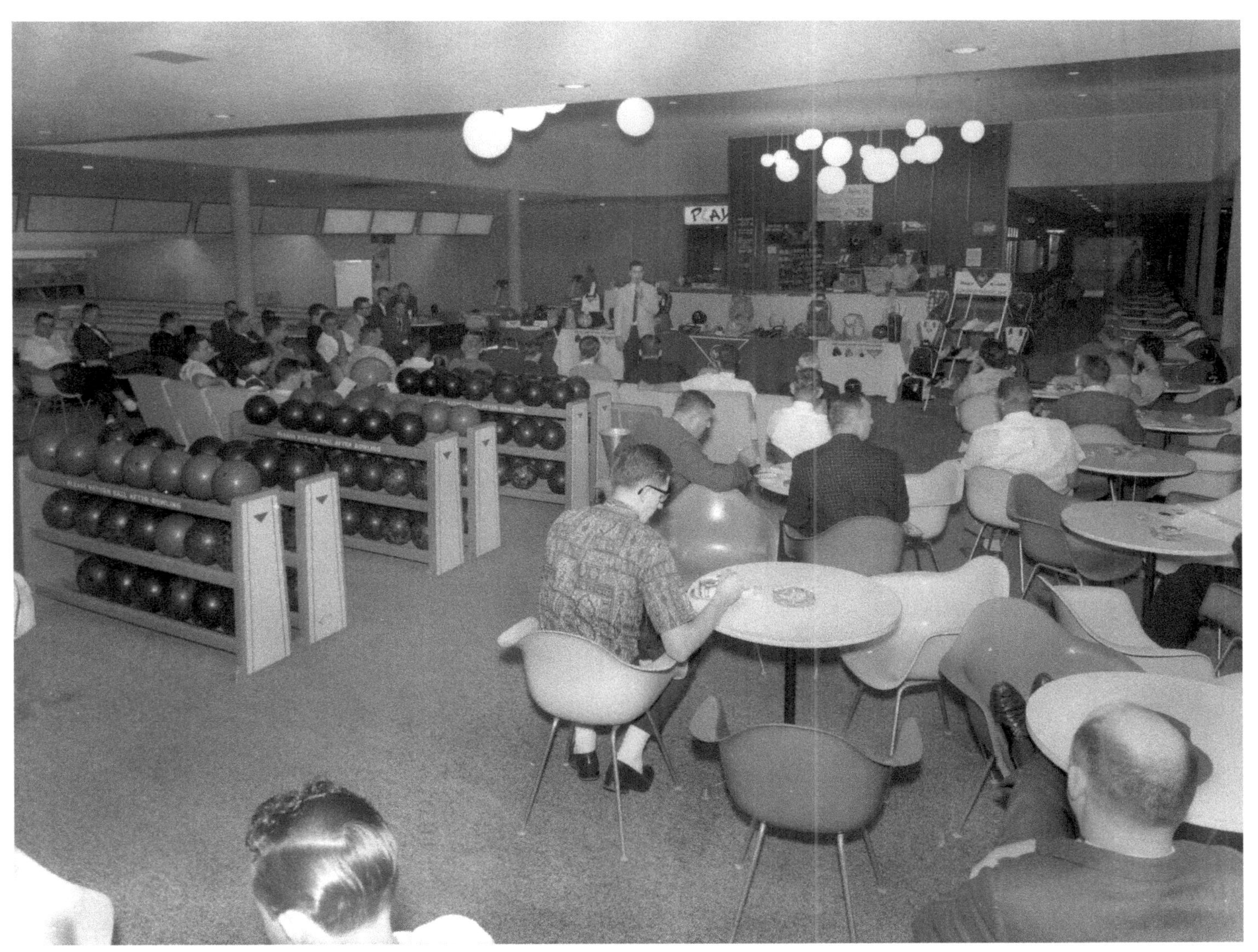

Ready to bowl at Eastwood.

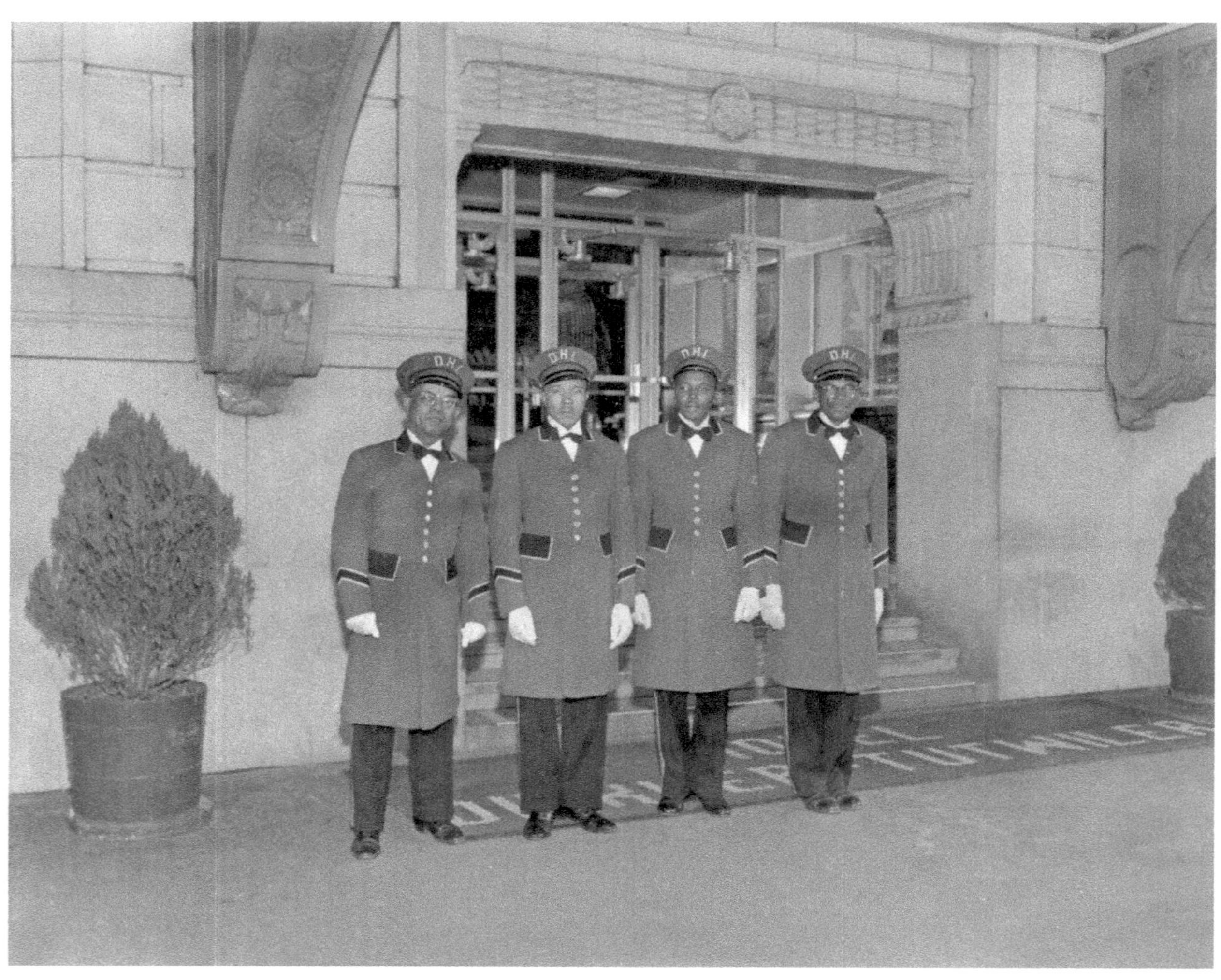

Bellhops at the Tutwiler Hotel, 1954.

Teenagers gather to hear WSGN radio broadcasting from the Sky Castle, 1956.

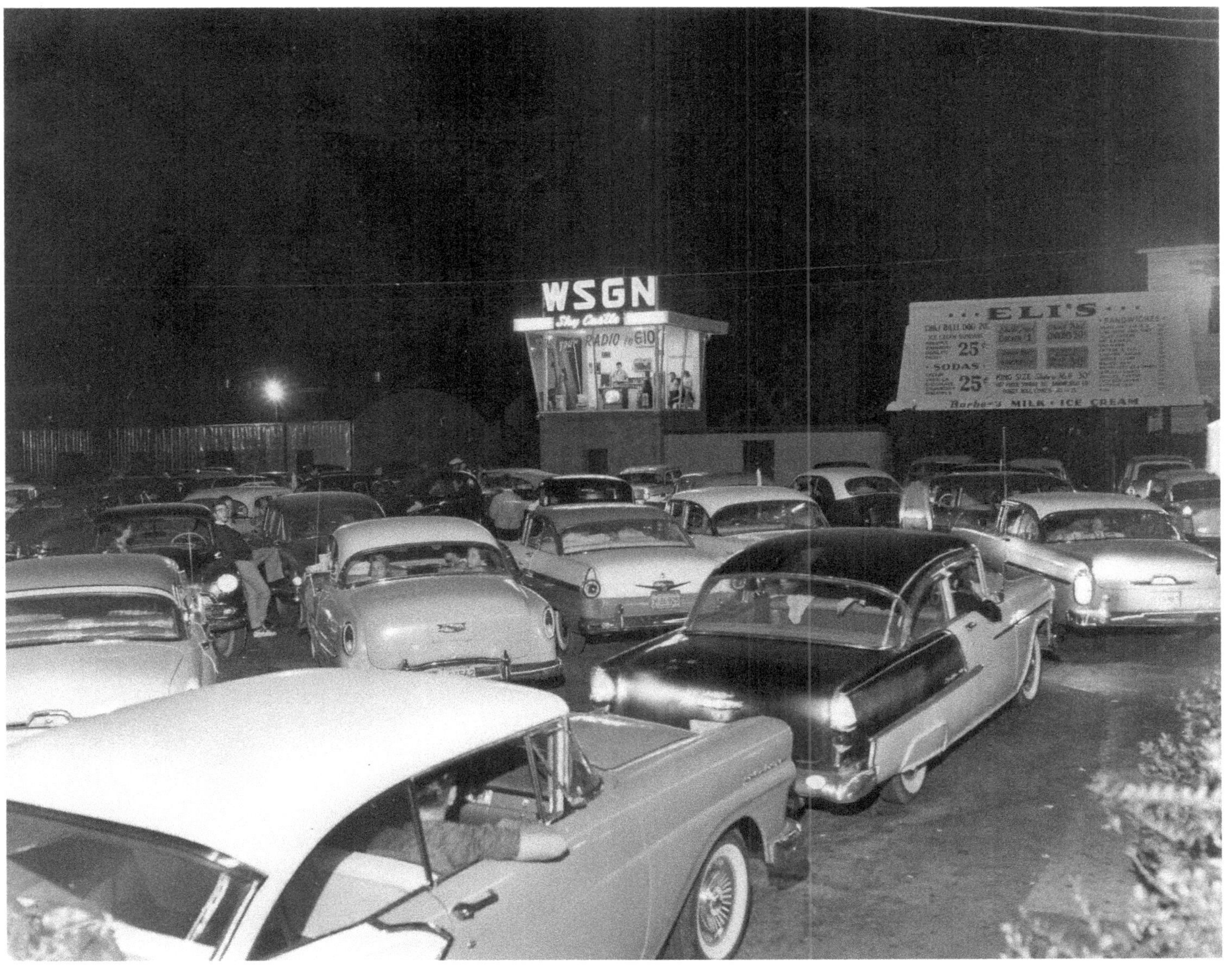

Soap Box Derby race, July 1956.

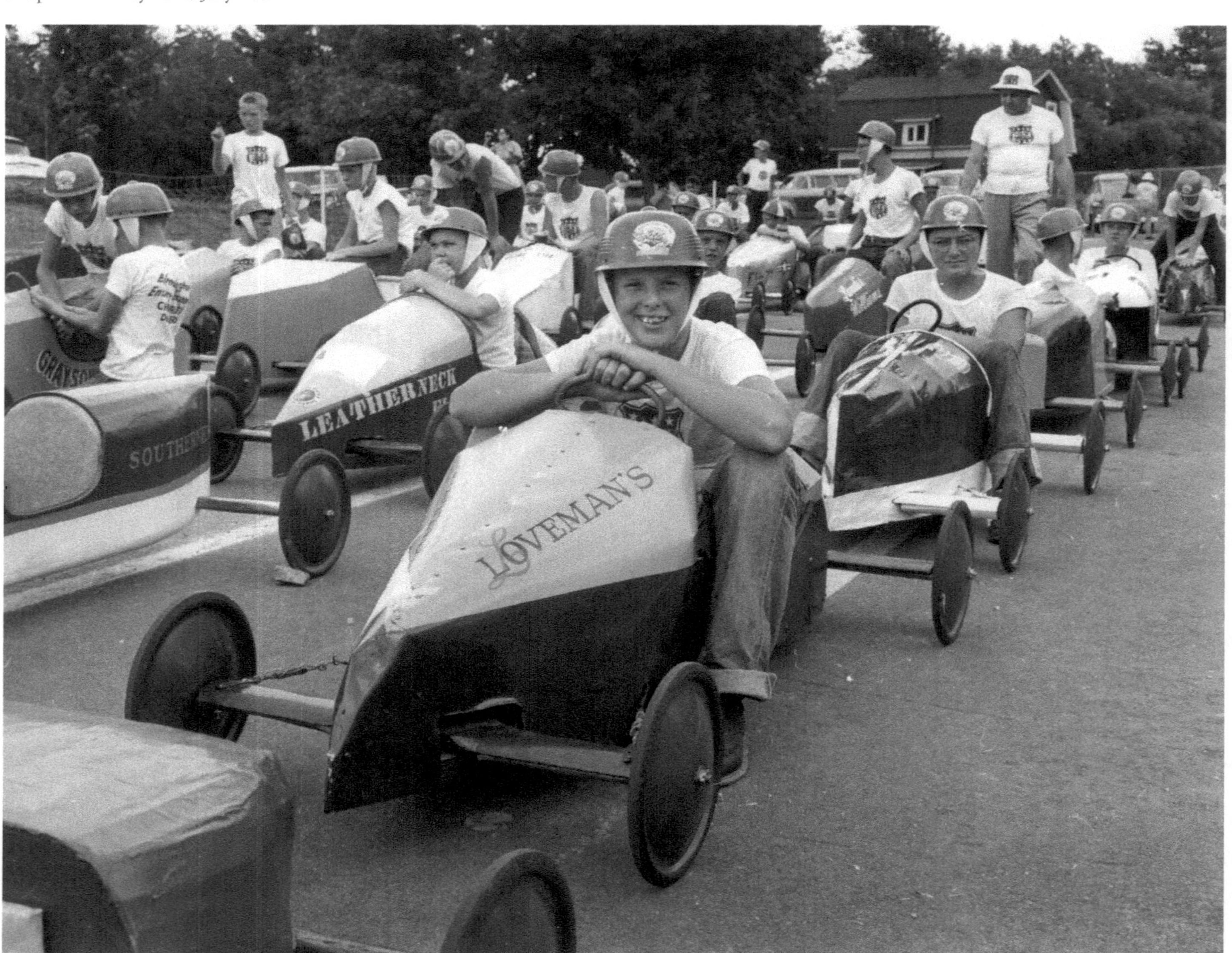

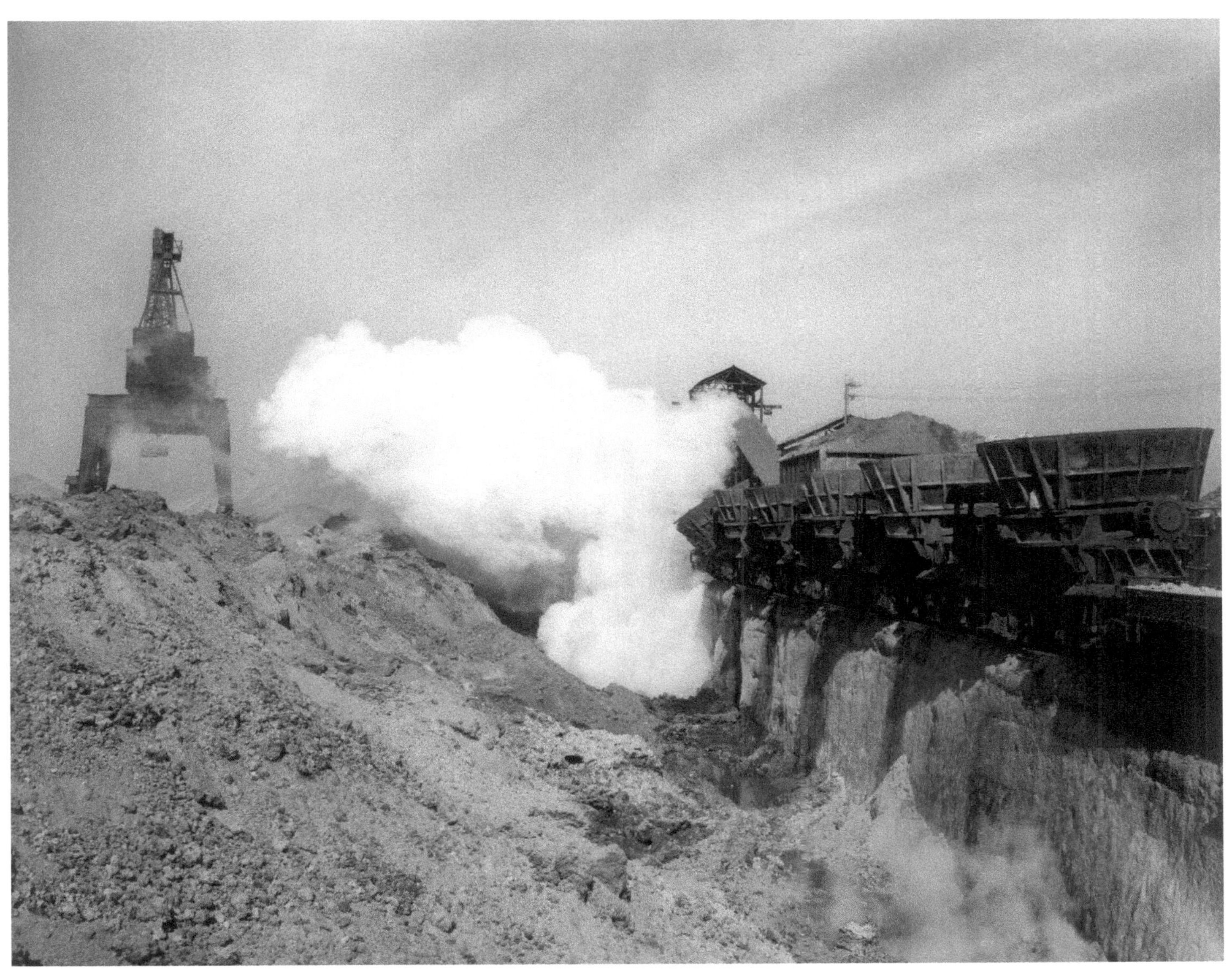

Expanded slag pit at Ensley. Vulcan Materials Company's predecessor, Birmingham Slag, took slag, a waste product from Birmingham's steel industry, and processed it for use as railroad ballast and an aggregate in road building.

A concrete truck (with the Birmingham Slag Division logo) is loaded with ready-mixed concrete at a Vulcan Materials plant in Fairfield. The Birmingham Slag Division was in existence from 1956 to 1964, when it became a part of Vulcan's Southeast Division.

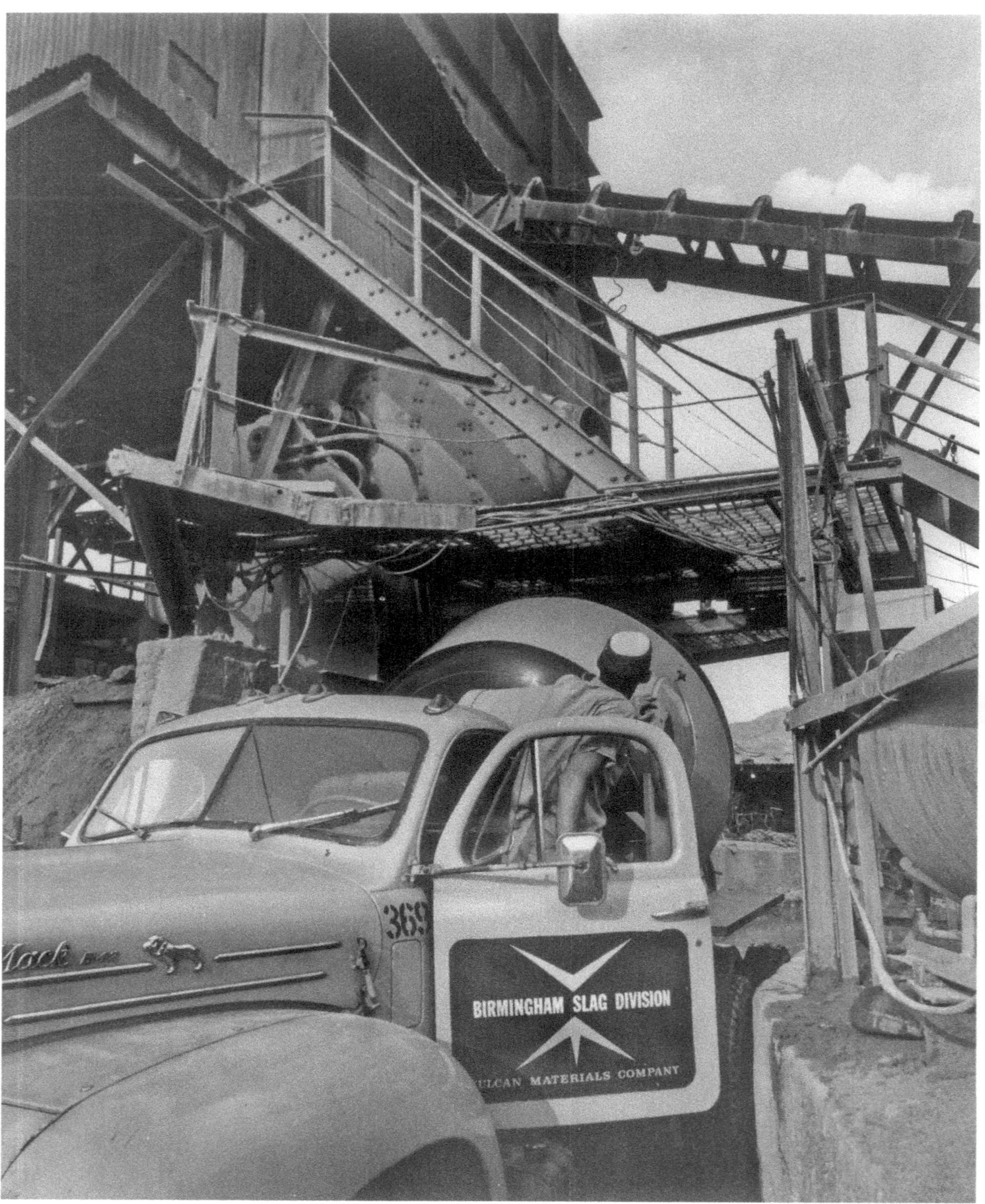

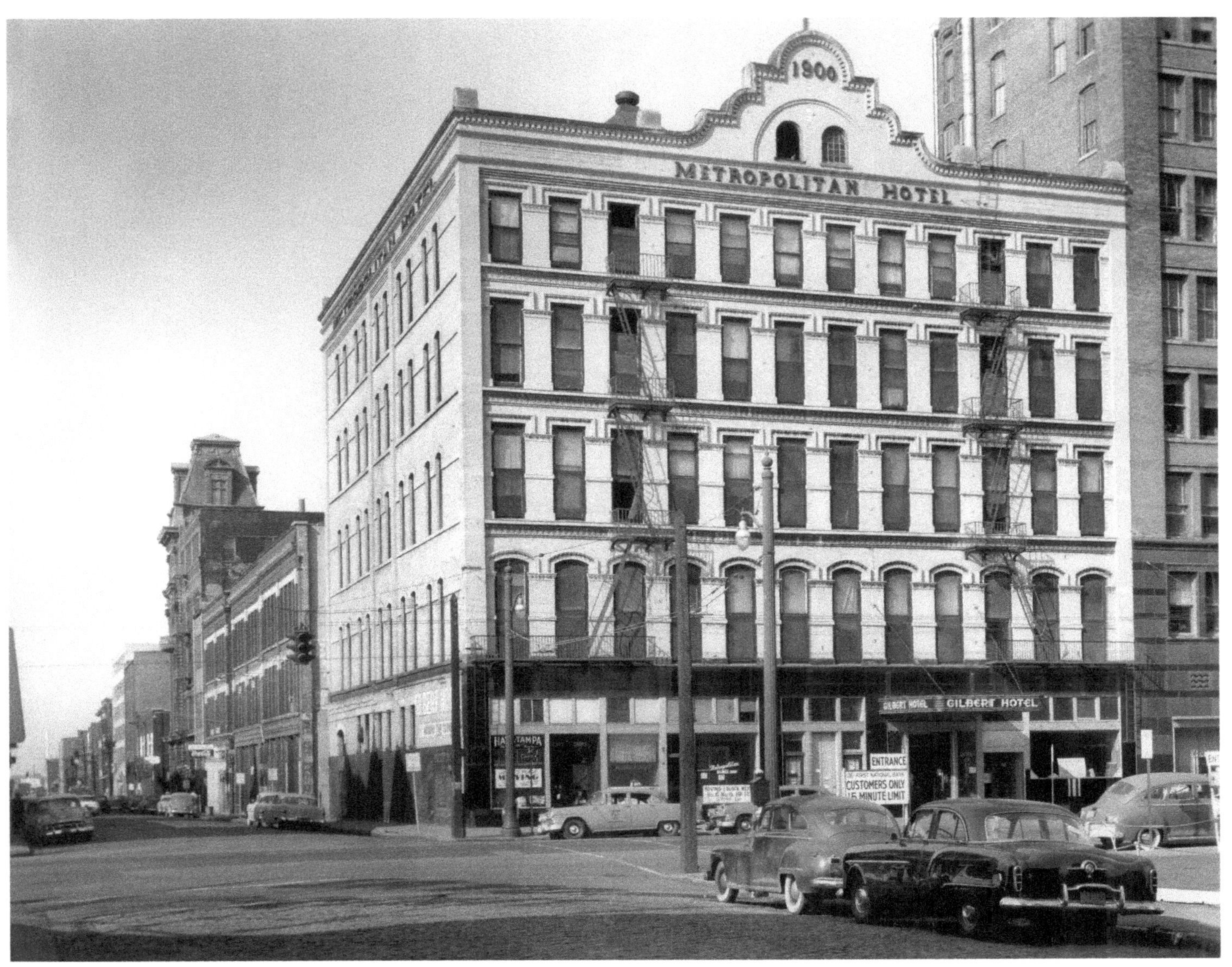

The old Metropolitan Hotel, well past its glory days and renamed the Gilbert, on the corner of Twentieth Street and Morris Avenue, 1950s.

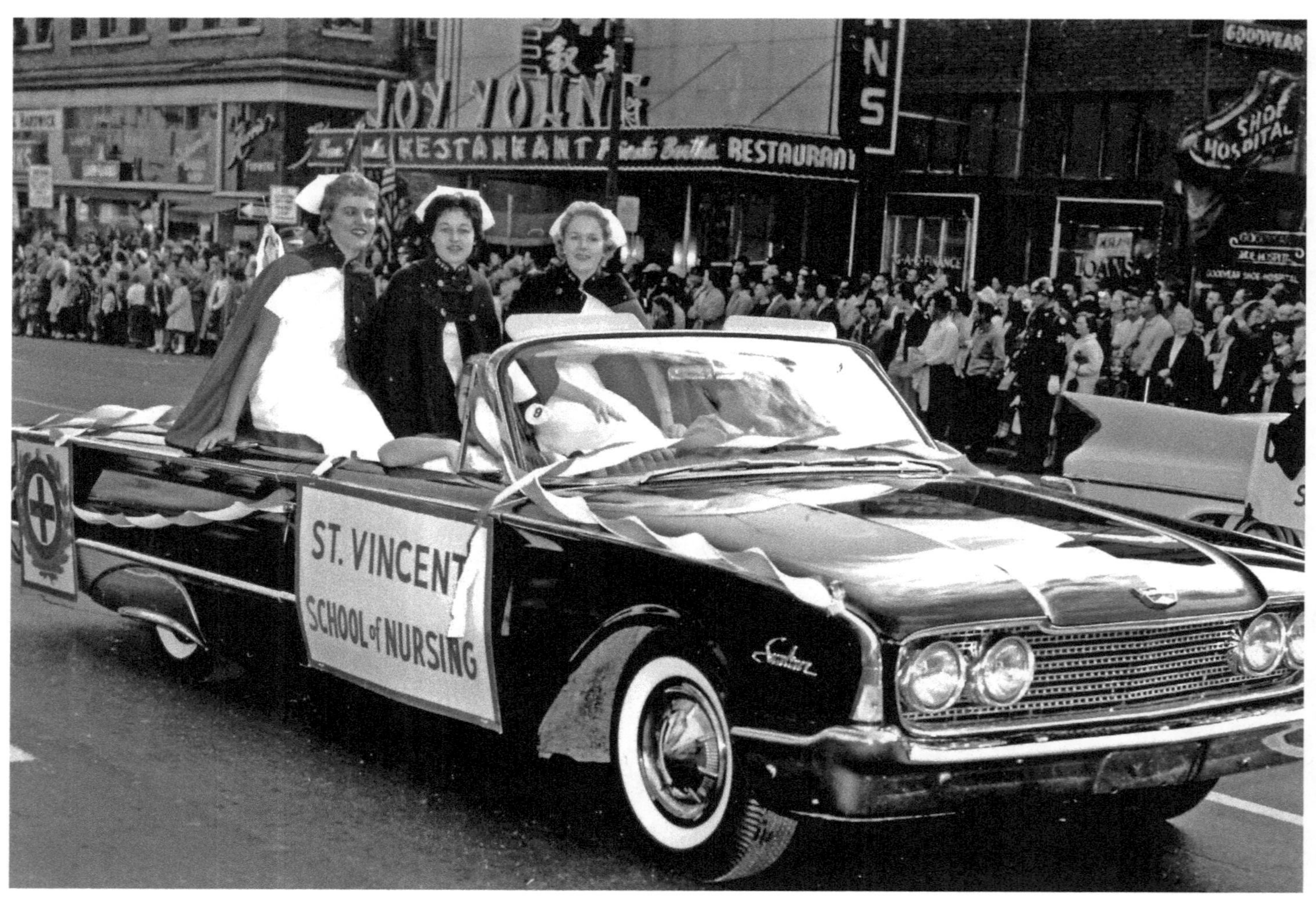

Students from St. Vincent's School of Nursing participate in the 1959 Veterans Day parade.

Pantages Theater on the corner of Third Avenue North and Seventeenth Street. Prior to 1963, most public facilities in Birmingham were racially segregated, and here the entrance to the "Colored Balcony" is visible on the side of the building.

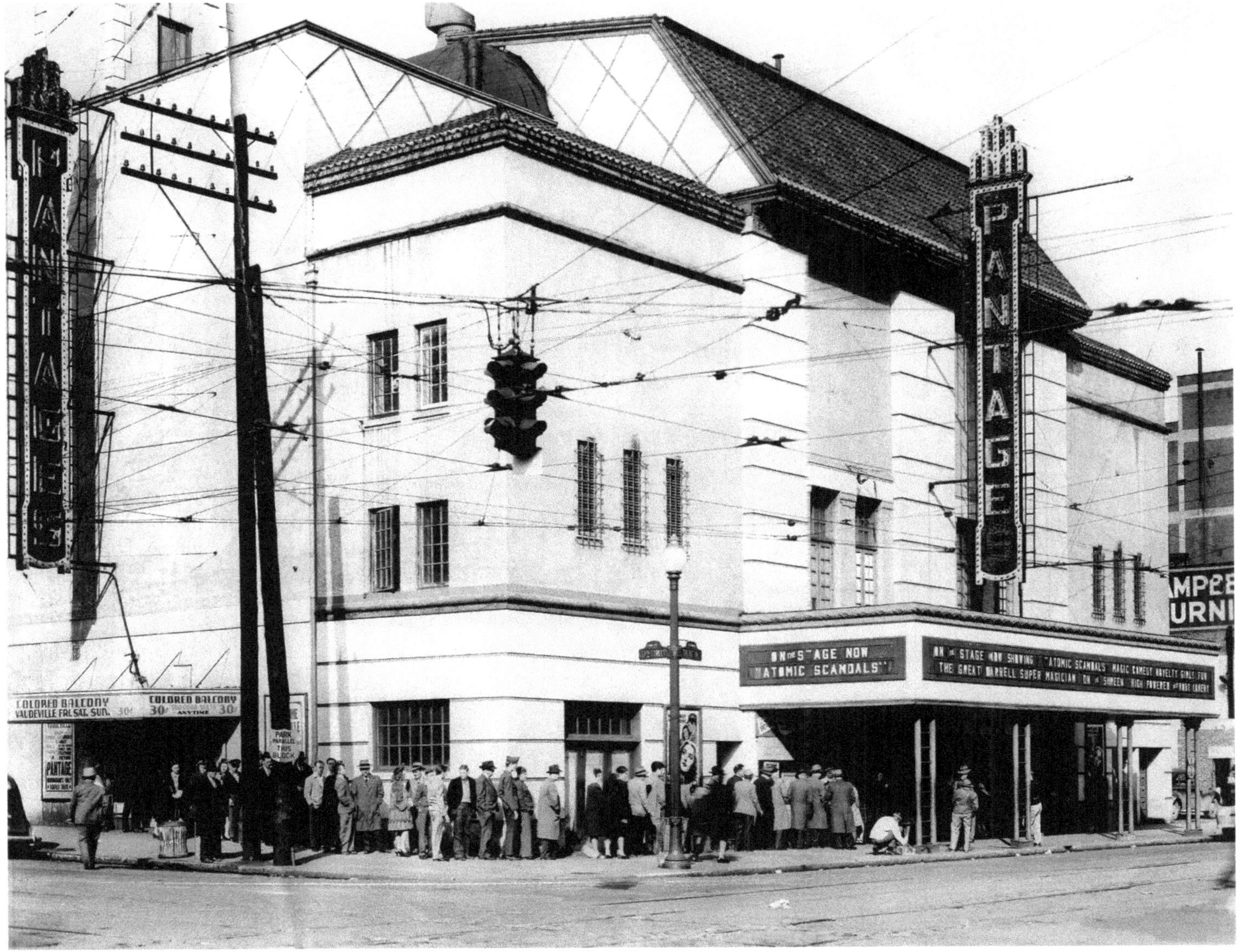

The Morris Hotel was demolished in 1959. A parking deck now occupies the site.

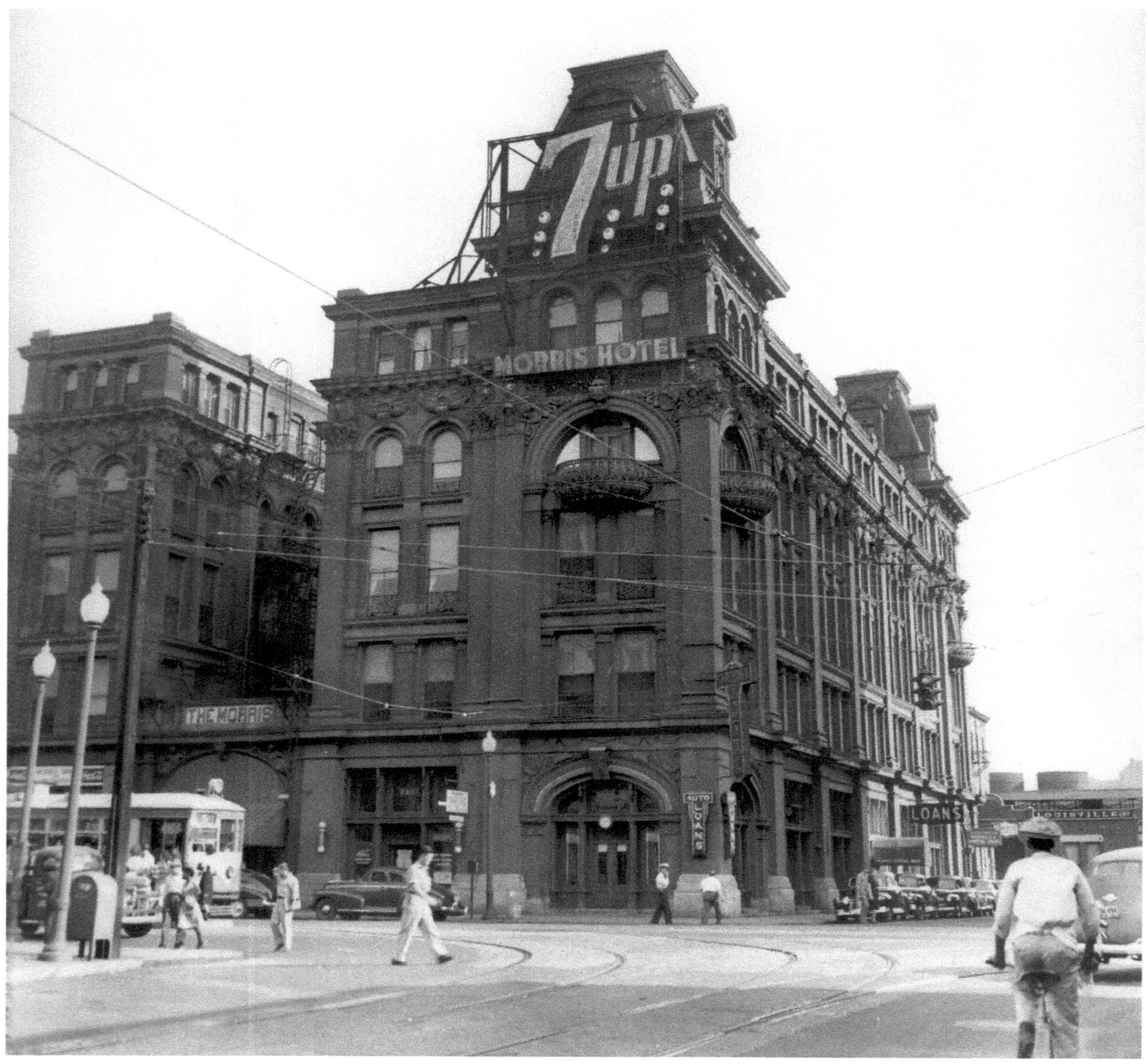

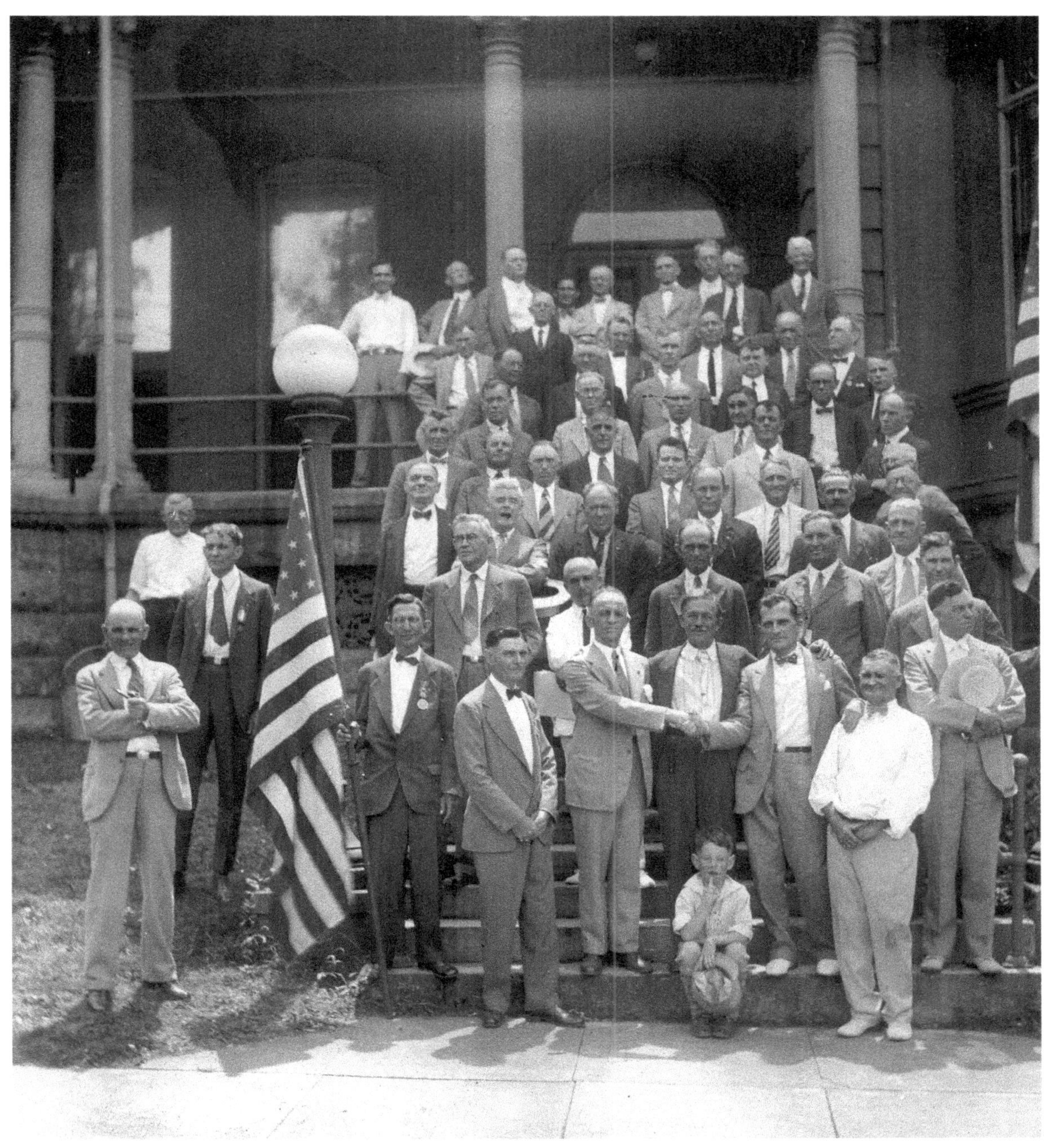

Spanish-American War veterans hold a reunion at the Fraternal Order of Elks clubhouse. The war had ended so quickly in 1898 that most Birmingham area veterans never saw combat, or even left the continental United States.

Sisters seated on the front steps of St. Vincent's Hospital.

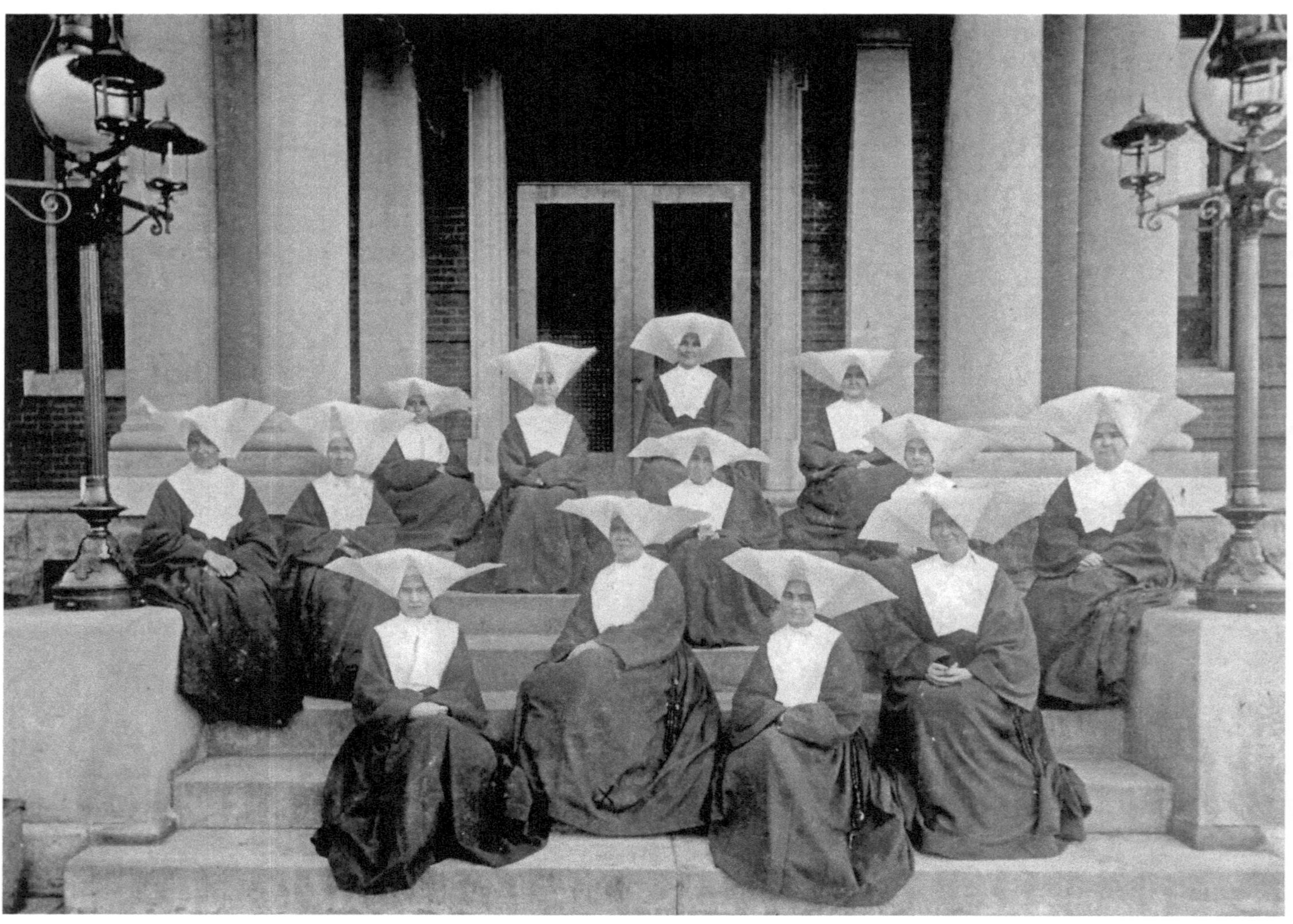

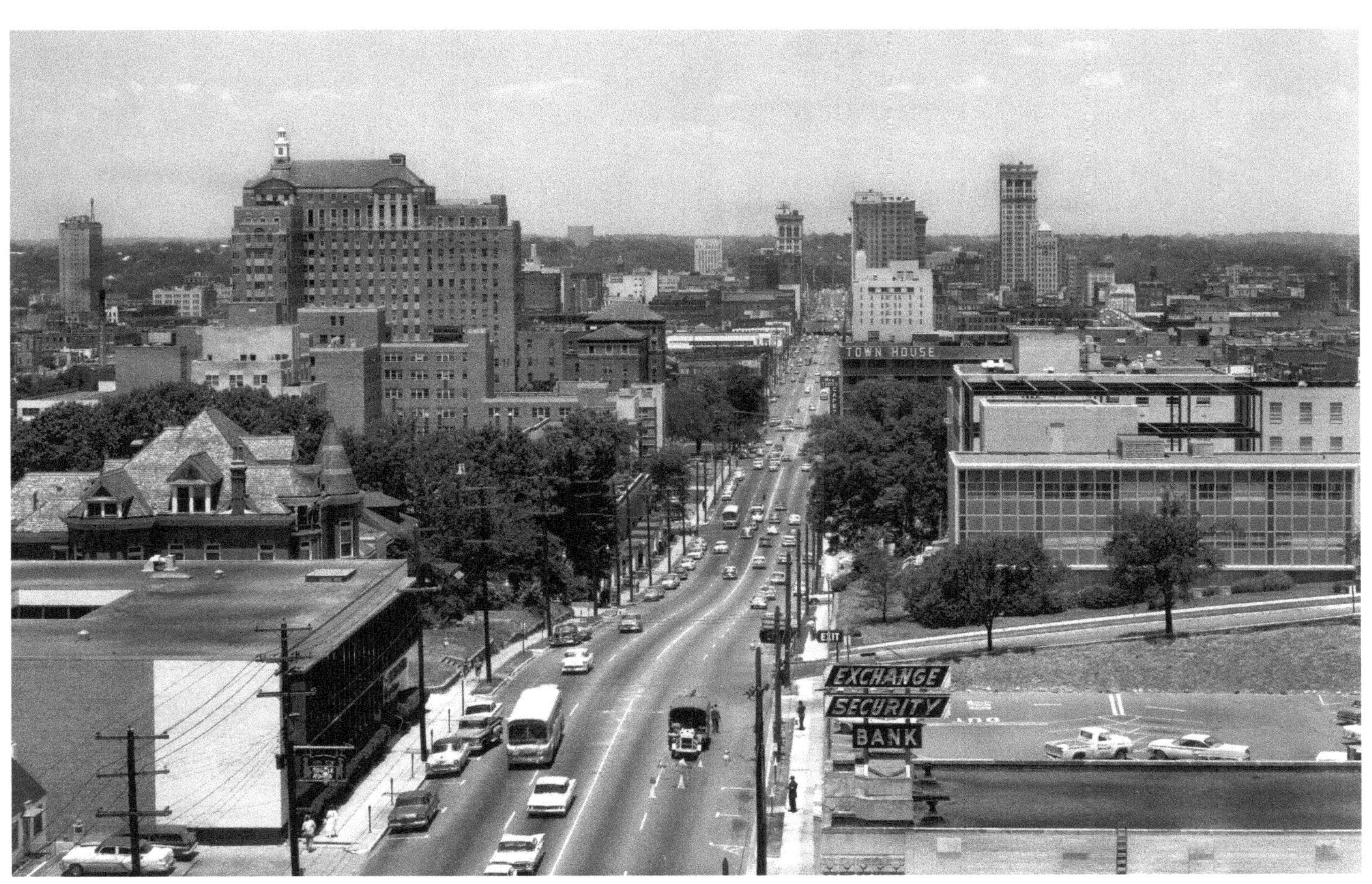

Looking down Twentieth Street from atop the Medical Arts Building (now the Pickwick Hotel), 1961.

For decades, Birmingham's African American community battled racial segregation. This man is protesting outside a downtown department store in the early 1960s.

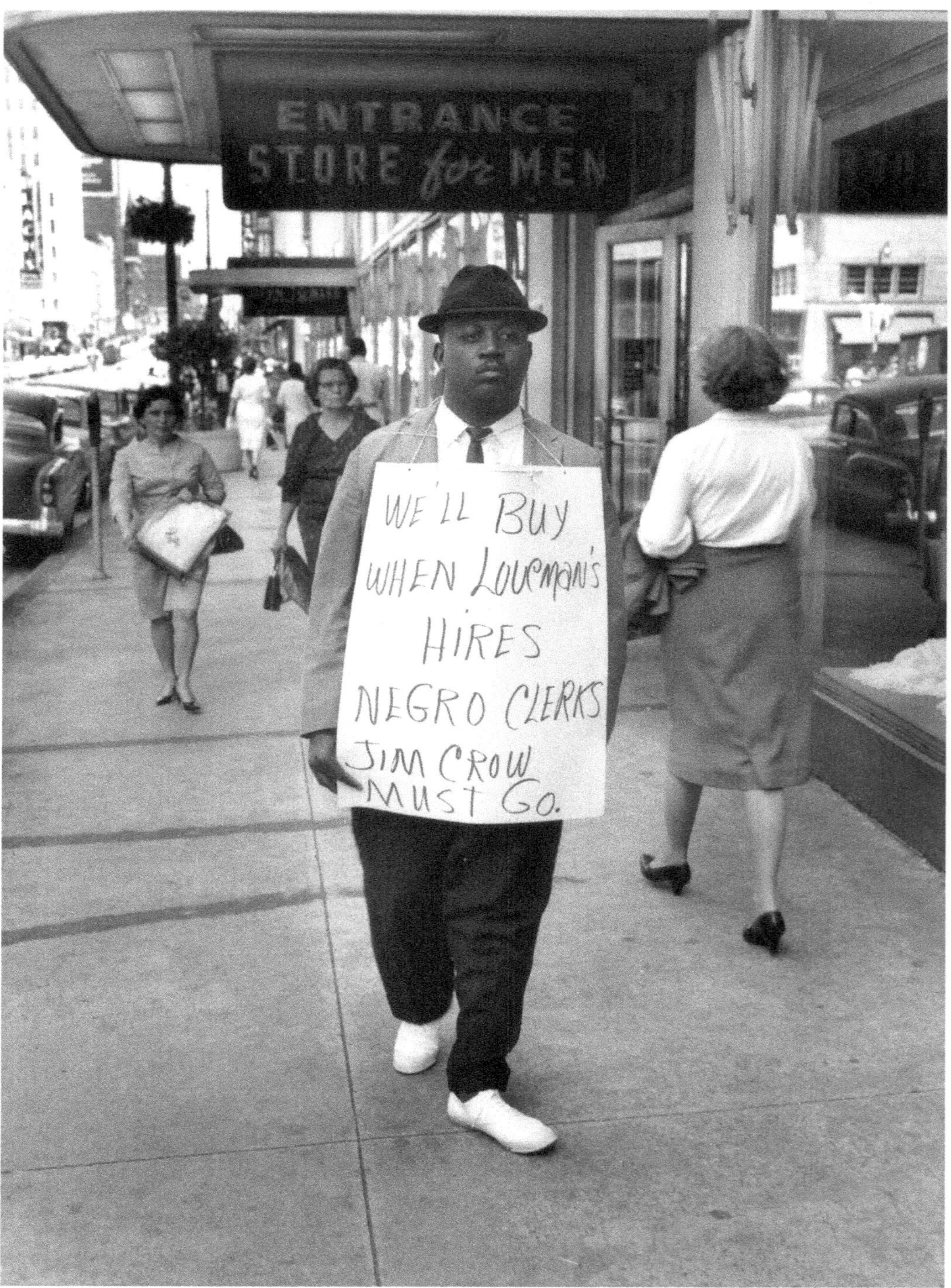

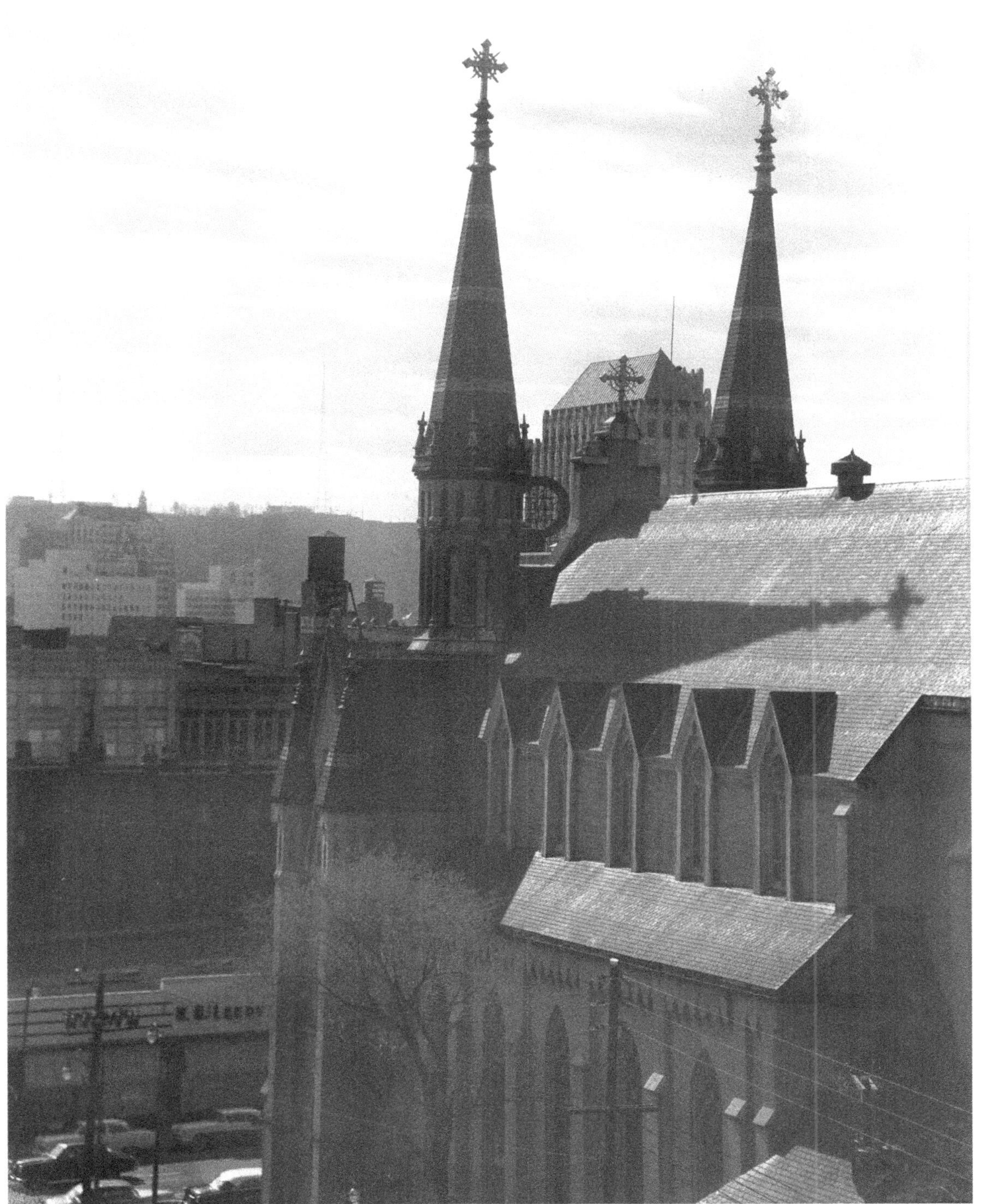

St. Paul's Catholic Church with shadows cast by the morning sun 1960s.

Enjoying cotton candy at the state fair, 1961.

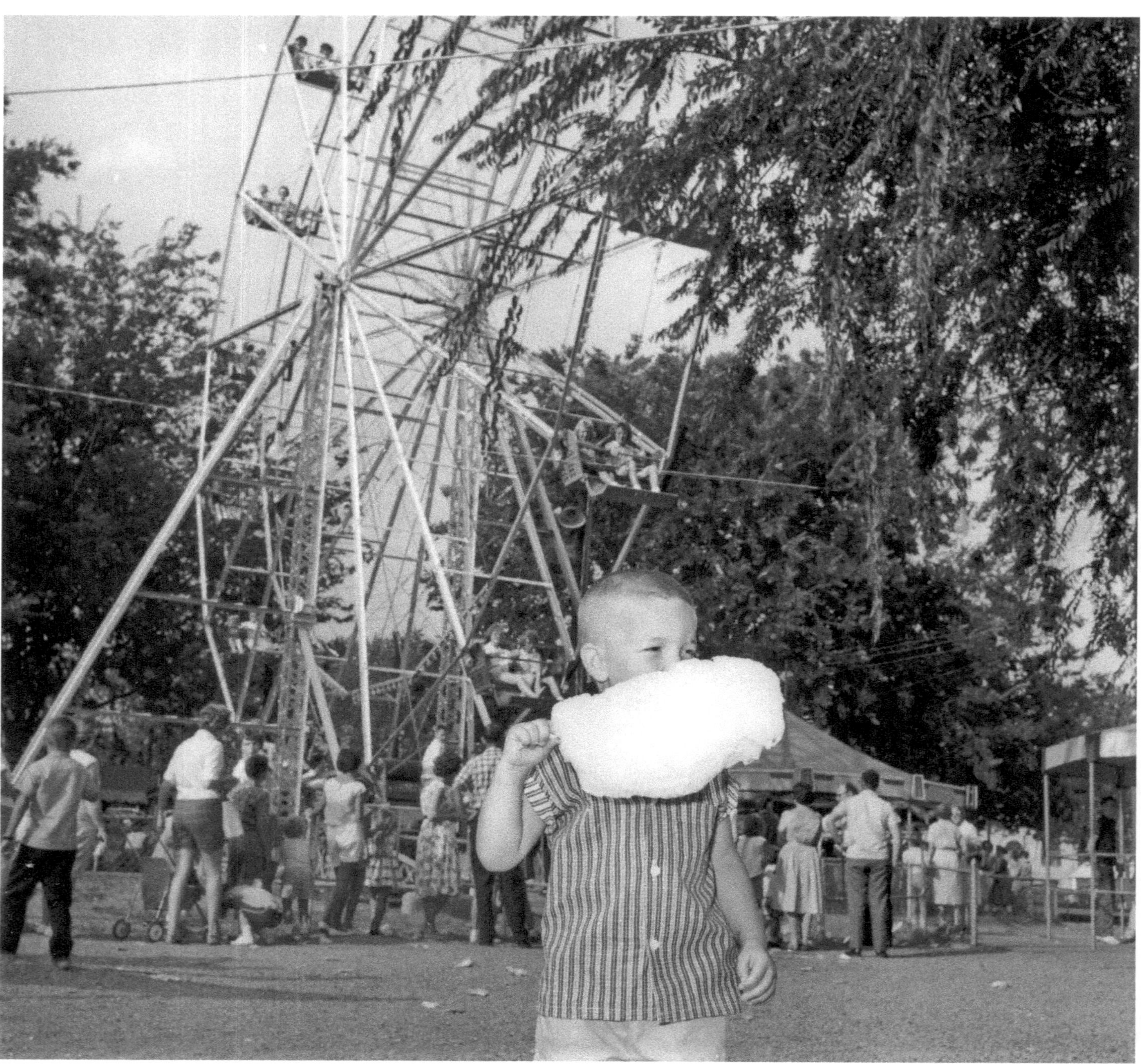

The Farmer's Market on Finley Avenue, June 1961.

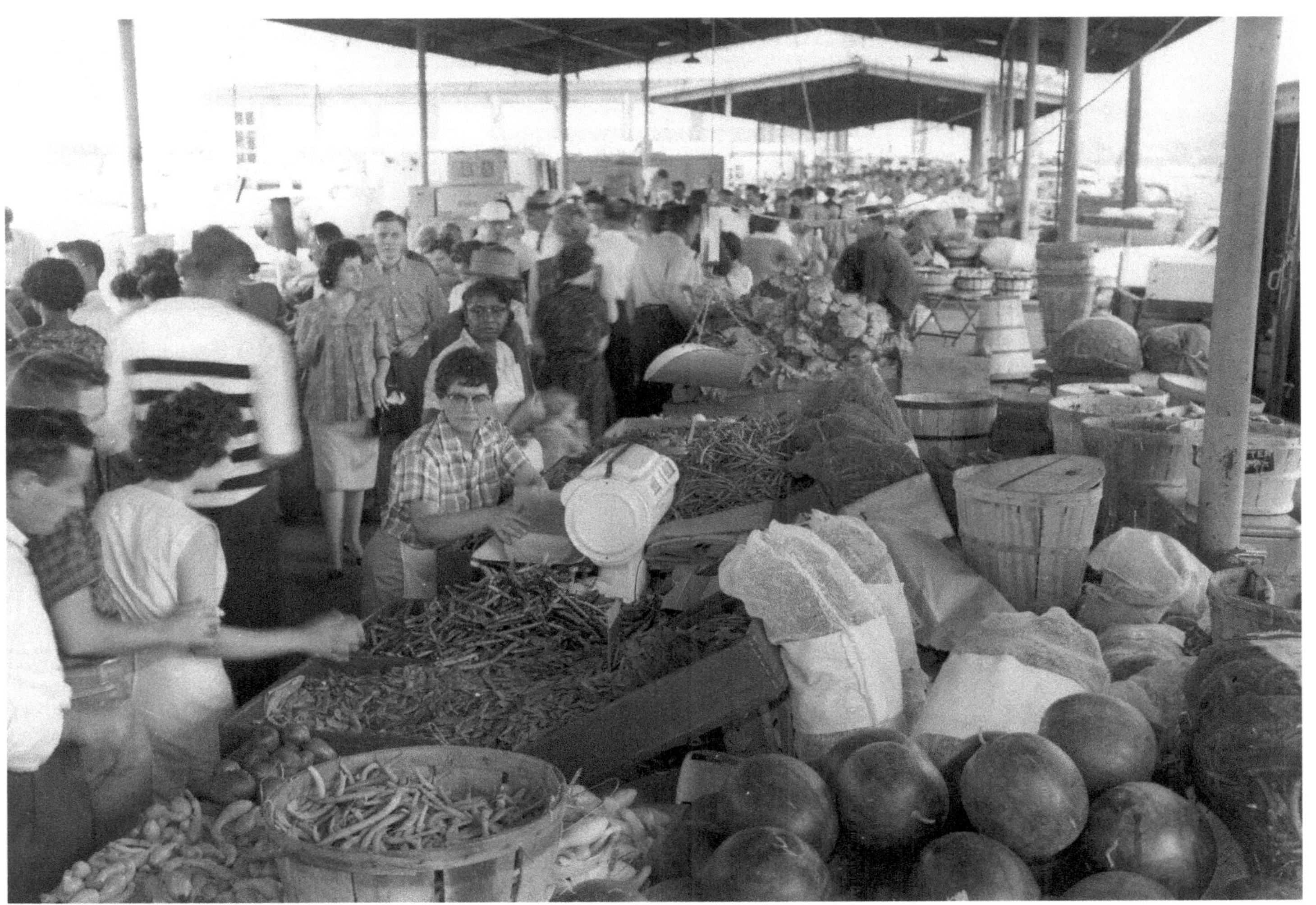

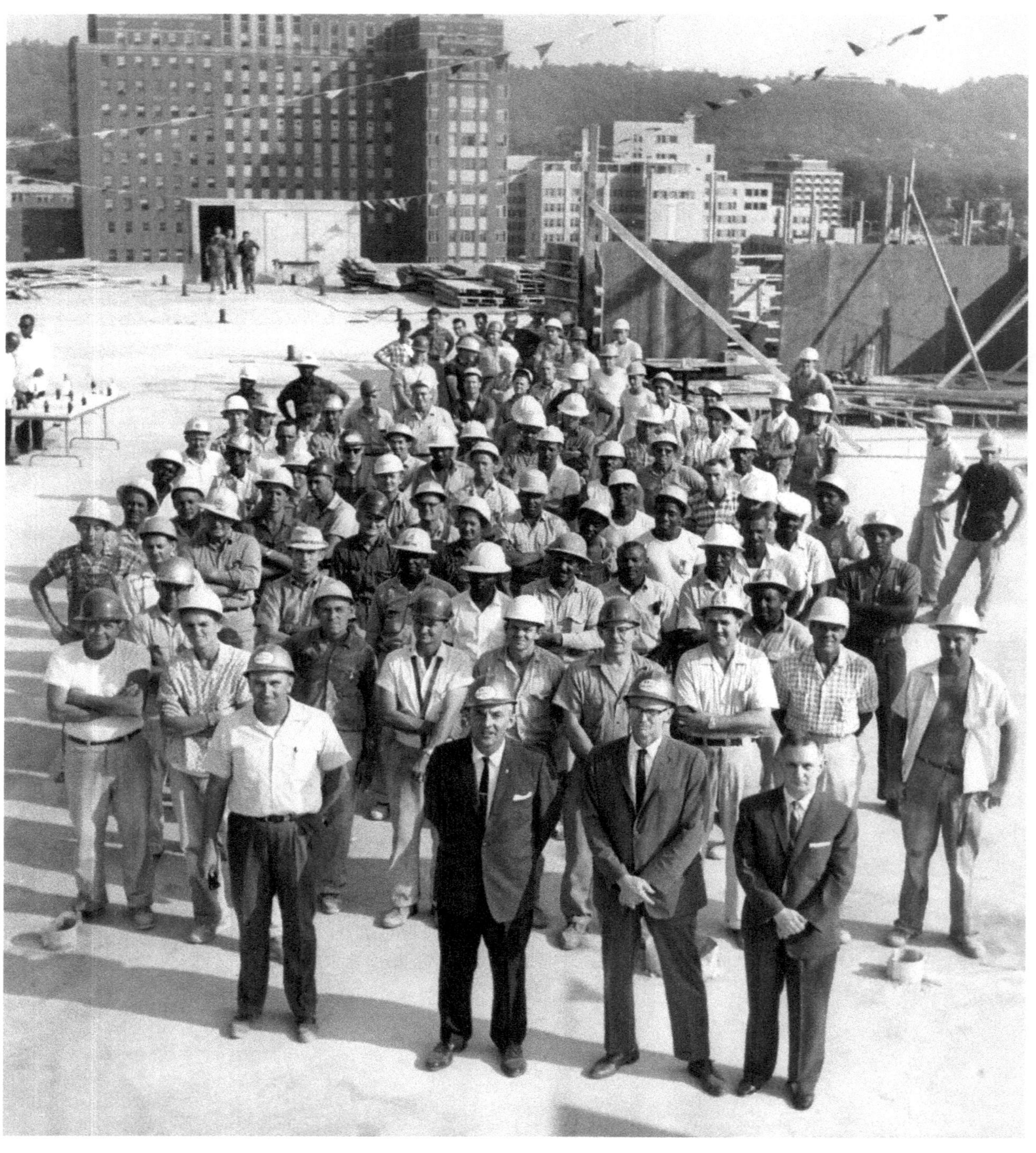

The Parliament House, 1962. Brice Building Company's construction team celebrates the topping out of Birmingham's first new multi-story motor hotel.

Hot rod and custom car show at the Alabama State Fairgrounds, May 1963.

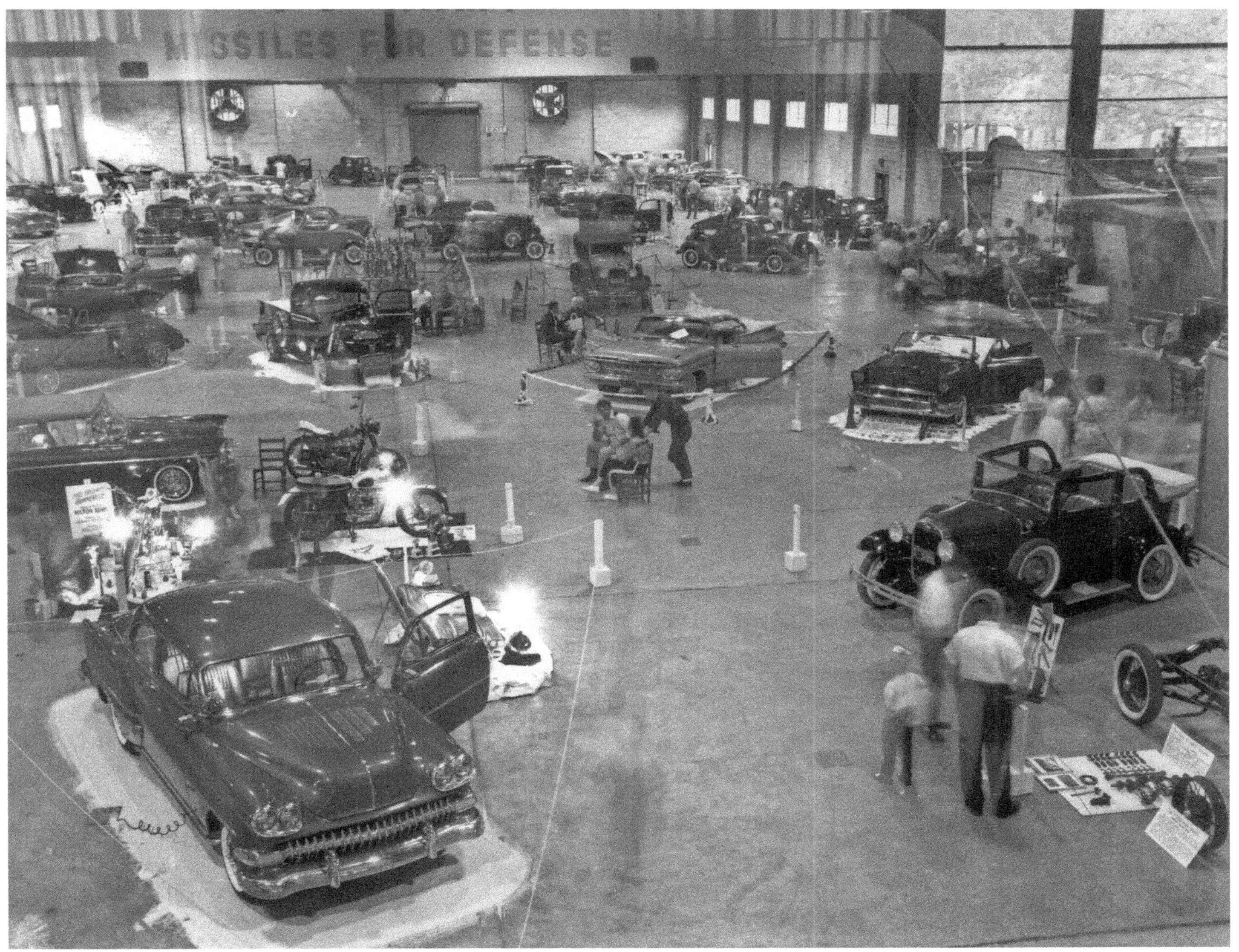

Cheerleaders at Legion Field for the 1964 Alabama versus Auburn game. In the first Iron Bowl to be televised to a national audience, quarterback Joe Namath led the Tide to a 21-14 victory.

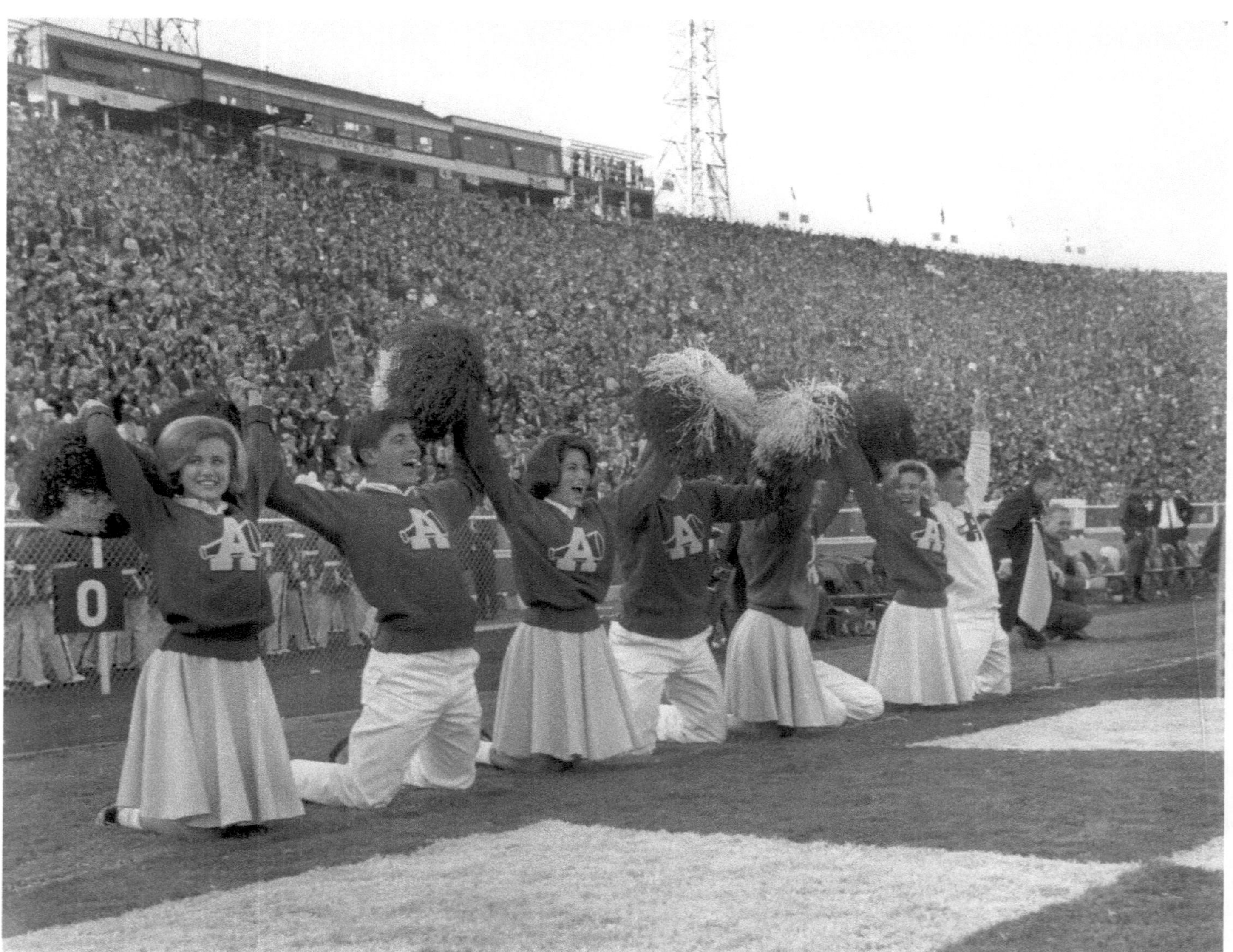

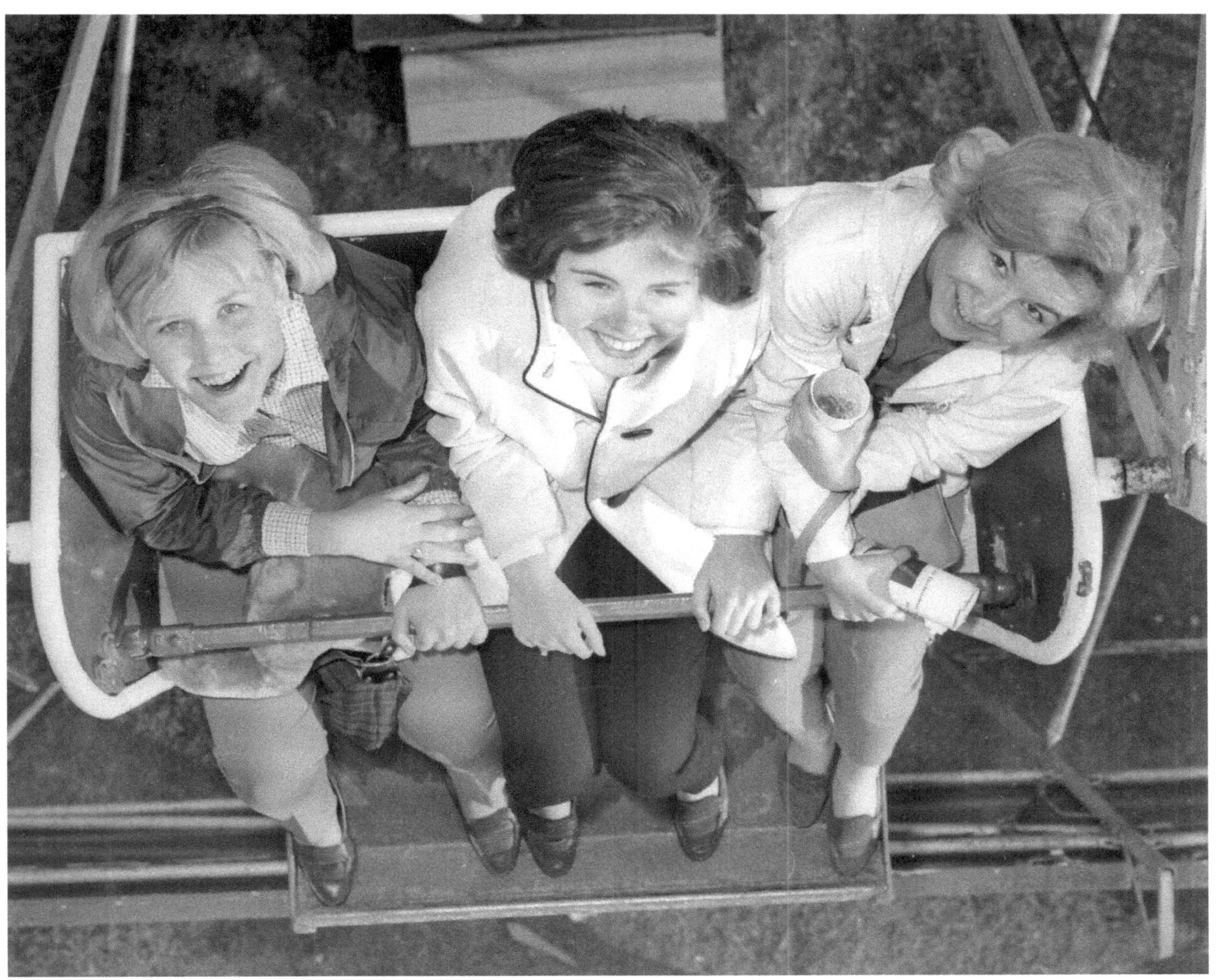

Riding the Ferris wheel at the state fair, 1964.

In addition to its long baseball tradition, Rickwood Field has hosted many events, even (gasp) football. Here, Birmingham's Roman Catholic community celebrates the Feast of Christ the King on the last Sunday in October, 1965.

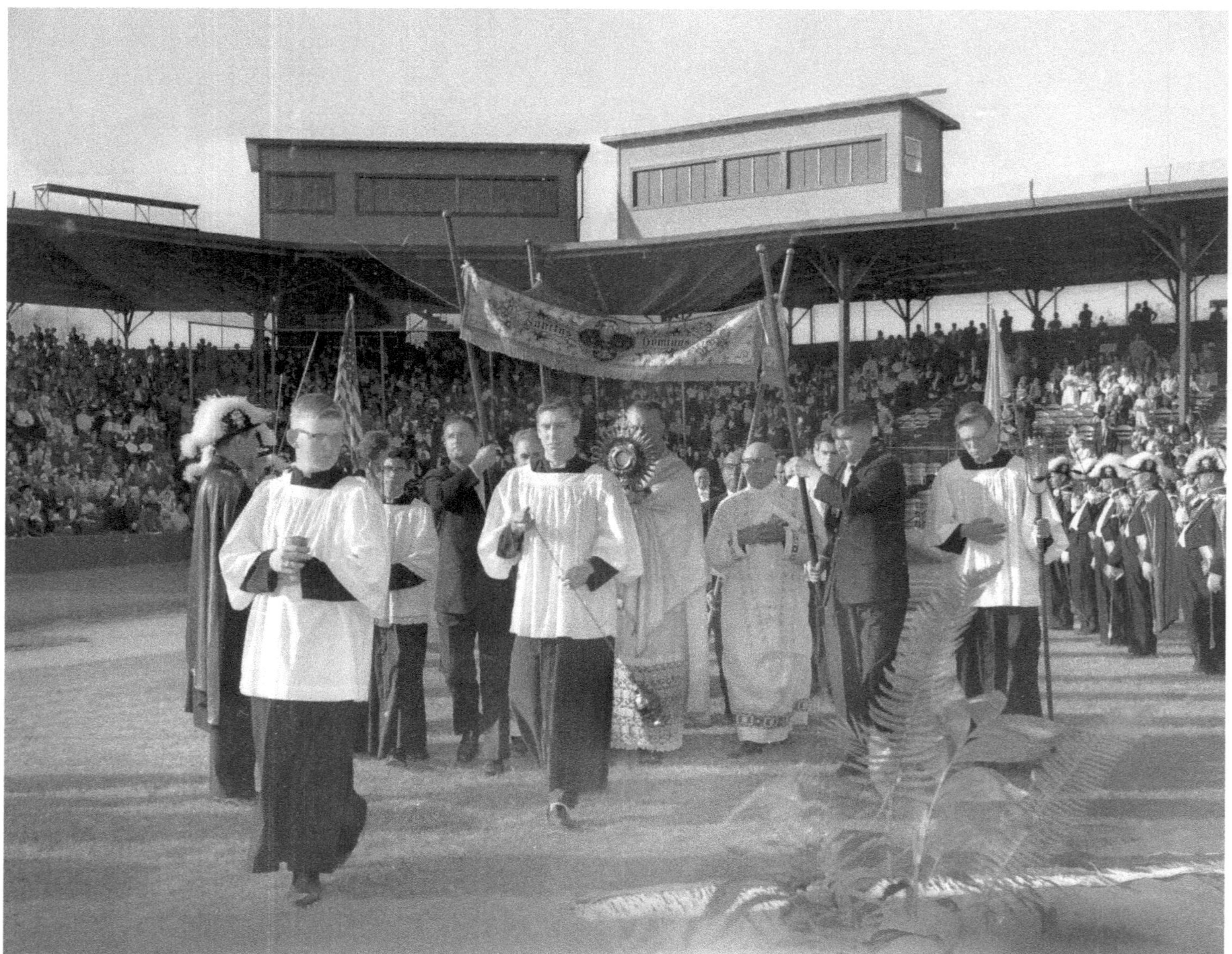

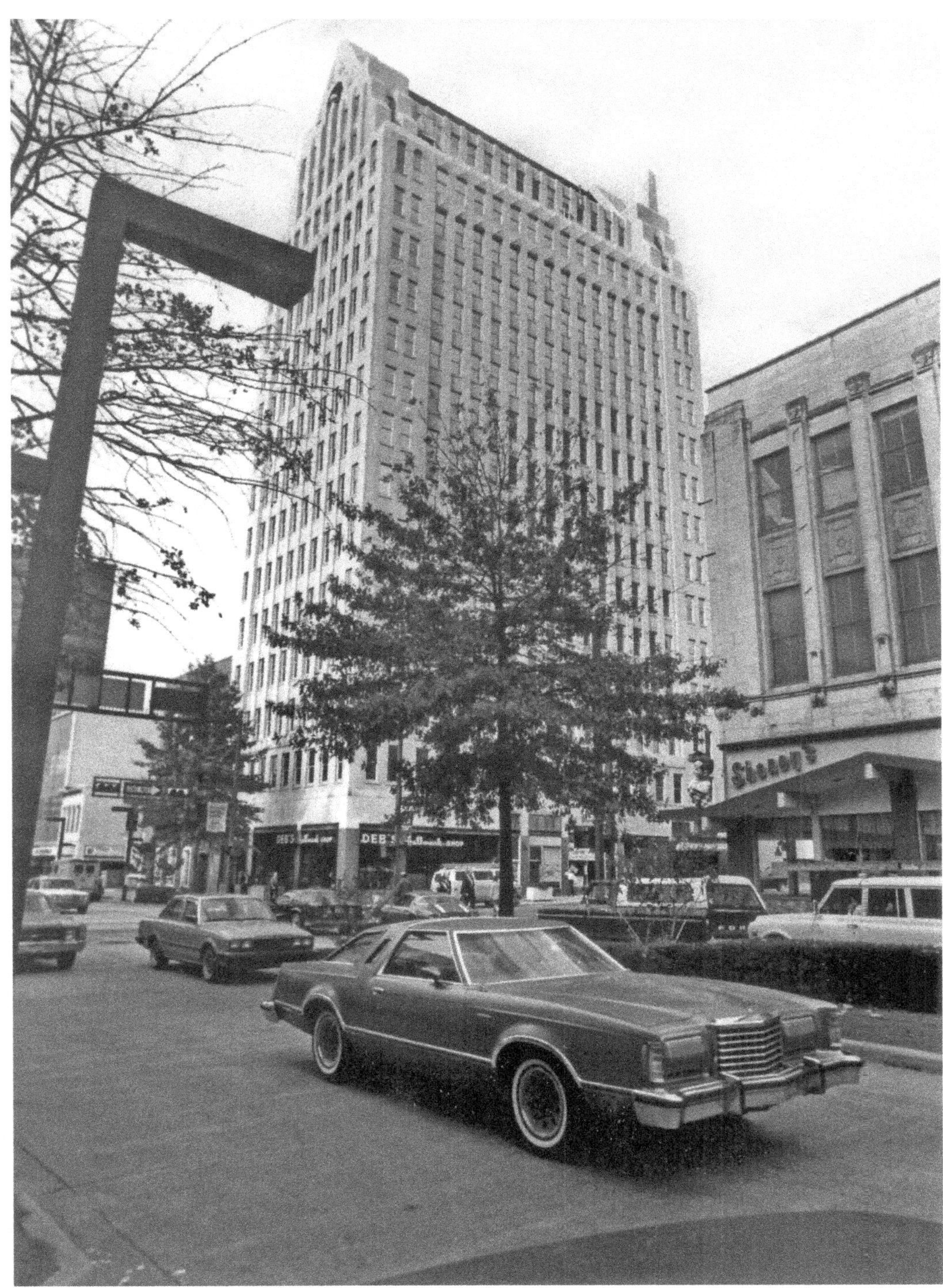

Twentieth Street and Third Avenue North in the late 1970s. The skyscraper in the background is the Watts Building.

Thompson's Restaurant located on Twentieth Street North, 1974.

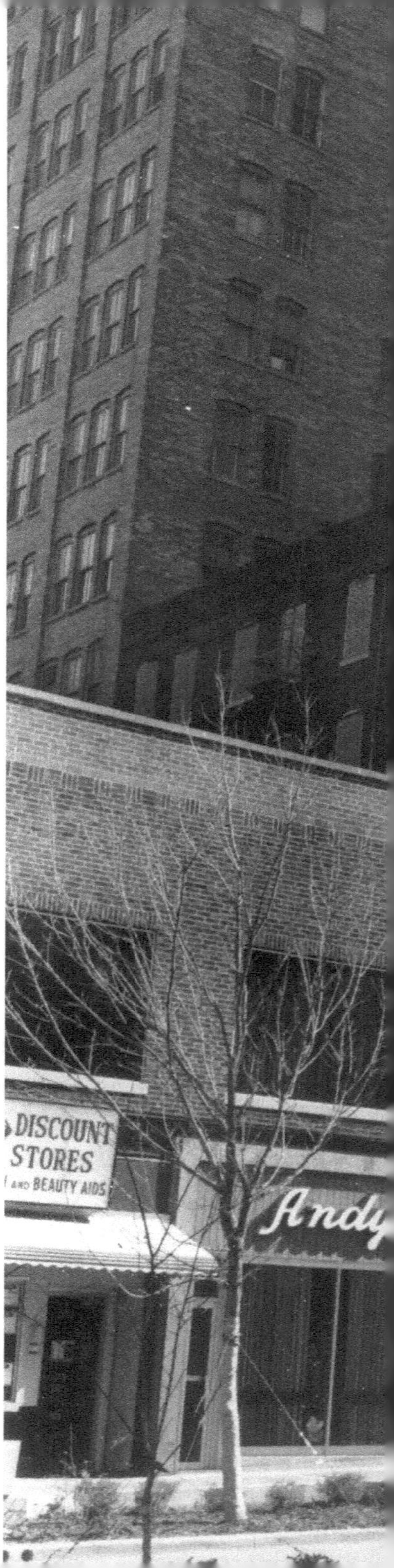

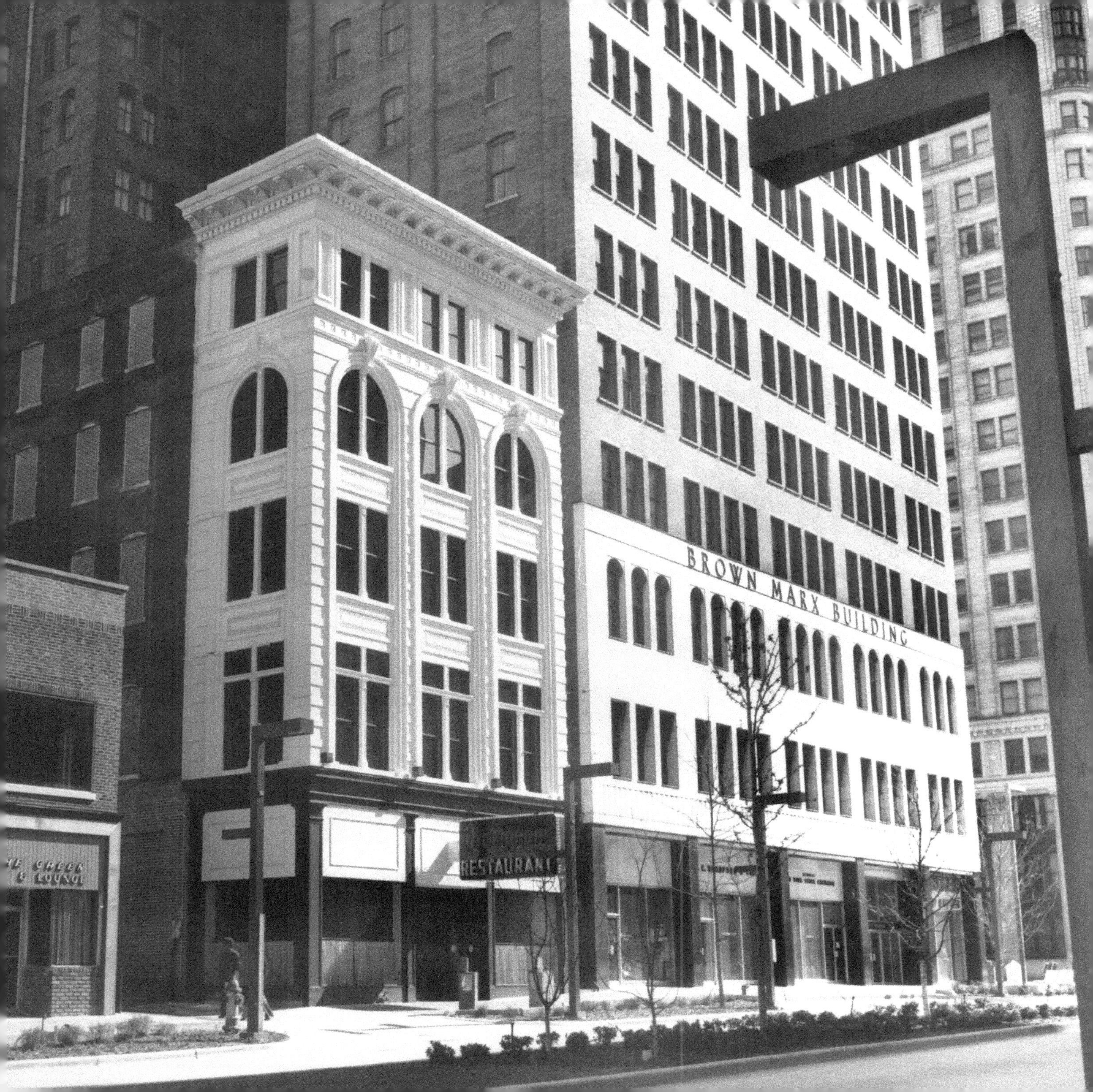
BROWN MARX BUILDING
RESTAURANT

Sorting papers at Flo's Newsstand downtown, 1982.

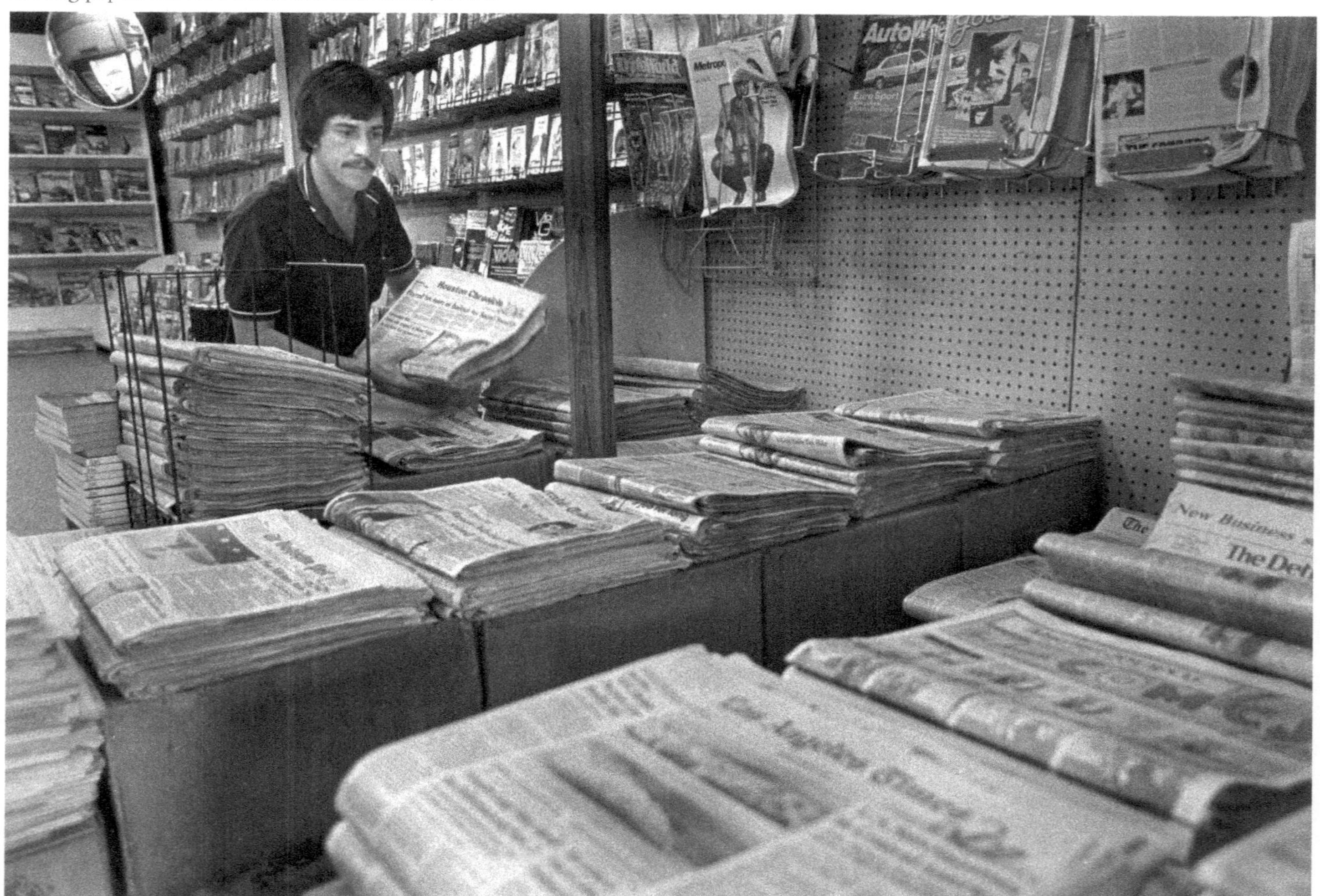

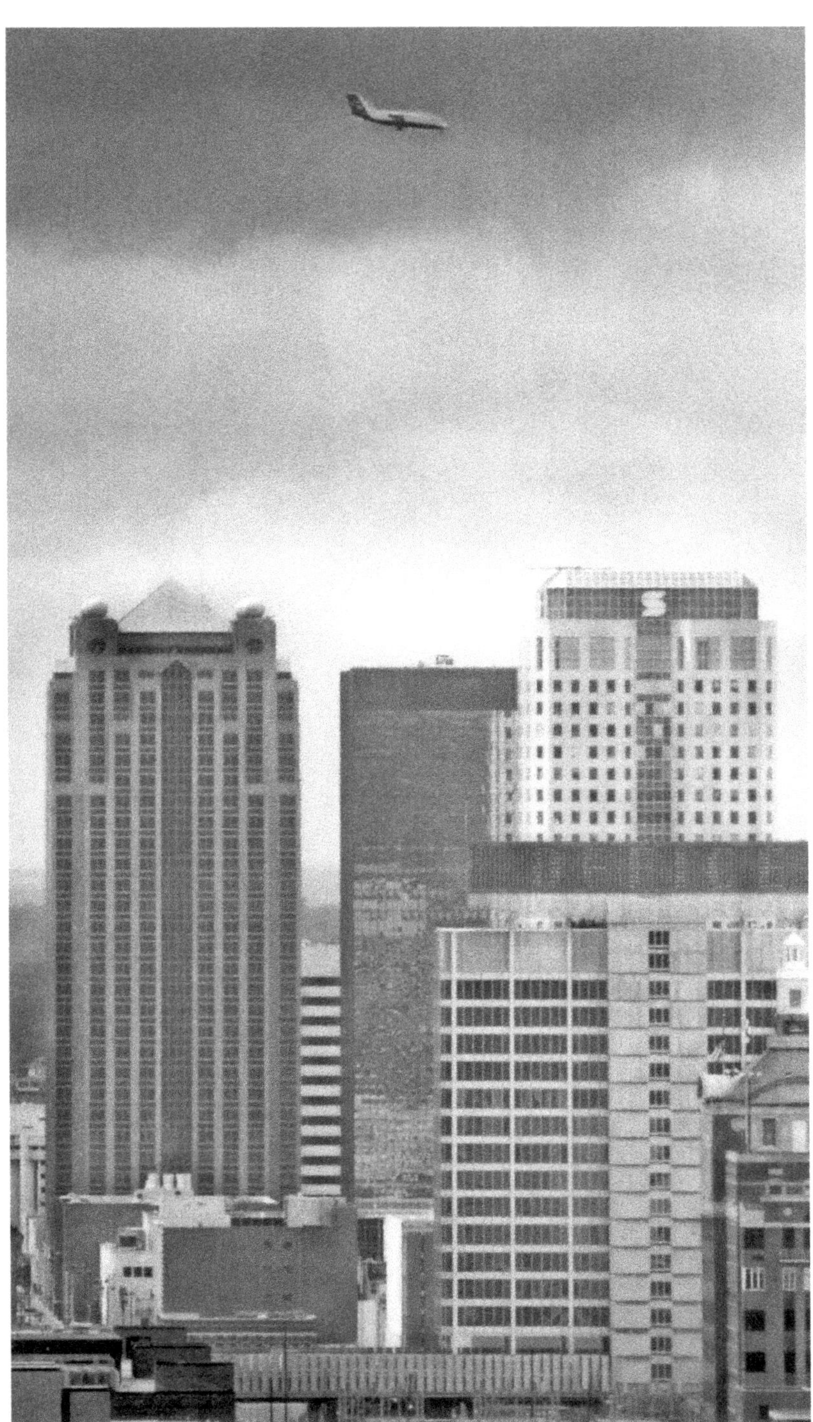

A jet flies over Birmingham's tallest skyscrapers and some of the city's major financial institutions in this view facing downtown from the south. Pictured are AmSouth-Harbert Plaza, the AmSouth Center, and SouthTrust Tower, now headquarters for Wachovia Bank.

Notes on the Photographs

These notes, listed by page number, attempt to include all aspects known of the photographs. Each of the photographs is identified by the page number, photograph's title or description, photographer and collection, archive, and call or box number when applicable. Although every attempt was made to collect all available data, in some cases complete data was unavailable due to the age and condition of some of the photographs and records.

II **Terminal Station with the Magic City Sign**
Photo by O.V. Hunt
Birmingham Public Library Archives
OVH 85

VI **Placing First Column for Tutwiler Hotel**
Photo by O.V. Hunt
Birmingham Public Library Archives
15.54

X **First Avenue North**
Photo by unknown photographer
Birmingham Public Library Archives
38.06

2 **Earliest Known Photograph of Birmingham**
Photo by A. C. Oxford
Birmingham Public Library Archives
6.57

3 **Jefferson County Courthouse**
Photo by unknown photographer
Birmingham Public Library Archives
34.05

4 **Mule-drawn Streetcar**
Photo by unknown photographer
Birmingham Public Library Archives
43.01

5 **Georgia-Pacific Railroad Engine**
Photo by A. C. Oxford
Birmingham Public Library Archives
37.17

6 **Passenger Train**
Photo by unknown photographer
Birmingham Public Library Archives
17.68

7 **Lakeview**
Photo by unknown photographer
Birmingham Public Library Archives
17.08

8 **Roden's Book Store**
Photo by Bob Baker
Birmingham Public Library Archives
4.91

9 Home of Robert Jemison, Sr.
Photo by unknown photographer
Birmingham Public Library Archives
15.28

10 Jefferson County Courthouse
Photo by J. Horgan, Jr.
Birmingham Public Library Archives
14.47

11 Nineteenth Street North at Second Avenue
Photo by J. Horgan, Jr.
Birmingham Public Library Archives
20.28

12 Third Avenue North and Twenty-second Street
Photo by J. Horgan, Jr.
Birmingham Public Library Archives
9.81

13 Gate City Streetcar
Photo by O.V. Hunt
Birmingham Public Library Archives
8.06

14 Going for a Ride
Photo by unknown photographer
Birmingham Public Library Archives
1.14

15 Team Photo at Lakeview
Photo by Bob Baker
Birmingham Public Library Archives
1.1

16 Shriners on Parade
Photo by O.V. Hunt
Birmingham Public Library Archives
OVH 450

17 Birmingham Streetcars
Photo by J. Horgan, Jr.
From a copy by O. V. Hunt
Birmingham Public Library Archives
OVH 434

18 Pioneer Mining and Manufacturing Company
Photo by unknown photographer
Erskine Ramsay Papers
Birmingham Public Library Archives
1.3.61

19 Jefferson Volunteers
Photo by D. C. Redington
From a copy by O. V. Hunt
Birmingham Public Library Archives
OVH 198

20 Picnickers to East Lake Park
Photo by O.V. Hunt
Birmingham Public Library Archives
OVH 100

21 First Avenue North
Photo by O.V. Hunt
Birmingham Public Library Archives
OVH 298

23 Birmingham Traction Company
Photo by O.V. Hunt
Birmingham Public Library Archives
OVH 99

24 Penny Savings Bank
Photo by unknown photographer
Birmingham Public Library Archives
829.1.21

25 Birmingham Fire Department
Photo by unknown photographer
Birmingham Public Library Archives
25.82

26 L & N Train Station
Photo by unknown photographer
Birmingham Public Library Archives
32.29

27 Kentucky Horse Shoeing
Birmingham Public Library Archives
43.18

28 Cornerstone Laying
St. Vincent's Hospital

29 Old Watts Building
Photo by O.V. Hunt
Birmingham Public Library Archives
OVH 37

30 Rooftop View of Downtown
Photo by unknown photographer
Birmingham Public Library Archives
29.88

32 Birmingham Railway, Light and Power Company
Photo by unknown photographer
Birmingham Public Library Archives
27.41

33 Bessemer Furnaces
Photo by unknown photographer
Birmingham Public Library Archives
17.02

34 Irondale Ore Mines
Photo by J. Horgan, Jr.
Birmingham Public Library Archives
7.06

35 Unidentified Coal Mine
Photo by J. Horgan, Jr.
Birmingham Public Library Archives
5.63

36 Bicycle Race
Photo by O.V. Hunt
Birmingham Public Library Archives
OVH 649

37 Twentieth Street from Morris Avenue
Photo by O.V. Hunt
Birmingham Public Library Archives
OVH 57

39 St. Vincent's Hospital
St. Vincent's Hospital

40 Three-Story Mansion
St. Vincent's Hospital

41 Nurses
St. Vincent's Hospital

42 Loveman's Department Store
Photo by O.V. Hunt
Birmingham Public Library Archives
OVH 53

43 Vaudeville Show Lyric Theatre
Photo by O.V. Hunt
Birmingham Public Library Archives
OVH 484

44 Vulcan at the State Fair
Photo by O.V. Hunt
Birmingham Public Library Archives
21.08

45 Early Airplane
Photo by O.V. Hunt
Birmingham Public Library Archives
OVH 582

46 East Lake Amusement Park
Photo by O.V. Hunt
Birmingham Public Library Archives

47 Five Points South
Photo by Birmingham View Company
Birmingham Public Library Archives
35.51

48 Road Crew Lays Tracks
Photo by O.V. Hunt
Birmingham Public Library Archives
OVH 86

49 American Trust & Savings Bank
Brice Building Corp.

50 A Daring Worker
Photo by O.V. Hunt
Birmingham Public Library Archives
21.48

51 Construction Workers
Photo by O.V. Hunt
Birmingham Public Library Archives
OVH 723

52 The Tutwiler
Birmingham Public Library Archives
OVH 330

53 O.V. Hunt Studio
Photo by O.V. Hunt
Birmingham Public Library Archives
OVH 3

54 Motorcyclists Along Seventh Avenue N.
Photo by O.V. Hunt
Birmingham Public Library Archives
OVH 503

55 Moore & Handley Hardware
Photo by unknown photographer
Birmingham Public Library Archives
4.78

56 Advertising Indian Motorcycles
Photo by O.V. Hunt
Birmingham Public Library Archives
OVH 644

58 Delivery Men on Motorcycles
Photo by O.V. Hunt
Birmingham Public Library Archives
OVH 493

59 Young Woman at East Lake
Photo by O.V. Hunt
Birmingham Public Library Archives
OVH 385

60 Motorcyclists Gather
Photo by O.V. Hunt
Birmingham Public Library Archives
OVH 345

61 Birmingham Firemen
Photo by O.V. Hunt
Birmingham Public Library Archives
OVH 410

62 Confederate Veterans
Photo by O.V. Hunt
Birmingham Public Library Archives
OVH 128

63 **Jefferson County Savings Bank Building**
Photo by O.V. Hunt
Birmingham Public Library Archives
OVH 44

64 **St. Vincent's Medical Staff**
St. Vincent's Hospital

65 **Transmission Line Workers**
Alabama Power Company

67 **Harley Davidson**
Photo by O.V. Hunt
Birmingham Public Library Archives
OVH 803

68 **U.S. Marshals**
Alabama Power Company

69 **Second Avenue North**
Photo by unknown photographer
Birmingham Public Library Archives
36.78

70 **Harley-Davidson Motorcycles**
Photo by O.V. Hunt
Birmingham Public Library Archives
OVH 519

71 **Swimming at East Lake Park**
Photo by O.V. Hunt
Birmingham Public Library Archives
OVH 774

72 **Drivers and Crew**
Photo by O.V. Hunt
Birmingham Public Library Archives
14.15

74 **Boating at East Lake Park**
Photo by O.V. Hunt
Birmingham Public Library Archives
OVH 775

75 **Tipple at Pratt Mines**
Photo by unknown photographer
Erskine Ramsay Papers
Birmingham Public Library Archives
1.3.25

76 **Police Officers**
Birmingham Public Library
17.86

77 **Sixteenth Street Baptist Church Choir**
Photo by unknown photographer
Birmingham Public Library Archives
829.1.48

79 **Industrial High School Band**
Photo by unknown photographer
Birmingham Public Library Archives
829.1.10

80 **Birmingham during World War I**
Photo by unknown photographer
Birmingham Public Library Archives
28.56

81 **Downtown Post Office**
Birmingham Public Library Archives
OVH 72

82 **Empire Building**
Photo by O.V. Hunt
Birmingham Public Library Archives
OVH 61

83 **YWCA**
Photo by O.V. Hunt
Birmingham Public Library Archives
OVH 414

84 **Warrior Reserve Steam Plant**
Alabama Power Company

85 **Rainbow Division Parade**
Photo by O.V. Hunt
Birmingham Public Library Archives
OVH 510

86 **Providing Drivers with Some Direction**
Photo by O.V. Hunt
Birmingham Public Library Archives
OVH 243

88 **Second Avenue North**
Photo by unknown photographer
Birmingham Public Library Archives
29.83

89 **Balloon Race**
Photo by O.V. Hunt
Birmingham Public Library Archives
28.04

90 **Floodwaters on Fifth Avenue**
Photo by O.V. Hunt
Birmingham Public Library Archives
OVH 448

91 **Sloss-Sheffield Truck**
Photo by O.V. Hunt
Birmingham Public Library Archives
OVH 755

92 Twenty-second Street Overpass
Photo by unknown photographer
Birmingham Public Library Archives
20.35

94 Lay Dam Power House Crew
Alabama Power Company

95 Graduating Nurses
St. Vincent's Hospital

96 Old Birmingham City Hall
Photo by O.V. Hunt
Birmingham Public Library Archives
OVH 14

97 Traffic Cop on Twentieth Street
Photo by O.V. Hunt
Birmingham Public Library Archives
OVH 190

98 President Warren G. Harding
Photo by O.V. Hunt
Birmingham Public Library Archives
OVH 119

99 Viola Dana Receives Key to City
Photo by O.V. Hunt
Birmingham Public Library Archives
OVH 356

100 Traffic cop
Photo by unknown photographer
Birmingham Public Library Archives
29.47

101 Board of Directors
Alabama Power Company

102 Building on Fire
Vulcan Materials Company

103 Traffic Tower
Photo by unknown photographer
Birmingham Public Library Archives
7.33

104 Celebrating Casey Jones
Birmingham Public Library Archives
28.25

105 Elegant Morris Hotel
Alfred C. Keily Collection
Birmingham Public Library Archives
15.42

106 The Spirit of St. Louis
Photo by unknown photographer
Birmingham Public Library Archives
14.39

107 Jefferson County Courthouse
Photo by O.V. Hunt
Birmingham Public Library Archives
3.14

108 Notorious Jitney
Photo by unknown photographer
Birmingham Public Library Archives
1.85

109 Heinz Company on Morris Avenue
Photo by O.V. Hunt
Birmingham Public Library Archives
OVH 802

110 Boy Scouts at the Odeon Theatre
Photo by O.V. Hunt
Birmingham Public Library Archives
OVH 526

111 First Avenue North
Photo by O.V. Hunt
Birmingham Public Library Archives
OVH 49

112 General Office
Alabama Power Company

113 Alabama Power Building
Alabama Power Company

114 Northwest View of General Office
Alabama Power Company

115 Concert in Avondale Park
Photo by O.V. Hunt
Birmingham Public Library Archives
OVH 197

116 Confederate Veterans
Photo by unknown *Birmingham News* photographer
Birmingham Public Library Archives
BN 6

117 Post Office
Photo by O.V. Hunt
Birmingham Public Library Archives
OVH 56

118 Firestone Tires
Birmingham Public Library Archives
OVH 471

119 Brown-Marx Building
Photo by unknown photographer
Birmingham Public Library Archives
20.74

120 Twentieth and Second Intersection
Photo by unknown Photographer
Birmingham Public Library Archives

121 Spring Festival
Photo by Walter Rosser
Birmingham Public Library Archives
2.48

122 Birmingham Barons at Rickwood
Photo by O.V. Hunt
Birmingham Public Library Archives
OVH FF 14.42

124 Aerial View of Birmingham Business
Alabama Power Company

125 Loveman's Fire
Birmingham Public Library Archives
12.91

126 Fire Fighters
Birmingham Public Library Archives
12.72

127 Miners Ending Their Shift
Photo by Arthur Rothstein
Library of Congress
LC-74

128 Miners Heading Home
Photo by Arthur Rothstein
Library of Congress
LC-75

129 Company Guard Watching Over Village
Photo by Arthur Rothstein
Library of Congress
LC-72

130 Shopping Along Second Avenue North
Photo by unknown *Birmingham News* photographer
Birmingham Public Library Archives
BN 364

131 Business District of Ensley
Photo by O.V. Hunt
Birmingham Public Library Archives
OVH 41

132 Twentieth Street at Second Avenue North
Photo by O.V. Hunt
Birmingham Public Library Archives
OVH 36

133 Cotton Ties
Photo by unknown photographer
Birmingham Public Library Archives
31.42

134 Black Barons at Rickwood
Photo by unknown photographer
Tom Hayes Collection
Memphis-Shelby County Public Library
(Copy available Birmingham Public Library Archives)
1436.1.16A

135 Birmingham Public Library
Photo by unknown photographer
Birmingham Public Library Archives
16.08

136 City Hall and Courthouse
Photo by unknown photographer
Birmingham Public Library Archives
17.89

138 Looking South Down Twentieth Street
Photo by O.V. Hunt
Birmingham Public Library Archives
OVH 19

139 Looking North Down Twentieth Street
Photo by O.V. Hunt
Birmingham Public Library Archives
OVH 22

140 First Presbyterian Church
Photo by O.V. Hunt
Birmingham Public Library Archives
OVH 50

141 Easter Egg Hunt at Avondale Park
Photo by Charlie Preston
Birmingham Public Library Archives
98.2054

142 Tom's Real Shine
Photo by O.V. Hunt
Birmingham Public Library Archives
OVH 185

143 Sixteenth Street Baptist Church
Photo by O.V. Hunt
Birmingham Public Library Archives
OVH 77

144 Bob Hope and Doris Day
Photo by Charlie Preston
Birmingham Public Library Archives
98.3945A

145 Birmingham Mop Manufacturing Company
Photo by Charlie Preston
Birmingham Public Library Archives
98.3907

146 Loveman's Department Store
Photo by A. C. Keily
Birmingham Public Library Archives
31.06

147 Liberty National Is Growing
Brice Building Corp.

148 Liberty National
Brice Building Corp.

149 McWane Cast-iron Pipe
Brice Building Corp.

150 Joe Rumore
Photo by Charlie Preston
Birmingham Public Library Archives
98.3063

151 Washington Branch Library
Photo by unknown photographer
Birmingham Public Library Archives
18.30

152 Jemison Company
Photo by unknown photographer
Birmingham Public Library

154 Woman Taxi Driver
Photo by Charlie Preston
Birmingham Public Library Archives
98.6897

155 Yolanda Betbeze
Photo by Charlie Preston
Birmingham Public Library Archives
98.6479C

156 WBRC Television
Photo by Charlie Preston
Birmingham Public Library Archives
98.8528

157 Willie B. Smith
Photo by unknown photographer
Birmingham Public Library Archives
24.78

158 Woodrow Wilson Park
Photo by Charlie Preston
Birmingham Public Library Archives
98.8164

159 Bookmobile
Photo by unknown photographer
Birmingham Public Library Archives
16.21

160 City Farmer
Photo by Bill Mobley for the
Birmingham Post-Herald
Birmingham Public Library Archives

161 A Rainy Day on Twentieth Street
Photo by *Birmingham Post-Herald* photographer
Birmingham Public Library Archives

162 Miss Alabama Gwen Harmon
Photo by Charlie Preston
Birmingham Public Library Archives
98.8312

163 Bowling at Eastwood
Birmingham Public Library Archives
820.15.45

164 Bellhops at Tutwiler Hotel
Photo by Charlie Preston
Birmingham Public Library Archives
98.10314

165 WSGN Radio
Photo by Charlie Preston
Birmingham Public Library Archives
98.14314

166 Soap Box Derby
Photo by Charlie Preston
Birmingham Public Library Archives
98.14001

167 Slag Pit
Vulcan Materials Company

168 Concrete Truck
Vulcan Materials Company

169 Metropolitan Hotel
Photo by O.V. Hunt
Birmingham Public Library Archives
OVH 282

170 Nursing Beauties
St. Vincent's Hospital

171 Pantages Theater
Photo by O.V. Hunt
Birmingham Public Library Archives
OVH 80

172 Morris Hotel
Photo by Charlie Preston
Birmingham Public Library Archives
98.1566A

173 Spanish-American War Veterans
Photo by unknown photographer
Birmingham Public Library Archives
13.47

174 Sisters
St. Vincent's Hospital

175 Looking Down Twentieth Street
Birmingham Public Library Archives
36.86

176 Civil Rights Protest
Photo by unknown photographer
Birmingham Public Library Archives
639.1.25

177 St. Paul's Catholic Church
Photo by *Birmingham Post-Herald* photographer
Birmingham Public Library Archives

178 Enjoying Cotton Candy at the State Fair
Photo by *Birmingham Post-Herald* photographer
Birmingham Public Library Archives

179 Farmer's Market
Photo by *Birmingham Post-Herald* photographer
Birmingham Public Library Archives

180 Parliament House
Brice Building Corp.

181 Custom Car Show
Photo by Charlie Preston
Birmingham Public Library Archives
98.23120

182 Cheerleaders at Legion Field
Photo by *Birmingham Post-Herald* photographer
Birmingham Public Library Archives

183 Riding the Rides at the State Fair
Photo by *Birmingham Post-Herald* photographer
Birmingham Public Library Archives

184 Catholics at Rickwood Field
Photo by *Birmingham Post-Herald* photographer
Birmingham Public Library Archives

185 Twentieth and Second
Photo by *Birmingham Post-Herald* Photographer
Birmingham Public Library Archives

187 Thompson's Restaurant
Brice Building Corp.

188 Flo's Newsstand
Photo by *Birmingham Post-Herald* Photographer
Birmingham Public Library Archives

189 Tallest Skyscrapers
Photo by *Birmingham Post-Herald* Photographer
Birmingham Public Library Archives

198 Britling Cafeteria
Photo by *Birmingham Post-Herald* Photographer
Birmingham Public Library

Following Page: Britling Cafeteria, shown here in 1951, was a favorite place to eat downtown.

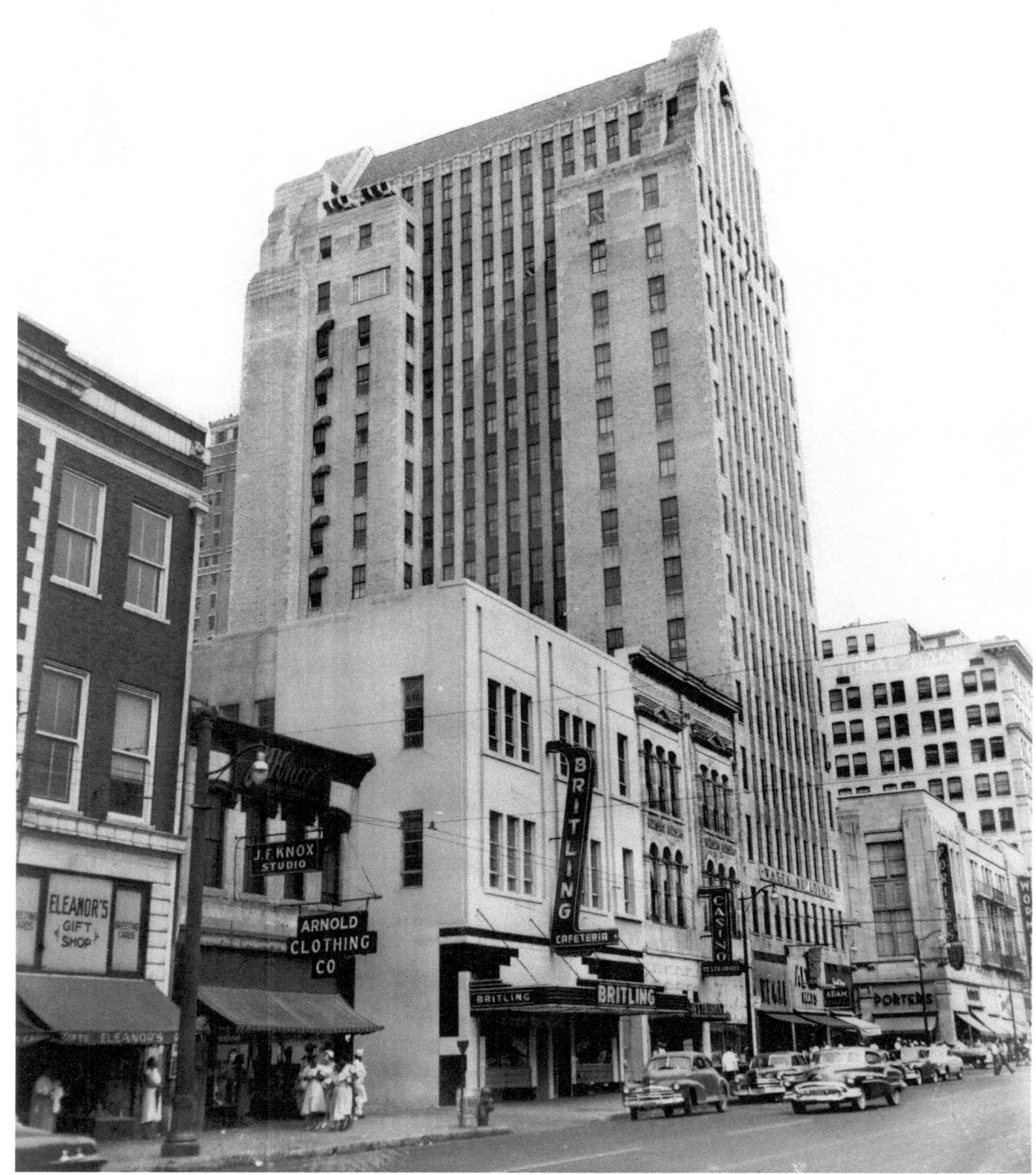

ELEANOR'S GIFT SHOP
J.F. KNOX STUDIO
ARNOLD CLOTHING CO
BRITLING
CAFETERIA
BRITLING
BRITLING
CASINO
PORTERS

HISTORIC PHOTOS OF BIRMINGHAM

By the mid nineteenth century, the city of Birmingham was a vibrant cultural center of the South. Through the late 1800s, the Roaring Twenties, two World Wars, and into the modern era, Birmingham has continued to grow and prosper by overcoming adversity and maintaining the strong independent culture of its citizens.

Historic Photos of Birmingham, captures this journey through still photography from the finest archives of city and private collections. From the Reconstruction era to the building of a modern metropolis, *Historic Photos of Birmingham* follows life, government, education, and events throughout Birmingham's history. The book captures unique and rare scenes through the original lens of hundreds of historic photographs. Published in striking black and white, these images communicate historic events and everyday life of several generations of people building a unique and prosperous city.

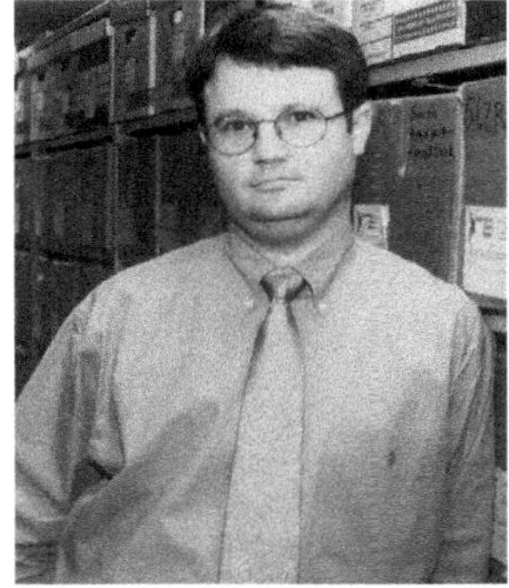

James L. Baggett is Head of the Department of Archives and Manuscripts at the Birmingham Public Library, and Archivist for the City of Birmingham.

A past president of the Society of Alabama Archivists and past Chair of the Jefferson County Historical Commission, he is the editor of three previous books, including *A Woman of the Town: Louise Wooster, Birmingham's Magdalen.*

WWW.TURNERPUBLISHING.COM

www.ingramcontent.com/pod-product-compliance
Lightning Source LLC
LaVergne TN
LVHW070919120826
845154LV00019BB/27

9781683369110